D0521545

The Complete Golden Retriever Handbook

BY

LINDA WHITWAM

ISBN- 13: 978-1979837125

Copyright

Acknowledgements

My sincere thanks to the dedicated Golden Retriever breeders, owners and canine experts who have generously contributed their time and expertise to this book. Their knowledge and love of their dogs shines through; without them, this book would not have been possible.

Specialist Contributors

HELEN DORRANCE

SUE PAGE

LIZ SPICER-SHORT

Contributors

Special thanks to (in alphabetical order): Angie and Ray Gait, Anna Cornelius-Jones, Claire Underwood, Dee Johnson, George and Val Coxwell, Helen Dorrance, Jan Schick, Jessica and Stephen Webb, Julian Pottage, Karen Ireland, Karen Moore, Karen Parsons, Kelly Sisco, Lesley Gunter and Geoff Brown, Lisa and Mark Mellor, Liz Spicer-Short, Lorna Bishop, Nicholas Lock and Elaine Griffiths, Richard and Suzanne Clear, Sue Page, Tim Hoke, Wendy Pickup, and Dr Sara Skiwski

(Full details of the breeders appear at the back of the book)

TABLE OF CONTENTS

1. Meet the Golden Retriever

This strikingly handsome dog with a wonderful temperament, intelligence, love of humans and great desire to please his owners has become one of the most popular breeds on the planet. When listing the attributes of all the different dog breeds, it's hard – if not impossible - to think of one with a better temperament, or a dog that is more family friendly.

He is affectionate and loyal, gentle, honest, good-natured and gets on well with people of all ages, as well as other animals.

As with all dogs with sporting origins, Goldens or Goldies, as they are often called, love a challenge – both physical and mental. Given enough exercise, they are happy, biddable and laid-back - at least when they are adults; youngsters can be boisterous!

This large canine with the big heart and flowing golden coat is one of the most versatile of dogs. His intelligence and eagerness to please mean he can be trained to a high level. As well as family pets and working retrievers, Goldens also become Guide Dogs for the Blind, Hearing Dogs for the Deaf, certified therapy dogs that 'read' to children at libraries, visit the sick in hospital and the elderly in nursing homes. They bring companionship and happiness to autistic children, and even take part in search and rescue operations.

They excel in the show ring – visit any conformation show and you are guaranteed to see a large entry of Golden Retrievers - and at obedience events, and do well at agility and other canine competitions. Above all, they are the most willing and devoted companions. The breed's stellar, sunny temperament has made the Golden Retriever the dog of choice for countless households and his retrieving instincts mean that he is popular with field sport enthusiasts as well.

The Golden Retriever's heritage is as a working dog, bred to pick up game - from land and water. Some of the breed's ancestors were Water Spaniels, and all types of retriever are descended from a breed known hundreds of years ago as the Lesser Newfoundland or St. John's Dog, from Newfoundland in Canada. These hardy dogs worked alongside fishermen, pulling carts, retrieving fallen fish and hauling fishing nets through water – even in icy conditions. No wonder the Golden has inherited an instinctive love of water (and mud!).

The very first Golden Retrievers were created in the 1860s by the First Lord Tweedmouth to retrieve game from marshy land and water on his Guisachan Estate in the Scottish Highlands. But it took nearly half a century for breeders to consistently produce yellow Retriever pups and the breed to be officially recognised – not until 1913 in the UK and 1925 in the USA.

As a sporting dog, the breed needs both physical and mental exercise – how much depends on the individual dog, his ancestry and the amount of exercise he gets used to as a young dog. The (UK) Kennel Club recommends "more than two hours per day" for adult dogs.

The double coated Golden Retriever has a soft, dense undercoat and a coarser outer coat which repels water. Coat colour can vary; the UK Kennel Club Breed Standard states: "Any shade of gold or cream, neither red nor mahogany" - the reds are not accepted in the UK show ring. This is slightly different in the USA, where red is more acceptable; the American Kennel Club states: "Rich, lustrous golden of various shades."

Types of Golden Retriever

There is a difference between 'show' and 'working' (or 'field') Golden Retrievers, both in appearance and nature. The Golden Retriever bred from working bloodlines generally has a lighter, leaner frame and longer leg than a show Golden. He has a less dense coat, which is often darker or slightly redder, and a narrower head. The show type has a more powerful appearance, shorter muzzle and more feathering on the coat.

Retrievers that take part in field sports can work up to eight or more hours a day. Mentally, they have to be highly alert and use all their senses to locate game from land or water, so a dog bred purely from working stock may require more exercise and mental challenges than a show Golden. Dogs bred for the bench have to be patient enough to wait for hours until it's their turn to be inspected by the judge, and then to remain composed once inside the show ring.

In reality, the litters from many modern breeders, in both the UK and USA, are often a mixture of show and working bloodlines. It pays to find out as much as you can from the breeder about what your dog's parents and ancestors were bred for. If you already have your Golden Retriever, contact your breeder to find out what type he is to help you better understand and train him.

This photo shows (top, left to right): Zane, an 'English Cream' bred by Icewind Goldens, USA, Ruby, bred from working stock by Karen Parsons, West Sussex, UK, and Parsnip, bred from show lines, Bowcombe Golden Retrievers, Isle of Wight, UK. Below: two Goldens from George and Val Coxwell's Revaliac Golden Retrievers, Devon, UK, six-month-old Millie on the left is from working lines and three-year-old Phoebe is from show lines.

In the USA, the terms 'English Cream' or 'English Crème' and 'American Golden Retriever' are also used. The English Creams, so called because they originate from imported European stock, are light coloured, from cream to almost white. (White is not an accepted colour for the breed). English Creams tend to have bigger bones and 'chunkier' heads than the American. Statistically, the American Golden Retrievers are more prone to cancer. Whatever type you buy - and it's all down to personal preference - check out the health clearances and temperaments of the parents.

Downsides to Golden Retrievers?

Does the Golden Retriever have any downsides, and with all of these amazing talents, how come some Golden Retrievers end up in rescue centres? Well, sometimes people enter into dog ownership without considering all of the consequences, and although Golden Retrievers have all of the qualities listed, this is also an active breed which needs a fair bit of space inside and outside the home and plenty of exercise. Here are some things to consider:

- Goldens love swimming and they seem to be attracted to mud. They often return home after walks wet and/or dirty as their long coat traps the dirt
- This is definitely not a breed for the house-proud. As well as getting wet and dirty, they shed lots of long hair around the house for months, some shed all year round
- Many love digging up the garden
- Some Goldens can be stubborn, requiring a lot of patience and repetition when training
- Goldens are great with children, but a lively young Golden Retriever combined with lively young children can be a recipe for disaster if none is well-trained!

- Golden Retrievers love running off the lead (leash), but they can also roam, so need to be taught the recall from an early age
- This breed is time-consuming. It needs a lot of exercise - more than two hours a day is what the Kennel Club recommends
- Left alone too long or under-exercised, a Golden can become bored and destructive
- Goldens are not cheap to keep. They are big dogs with big appetites. You also need to have the finances for proper veterinary care, regular worming and de-fleaing treatments, pet insurance, and so on
- Some lines of Golden Retrievers have a high incidence of cancer, particularly in the USA; ask the breeder about the lifespan of his or her dogs

And, like any breed, the Golden Retriever can be a challenge. Often Goldens are extremely boisterous for the first two or three years of their lives. Sometimes described as 'goofy', this belies their intelligence, but they seem to have little spatial awareness and can be clumsy. You and the kids can get bowled over as your adolescent canine enthusiastically races around and jumps up at people, full of the joys of life and everything and everyone in it. Without proper training and sufficient exercise and play time, this unfocused energy can lead to a lively dog which is too much to handle for some families.

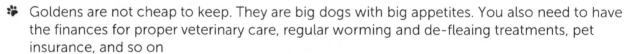

Breeders on Golden Retrievers

Despite all of this, ask anyone who has spent any time with a Golden Retriever and they all say the same: there is something really special about this breed. Some 21 breeders have been involved in the writing of this book and between them they have hundreds of years' experience of Goldens. We asked what first attracted them to the Golden Retriever and how they would describe the typical temperament. Here are their replies (breeders are in the UK unless otherwise stated):

Angie and Ray Gait, Sonodora Golden Retrievers, Hampshire, breeders for 27 years: "Goldens are a complete dog. They have the most wonderful temperament, they are extremely good looking and can turn their hand to anything, from a job of work, i.e. guide dogs, assistance or retrieving on the shooting field - or they can be just a faithful companion or hearth rug! A Golden's temperament should be loving, biddable, willing to please, confident in all situations. Their only behaviour quirk would be their need to be friends with anyone."

Wendy Pickup, Blenstone Golden Retrievers, Flintshire, a breeder of 26 years says: "I was attracted to the breed for its temperament, size, beauty and brains. They are biddable, eager to please, intelligent, and playful – they can sometimes be stubborn."

Liz Spicer-Short, Priorschest Golden Retrievers, Dorset: "Our wider family had Goldens, who had proved to be fantastic family dogs, so when (aged eight) I was told I could have a dog of my own it was a 'no brainer' that he would be a Golden Retriever. Goldens are generally placid, easy-going dogs. They are adaptable and settle to a new situation easily. They are affectionate and seek out human company, often being happy just to lie beside their owner. They are great fun and love life, usually running along with a smile on their face. They love water (and if it is muddy, so much the better!) and are good at swimming. They are gentle and patient (mine work with autistic and learning difficulty children), though they are also protective and bark if strangers approach me or the house."

Lisa and Mark Mellor, Goodgrace Retrievers, Essex, breeders with 23 years' experience: "They have a warmth and beauty about them; the dogs are strong and majestic and the bitches capture the lovely gentle nature of the breed. They are very family-oriented, and (unlike some breeds) love all the family, rather than attaching themselves to one particular person. They are seen as safe and dependable, they are not a high maintenance dog and so for families buying their first dog they are a natural choice. Once a family has a Goldie, they are unlikely to change, in our experience, as the breed lives up to its good reputation.

"They are very patient, biddable and intuitive. Whilst they are most definitely a very happy-go-lucky breed, they also have a wonderful sense of empathy, and so when things are affecting you and you are unhappy, they sense and pick up on that and it shows in their behaviour towards you. We have never heard of a bad word said about a Golden Retriever's temperament."

Sue Page, Dormansue Golden Retrievers, Surrey, a breeder since 2004: "How can you put the sheer joy of owning a Golden Retriever into words, as they enrich the lives of their owners in so many different ways? Their kind, gentle, sensitive natures make them the ideal companion and they want to be friends with everyone. They are intelligent and so they are easy to train, which is why they make such good Guide Dogs. There is something so special about Golden Retrievers and they really get into your heart. As Golden Retrievers are such happy dogs, it is difficult for their happiness not to rub off on to their owners. They have everything going for them. They are great fun, always doing something you don't expect, amazingly attuned to your moods and all they ever want to do is to please."

Claire Underwood, Bowcombe Golden Retrievers, Isle of Wight: "I met a lovely retriever where I used to work, and loved his temperament. He was laid-back, he loved everyone, but was also independent and not needy. Golden Retrievers have a stand-by mode, where people can walk over them, visitors can be undisturbed by them, but they respond to anyone who wants to say hello with a gentle waving of their tails. They are not anxious and can be self-contained and settle quickly wherever you take them. At events like county shows, etc. I receive a lot of comments on how good the dogs are; it's not me, it's the dogs that make it look like they are well-trained. They are good at puppy training.

"All the ones I have had wander given half a chance; they are quite happy to take themselves off or escape, which is not always a good trait! They steal food, and will jump up to work surfaces to reach food. They dig and can chew plants and shrubs, but this is common amongst many dogs... probably all!"

Anna Cornelius-Jones, Mindieslodge Golden Retrievers, Dorset: "I was attracted to the breed because of their good nature and temperament. We had young children when we acquired our first Golden and that was an important factor when choosing our family pet. I think their reputation for this, along with the fact that they are easy to train both as family and working/show dogs has made them popular all over the world.

"Goldens are very loving and loyal dogs. They are very family-orientated and are always wanting to please their owners and lavish you with unconditional love. They are always picking up toys or clothing and bringing them to you as a sign of their love. I haven't found, in the 13 years that I have been breeding, a bad quirk in this breed at all."

Nicholas Lock, Bonsaviour Retrievers, Shropshire: "They are intelligent, gentle, loving and loyal. All Goldies have a personality suited to family life. A Goldie will always show you affection and dig up your garden!"

Julian Pottage, Yorkbeach Golden Retrievers, Mid Glamorgan, Wales: "Goldens are well known for having a lovely temperament. At the time I acquired my foundation bitch, my daughter was not yet two and it was important to have a breed suitable for living with young children. The Golden has a lovely coat for admiring and stroking – short-coated breeds do not appeal to me. A traditionally docked breed did not appeal either, because I like to see a dog's tail wag.

"I like the size of a Golden – smaller breeds lack the same appeal and, while I would not mind a bigger dog, the size of a Golden is practical – you can lift one up if you have to without breaking your back. The colour is something I like too, when it is golden, rather than cream. The typical show line Golden should be biddable, laid-back, friendly with both people and other dogs. Many Goldens are keen on their food and some will scavenge or even steal food. Many Goldens like getting themselves wet in a river, the sea, a lake or pool."

Photo of five-month-old Abbie, courtesy of Julian.

Dee Johnson, Johnsongrace Golden Retrievers, North Cornwall: "My sister-in-law had a female Golden Retriever and I fell in love with her gentle nature. I noticed how much she seemed to be more human-like than any other breed. They are gentle, inquisitive, loyal and playful. Goldens have a particular trait that they don't show when they are in pain very often."

George Coxwell, Revaliac Golden Retrievers, Devon: "My grandmother had a Golden when I was a child, and when our German Shepherd Dog died in 1986, we bought our first Golden. They are without doubt the best breed for children. They will be whatever you wish them to be, trainable, lazy or full of energy; the ideal family pet."

Stephen and Jessica Webb, HollyRoseFen Golden Retrievers, Lincolnshire: "The dogs are pretty, loyal, easy to train and ideal family pets. They are predictable, a good all round dog; calm and laid-back. Goldies are very intelligent and love to be off-lead."

Karen Parsons, Arundel, West Sussex: "I love their happy faces and outlook on life. They are always ready to do whatever you want and are just the best friends when life is getting you down. They understand and do not judge you; they just love you. They are calm, intelligent and loyal. They often ask for a paw to be held and stroked - and if you ignore that, they nudge you with their noses!

"I was attracted to the breed because of their 'goofy' nature, their size and general appearance. I like a dog to look like a dog — big and fluffy. Their popularity is obvious - to me anyway, it's their nature. To be with you, to do your bidding, to accept what you give them and not be too demanding. Their temperament is brilliant; gentle, loving and intelligent. They seem to know how to behave around different types of people: children and oldies — careful and considerate; teenagers and young adults — more bouncy; general types — sedate and calm."

Jan Schick, Mildenhall, Suffolk: "I was attracted to Golden Retrievers because of their friendly nature and their 'natural' good looks, i.e. no squashed noses or abnormal head size! Also, their ability to go on long walks and their fondness for swimming. I believe that they are so popular worldwide because they are so good with children and are therefore an ideal choice for families. They enjoy energetic play, but are fundamentally calm and chilled, but, as they have a sense of humour, they can be mischievous. They do not tend to bark when there is a knock at the door and they would make poor guard dogs - they would welcome thieves as enthusiastically as they would any visitor."

Lesley Gunter, Moorvista, Derbyshire, who has recently bred her first litter after many years' experience with Goldens: "I had Staffordshire Bull Terriers when I was growing up and later Border Collies and a Lab/Setter cross. Since having our first Golden 20 years ago, we haven't thought of moving to any other breed. We are now on our fourth and for the last few years have had two together. They fit in with family life very well. Our children grew up with them, and we have never had any problematic behaviour to deal with. I think their reliability as a steady family dog, combined with their attractiveness, is what attracts people to them. They are generally very good-natured with both people, including children, and other dogs - though there are obviously exceptions."

"As far as temperament goes, Golden Retrievers are generally kind and friendly with everyone; sometimes a little over-exuberant, so training is important to ensure they behave calmly when around people. I understand that they can be possessive of toys and food, but I have to say that none of the Retrievers I've owned have had that trait. I have recently sustained a broken wrist when my lovely calm three-year-old bitch knocked me off my feet in her enthusiasm to retrieve a stick from the river! I've heard of other people who have had similar incidents. They do seem to have quite poor spatial awareness.

"Barging and over-exuberance, as already mentioned, does need to be considered. My three current dogs don't bark when someone comes to the door. They don't bark much at all in fact, but our first Golden Retriever did alert bark. I think it is more usual for them not to, so this is not a breed to choose if you want a guard dog."

Richard and Suzanne Clear, Arunsglory Golden Retrievers, West Sussex, bred their first litter three years ago, having had Goldens for 25 years: "They are such easy-going dogs with a laid-back attitude to life. They are placid, loving, funny and, above all, caring - although they can be stubborn, too."

Helen Dorrance, of Ducat Goldens, Texas, USA, has 42 years' experience of breeding Goldens and says: "I think the fact that Goldens are known as 'the family-friendly breed' is what has made them so popular. They are also a very beautiful breed. I was attracted by their trainability and eager-to-please nature. When I first got into the breed, Goldens tended to be more laid-back, but always ready to work at whatever activity their owner suggested. I think originally the Golden truly was the gentleman's hunting dog, easy to work with and train but also able to think for themselves."

Helen added that she owns a boarding kennel and had come across an increasing number of Goldens that were not as trainable and "some are quite wild." She no longer recommends Goldens for older people or puppies for children under five years of age.

Tim Hoke, Golden Meadows Retrievers, California, has bred Goldens for 25 years and been involved with them for even longer: "I had a Golden as a child, I have always loved them. They are so smart, affectionate and easy-going that they make a wonderful family companion. The typical Golden is easy-going, mild-mannered, cautiously curious, interested in the world around him and eager to meet new people."

Kelly Sisco, Show Me Goldens, Missouri: "Goldens are extremely loving, very trainable and beautiful, of course! I believe their easy-going and fun-loving nature makes them an ideal family or first pet. They are ready to play and have fun, but also very happy to crawl in your lap for a night of watching movies. My gals and guys tend to be happy when they are by my side, no matter what we are doing."

We also asked the breeders to sum up their Golden Retrievers in a few words. This is what they said:

- Affectionate, loyal, attractive
- Angels with golden fur
- Fun-loving, family-centred and gentle
- Hearts of gold
- Intelligent, loving, loyal, fantastic
- Loving, obedient, family-orientated faithful
- Loving, gentle, trainable, affectionate
- Hairy specimens of love!
- Gentle, welcoming and trainable
- Best family dog!
- Individual, funny, devoted, stubborn
- Loyal, fun, friendly
- Gorgeous, striking, obedient, perfect
- Family-friendly, amenable, fun
- Beautiful, independent, mud-loving, friendly
- Everything you could wish for

Read on to find the right puppy and then learn how to take good care of the newest member of the family for the rest of his or her life, and how to build a unique bond that will become one of the most important things in your life - and certainly his or hers.

2. History of the Golden Retriever

Today, the Golden Retriever is one of the most popular dog breeds in Europe and North America. But the true history of the Golden was only discovered in 1952.

The origins of the breed lie with Dudley Coutts Marjoribanks (pronounced Marchbanks) - pictured. He was a Liberal politician and a Scottish businessman whose father was a senior partner in Coutts Bank. He sat in the House of Commons from 1853 until 1881, when he was elevated to the House of Lords as the First Baron Tweedmouth.

Lord Tweedmouth, as he then became known, acquired considerable family wealth after the purchase of Meux Brewery, of which he became chairman, and later as a director of the East India Company. With some of his riches he built the mansion of Brook House in London's fashionable Park Lane and also purchased the Scottish Highlands deer forest of Guisachan (pronounced *GOOSH-a-gan* meaning 'place of the fir' in Gaelic).

The Baron undertook a vast building programme during which he built Guisachan House (pictured below in its heyday in the 1890s) and service buildings for the estate. These included a farm steading, dairy, stables, laundry, brewery, meal mill, school (which doubled as a church), meeting house, hot house, deer rendering hut, houses in and around the village of Tomich. He also built kennels and it was here that the Golden Retriever breed was created.

Although Guisachan House is today a ruin, the dairy and steading have been converted to self-catering residences known as Tomich Holidays and the estate has become a place of pilgrimage for Golden Retriever lovers who travel from far and wide to see the ancestral home of their beloved breed. In July 2006, the Golden Retriever Club of Scotland organised a gathering of Golden Retriever owners at Guisachan. The commemorative photograph captured 188 Goldens, and so holds the record for the most Golden Retrievers in one image.

In 1868 the Baron mated a yellow Wavy-Coated Retriever, Nous, to liver-coloured Tweed Water Spaniel, Belle, from Ladykirk on the Tweed in the Scottish Borders. In those days the word 'liver' signified any shade of coat from yellow to brown. This created the foundation litter of Golden Retrievers, three yellow wavy-coated puppies called Crocus (male), Cowslip and Primrose (females). Lord Tweedmouth's grandson told an interesting story as to Nous's origins (in the UK Nous means common sense!).

He said that one Sunday when his grandfather and father were at Brighton in the late 1860s, they met a good looking yellow retriever and approached the man who had it. This man, a cobbler, said that he had got the dog in lieu of a bad debt from a local keeper and that it was the only yellow puppy out of a black Wavy-Coated Retriever litter (the Flat Coats were then called Wavy). The bitch, Belle, was a Tweed Water Spaniel, which was a rare breed, even in those days, except in the Scottish Borders.

They were described as small liver-coloured and curly-coated Retrievers. According to his journals, between 1868 and 1890 Lord Tweedmouth methodically line-bred down from this original mating using another Tweed Water Spaniel and outcrosses of two black Retrievers, an Irish Setter and a sandy-coloured Bloodhound. The Bloodhound connection was later refuted by Lord Tweedmouth's grandson, the Third Lord Tweedmouth.

(This 1864 painting 'Water Spaniel' by John Carlton is thought to represent the now extinct Tweed Water Spaniel).

For many decades it was thought that there was a fourth puppy from this first litter, Ada. But Ada was from a second mating of Nous and Belle and was given to Lord Tweedmouth's nephew, the Fifth Lord Ilchester, thus beginning the famous Ilchester line of retrievers. A few of the Tweedmouth dogs were given to the Earl of Shrewsbury, whose Ingestre Kennel became well known for its Flat-Coats - both black and yellow – and which appears in the background of many of today's Goldens.

None of this came to light until 1952 when Lady Pentland, granddaughter of Lord Tweedmouth, made the Guisachan Record Book (1865 to 1890) available. Her friend the Sixth Earl of Ilchester published a famous article in the July 25, 1952 edition of Country Life magazine. The following year noted Golden Retriever historian Elma Stonex published a book entitled "The Golden Retriever."

Until the Record Book was made public, the breed was said to have originated from a troupe of Russian circus dogs which the Lord saw performing in Brighton in 1858! The story went that the Baron was so impressed by their intelligence, looks and docility, that he purchased all eight of them and had them transported to Guisachan, where they were used for tracking deer.

In his Country Life article, the Sixth Earl wrote: *"For some years I have been intending to put on paper my recollections of the earliest history of the yellow, wavy-coated retrievers, which have, in recent years, become so numerous and so popular in this country. Up to the end of the last century they were a rarity, and I am probably the only person alive who can remember even the second generation of the yellow breed which belonged to Sir Dudley Coutts Marjoribanks, of Guisachan, Inverness-shire.*

"The name yellow retriever was the original name of the breed, but this has been largely superseded in later years by that of golden retriever, one coined by the late Lord Harcourt, after he had bought one or more puppies from a keeper, and after he had been given a number of those dogs which remained in the Guisachan kennels by Lord Tweedmouth, when he sold the property in 1905 or 1906.

"Lord Harcourt immediately began to exhibit his dogs on the show-bench, and was no doubt in search of a new title in order to form a new class, for neither Tweedmouth nor Ilchester breeds had ever been shown. However, it is fair to add that the Guisachan dogs had generally become darker in colour in the intervening years.

"Even at the beginning of this century, there was confusion about the origin of the breed. Black, wavy-coated retrievers, and in certain circles in the south of Scotland, black Labradors, were in great vogue. Indeed, except among members of the Tweedmouth and Ilchester families and their intimate friends, yellow retrievers were little known. Consequently their subsequent spread to all parts of the country was not easily foreseen."

"One story is that Sir Dudley purchased at Brighton about the year 1868, from a dog trainer in a travelling circus, three yellow dogs. These animals, no doubt sheep dogs, were said to have been

brought from the Region of the Caucasus and one of them, specified as Nous, was said to have been taken to Guisachan, and in due course to have become the first of the yellow breed.

"Everyone, I think, agrees that Nous was yellow, and that he was the first. But the belief that a Russian dog originated the strain is not borne out by dates, for Nous is to be found in the studbook as early as 1865, where he is described as "Lord Chichester's breed. June, 1864, purchd. At Brighton." He had no connection at all with any Russian dogs, if indeed they existed, for he had already been at Guisachan for some years."

"In 1865 Nous appears in the book as having been bought in the previous year. A photograph of him, probably taken in 1872, with a Guisachan keeper, Simon Munro, who died who died the following year, appears in Hutchinson's Dog Encyclopaedia, p. 742, and shows a very definite yellow dog."

(Photo shown right with Nous at the feet of Simon Munro).

He goes on to say that Crocus, the male offspring of the first litter of three: "*produced three yellow puppies in 1881 out of Zoe. I have given these names since they will be referred to again when discussing the Ladykirk (Tweed Water Spaniel) breed, and also to show that the cross of a black dog with a yellow bitch almost invariably produced yellow puppies. We also found these characteristics most strongly marked in the Ilchester breed. After about 1890, the bloodhound cross was introduced at Guisachan, largely for tracking purposes, and there is a definite mention also, on a loose sheet, of a sandy coloured bloodhound having been used.*"

Another Tweed Water Spaniel, named Tweed, was mentioned in Lord Tweedmouth's handwritten notes, but is believed to have died, and the Earl of Ilchester writes: "*So Tweed and Belle were Tweed Water Spaniels! But what was that Tweed variety? There even seems great doubt as to what a water spaniel in 1868 looked like. No one seems able to tell me. The Natural History Museum has no record, but Dr. Parker, Keeper of Zoology, has sent me a quotation from Ash, 1927, Dogs, Their History and Development.... the English water-spaniel, first depicted by Bewick, a collie-like dog, was probably a cross between the rough waterdog, or poodle, and the springer spaniel or setter.*

"*Between Bewick's time and that of Toplin, to judge from the illustration in Toplin's work, the water-spaniel had been so constantly crossed with the springer as to result in a dog of spaniel type, yet retaining the curly coat of the waterdog to some extent.*"

He then goes on to talk about the Ilchester Golden Retrievers, which his father, the Fifth Earl, bred from Ada, and which founded the line later known as Melbury: "*This strain my father proceeded to develop on lines quite different from those employed at Guisachan. From the first he bred from black dogs. One of my earliest recollections was of my father coming into lunch at Melbury, suffering from many wasp stings. Ada had walked into a nest, luckily on the bank of a pond, and my father had thrown her into the water to get rid of her assailants!*

"*Unfortunately no record was kept of how our crosses were arranged. Certainly at first, black wavy-coats were used, and later, black Labradors. Mr. Montague Guest's Sweep, a smooth-coat, sired more than one litter, and was probably the father of the best of our second generation, Robin, a first class worker, with a beautiful nose and mouth, and a splendid water dog.*"

Early Retrievers and the Aristocratic Connection

The 19th century was a time of great interest in dog breeding in England. Unusually for the time, it was a hobby enjoyed right across the social spectrum, from working men to aristocrats. The working "fanciers" often favoured the smaller breeds, as they were inexpensive to keep and could live in cramped little houses with the family. Those of noble birth were more often associated with larger, sporting dogs, and this was the case with Retrievers, including Goldens.

Country Life magazine explained why there was such interest in breeding the perfect retriever: "*Previous to 1850, setters, pointers, etc., were used to retrieve, as they are still in this country, but English sportsmen felt the need for one dog to find the game and another to retrieve it. At some time in the (18)50's the Labrador dog was introduced into England and was found to be a natural retriever. He was a black, close-coated water dog, classed then as a spaniel.*

"*Various writers have attributed Labrador, collie, setter, spaniel, and Newfoundland blood to the flat-coated retriever, but the weight of evidence seems to favour a fairly clean Labrador-setter cross. He exhibits some spaniel characteristics, to be sure, but they may well have come from the Labrador strain, while his head is decidedly setter-like.*

"*The flat-coated retriever was made popular among British fanciers about 1870 by Dr. Bond Moore,*

FLAT-COATED RETRIEVER.

CURLY-COATED RETRIEVER.

Mr. S. E. Shirley, and others, the pure black and liver colours being favoured. There has also been produced a so-called golden retriever, varying in colour from fawn to Irish setter red. The brown colours are difficult to breed true, however, and the blacks have always been more popular.

The Encyclopaedia of Sport and Games, Volume 2, edited by the Earl of Suffolk and Berkshire 1911 states: "*With many sportsmen, the retriever is the up and coming dog, as, in many cases where grouse and partridge are "driven" or "walked up," a retriever is more useful than pointer, setter, or spaniel; besides, he is a good all-round dog for a shooting man.*

"*There are three varieties of the retriever proper, the curly coated, which may originally have been produced from the Irish water spaniel or the poodle; the flat or wavy-coated, (ancestor of the Golden Retriever) which is no doubt a cross between the Labrador dog, the collie, and the setter. Black is the prevailing colour of each, though, in the first-named variety liver or browns are not uncommon, and black and tan are sometimes seen. Of the flat-coated variety, liver coloured specimens are unusual, though puppies of that hue are sometimes produced from black parents.*"

In the *Complete Book of the Dog*, published in 1922, author Leighton Robert, gives a description of the early Golden Retrievers (although his account of the origins is now known to be incorrect): "*This is a variety which is becoming increasingly popular. Introduced forty or fifty years ago as the Yellow Russian Retriever, they are neither yellow nor Russian. They are really Labradors, and they have all the intelligence of the Labrador. Their colour is a pale golden tan. Black has always been the recognized colour of the Labrador, but the early Retrievers were by no means fixed in colour.*

"In 1876 Dr. Bond Moore's black bitch Midnight whelped a litter of pale golden puppies, and somewhat later Captain Radcliffe owned several Golden Labradors at Wareham. It is stated by some writers that the black Labrador was designedly crossed with the Bloodhound, and by others that the Irish Setter has been used as an outcross. But if this was in order to get the golden colouring it was surely a roundabout method, considering that yellow Retrievers already existed on the (Scottish) Borders.

"In any case, the Golden Retriever is now a dog of fixed type. He is somewhat heavier than the ordinary flat-coated Retriever, but not very different in shape and quite as handsome, and he has proved himself a capable worker in the retrieving of game. At recent field trials Mr. J. Compton's Balbeardie and Mr. T. W. Twyford's Tatler and Titus distinguished themselves in close competition, and an increasing number of the variety are to be seen at important dog shows. Mr. Hermon's Balcombe Boy and Mr. Braybrook's Ballingdon Floss are notable prize-winners, and Mrs. W. M. Charlesworth's Golden Retrievers bearing her Noranby prefix are always especially good representatives of the variety.

"The description of the flat-coated variety applies to the Golden Retriever, with the exception that the latter has rather larger ears and is, of course, lighter in eye."

The first Conformation Dog Show was held from June 28th to 29th, 1859, at Newcastle-upon-Tyne. It was an added attraction to the annual cattle show and only the sporting breeds of setters and pointers were allowed to enter - the prizes were guns! But, despite this limited beginning, the genie was out of the bag and the Conformation Dog Show went on to become hugely popular in Victorian times – and still is.

Culham Brass and Culham Rossa, registered under the famous Culham prefix, were among the earliest dogs to be shown as yellow or golden Retrievers. These two dogs had been raised by Mr. John McLennan, former keeper at the Guisachan estate, and were sold as puppies to Lord Harcourt, who owned the Culham Kennel. Lord Harcourt had also received other Guisachan Retrievers from Lord Tweedmouth II, after his father's death, and these he also showed.

From Brass and Rossa came Culham Copper, sire of Ch. Noranby Campfire, the first Golden ever to win a bench title. Copper also sired Culham Tip, out of Beena of Ingestre parentage, said to have been dark red in colour. Campfire's dam was the great foundation bitch of the Noranby Kennel, Normanby Beauty. In a later mating with Culham Brass, Beauty produced the famous Noranby Balfour.

The first dog show was followed 14 years later by the formation of The Kennel Club and 11 years after that (1884) by the American Kennel Club. These organisations began to draw up Breed Standards which stated how a particular breed of dog should look and act. Before that, the same breed of dog could come in varying shapes, sizes and colours. The 19th and early 20th centuries saw much experimentation by fanciers with different dogs from varied backgrounds. New breeds were being created from the bloodlines of several types of dogs and it was often not until the late 19th and turn of the 20th century that the first Breed Standards were drawn up.

As we have read, several aristocrats were involved in creating the dog we know today as The Golden Retriever. Throughout the end of the 19th century and early 20th century, the aristocrats continued to experiment with various pairings, introducing Setters and Spaniels into the mix, until they could fairly consistently produce a dog which was then known as the yellow Retriever. This dog became particularly popular in the Scottish Borders, where there are many large shooting estates.

Golden coloured Retrievers were first accepted as 'Flat Coats – Golden' by the (UK) Kennel Club in 1903. They were first exhibited in 1908, and in 1913 were officially recognised by the Kennel Club as a unique breed, described as Retriever (Golden and Yellow). When the Golden Retriever Club was formed in 1920, the breed's name was changed to Golden Retriever.

The St John's Water Dog

To truly understand the nature of today's Golden Retriever, the breed's love of water, huge heart and great desire to please its owners, I think it is beneficial to get an insight into the dog which was the founding stock of ALL retrievers. That was the rugged St John's Water Dog (also called the St. John's Dog or Lesser Newfoundland) that emerged through ad-hoc breedings by early settlers of the island in the 16th century. This dog was black in colour with white "tuxedo" markings on the chest, muzzle and feet – occasionally, these markings can still be seen on some of today's Labrador Retrievers, when the white chest mark is known as a "medallion." They are often more pronounced on crossbreeds.

The ancestors of the St. John's Water Dog are not entirely known; it is likely they were a random-bred mix of English, Irish and Portuguese working breeds. The dog is often referred to as a "landrace," i.e. it was not a pedigree; it was bred for a job, rather than for a specific look. The dogs were described as having a short thick coat, rudder-like tail, high endurance and a great love of swimming.

Newfoundland was settled by English fisherman as early as the 1500s and the St. John's Water Dogs developed alongside the fishing industry. The English fisherman working in Newfoundland used the dog to retrieve fish that had fallen off their hooks, as well as to help haul nets and long fishing lines through the water back to their boats. These dogs were considered workaholics and enjoyed their retrieving tasks – even in freezing weather and icy water.

They would work long hours in the cold waters and then be brought home to play with the fisherman's children. The breed was very eager to please and its retrieving abilities made an ideal hunting companion and sporting dog; it was known to retrieve ptarmigan and even seal. So, even in these early days, the Golden Retriever's ancestors had a reputation as keen, versatile workers with excellent temperaments.

The St. John's Water Dog was the ancestor of all present-day retrievers, including the Flat Coated Retriever, Chesapeake Bay Retriever, Golden Retriever and Labrador Retriever. It was also an ancestor of the larger, gentle Newfoundland dog, probably through breeding with Mastiffs brought to the island by the generations of Portuguese fishermen who had fished offshore since the 15th century.

The breed survived until the early 1980s. Our photo, dating back to the late 1970s, shows the last two St. John's Water Dogs – unfortunately both were male (despite one of them being called Lassie!) and the breed became extinct upon their deaths. The decline was caused by a combination of two factors. In an attempt to encourage sheep raising, heavy restrictions and taxes were placed on any dogs not used in the production of sheep during the 19th century.

Secondly, their main overseas destination - England - imposed rigorous long-term quarantine on imported dogs after a rabies outbreak in 1885 – but not before many Newfoundland fishermen had sold their water dogs to British dog dealers, who then sold them on to people wanting to improve their retriever lines.

In 1807 a ship called Canton from Baltimore carried some St. John's Water Dogs destined for Poole, England, probably as breeding stock for what was to become a British aristocrat's retriever kennel. The Canton shipwrecked, but not before the crew were saved, along with two dogs - a black bitch called Canton and a "dingy red" dog, Sailor. The captain sold them back in the USA for a guinea each and these two are believed to be the foundation stock of the Chesapeake Bay Retriever.

This "dingy red" is what we today refer to as "chocolate" or "liver" in the Labrador. We know from Sailor that this was a natural colour in the original St. John's Water Dog. Along with yellow, the chocolate was a recessive colour which would occasionally appear in litters.

In 1822, explorer W.E. Cormack crossed the island of Newfoundland by foot. In his journal he wrote: *"The dogs are admirably trained as retrievers in fowling, and are otherwise useful.....The smooth or short haired dog is preferred because in frosty weather the long haired kind become encumbered with ice on coming out of the water."*

An early report by a Colonel Hawker described the dog as: *"By far the best for any kind of shooting. He is generally black and no bigger than a Pointer, very fine in legs, with short, smooth hair and does not carry his tail so much curled as the other; is extremely quick, running, swimming and fighting....and their sense of smell is hardly to be credited."*

The first St. John's dog was said to be brought to England in or around 1820, but the breed's reputation had already spread to England; there is a story that the 2nd Earl of Malmesbury saw a St. John's Water Dog on a fishing boat and immediately made arrangements with traders to have some of these dogs imported to England. (Pictured is Lassie, aged 13).

In his book *"Excursions In and About Newfoundland During the Years 1839 and 1840"*, the geologist Joseph Beete Jukes describes the St. John's Water Dog: *"A thin, short-haired, black dog came off-shore to us to-day. The animal was of a breed very different from what we understand by the term Newfoundland dog in England. He had a thin, tapering snout, a long thin tail, and rather thin, but powerful legs, with a lank body, – the hair short and smooth.*

"These are the most abundant dogs in the country...They are no means handsome, but are generally more intelligent and useful than the others...I observed he once or twice put his foot in the water and paddled it about. This foot was white, and Harvey said he did it to "toil" or entice the fish. The whole proceeding struck me as remarkable, more especially as they said he had never been taught anything of the kind."

Today, in both Newfoundland and the Maritime provinces, there are still large black mixed-breed dogs with many characteristics of the original St. John's Water Dog.

Golden Retrievers in North America

In the late 19th century, American hunters used Setters and Pointers to cover large areas and heavy cover. Although there was – and still is - a difference between British shoots and American hunts, the Golden Retriever's popularity as a sporting dog increased throughout the 20th century. At the British 'driven' shoots, dogs walked at heel, before 'marking' (being trained to note where the bird has fallen), then retrieving game. However, the size and variations of American terrain, combined with the many different types of cover, made more demands on the working dog.

At that time, American hunters were using Springer Spaniels to find upland game and Chesapeake Bay Retrievers to retrieve birds from water. They began taking an interest in Retrievers when they realised that they were as good as Springers on the uplands and Chesapeakes in the water. The Retriever had the added bonus of an excellent and willing temperament.

The first Golden Retriever in North America was Lady, who was imported into Canada by The Honourable Archie Marjoribanks, son of Lord Tweedmouth in 1881. Lady and other Tweedmouth Retrievers went to Coldstream Ranch in British Columbia, owned by the Marquis of Aberdeen, Archie's brother-in-law and Canada's Governor General from 1893 to 1898.

The first Golden Retriever registered with the Canadian Kennel Club was Judy of Westholme, born May 8, 1926, by Buckham ex Hersham Primula, owned by B.M. Armstrong of Manitoba, and bred by G.A.S. Wylys. The first champion of record was Ch. Foxbury Peter. He was imported to Quebec from Great Britainby Mrs. Alex MacLaren.

GOLDEN RETRIEVERS

ROCKHAVEN
KENNELS
(Reg'd)

NORTH
VANCOUVER, B.C.

GILNOCKIE
KENNELS
(Reg'd)

ADRIAN, OREGON

Can. and Am. Ch. SPEEDWELL PLUTO (Imp.)
Ch. Michael of Moreton ex Speedwell Emerald.

At Stud:
Can. & Am. CH. SPEEDWELL PLUTO (Imp.);
CH. ROCKHAVEN HAROLD;
CH. ROCKHAVEN ROCKET.

Puppies For Sale from proven bloodlines as workers and winners on the bench. Kindly and affectionate dispositions, easy to train and handle, and all perfectly conditioned and developed.

Correspondence a pleasure.

In 1928, Mr. M.M. Armstrong of Winnipeg took an interest in the breed and his Gilnockie kennel was started. At his death, Gilnockie was transferred to Col. Samuel Magoffin's kennel in Denver, Colorado, and from this he eventually imported his first Golden, Am/Can CH Speedwell Pluto.

It took some years before the early Golden Retrievers which had first appeared in Canada and then the USA to be recognised in these countries. Kennel Club recognition for the breed was eventually given by in 1925 in Canada and 1932 in the USA. In 1938, a group of Golden Retriever fanciers formed the Golden Retriever Club of America (GRCA) which is today among the largest of the parent breed clubs in the AKC, with more than 5,000 members. (Pictured is an advertisement for Rockhaven Kennels from the February 1934 issue of Kennel and Bench, the Canadian Kennel Club magazine. The Rockhaven dogs not only competed in conformation shows, but also regularly hunted and competed in field trials).

During the latter part of the 20th century, the breed's appeal as a pet, as well as a working dog, rapidly increased. The Golden Retriever has consistently been in the top three or four places since the end of the 20th century in the USA and top 10 in the UK.

3. Breed Standard

The **breed standard** is what makes a Great Dane a Great Dane and a Chihuahua a Chihuahua. It is a blueprint not only for the appearance of each breed, but also for character and temperament, how the dog moves and what colours are acceptable. In other words, it ensures that the Golden Retriever looks and acts like a Golden Retriever and is 'fit for function'. The 'Golden' or 'Goldie' is listed in the Gundog Group in the UK and the Sporting Group in the USA.

The breed standard is laid down by the breed societies. In the UK it's the Kennel Club, and in the USA it's the AKC (American Kennel Club) that keeps the register of pedigree (purebred) dogs. Dogs entered in conformation shows run under Kennel Club and AKC rules are judged against this ideal list of attributes. Breeders approved - or 'Assured' in the UK - by the Kennel Clubs agree to produce puppies in line with the breed standard and maintain certain welfare conditions.

Good breeders, such as Kennel Club Assured Breeders, select only the best dogs for reproduction, based on factors such as the health, looks, temperament and the character of the parents and their ancestors. They do not simply take any available male and female and allow them to randomly breed.

The same is true of AKC Breeders of Merit in the USA: "AKC Breeders are dedicated to breeding beautiful purebred dogs whose appearance, temperament, and ability are true to their breed." The Kennel Clubs all have lists of breeders, and if you have not yet got a puppy, this is a good place to start looking for one. Visit the Kennel Club website or breed club in your country for details of approved breeders.

Responsible breeders also aim to reduce or eradicate genetic illnesses, which in the case of Golden Retrievers include joint, eye and heart disease. In the past, breeders of some types of dog have concentrated too closely on the physical appearance of the animal without paying enough attention to soundness and health. In response, the Kennel Club set up Breed Watch, which serves as an 'early warning system' to identify points of concern for individual breeds. In the UK the Golden Retriever is listed in Category 2, with Category 1 being the breeds with "no major points of concern" and Category 3 being: "Breeds where some dogs have visible conditions or exaggerations that can cause pain or discomfort." Goldens have the following "Points of concern for special attention by judges:"

- Legs too short in proportion to depth of body and to length of back
- Significantly overweight

Golden Retrievers are bred from a fairly large gene pool, compared with some other breeds. However, the Kennel Club average COI (Coefficient of Inbreeding) for the breed is 9.4%, which is some way above the ideal of 6.25%. UFAW (Universities Federation for Animal Welfare) says: "Essentially, COI measures the common ancestors of dam and sire, and indicates the probability of how genetically similar they are. There are consequences to being genetically similar, some good, some bad. The fact that dogs within individual breeds are so genetically similar is what makes them

that breed." Which is why when you breed any Golden Retriever to any other Golden Retriever, the puppies will look recognisably like Golden Retrievers.

It goes on to explain why a high COI can be a problem: "Inbreeding will help cement 'good' traits but there's a danger of it also cementing bad ones. In particular, it can cause the rapid build-up of disease genes in a population. Even if a breed of dog is lucky enough to be free of serious genetic disorders, inbreeding is likely to affect our dogs in more subtle, but no less serious, ways."

Anyone buying a puppy is advised to ask to see the relevant health certificates for the pup and his or her parents before committing. Prospective UK owners can also check the COI of their chosen puppy and parents using the Kennel Club's **Mate Select** programme at www.thekennelclub.org.uk/services/public/mateselect

If you are serious about getting a Golden Retriever, then study the breed standard before visiting any puppies, so you know what a well-bred example should look like. There may be some slight variation in coat colour and appearance between working and show dogs, but the main points remain the same. And if you've already got your dog, these are the desired features he or she should display:

Kennel Club Breed Standard (UK)

General Appearance - Symmetrical, balanced, active, powerful, level mover; sound with kindly expression.

Characteristics - Biddable, intelligent and possessing natural working ability.

Temperament - Kindly, friendly and confident.

Head and Skull - Balanced and well chiselled, skull broad without coarseness; well set on neck, muzzle powerful, wide and deep. Length of foreface approximately equals length from well-defined stop to occiput. Nose preferably black.

Eyes - Dark brown, set well apart, dark rims.

Ears - Moderate size, set on approximate level with eyes.

Mouth - Jaws strong, with a perfect, regular and complete scissor bite, i.e. upper teeth closely overlapping lower teeth and set square to the jaws.

Neck - Good length, clean and muscular.

Forequarters - Forelegs straight with good bone, shoulders well laid-back, long in blade with upper arm of equal length placing legs well under body. Elbows close fitting.

Body - Balanced, short-coupled, deep through heart. Ribs deep, well sprung. Level topline.

Hindquarters - Loin and legs strong and muscular, good second thighs, well bent stifles. Hocks well let down, straight when viewed from rear, neither turning in nor out. Cow-hocks highly undesirable.

Feet - Round and cat-like.

Tail - Set on and carried level with back, reaching to hocks, without curl at tip.

Gait/Movement - Powerful with good drive. Straight and true in front and rear. Stride long and free with no sign of hackney action in front.

Coat - Flat or wavy with good feathering, dense water-resisting undercoat.

Colour - Any shade of gold or cream, neither red nor mahogany. A few white hairs on chest only, permissible.

Size - Height at withers: dogs: 56-61 cms (22-24 ins); bitches: 51-56 cms (20-22 ins).

Faults - Any departure from the foregoing points should be considered a fault and the seriousness with which the fault should be regarded should be in exact proportion to its degree and its effect upon the health and welfare of the dog and on the dog's ability to perform its traditional work.

Note - Male animals should have two apparently normal testicles fully descended into the scrotum.

American Kennel Club Breed Standard

General Appearance: A symmetrical, powerful, active dog, sound and well put together, not clumsy nor long in the leg, displaying a kindly expression and possessing a personality that is eager, alert and self-confident. Primarily a hunting dog, he should be shown in hard working condition. Overall appearance, balance, gait and purpose to be given more emphasis than any of his component parts.

Faults - Any departure from the described ideal shall be considered faulty to the degree to which it interferes with the breed's purpose or is contrary to breed character.

Size, Proportion, Substance: Males 23 to 24 inches in height at withers; females 21½ to 22½ inches. Dogs up to one inch above or below standard size should be proportionately penalized. Deviation in height of more than one inch from the standard shall disqualify. Length from breastbone to point of buttocks slightly greater than height at withers in ratio of 12:11. Weight for dogs 65 to 75 pounds; bitches 55 to 65 pounds.

Head: Broad in *skull,* slightly arched laterally and longitudinally without prominence of frontal bones (forehead) or occipital bones. Stop well defined but not abrupt. Foreface deep and wide, nearly as long as skull. *Muzzle* straight in profile, blending smooth and strongly into skull; when viewed in profile or from above, slightly deeper and wider at stop than at tip. No heaviness in flews. Removal of whiskers is permitted but not preferred. *Eyes* friendly and intelligent in expression, medium large with dark, close-fitting rims, set well apart and reasonably deep in sockets. Color preferably dark brown; medium brown acceptable. Slant eyes and narrow, triangular eyes detract from correct expression and are to be faulted. No white or haw visible when looking straight ahead. Dogs showing evidence of functional abnormality of eyelids or eyelashes (such as, but not limited to, trichiasis, entropion, ectropion, or distichiasis) are to be excused from the ring.

Ears rather short with front edge attached well behind and just above the eye and falling close to cheek. When pulled forward, tip of ear should just cover the eye. Low, hound-like ear set to be faulted. Nose black or brownish black, though fading to a lighter shade in cold weather not serious. Pink nose or one seriously lacking in pigmentation to be faulted. Teeth scissors **bite**, in which the outer side of the lower incisors touches the inner side of the upper incisors. Undershot or overshot bite is a disqualification. Misalignment of teeth (irregular placement of incisors) or a level bite (incisors meet each other edge to edge) is undesirable, but not to be confused with undershot or overshot. Full dentition. Obvious gaps are serious faults.

Neck, Topline, Body: *Neck* medium long, merging gradually into well laid-back shoulders, giving sturdy, muscular appearance. No throatiness. *Backline* strong and level from withers to slightly sloping croup, whether standing or moving. Sloping backline, roach or sway back, flat or steep croup to be faulted.

Body well balanced, short coupled, deep through the chest. Chest between forelegs at least as wide as a man's closed hand including thumb, with well-developed forechest. Brisket extends to elbow. Ribs long and well sprung but not barrel shaped, extending well towards hindquarters. Loin short, muscular, wide and deep, with very little tuck-up. Slabsidedness, narrow chest, lack of depth in brisket, excessive tuck-up to be faulted. *Tail* well set on, thick and muscular at the base, following the natural line of the croup. Tail bones extend to, but not below, the point of hock. Carried with merry action, level or with some moderate upward curve; never curled over back nor between legs.

Forequarters: Muscular, well-coordinated with hindquarters and capable of free movement. Shoulder blades long and well laid-back with upper tips fairly close together at withers. Upper arms appear about the same length as the blades, setting the elbows back beneath the upper tip of the blades, close to the ribs without looseness. Legs, viewed from the front, straight with good bone, but not to the point of coarseness. Pasterns short and strong, sloping slightly with no suggestion of weakness. Dewclaws on forelegs may be removed, but are normally left on. Feet medium size, round, compact, and well knuckled, with thick pads. Excess hair may be trimmed to show natural size and contour. Splayed or hare feet to be faulted.

Hindquarters: Broad and strongly muscled. Profile of croup slopes slightly; the pelvic bone slopes at a slightly greater angle (approximately 30 degrees from horizontal). In a natural stance, the femur joins the pelvis at approximately a 90-degree angle; stifles well bent; hocks well let down with short, strong rear pasterns. Feet as in front. Legs straight when viewed from rear. Cow-hocks, spread hocks, and sickle hocks to be faulted.

Coat: Dense and water-repellent with good undercoat. Outer coat firm and resilient, neither coarse nor silky, lying close to body; may be straight or wavy. Untrimmed natural ruff; moderate feathering on back of forelegs and on underbody; heavier feathering on front of neck, back of thighs and underside of tail. Coat on head, paws, and front of legs is short and even. Excessive length, open coats, and limp, soft coats are very undesirable. Feet may be trimmed and stray hairs neatened, but the natural appearance of coat or outline should not be altered by cutting or clipping.

Color: Rich, lustrous golden of various shades. Feathering may be lighter than rest of coat. With the exception of graying or whitening of face or body due to age, any white marking, other than a few white hairs on the chest, should be penalized according to its extent. Allowable light shadings are not to be confused with white markings. Predominant body color which is either extremely pale or extremely dark is undesirable. Some latitude should be given to the light puppy whose coloring shows promise of deepening with maturity. Any noticeable area of black or other off-color hair is a serious fault.

Gait: When trotting, gait is free, smooth, powerful and well-coordinated, showing good reach. Viewed from any position, legs turn neither in nor out, nor do feet cross or interfere with each other. As speed increases, feet tend to converge toward center line of balance. It is recommended that dogs be shown on a loose lead to reflect true gait.

Temperament: Friendly, reliable, and trustworthy. Quarrelsomeness or hostility towards other dogs or people in normal situations, or an unwarranted show of timidity or nervousness, is not in keeping with Golden Retriever character. Such actions should be penalized according to their significance.

Disqualifications: Deviation in height of more than one inch from standard either way. Undershot or overshot bite.

Approved October 13, 1981. Reformatted August 18, 1990.

Glossary:

Dew claw – claw on the inside of the leg in a similar corresponding position to the human thumb

Hackney action - exaggerated high knee and hock action (like that of a Hackney trotting horse)

Hock - tarsal joint of the hind leg corresponding to the human ankle, but bending in the opposite direction

Occiput - bony bump seen at the top rear of the skull on some breeds

Stifle - knee

Stop - area between a dog's eyes, below the skull

Withers – shoulders

4. Choosing a Puppy

Once you have decided that the Golden Retriever is the dog for you, the best way to select a puppy is with your head - and not with your heart. With their beautiful big eyes, velvet coats, comical antics and eagerness to please, there are few more endearing things on this Earth than a litter of Golden Retriever puppies. If you go to view a litter, the pups are sure to melt your heart and it is extremely difficult – if not downright impossible - to walk away without choosing one.

So, it's essential to do your research before you visit any litters, then select **a responsible breeder with health-tested parents** (of the puppy, not the breeder!) and one who knows Goldens inside out. After all, apart from getting married or having a baby, getting a puppy is one of the most important, demanding, expensive and life-enriching decisions you will ever make.

Just like babies, puppies will love you unconditionally - but there is a price to pay. In return for their loyalty and devotion, you have to fulfil your part of the bargain.

In the beginning, you have to be prepared to devote much of your day to your new puppy. You have to feed him several times a day and housetrain virtually every hour; you have to give him your attention and start to gently introduce the rules of the house as well as take care of his health and welfare. You also have to be prepared to part with hard cash for regular healthcare and pet insurance.

If you are not prepared, or unable, to devote the time and money to a new arrival, if you have a very young family or if you are out at work all day, then now might not be the right time to consider getting a puppy. Golden Retrievers, like all breeds with working origins, are happiest when they are mentally and physically stimulated.

If left alone too long or under-exercised, these large, intelligent and loyal dogs can become bored and even destructive. This is a natural reaction and is not the dog's fault; it is simply a response to his environment, which is failing to meet his needs. Golden Retrievers want to be involved in your life and enjoy having something to do, such as retrieving a stick, swimming, picking up on a shoot, or learning new tasks. Pick a healthy pup and he or she should live for more than a decade, maybe even into the early teens if you're lucky, so this is definitely a long-term commitment. Before taking the plunge, ask yourself some questions:

Have I Got Enough Time?

In the first days after leaving his - or her - mother and littermates, your puppy will feel very lonely and probably even a little afraid. You and your family have to spend time with your new arrival to make him feel safe and sound. Ideally, for the first few days you will be around all of the time to help him settle and to start bonding with him. If you work, book a couple of weeks off - this may not be possible for some of our American readers who get shorter vacations than their European counterparts - but don't just get a puppy and leave him or her all alone in the house a couple of days later. Housetraining (potty training) starts the moment your pup arrives home. Then, after the first few days and once he's feeling more settled, start to introduce short sessions of a couple of minutes of behaviour training. Golden Retriever puppies are known for being boisterous and early training to stop puppy biting, jumping up and running into people are a must.

Begin the socialisation process by taking him out of the home to see buses, trains, noisy traffic, kids, etc. - but make sure you CARRY HIM until the vaccinations have taken effect. Puppies can be very sensitive to all sorts of things and it's important to start the socialisation process as soon as possible. The more he is introduced to at this early stage, the better, and a good breeder will already have started the process.

Once he has had the all-clear following vaccinations, get into the habit of taking him out of the house and garden or yard for a short walk every day – more as he gets older. New surroundings stimulate interest and help to stop puppies becoming bored and developing unwanted behaviour issues. He also needs to get used to different noises. Golden Retrievers are high maintenance on the grooming front, so make time to gently brush your pup and check his ears are clean to get him used to being handled and groomed right from the beginning. It's a good idea to have your pup checked out by a vet within a few days of taking him home – many breeders recommend this. You'll also need to factor in time to visit the vet's surgery for regular healthcare visits and annual vaccinations.

How Long Can I Leave Him?

This is a question we get asked all of the time and one that causes much debate among new and prospective owners. All dogs are pack animals; their natural state is to be with others. So being alone is not normal for them, although many have to get used to it. The Golden Retriever has not been bred to be a guard dog; he or she wants to be around you or other dogs.

Another issue is the toilet; all Golden Retrievers have smaller bladders than humans. Forget the emotional side of it, how would you like to be left for eight hours without being able to visit the bathroom? So how many hours can you leave a dog alone?

Well, a useful guide comes from the canine rescue organisations. In the UK, they will not allow anybody to adopt if they are intending to leave the dog alone for more than four or five hours a day.

Dogs left at home alone a lot become bored and, in the case of Golden Retrievers and other intelligent breeds, they can become depressed and/or destructive. Of course, it depends on the character and temperament of your dog, but a lonely Golden may display signs of unhappiness by chewing, barking, digging, urinating, bad behaviour, or just being plain sad and disengaged.

A puppy or fully-grown dog must NEVER be left shut in a crate all day. It is OK to leave a puppy or adult dog in a crate if he or she is happy there, but all our breeders said the same, the door should never be closed for more than a few hours during the day. A crate is a place where a puppy or adult should feel safe, it's not a prison. Ask yourself why you want a dog – is it for selfish reasons or can you really offer a good home to a young puppy - and then adult dog - for a decade or longer?

Home Preparation

Golden Retrievers are adaptable. They usually live among families in homes across the globe, but some are working dogs that retrieve game in the field. The Golden is famed for his wonderfully soft mouth and the ability to return game intact. However, one thing they all have in common is that they need exercise and regular access to the Great Outdoors. Golden Retrievers are not lap dogs, they love being outdoors, and some of this exercise time should be spent off the lead (leash). They also have an instinctive love of swimming; not surprising when you consider that the breed was created by breeding existing retrievers with water spaniels in the mid-19th century. One reason why some Goldens end up in rescue centres is that their owners did not realise how much exercise and stimulation these dogs need.

Golden Retrievers are highly intelligent, and breeders find them one of the easiest breeds to housetrain – provided you are diligent in the beginning. At a minimum, puppies should go out immediately after waking up, about 20-30 minutes after eating each meal, and right before bed. See **Chapter 6** for more information on how to housetrain your puppy.

Make sure there are no poisonous plants or chemicals in your garden. Common plants toxic to dogs include crocus, daffodil, azalea, wisteria, cyclamen, sweet pea, lily of the valley, tulips, hyacinth and lily. The Kennel Club has a list of poisonous house and garden plants here: http://bit.ly/1nCv1qJ A word of warning: don't leave your puppy unattended in the garden or yard, as dognapping is on the increase.

Golden Retriever puppies are little chewing machines and puppy-proofing your home should involve moving anything sharp, breakable or chewable - including your shoes - out of reach of sharp little teeth. Lift electrical cords, mobile phones and chargers, remote controls, etc. out of reach and block off any off-limits areas of the house - such as upstairs or your bedroom - with a child gate or barrier, especially as he will probably be following you around the house in the first few days. There's more specific advice from breeders on preparing your home later in this chapter.

Family and Children

One of the reasons you have decided on a Golden Retriever may well be because you have children. With their easy-going and loving personalities, Goldens make excellent family pets. Your children will, of course, be delighted about your new arrival. But remember that puppies are small and delicate, as are babies, so you should never leave babies or young children and dogs alone together – no matter how well they get along. Small kids lack co-ordination and a young pup may inadvertently get poked in the eye, trodden on or pulled about if you don't keep watch.

Often puppies regard children as playmates (just like a small child regards a puppy as a playmate) and young Goldens are both playful and boisterous. They may chase, jump, bump and nip a small child if left together unsupervised. This is not aggression; this is normal play for puppies. Train your pup to be gentle with your children and your children to be gentle with your puppy. If your puppy is getting too frisky when playing, say NO! or ACK! in a firm voice and stop all play until the pup has calmed down. He or she should learn that when you use your reprimand word (firmly, not shouted), the fun stops. If necessary, remove yourself and the kids – or the puppy - from the room for a short period. See **Chapter 10. Training** on how to deal with puppy biting.

Discourage the kids from constantly picking up your gorgeous new puppy. They should learn respect for the dog, which is a living creature with his or her own needs, not a toy. Make sure your puppy gets enough time to sleep – **which is most of the time in the beginning** - so don't let children - or adults! - constantly pester him. Sleep is very important to puppies, just as it is for babies.

Also, allow your Golden Retriever to eat at his or her own pace uninterrupted; letting youngsters play with the dog while eating is a no-no as it may promote gulping of food or food aggression. Another reason some dogs end up in rescue centres is that owners are unable to cope with the demands of small children AND a dog.

On the other hand, it is also a fantastic opportunity for you to educate your little darlings (both human and canine) on how to get along with each other and set the pattern for wonderful life-long friendships.

Single People

Many single adults own dogs, but if you live alone, getting a puppy will require a lot of dedication on your part. There will be nobody to share the responsibility, so taking on a dog requires a huge commitment and a lot of your time if the dog is to have a decent life. If you are out of the house all day as well, it is not really fair to get a puppy, or even an adult dog. Left alone all day, they will feel isolated, bored and sad. However, if you work from home or are at home all day and you can spend considerable time with the dog, then great; a Golden Retriever will undoubtedly become your most loyal friend.

Older People

If you are older, make sure you have the energy and patience to deal with a young puppy and then a large dog. All Goldens need plenty of daily exercise, so if you are not up to lots of daily outdoor exercise, a smaller companion dog (rather than a large breed from working stock) might be a better option – or an older Golden Retriever. A young, bouncy Golden is, in all honesty, probably a step too far for an elderly person or couple.

Dogs can, however, be great for fit, older people. My father is in his mid-80s, but takes his dog out walking for an hour or more every day - a morning and an afternoon walk and then a short one last thing at night – even in the rain or snow. He grumbles occasionally, but it's good for him and it's good for the dog, helping to keep both of them fit and socialised! They get fresh air, exercise and the chance to communicate with other dogs and their humans.

Dogs are also great company indoors – you're never alone when you've got a dog. Many older people get a canine companion after losing a loved one (a husband, wife or previous much-loved dog). A pet gives them something to care for and love, as well as a constant companion. However, owning a dog is not cheap, so it's important to be able to afford annual pet insurance, veterinary fees, a quality pet food, etc. The RSPCA in the UK has estimated that owning a dog costs an average of around £1,300 ($1,700) a year – and it's more for a big dog.

Show or Working?

All Golden Retrievers require a fair amount of exercise. After all, they were originally bred not as companions to humans, but to work all day retrieving game. Although these days many Goldens have a mixture of bloodlines in their make-up, there are still plenty that are bred from predominantly either show or working lines - and there are differences between the two.

Physically, show-type Goldens are often larger and heavier than their working counterparts, who have a leaner, more athletic appearance. Another difference is in natural temperament. A dog bred to be successful in the show ring has to be patient and wait in a kennel or crate until it's time to perform for a few brief minutes in the ring. He or she then has been bred to stand quietly while the judge prods and pokes, looks at teeth, etc. to determine if he or she is a good specimen of the breed.

In contrast, a working Retriever has to be mentally alert and physically on the go for hours on end. They are constantly paying attention to what is going on at the shoot, waiting for that command to retrieve the game and then they are off, bounding through the countryside and using all of their senses to locate the bird, which they bring back undamaged in their wonderfully soft mouths.

The consequence of this is that working dogs are often more driven that their show-type cousins. They require more physical and mental stimulation to keep their minds and bodies occupied. All Goldens like exercise - and especially running off the lead (leash) and swimming; it's in their DNA. A big generalisation would be that if you've been out on a long walk with your dog, a show-type is more likely to curl up at your side and have a snooze, whereas a working Retriever may still want to be on the go, looking for mental stimulation or the next new challenge.

Both types will thrive in active families where they are getting plenty of regular daily exercise. If you are specifically looking for a Retriever or intend taking part in field trials, then the working Golden is the dog for you. If you are a less active family, then a dog from show or mixed bloodlines might suit you better than one bred purely from working Retrievers.

Other Pets

One of the wonderful things about Golden Retrievers is how they generally get on well with everybody and everything - although it might not be a good idea to leave your hamster or pet rabbit running loose with your pup; most lively young Goldens have play or prey instincts! And if you already have other pets in your household, bear in mind that they may not be too happy at the new arrival, no matter how friendly your puppy is. Just type 'Golden Retriever puppy and cat' into YouTube to see how the two might interact; there are some amusing videos.

Spend time to introduce your pets to each other gradually and supervise the sessions in the beginning. Puppies are naturally curious and playful and they will sniff and investigate other pets. Depending on how lively your pup is, you may have to separate them to start off with, or put your high spirited Golden Retriever puppy into a pen or crate initially to allow a cat to investigate without being mauled by a hyperactive pup who thinks the cat is a great playmate.

This will also prevent your puppy from being injured. If the two animals are free and the cat lashes out, he or she could scratch your pup's eyes. A timid cat might need protection from a bold, playful Golden Retriever - or vice versa. A bold cat and a timid young Golden will probably settle down together quickest!

If things seem to be going well with no aggression after one or two supervised sessions, then let them loose together. Take the process slowly, if your cat is stressed and frightened he may decide to leave. Our feline friends are notorious for abandoning home because the food and facilities are better down the road. Until you know that they can get on, don't leave them alone together.

Gender

You have to decide whether you want a male or a female puppy. In terms of gender, much depends on the temperament of the individual dog - the differences WITHIN the sexes are greater than the differences BETWEEN the sexes. One difference, however, is that males are usually larger and heavier than females.

Another is that females have heat cycles and, unless you have her spayed, you will have to restrict your normal exercise routine when she comes into heat (every six months or so) to stop unwanted attention from other dogs. Your main point of reference in terms of size and temperament is to look at the puppy's parents; see what they are like and discuss with your breeder which puppy would best suit you.

Coat Colour

The colour of the coat is in the breed name – "Golden" Retriever. However, as breeders have developed their individual bloodlines and bred for features they consider desirable, this "Golden" now takes on many hues. Today a Golden can look almost pure white - although there is no such thing as a "white" Golden Retriever. Some puppies may appear white when born, but they will grow a light golden topcoat.

These light Golden Retrievers are sometimes known as 'English Creams' in the United States, since the majority of them originate from European Golden Retrievers. One US breeder has warned buyers to beware of inaccurate claims from some of the people who import these dogs, such as saying that these English dogs don't get cancer. She added: "The importers/breeders also tend to do less (health) testing compared with breeders who are breeding for other traits besides color."

Karen Moore, of Icewind Goldens, New Jersey, added: "I know there is only one Golden Retriever because no matter what the color, the breed originated in Scotland. But recently many people in America are calling the light gold and cream/white colored Golden Retriever the 'English Cream Golden' or the 'English Golden'. This has caused some American breeders who can't seem to see past the color to not appreciate the other good qualities of the dog.

"In my opinion color is a personal preference of the breeder as long as the dog has the excellent qualities it was originally bred for. Also all OFA and genetic health clearances must be done. During my search looking for excellent quality Goldens with health clearances, I was disappointed to learn that not all breeders do them."

Some breeders make other extravagant claims, people advertising these light US dogs as "Rare White European Golden Retrievers" or "Exclusive Platinum Imported Golden Retrievers," or similar. Don't be taken in by the hype! These light colours have always been a part of the Golden Retriever colour spectrum, there is nothing special or rare about them. Remember that good breeders don't breed purely for colour – they consider health and temperament to be important factors, and this often throws several different shades of coat within the same litter.

The full coat colour range runs from nearly white, through beige and golden right through to red, similar to the colouring of an Irish Setter. The UK Breed Standard accepts: "Any shade of gold or cream, neither red nor mahogany." So if you live in the UK and buy a red Golden, you would not be able to enter conformation shows under KC rules - although there are plenty of other events and agility competitions, etc. that you could take part in. Red Golden Retrievers often have some working stock in their heritage.

The FCI (Federation Cynologique Internationale) also bans red Goldens from their shows. The AKC (American Kennel Club) does not ban them, but the Breed Standard states: "Predominant body color which is either extremely pale or extremely dark is undesirable." So you could enter a deep red Golden under AKC rules, but the judge is less likely to award your dog a prize.

Even within the same litter, you will see puppies of different shades; this is perfectly normal. One tip when choosing your pup is to look at the colour of the tip of the ears, as this is likely to be close to the dog's colouring once fully grown. Even if you have your heart set on a particular shade of Golden, we would advise you to concentrate on important factors, such as whether the breeder is a good one and health screens his or her dogs, whether the dog is from working or show stock or a mixture, and picking a puppy with a temperament suited to your family or lifestyle.

Photo by Elizabeth Russell for the Golden Retriever Club of Canada

More Than One Dog

Well-socialised Golden Retrievers have no problem sharing their home with other dogs. Supervised sessions from an early age help everyone to get along and for the other dogs to accept your friendly new puppy. It's a good idea to introduce your pup to your other dog(s) for the first time outdoors, rather than in the house or in a specific area one dog regards as his own. You don't want the established dog to feel he has to protect his territory, nor the puppy to feel he is in an enclosed space and can't get away.

If you are thinking about getting more than one pup, consider waiting until your first Golden Retriever is at least a couple of years old before getting a second, so your older dog is calmer and can help train the younger one. Coping with, training and housetraining one puppy is hard enough, without having to do it with two. On the other hand, some owners prefer to get the messy part over and done with in one go – but this will require a lot of your time for the first few weeks and months. Owning two dogs can be twice as nice - or double the trouble, and double the vet's bills. There are a number of factors to consider. This is what one UK rescue organisation has to say: "Think about why you are considering another dog. If, for example, you have a dog that suffers from separation anxiety, then rather than solving the problem, your second dog may learn from your first and you then have two dogs with the problem instead of one. The same applies if you have an unruly adolescent; cure the problem first and only introduce a second dog when your first is balanced.

"A second dog will mean double vet's fees, insurance and food. You may also need a larger car, and holidays will be more problematic. Sit down with a calculator and work out the expected expense – you may be surprised. Two dogs will need training, both separately and together. If the dogs do not receive enough individual attention, they may form a strong bond with each other at the expense of their bond with you. If you are tempted to buy two puppies from the same litter - DON'T! Your chances of creating a good bond with the puppies are very low and behaviour problems with siblings are very common.

"Research your considered breed well, it may be best to buy a completely different breed to add balance. If you have a very active dog, would a quieter one be best to balance his high energy or would you enjoy the challenge of keeping two high energy dogs? You will also need to think of any problems that may occur from keeping dogs of different sizes and ages. If you own an elderly Chihuahua, then a large adolescent may not be a good choice! If you decide to purchase a puppy, you will need to think very carefully about the amount of time and energy that will be involved in caring for two dogs with very different needs. A young puppy will need to have his exercise restricted until he has finished growing and will also need individual time for training. If you decide to keep a dog and bitch together, then you will obviously need to address the neutering issue."

You can't expect an un-neutered male to live with an unspayed female without problems. Similarly, two uncastrated males may not always get along; there may simply be too much testosterone and competition. If an existing dog is neutered (male) or spayed (female) and you plan to have your puppy neutered or spayed, then gender should not be an issue. Many breeders will specify that your pup has to be spayed or neutered within a certain time frame. This is not because they want to make more money from breeding; it is to protect Golden Retrievers from indiscriminate breeding.

One UK breeder added: "Some breeders will sell two puppies from the same litter to one family. In my experience this is a very bad idea as the puppies focus on each other and it makes them very difficult to train. I wouldn't sell two puppies to one family."

Top 10 Tips For Working Golden Retriever Owners

We wouldn't recommend getting a Golden if you are out at work all day. But if you're determined to get one when you're out for several hours at a time, here are some useful points:

1. Take him for a walk before you go to work – even if this means getting up at the crack of dawn – and spend time with him as soon as you get home. Exercise generates serotonin in the brain and has a calming effect. A dog that has been exercised will be less anxious and more ready for a good nap.

2. Leave him in a place of his own where he feels comfortable. If you use a crate, leave the door open, otherwise his favourite dog bed or chair. You may need to restrict access to other areas of the house to prevent him coming to harm or chewing things you don't want chewed. If possible, leave him in a room with a view of the outside world; this will be more interesting than staring at four blank walls.

3. Make sure that it does not get too hot during the day and there are no cold draughts in the place where you leave him.

4. Either come home at lunchtime or employ a dog walker (or neighbour) to exercise him. If you can afford it, leave him at doggie day care where he can socialise with other dogs.

5. If not, do you know anybody you could leave your dog with during the day? Consider leaving your dog with a reliable friend, relative or neighbour who would welcome the companionship of a dog without the full responsibility of ownership.

6. Food and drink: Although most Golden Retrievers love their food, it is still generally a good idea to put food down at specific meal times and remove it after 15 or 20 minutes if uneaten to prevent your dog becoming fussy or 'punishing' you for leaving him alone by refusing to eat. **Make sure he has access to water at all times.** Dogs cannot cool down by sweating; they do not have many sweat glands (which is why they pant, but this is much less efficient than perspiring) and can die without sufficient water.

7. Consider leaving a radio or TV on very softly in the background. The 'white noise' can have a soothing effect on some pets. If you do this, select your channel carefully – try and avoid one with lots of bangs and crashes or heavy metal music!

8. Stick to the same routine before you leave your dog home alone. This will help him to feel secure. Before you go to work, get into a daily habit of getting yourself ready, then feeding and exercising your Golden Retriever. Dogs love routine. But don't make a huge fuss of him when you leave as this can also stress the dog; just leave the house calmly.

9. Leave toys available to play with to prevent destructive chewing (a popular occupation for bored Golden Retrievers). Stuff a Kong toy – pictured - with treats to keep him occupied for a while. Choose the right size of Kong; you can even smear the inside with peanut butter or another favourite to keep him busy for longer.

10. Consider getting a companion for your Golden. This will involve even more of your time and twice the expense, and if you have not got time for one dog, you have hardly time for two. A better idea is to find someone you can leave the dog with during the day.

Similarly, when you come home, your Golden Retriever will feel starved of attention and be pleased to see you. Greet him normally, but try not to go overboard by making too much of a fuss as soon as you walk through the door. Give him a pat and a stroke then take off your coat and do a few other things before turning your attention back to him. Lavishing your Golden Retriever with too much attention the second you walk through the door may encourage needy behaviour or separation anxiety.

Puppy Stages

It is important to understand how a puppy develops into a fully-grown dog. This knowledge will help you to be a good owner. **The first few months and weeks of a puppy's life will have an effect on his behaviour and character for the rest of his life.** This Puppy Schedule will help you to understand the early stages:

Birth to seven weeks	A puppy needs sleep, food & warmth. He needs his mother for security & discipline and littermates for learning & socialisation. The puppy learns to function within a pack & learns the pack order of dominance. He begins to become aware of his environment. During this period, puppies should be left with their mother.
Eight to 12 weeks	A puppy should NOT leave his mother before eight weeks. At this age the brain is fully developed & **he now needs socialising with the outside world.** He needs to

	change from being part of a canine pack to being part of a human pack. This period is a fear period for the puppy, avoid causing him fright and pain.
13 to 16 weeks	Training & formal obedience should begin. **This is a critical period for socialising with other humans, places & situations.** This period will pass easily if you remember that this is a puppy's change to adolescence. Be firm & fair. His flight instinct may be prominent. Avoid being too strict or too soft with him during this time & praise his good behaviour.
Four to eight months	Another fear period for a puppy is between seven to eight months of age. It passes quickly, but be cautious of fright or pain that may leave the puppy traumatised. The puppy reaches sexual maturity & dominant traits are established. Your Golden Retriever should now understand the following commands: Sit, Down, Come & Stay

Plan Ahead

Most puppies leave the litter for their new homes when they are around eight weeks old. It is important that they have enough time to develop and learn the rules of the pack from their mothers and litter mates. Golden puppies take a little longer to develop than some other breeds, and a puppy that leaves the litter too early may suffer with issues, for example a lack of confidence and/or problems interacting with other dogs, throughout life. Breeders who allow their pups to leave home before eight weeks are probably more interested in a quick buck than a long-term puppy placement. In the USA, many states specify that a puppy may not be sold before eight (or sometimes seven) weeks of age. And if you want a well-bred puppy, it certainly pays to plan ahead as most good Golden Retriever breeders have waiting lists.

Choosing the right breeder is one of the most important decisions you will make. Like humans, your puppy will be a product of his or her parents and will inherit many of their characteristics. His temperament and how healthy your puppy will be now and throughout his life will largely depend on the genes of his parents. Responsible breeders health test their dogs, they check the health records and temperament of the parents and only breed from suitable stock - and good breeding comes at a price.

Prices vary a great deal for Golden Retriever puppies. As a very broad rule of thumb, for a fully health-tested pet puppy from a good breeder, expect to pay from around £850 to £1,200 in the UK and around $2,000 in the USA, but this varies a lot depending on where you live. If a Golden Retriever pup is being sold for much less, you have to ask why. Dogs with some show or working potential may cost 50% to 100% more.

A healthy Golden Retriever will be your irreplaceable companion for the next decade or more, so why buy an unseen puppy, or one from a pet shop or general advertisement? Would you buy an old wreck of a car or a house with structural problems just because it was cheap? The answer is probably no, because you know you would be storing up stress and expense in the future. (Pictured is the handsome Beren, aged seven weeks and two days, courtesy of Suffolk breeder Jan Schick).

If a healthy Golden is important to you, wait until you can afford one. Good breeders do not sell their dogs on general sales websites or in pet shops. Many reputable breeders do not have to advertise, such is the demand for their puppies. Many have their own websites; you must learn to spot the good ones from the bad ones, so do your research. We strongly recommend visiting the breeder personally at least once and follow our **Top 12 Tips for Selecting a Good Breeder** to help you make the right decision. Buying a poorly-bred puppy may save you a few hundred pounds or dollars in the short term, but could cost you thousands in extra veterinary bills in the long run - not to mention the terrible heartache of having a sickly dog. Rescue groups know only too well the dangers of buying a poorly-bred dog; years of problems can arise, usually health-related, but there can also be temperament issues, or poor behaviour due to lack of socialisation at the breeder's.

Where NOT to buy a Golden Retriever Puppy

There are no cast iron guarantees that your puppy will be 100% healthy and have a good temperament, but choosing a Golden Retriever breeder who is registered with the Kennel Club in your country or who belongs to a Golden Retriever club increases these chances enormously. There are several regional and national Golden Retriever clubs in the UK and USA and most have strict entry guidelines and Code of Ethics; see back of book for details.

If, for whatever reason, you're not able to buy a puppy from a breeder with a proven track record, how do you avoid buying one from a 'backstreet breeder' or puppy mill (puppy farm)? These are people who just breed puppies for profit and sell them to the first person who turns up with the cash. Unhappily, this can end in heartbreak for a family months or years later when their puppy develops problems due to poor breeding.

Price is a good guide, and with Golden Retrievers you often do get what you pay for. A cheap puppy usually means that corners have been cut somewhere along the line – and it's often health. If a pup is advertised at a price that seems too good to be true, then it is. You can bet your last dollar that the dam and sire are not superb examples of their breed, that they haven't been fully health tested, and that often the puppies are not being fed premium quality food or even kept in the house with the family where the breeder should start to socialise and housetrain them.

Here's some advice on what to avoid:

The Golden Retriever is one of the most popular of all the breeds and unscrupulous breeders have sprung up to cash in on its popularity. While new owners might think they have bagged 'a bargain,' this more often than not turns out to be false economy and an emotionally disastrous decision when the puppy develops health problems due to poor breeding, or behavioural problems due to lack of socialisation during the critical early phase of his or her life. Buying from a puppy mill or someone breeding for profit means that you are condemning other dogs to a life of misery. If nobody bought these cheap puppies, there would be no puppy mills.

In September 2013, The UK's Kennel Club issued a warning of a puppy welfare crisis, with some truly sickening statistics. As many as one in four puppies bought in the UK may come from puppy farms - and the situation is no better in North America. The Press release stated: "**As the popularity of online pups continues to soar:**

- **Almost one in five pups bought (unseen) on websites or social media die within six months**
- One in three buy online, in pet stores and via newspaper adverts - outlets often used by puppy farmers – this is an increase from one in five in the previous year
- The problem is likely to grow as the younger generation favour mail order pups, and breeders of fashionable breeds flout responsible steps."

The Kennel Club said: "We are sleepwalking into a dog welfare and consumer crisis as new research shows that more and more people are buying their pups online or through pet shops, outlets often used by cruel puppy farmers, and are paying the price with their pups requiring long-term veterinary treatment or dying before six months old. The increasing popularity of online pups is a particular concern. Of those who source their puppies online, half are going on to buy 'mail order pups' directly over the internet." The KC research found that:

- One third of people who bought their puppy online, over social media or in pet shops failed to experience 'overall good health'
- Almost one in five puppies bought via social media or the internet die before six months old
- Some 12% of puppies bought online or on social media end up with serious health problems that require expensive on-going veterinary treatment from a young age

Caroline Kisko, Kennel Club Secretary, said: "More and more people are buying puppies from sources such as the internet, which are often used by puppy farmers. Whilst there is nothing wrong with initially finding a puppy online, it is essential to then see the breeder and ensure that they are doing all of the right things. This research clearly shows that too many people are failing to do this, and the consequences can be seen in the shocking number of puppies that are becoming sick or dying. We have an extremely serious consumer protection and puppy welfare crisis on our hands."

The research revealed that the problem was likely to get worse as mail order pups bought over the internet are the second most common way for the younger generation of 18 to 24-year-olds to buy a puppy (31%). Marc Abraham, TV vet and founder of Pup Aid, said: "Sadly, if the 'buy it now' culture persists, then this horrific situation will only get worse. There is nothing wrong with sourcing a puppy online, but people need to be aware of what they should then expect from the breeder.

"For example, you should not buy a car without getting its service history and seeing it at its registered address, so you certainly shouldn't buy a puppy without the correct paperwork and health certificates and without seeing where it was bred. However, too many people are opting to buy directly from third parties such as the internet, pet shops, or from puppy dealers, where you cannot possibly know how or where the puppy was raised.

"Not only are people buying sickly puppies, but many people are being scammed into paying money for puppies that don't exist, as the research showed that 7% of those who buy online were scammed in this way." The Kennel Club has launched an online video and has a Find A Puppy app to show the dos and don'ts of buying a puppy. View the video at www.thekennelclub.org.uk/paw

Caveat Emptor – Buyer Beware

Here are some signs that a puppy may have arrived via a puppy mill, a puppy broker (somebody who makes money from buying and selling puppies) or even an unscrupulous importer. Our strong advice is that if you suspect that this is the case, walk away. You can't buy a Rolls Royce or a Lamborghini for a couple of thousand pounds or dollars - you'd immediately suspect that the 'bargain' on offer wasn't the real thing. No matter how lovely it looked, you'd be right - and the same applies to Golden Retrievers.

- Websites – buying a puppy from a website does not necessarily mean that the puppy will turn out to have problems. But avoid websites where there are no pictures of the home, environment and owners. If they are only showing close-up photos of cute puppies, click the **X** button

- Don't buy a website puppy with a shopping cart symbol next to his picture

- Don't commit to a website puppy unless you have seen it face-to-face. If this is not possible, at the very least you must speak (on the phone) with the breeder and ask questions; don't deal with an intermediary

- At the breeder's, you hear: "You can't see the parent dogs because......" ALWAYS ask to see the parents and, as a minimum, see the mother and how she looks and behaves

- If the breeder says that the dam and sire are Kennel Club or AKC registered, insist on seeing the registration papers

- Ignore photographs of so-called 'champion' ancestors (unless you are buying from an approved breeder), in all likelihood these are fiction

- The puppies look small for their stated age. A committed Golden Retriever breeder will not let her puppies leave before they are eight weeks old. Many poorly bred Goldens are smaller than the Breed Standard

- The person you are buying the puppy from did not breed the dog themselves

- The place you meet the puppy seller is a car park or place other than the puppies' home

- The seller tells you that the puppy comes from top, caring breeders from your or another country. Not true. There are reputable, caring breeders all over the world, but not one of them sells their puppies through brokers

- Ask to see photos of the puppy from birth to present day. If the seller has none, there is a reason – walk away

- Price – if you are offered a very cheap Golden Retriever, he or she almost certainly comes from dubious stock. Careful breeding, taking good care of mother and puppies and health screening all add up to one big bill for breeders. Anyone selling their puppies at a knock-down price has certainly cut corners

- If you get a rescue Golden Retriever, make sure it is from a recognised rescue group – see **Chapter 15. Golden Retriever Rescue** for details - and not a 'puppy flipper' who may be posing as a do-gooder, but is in fact getting dogs (including stolen ones) from unscrupulous sources

In fact, the whole brokering business is just another version of the puppy mill and should be avoided at all costs. Bear in mind that for every cute puppy you see from a puppy mill or broker, other puppies have died.

Cautionary Tales

Wendy Pickup, of Blenstone Golden Retrievers, Flintshire, Wales, has been breeding Goldens for 26 years and had this story: "A lovely family went to buy a puppy from a person who claimed to be the breeder. The same family had been in contact with this 'breeder' some four weeks previously, and at that time she said that she did not have any puppies left. On the second occasion the family were in touch, it was in response to an advert from the same breeder for eight-week-old puppies. The family did not see the mother with the puppies. The breeder told them that the reason she had not told them about this second litter when they enquired the first time was because she did not believe in keeping purchasers waiting – that she only ever advertised puppies when they were ready to go.

"It turned out that the lady had not bred the puppies herself, but was acting as an agent for the actual breeder who had passed the whole litter over to be sold as though they had been born at the premises belonging to the agent. This appears to be one example of how puppy farmers ply their trade."

Anna Cornelius-Jones, of Mindieslodge Golden Retrievers, Dorset, added: "I think there will always be a few breeders that give a bad impression. They normally do it more for the money and tend not to put the wellbeing of their litters first. This can be found with over-breeding, dirty and cramped conditions and missing health certifications."

("We don't suppose you have any treats, have you?!" Photo of Lexy, aged three and Candie, aged 12, enjoying life in the family home courtesy of Anna).

Sue Page, Dormansue Golden Retrievers, Surrey, said: "I have visited an unscrupulous breeder. He kept a litter of about seven puppies in an area about five feet by five feet. He knew this was wrong as he said in my hearing that they would have to increase the area when an important Golden Retriever breeder was going to visit him the following week. He never let his puppies have access to a garden and so the puppies spent their first eight weeks cooped up in a small space which meant that the puppies' muscles wouldn't develop properly."

Some breeders may have unwittingly added to the problem, as one experienced UK breeder explained: "It is fair to say that the take-up of the available health tests has been slow. Some breeders are reluctant for their dogs to take a voluntary test for fear that an imperfect score may result in a big loss in stud fees. This attitude needs to change. I have heard of one big-name breeder (now deceased) who threatened bitch owners with a lawsuit if they disclosed that one of her stud dogs had produced a wet puppy (with an ectopic ureter)."

Kelly Sisco, of Show Me Goldens, Missouri, USA, said: "Thankfully I have not had direct experiences. However I have had many of my puppy parents express their frustration that during their puppy-looking process they came across several breeders that would claim their parent dogs had all of their (health) clearances. Upon further research, they discovered that the dogs would either have missing clearances or non-passing clearances.

"I HIGHLY recommend not taking a breeders word, sadly enough. Go to OFA's website (if you live in the USA) and search the parents or ask to see copies of clearances. Any reputable breeder will provide these happily as they are interested in only producing top quality dogs. If they seem hesitant or bothered by providing this information, move on. Where will they be when you need help with potty training or questions regarding food, etc?"

A relatively new UK breeder added: "Luckily, I have not come across any unscrupulous breeders. When looking for my first pup, I used the Kennel Club website to find a reputable breeder and went from there."

There are plenty of good Golden Retriever breeders out there, spend the time to find one.

Top 12 Tips for Choosing a Good Breeder

1. Choose a breeder whose dogs are health tested with certificates to prove it.

2. Visit the Kennel Club and Golden Retriever clubs' websites in your country to find a good breeder in your area.

3. Good breeders keep the dogs in the home as part of the family - not outside in kennel runs, garages or outbuildings. Check that the area where the puppies are kept is clean and that the puppies themselves look clean. (Photo of Ellie courtesy of Alan and Lorna Bishop, West Midlands).

4. Their Golden Retrievers appear happy and healthy. Check that the pup has clean eyes, ears, nose and bum (butt) with no discharge. The pups are alert, excited to meet new people and don't shy away from visitors.

5. A good breeder will encourage you to spend time with the puppy's parents - or at least the mother - when you visit. They want your family to meet the puppy and are happy for you to visit more than once.

6. They are very familiar with Golden Retrievers, although some may also have other breed(s).

7. All responsible breeders should provide you with a written contract and health guarantee. They will also show you records of the puppy's visits to the vet, vaccinations, worming medication, etc. and explain what other vaccinations your puppy will need. They will agree to take a puppy back within a certain time frame if it does not work out for you, or if there is a health problem.

8. They feed their adults and puppies high quality dog food and give you some to take home and guidance on feeding and caring for your puppy. They will also be available for advice after you take your puppy home.

9. They don't always have pups available, but keep a list of interested people for the next available litter. They don't over-breed, but do limit the number of litters from their dams. Over-breeding or breeding from older females can be detrimental to the female's health.

10. If you have selected a breeder and checked if/when she has puppies available, go online to the Golden Retriever forums before you visit and ask if anyone already has a dog from this breeder. If you are buying from a good breeder, the chances are someone will know her dogs or at least her reputation. If the feedback is negative, cancel your visit and start looking elsewhere.

11. Good breeders will, if asked, provide references from other people who have bought their puppies; call at least one before you commit. They will also agree to take a puppy back within a certain time frame if it does not work out for you, or if there is a health problem.

12. And finally ... good Golden Retriever breeders want to know their beloved pups are going to good homes and will ask YOU a lot of questions about your suitability as owners. DON'T buy a puppy from a website or advert where a PayPal or credit card deposit secures you a puppy without any questions.

Golden Retriever puppies should not be regarded as must-have accessories. They are not objects; they are warm-blooded, living, breathing creatures. Happy, healthy dogs are what everybody wants. Taking the time now to find a responsible and committed breeder with healthy pups is time well spent. It could save you a lot of time, money and heartache in the future and help to ensure that you and your chosen dog are happy together for many years to come.

....

Important Questions to Ask a Breeder

Some of these points have already been covered, but here's a reminder and checklist of the questions you should be asking.

Have the parents been health screened? Buy a Golden Retriever pup with health tested parents – hips and eyes at the very minimum, with certificates to prove it. Ask what guarantees the breeder or seller is offering in terms of genetic illnesses, and how long these guarantees last – 12 weeks, a year, a lifetime? It will vary from breeder to breeder, but good ones will definitely give you some form of guarantee, and this should be stated in the puppy contract.

They will also want to be informed of any hereditary health problems with your puppy, as they may choose not to breed from the dam or sire (mother or father) again. Some breeders keep a chart documenting the full family health history of the pup – ask if one exists and if you can see it.

Are you registered with the Kennel Club (UK) or AKC (USA) or a member of a Golden Retriever breed club? Not all good Golden Retriever breeders are members, but this is a good place to start.

How long have you been breeding Golden Retrievers? You are looking for someone who has a track record with the breed.

How many litters has the mother had? Females should not have litters until they are two years old and then only have a few litters in their lifetime. The UK Kennel Club will not register puppies from a dam who has had more than four litters. Check the age of the mother; too young or too old is not good for her health.

Can you put me in touch with someone who already has one of your puppies?

What happens to the female(s) once she/they have finished breeding? Are they kept as part of the family, rehomed in loving homes or sent to animal shelters?

Do you breed any other types of dog? Buy from a Golden Retriever specialist, preferably one who does not produce lots of other breeds of dog - unless you know they have a good reputation.

What is so special about this litter? You are looking for a breeder who has used good breeding stock and his or her knowledge to produce healthy, handsome dogs with good temperaments, not just cute puppies. (Picture of 10-week-old Ellie courtesy of KC Approved Breeders Jessica and Stephen Webb, HollyRoseFen Golden Retrievers, Lincolnshire). Golden Retriever puppies look cute, don't buy the first one you see – be patient and pick the right one. If you don't get a satisfactory answer, look elsewhere.

What do you feed your adults and puppies? A

reputable breeder will feed a top quality dog food and advise that you do the same.

What special care do you recommend? Your Golden Retriever will need regular grooming, and possibly ear cleaning.

What is the average lifespan of your dogs? Generally, pups bred from healthy stock tend to live longer.

How socialised and housetrained is the puppy? Good breeders will raise their puppies as part of the household and start the socialisation and housetraining process before they leave.

What healthcare have the pups had so far? Ask to see records of flea treatments, wormings and vaccinations.

Has the puppy been microchipped?

Why aren't you asking me any questions? A good breeder will be committed to making a good match between the new owners and their puppies. If the breeder spends more time discussing money than the welfare of the puppy and how you will care for him, you can draw your own conclusions as to what his or her priorities are – and they probably don't include improving the breed. Walk away.

 Take your puppy to a vet to have a thorough check-up within 48 hours of purchase. If your vet is not happy with the health of the dog, no matter how painful it may be, return the pup to the breeder. Keeping an unhealthy puppy will only cause more distress and expense in the long run.

Puppy Contracts

All good Golden Retriever breeders should provide you with an official Puppy Contract. This protects both buyer and seller by providing information on diet, worming, vaccination and veterinary visits from the birth of the puppy until he or she leaves the breeder. You should also have a health guarantee for a specified time period. A Puppy Contract will answer such questions as to whether the puppy:

* Can be returned if there is a health issue within a certain period of time
* Was born by Caesarean section
* Has been micro-chipped and/or vaccinated and details of worming treatments
* What health issues the pup and parents have been screened for
* Has been partially or wholly toilet trained (not always included)
* Has been socialised and where it was kept
* What the puppy is currently being fed by the breeder and if any food is being supplied
* Details of the dam and sire

It's not easy for caring breeders to part with their puppies after they have lovingly bred and raised them to eight weeks of age or older, and so many supply extensive care notes for new owners, which may include details such as:
* The puppy's daily routine
* Feeding schedule

- Vet and vaccination schedule
- General puppy care
- Toilet training
- Socialisation

New owners should do their research before visiting a litter as once there, the cute Golden Retriever puppies will undoubtedly be irresistible and you will buy with your heart rather than your head. If you have any doubts at all about the breeder, seller or the puppy, WALK AWAY.

Spend time beforehand to research a good breeder with a proven track record. In the UK, The Royal Society for the Prevention of Cruelty to Animals (RSPCA) has a downloadable puppy contract endorsed by vets and animal welfare organisations .You can see a copy here and should be looking for something similar from the breeder or seller of the puppy: http://puppycontract.rspca.org.uk/webContent/staticImages/Microsites/PuppyContract/Downloads/PuppyContractDownload.pdf

Top 12 Tips for Choosing a Healthy Golden Retriever

Once you've selected your breeder and a litter is available, you then have to decide WHICH puppy to pick. A good breeder will ask questions about you, your family and lifestyle in order to try and match you with a puppy to fit in with your schedule. Here are some signs to look for when selecting a puppy:

1. Your chosen puppy should have a well-fed appearance. He or she should not, however, have a distended abdomen (pot belly) as this can be a sign of worms - or other illnesses (such as Cushing's disease in adults). The ideal puppy should not be too thin either, you should not be able to see his ribs.

   (This healthy and hungry litter was bred by Liz Spicer-Short, Priorschest Golden Retrievers, Dorset).

2. His or her nose should be cool, damp and clean with no discharge.

3. The pup's eyes should be bright and clear with no discharge or tear stain. Steer clear of a puppy that blinks a lot, as this could be the sign of a problem.

4. His gums should be clean and pink.

5. The pup's ears should be clean with no sign of discharge, soreness or redness and no unpleasant smell.

6. Check the puppy's rear end to make sure it is clean and there are no signs of diarrhoea.

7. The pup's coat should look clean, feel soft, not matted - and puppies should smell good! The coat should have no signs of ticks or fleas. Red or irritated skin or bald spots could be a

sign of infestation or a skin condition. Also, check between the toes of the paws for signs of redness or swelling.

8. Choose a puppy that moves freely without any sign of injury or lameness. It should be a fluid movement, not jerky or stiff, which could be a sign of joint problems.

9. When the puppy is distracted, clap or make a noise behind him - not so loud as to frighten him - to make sure he is not deaf.

10. Finally, ask to see veterinary records to confirm your puppy has been wormed and had his first injections.

If you are unlucky enough to have an early health problem with your pup, a reputable breeder will usually allow you to return the pup - the timescale varies from breeder o breeder. Also, if you get your puppy home and things don't work out for whatever reason, good breeders should also take the puppy back or try to rehome him or her. Make sure this is the case before you commit.

Picking the Right Temperament

You've picked a Golden Retriever, presumably, because you like the way they look and you love this breed's outstanding temperament, its willingness to please and learn, its intelligence, calm demeanour (once past that boisterous puppy and adolescent stage!) and friendly get-along-with-everybody nature. However, while Golden Retrievers share many common characteristics and temperament traits, each puppy also has his own individual character, just like humans.

The friendly, easy-going nature of the Golden suits most people. Visit the breeder to see how your chosen pup interacts and get an idea of his character in comparison to his littermates. Some puppies will run up to greet you, pull at your shoelaces and playfully bite your fingers. Others will be more content to stay in the basket sleeping. Watch their behaviour and energy levels.

Are you an active person who enjoys lots of daily exercise or would a less hyper puppy be more  suitable? Do you want a dog bred from working or show stock or a combination of both? Choose a puppy that will best fit in with your family and lifestyle.

A submissive dog will by nature be more passive, less energetic and also possibly easier to train. A dominant dog will usually be more energetic and lively. He or she may also be more stubborn and may need more patience when training. If you already have a dominant dog at home, you have to be careful about introducing a new dog into the household; two dominant dogs may not live together comfortably.

There is no good or bad, it's a question of which type of character will best suit you and your lifestyle. Here are a couple of quick tests to try and gauge your puppy's temperament; they should be carried out by the breeder in familiar surroundings so the puppy is relaxed. It should be pointed out that there is some controversy over temperament testing, as a dog's personality is formed by a combination of factors, which include inherited temperament, socialisation, training and environment (or how you treat your dog):

* ❧ The breeder puts the pup on his or her back on her lap and gently rests her hand on the pup's chest, or

* ❧ She puts her hands under the pup's tummy and gently lifts the pup off the floor for a few seconds, keeping the pup horizontal. A puppy that struggles to get free is less patient than one that makes little effort to get away. A placid, patient dog is likely to fare better in a home with young children than an impatient one. Here are some other useful signs to look out for –

* ❧ Watch how he interacts with other puppies in the litter. Does he try and dominate them, does he walk away from them or is he happy to play with his littermates? This may give you an idea of how easy it will be to socialise him with other dogs

* ❧ After contact, does the pup want to follow you or walk away from you? Not following may mean he has a more independent nature

* ❧ If you throw something for the puppy is he happy to retrieve it for you or does he ignore it? This may measure their willingness to work with humans

* ❧ If you drop a bunch of keys behind the Golden Retriever puppy, does he act normally or does he flinch and jump away? The latter may be an indication of a timid or nervous disposition. Not reacting could also be a sign of deafness

Decide which temperament would fit in with you and your family and the rest is up to you. Whatever hereditary temperament your Golden Retriever has, it is true to say that **dogs that have constant positive interactions with people and other animals during the first four months of life will generally be happier and more stable.** In contrast, a puppy plucked from its family too early and/or isolated for long periods will be less happy, less socialised, needier, and may display behaviour problems later in life.

Puppies are like children. Being properly raised contributes to their confidence, sociability, stability and intellectual development. The bottom line is that a pup raised in a warm, loving environment with people is likely to be more tolerant and accepting, and less likely to develop behaviour problems, than one which has spent much time alone..

For those of you who prefer a scientific approach to choosing the right puppy, we are including the full Volhard Puppy Aptitude Test (PAT). This test has been developed by the highly-respected Wendy and Jack Volhard who have built up an international reputation over the last 30 years for their invaluable contribution to dog training, health and nutrition. Their philosophy is: "We believe that one of life's great joys is living in harmony with your dog."

They have written several books and the Volhard PAT is regarded as an excellent method for evaluating the nature of young puppies. Jack and Wendy have also written the Dog Training for Dummies book. Visit their website at www.volhard.com for details of their upcoming dog training camps, as well as their training and nutrition groups.

The Volhard Puppy Aptitude Test

Here are the ground rules for performing the test: The testing is done in a location unfamiliar to the puppies. This does not mean they have to be taken away from home. A 10-foot square area is perfectly adequate, such as a room in the house where the puppies have not been.

- ✓ The puppies are tested one at a time. There are no other dogs or people, except the scorer and the tester, in the testing area
- ✓ The puppies do not know the tester
- ✓ The scorer is a disinterested third party and not the person interested in selling you a puppy
- ✓ The scorer is unobtrusive and positions himself so he can observe the puppies' responses without having to move

The puppies are tested before they are fed. (Photo of this hungry bunch courtesy of Dee Johnson, of Johnsongrace Golden Retrievers, North Cornwall, UK).

The puppies are tested when they are at their liveliest. Do not try to test a puppy that is not feeling well. Puppies should not be tested the day of or the day after being vaccinated. Only the first response counts! Tip: During the test, watch the puppy's tail. It will make a difference in the scoring whether the tail is up or down. The tests are simple to perform and anyone with some common sense can do them. You can, however, elicit the help of someone who has tested puppies before and knows what they are doing.

Social attraction - the owner or caretaker of the puppies places it in the test area about four feet from the tester and then leaves the test area. The tester kneels down and coaxes the puppy to come to him or her by encouragingly and gently clapping hands and calling. The tester must coax the puppy in the opposite direction from where it entered the test area. Hint: Lean backward, sitting on your heels instead of leaning forward toward the puppy. Keep your hands close to your body encouraging the puppy to come to you instead of trying to reach for the puppy.

Following - the tester stands up and slowly walks away encouraging the puppy to follow. Hint: Make sure the puppy sees you walk away and get the puppy to focus on you by lightly clapping your hands and using verbal encouragement to get the puppy to follow you. Do not lean over the puppy.

Restraint – the tester crouches down and gently rolls the puppy on its back for 30 seconds. Hint: Hold the puppy down without applying too much pressure. The object is not to keep it on its back but to test its response to being placed in that position.

Social Dominance - let the puppy stand up or sit and gently stroke it from the head to the back while you crouch beside it. See if it will lick your face, an indication of a forgiving nature. Continue stroking until you see a behaviour you can score. Hint: When you crouch next to the puppy avoid leaning or hovering over it. Have the puppy at your side, both of you facing in the same direction. During testing maintain a positive, upbeat and friendly attitude toward the puppies. Try to get each puppy to interact with you to bring out the best in him or her. Make the test a pleasant experience for the puppy.

Elevation Dominance - the tester cradles the puppy with both hands, supporting the puppy under its chest and gently lifts it two feet off the ground and holds it there for 30 seconds.

Retrieving - the tester crouches beside the puppy and attracts its attention with a crumpled up piece of paper. When the puppy shows some interest, the tester throws the paper no more than four feet in front of the puppy encouraging it to retrieve the paper.

Touch Sensitivity - the tester locates the webbing of one the puppy's front paws and presses it lightly between his index finger and thumb. The tester gradually increases pressure while counting to ten and stops when the puppy pulls away or shows signs of discomfort.

Sound Sensitivity - the puppy is placed in the center of the testing area and an assistant stationed at the perimeter makes a sharp noise, such as banging a metal spoon on the bottom of a metal pan.

Sight Sensitivity - the puppy is placed in the center of the testing area. The tester ties a string around a bath towel and jerks it across the floor, two feet away from the puppy.

Stability - an umbrella is opened about five feet from the puppy and gently placed on the ground. During the testing, make a note of the heart rate of the pup, this is an indication of how it deals with stress, as well as its energy level. Puppies come with high, medium or low energy levels. You have to decide for yourself, which suits your life style.

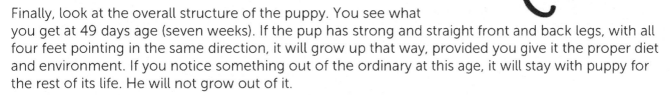

Dogs with high energy levels need a great deal of exercise, and will get into mischief if this energy is not channeled into the right direction.

Finally, look at the overall structure of the puppy. You see what you get at 49 days age (seven weeks). If the pup has strong and straight front and back legs, with all four feet pointing in the same direction, it will grow up that way, provided you give it the proper diet and environment. If you notice something out of the ordinary at this age, it will stay with puppy for the rest of its life. He will not grow out of it.

Scoring the Results

Following are the responses you will see and the score assigned to each particular response. You will see some variations and will have to make a judgment on what score to give them –

TEST	RESPONSE	SCORE
SOCIAL ATTRACTION	Came readily, tail up, jumped, bit at hands	1
	Came readily, tail up, pawed, licked at hands	2
	Came readily, tail up	3
	Came readily, tail down	4
	Came hesitantly, tail down	5
	Didn't come at all	6
FOLLOWING	Followed readily, tail up, got underfoot, bit at feet	1
	Followed readily, tail up, got underfoot	2
	Followed readily, tail up	3
	Followed readily, tail down	4
	Followed hesitantly, tail down	5
	Did not follow or went away	6
RESTRAINT	Struggled fiercely, flailed, bit	1
	Struggled fiercely, flailed	2

	Settled, struggled, settled with some eye contact	3
	Struggled, then settled	4
	No struggle	5
	No struggle, strained to avoid eye contact	6
SOCIAL DOMINANCE	Jumped, pawed, bit, growled	1
	Jumped, pawed	2
	Cuddled up to tester and tried to lick face	3
	Squirmed, licked at hands	4
	Rolled over, licked at hands	5
	Went away and stayed away	6
ELEVATION DOMINANCE	Struggled fiercely, tried to bite	1
	Struggled fiercely	2
	Struggled, settled, struggled, settled	3
	No struggle, relaxed	4
	No struggle, body stiff	5
	No struggle, froze	6
RETRIEVING	Chased object, picked it up and ran away	1
	Chased object, stood over it and did not return	2
	Chased object, picked it up and returned with it to tester	3
	Chased object and returned without it to tester	4
	Started to chase object, lost interest	5
	Does not chase object	6
TOUCH SENSITIVITY	8-10 count before response	1
	6-8 count before response	2
	5-6 count before response	3
	3-5 count before response	4
	2-3 count before response	5
	1-2 count before response	6
SOUND SENSITIVITY	Listened, located sound and ran toward it barking	1
	Listened, located sound and walked slowly toward it	2
	Listened, located sound and showed curiosity	3
	Listened and located sound	4
	Cringed, backed off and hid behind tester 5	5
	Ignored sound and showed no curiosity	6

SIGHT SENSITIVITY	Looked, attacked and bit object	1
	Looked and put feet on object and put mouth on it	2
	Looked with curiosity and attempted to investigate, tail up	3
	Looked with curiosity, tail down	4
	Ran away or hid behind tester	5
	Hid behind tester	6
STABILITY	Looked and ran to the umbrella, mouthing or biting it	1
	Looked and walked to the umbrella, smelling it cautiously	2
	Looked and went to investigate	3
	Sat and looked, but did not move toward the umbrella	4
	Showed little or no interest	5
	Ran away from the umbrella	6

The scores are interpreted as follows:

Mostly 1s - Strong desire to be pack leader and is not shy about bucking for a promotion.
Has a predisposition to be aggressive to people and other dogs and will bite.
Should only be placed into a very experienced home where the dog will be trained and worked on a regular basis. **Tip:** Stay away from the puppy with a lot of 1's or 2's. It has lots of leadership aspirations and may be difficult to manage. This puppy needs an experienced home. Not good with children.

Mostly 2s - Also has leadership aspirations. May be hard to manage and has the capacity to bite. Has lots of self-confidence. Should not be placed into an inexperienced home. Too unruly to be good with children and elderly people, or other animals. Needs strict schedule, loads of exercise and lots of training. Has the potential to be a great show dog with someone who understands dog behaviour.

Mostly 3s - Can be a high-energy dog and may need lots of exercise. Good with people and other animals. Can be a bit of a handful to live with. Needs training, does very well at it and learns quickly. Great dog for second-time owner.

Mostly 4s - The kind of dog that makes the perfect pet. Best choice for the first time owner.
Rarely will buck for a promotion in the family. Easy to train, and rather quiet.
Good with elderly people, children, although may need protection from the children.
Choose this pup, take it to obedience classes, and you'll be the star, without having to do too much work! **Tip:** The puppy with mostly 3's and 4's can be quite a handful, but should be good with children and does well with training. Energy needs to be dispersed with plenty of exercise.

Mostly 5s - Fearful, shy and needs special handling. Will run away at the slightest stress in its life. Strange people, strange places, different floor or surfaces may upset it. Often afraid of loud noises and terrified of thunderstorms. When you greet it upon your return, may submissively urinate. Needs a very special home where the environment doesn't change too much and where there are no children. Best for a quiet, elderly couple. If cornered and cannot get away, has a tendency to bite.

Mostly 6s – So independent that he doesn't need you or other people. Doesn't care if he is trained or not - he is his own person. Unlikely to bond to you, since he doesn't need you. A great guard dog for gas stations! Do not take this puppy and think you can change him into a lovable bundle -

you can't, so leave well enough alone. **Tip:** Avoid the puppy with several 6's. It is so independent it doesn't need you or anyone. He is his own person and unlikely to bond to you.

The Scores

Few puppies will test with all 2s or all 3s, there'll be a mixture of scores. For that first time, wonderfully easy to train, potential star, look for a puppy that scores with mostly 4s and 3s. Don't worry about the score on Touch Sensitivity - you can compensate for that with the right training equipment. It's hard not to become emotional when picking a puppy - they are all so cute, soft and cuddly. Remind yourself that this dog is going to be with you for eight to 16 years. Don't hesitate to step back a little to contemplate your decision. Sleep on it and review it in the light of day. Avoid the puppy with a score of 1 on the Restraint and Elevation tests. This puppy will be too much for the first-time owner. It's a lot more fun to have a good dog, one that is easy to train, one you can live with and one you can be proud of, than one that is a constant struggle.

Getting a Dog From a Shelter - Don't overlook an animal shelter as a source for a good dog. Not all dogs wind up in a shelter because they are bad. After that cute puppy stage, when the dog grows up, it may become too much for its owner. Or, there has been a change in the owner's circumstances forcing him or her into having to give up the dog. Most of the time these dogs are housetrained and already have some training. If the dog has been properly socialised to people, it will be able to adapt to a new environment. Bonding may take a little longer, but once accomplished, results in a devoted companion.

....

So you see, it's not all about the colour or the cutest face! When getting a puppy, your thought process should run something like this:

1. Decide to get a Golden Retriever.
2. Decide if you want one from show or working stock, or a mixture of both.
3. Find a good breeder whose dogs are health tested.
4. Find one with a litter available when you are ready for a puppy – or wait.
5. Decide on a male or female.
6. Pick one with a suitable temperament to fit in with your family.

Some people make the mistake of picking a puppy purely based on the look of the dog. If the shade of coat colour, for example, is very important to you, make sure the other boxes are ticked as well.

5. Bringing Your Puppy Home

Getting a new puppy is so exciting. You can't wait to bring your fluffy little bundle of joy home. Before that happens you probably dream of all the things you and your little soul mate are going to do together; going for walks in the countryside, snuggling down by the fire, playing games together, setting off on holiday, maybe even taking part in competitions, shoots or shows.

Your pup has, of course, no idea of your big plans, and the reality when he or she arrives can be a bit of a shock for some owners. Puppies are wilful little critters with minds of their own and sharp teeth. They leak at both ends, chew anything in sight, constantly demand your attention, nip the kids or anything else to hand, often cry a lot for the first few days and don't pay a blind bit of notice to your commands. There is a lot of work ahead before the two of you develop a unique bond. Your pup has to learn what is required of him or her before he or she can start to meet some of your expectations - and you have to understand what your pup needs from you.

....

Once your new arrival lands in your home, your time won't be your own, but you can get off to a good start by preparing things before the big day. Here's a list of things to think about getting beforehand (your breeder may supply some of these):

Puppy Checklist

- ✓ A dog bed or basket
- ✓ Bedding – a Vetbed or Vetfleece would be a good choice, you can buy them online
- ✓ If possible, a towel or piece of cloth which has been rubbed on the puppy's mother to put in the bed
- ✓ A manufactured or home-made puppy gate and/or pen to contain the pup in one area of the house initially
- ✓ A collar or harness and lead (leash)
- ✓ An identification tag for the collar or harness
- ✓ Food and water bowls, preferably stainless steel
- ✓ Puppy food – find out what the breeder is feeding and stick with it initially
- ✓ Puppy treats (preferably healthy ones, not rawhide)
- ✓ Lots of newspapers for housetraining
- ✓ Poo(p) bags
- ✓ Toys and chews suitable for puppies
- ✓ A puppy coat if you live in a cool climate
- ✓ A crate if you decide to use one
- ✓ Old towels for cleaning your puppy and partially covering the crate

AND PLENTY OF TIME!

Pictured almost ready to leave the litter is a seven-week-old puppy, bred by Icewind Goldens, New Jersey, USA. Photo courtesy of Karen Moore.

Later on you'll also need grooming brushes (possibly a Furminator – see **Chapter 13. Grooming**), dog shampoo, flea and worming products, which you can buy from your vet, and maybe a travel crate.

Good breeders provide Puppy Packs to take home; they contain some or all of the following items:

- ✓ Registration certificate
- ✓ Pedigree certificate
- ✓ Buyer's Contract
- ✓ Information pack with details of vet's visits, vaccinations and wormings, parents' health certificates, diet, breed clubs, etc.
- ✓ Puppy food
- ✓ ID tag/microchip info
- ✓ Blanket that smells of the mother and litter
- ✓ Soft toy that your puppy has grown up with, possibly a chew toy as well
- ✓ Collar and lead (sometimes)

Puppy Proofing Your Home

Before your puppy arrives, you may have to make a few adjustments to make your home safe and suitable. Puppies are small bundles of instinct and energy when they are awake, with little common sense and even less self-control. Young Goldens love to play and have a great sense of fun. They may have bursts of energy before they run out of steam and spend much of the rest of the day sleeping.

All young Goldens are curious and most of them are boisterous - especially when they grow into

adolescents and start throwing their weight around – literally. So, don't leave Grandma alone with a lively 'teenage' Golden if she's just had a hip operation – she's in danger of getting accidentally bowled over in all the excitement!

Puppies are like babies and it's up to you to look after them and set the boundaries – both physically, in terms of where they can wander, and also in terms of behaviour – but gently and one step at a time. Create an area where the puppy is allowed to go, perhaps one or two rooms, preferably with a hard floor which is easy to clean, and keep the rest of the house off-limits, at least until housetraining (potty training) is complete.

The designated area should be near a door to the garden or yard for housetraining. Restricting the area also helps the puppy settle in. At the breeder's he probably had a den and an area to run around in. Suddenly having the freedom of the whole house can be quite daunting - not to mention messy. You can buy a barrier specifically made for dogs or use a baby gate, which may be cheaper. Although designed for infants, they work perfectly well with dogs; you might even find a second-hand one on eBay. Choose one with narrow vertical gaps or mesh and check that your puppy can't get his head stuck between the bars, or put a covering or mesh over the bottom of the gate initially. You can also make your own barrier, but bear in mind that cardboard and other soft materials will almost certainly get chewed.

Gates can be used to keep the puppy enclosed in a single room or specific area or put at the bottom of the stairs. A puppy's bones are soft, and recent studies have shown that if pups are allowed to climb or descend stairs regularly, they can develop joint problems later in life. This is worth bearing in mind, especially as some Goldens can be prone to hip or elbow problems.

The puppy's designated area or room should not be too hot, cold or damp and it must be free from draughts. Little puppies can be sensitive to temperature fluctuations and don't do well in very hot or very cold conditions. If you live in a hot climate, your new pup may need air conditioning in the summertime.

Don't underestimate your puppy! Young Goldens are lively and very determined; they can jump and climb, so choose a barrier higher than you think necessary.

Just as you need a home, so your puppy needs a den. This den is a haven where your pup feels safe, particularly in the beginning after the traumatic experience of leaving his or her mother and littermates. Young puppies sleep for 18 hours or longer a day at the beginning; this is normal.

You have a couple of options with the den; you can get a dog bed or basket, or you can use a crate. Crates have long been popular in North America and are becoming increasingly used in the UK, particularly as it can be quicker to housetrain a puppy using a crate. It may surprise some American readers to learn that normal practice in the UK has often been to initially contain the puppy in the kitchen or utility room, and later to let the dog roam around the house. Some owners do not allow their dogs upstairs, but many do. The idea of keeping a dog in a cage like a rabbit or hamster is abhorrent to some animal-loving Brits.

However, a crate can be a useful aid if used properly. Using one as a prison to contain a dog for hours on end certainly is cruel, but the crate has its place as a sanctuary for your dog. It is the dog's own safe space and they know no harm will come to them in there. **See Chapter 6. Crate Training and Housetraining** for getting your Golden Retriever used to - and even to enjoy - being in a crate.

Most puppies' natural instinct is not to soil the area where they sleep. Put plenty of newspapers down in the area next to the den and your pup should choose to go to the toilet here if you are not quick enough to get outside. Of course, he or she may also decide to trash their designated area by chewing their blankets and shredding the newspaper – patience is the key!

Rather than using a crate, some owners prefer to create a safe penned area for their pup. You can make your own barriers or buy a manufactured playpen. Playpens come in two types - mesh or

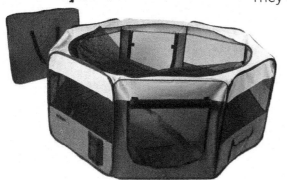

fabric. A fabric pen is easy to put up and take down, but can be chewed so may not last long. A metal mesh pen is a better bet; it can be expanded and will last longer, but is not quite as easy to put up or take down.

One breeder said: "A play pen can be used in much the same way as a crate and has an advantage of being very versatile in separating eating, sleeping and - in the early days - toileting. They are ideal for the busy Mum or Dad who has other things on their mind and can't possibly watch the puppy, children and try and tidy the house or prepare dinner. Again, it is peace of mind for the owner, knowing the pup is safe and not chewing anything it shouldn't."

With initial effort on your part and a willing pupil, housetraining a Golden Retriever should not take long. One of the biggest factors influencing the success and speed of housetraining is your commitment. You may also want to remove your Oriental rugs, family heirlooms and other treasured possessions until your little darling is fully housetrained and has stopped chewing everything in sight.

If you have young children, the time they spend with the puppy should be limited to a few short sessions a day. Plenty of sleep is **essential** for the normal development of a young dog. You wouldn't wake a baby every hour or so to play, and the same goes for puppies. Wait a day or two - preferably longer – before inviting friends round to see your gorgeous little puppy. However excited you are, your new arrival needs a few days to get over the stress of leaving mother and siblings and to start bonding with you.

If you have a garden or yard that you intend letting your puppy roam in, make sure that every little gap has been plugged. You'd be amazed at the tiny holes puppies can escape through. Don't leave your puppy unattended in the beginning, as they can come to harm. Also, dogs are increasingly being targeted by thieves, who are even stealing from gardens. Make sure there are no poisonous plants which your pup might chew and check there are no low plants with sharp leaves or thorns which could cause eye or other injuries. There are literally dozens of plants which can harm a puppy if ingested, including azalea, daffodil bulbs, lily, foxglove, hyacinth, hydrangea, lupin, rhododendron, sweet pea, tulip and yew. The Kennel Club has a list of some of the most common ones here: http://bit.ly/1nCv1qJ and the ASPCA has an extensive list for the USA at: http://bit.ly/19xkhoG

For puppies to grow into well-adjusted dogs, they have to feel comfortable and relaxed in their new surroundings and need a great deal of sleep. They are leaving the warmth and protection of their mother and littermates and for the first few days at least, most puppies may feel very sad. It is important to make the transition from the birth home to your home as easy as possible. Your pup's life is in your hands. How you react and interact with him in the first few days and weeks will shape your relationship and his character for the years ahead.

Chewing and Chew Toys

Like babies, most puppies are organic chewing machines and so remove anything breakable and/or chewable within the puppy's reach – including wooden furniture. Obviously you cannot remove your kitchen cupboards, doors, sofas and fixtures and fittings, so don't leave your new arrival unattended for any length of time where he can chew something which is hard to replace. Young

Goldens are enthusiastic chewers, so chew toys are a must. Don't give old socks, shoes or slippers or your pup will regard your footwear as fair game, and avoid rawhide chews as they can get stuck in the dog's throat or stomach. A safe alternative to real bones or plastic chew bones are natural reindeer antler chew toys (pictured), which have the added advantage of calcium.

Other good choices include Kong toys, which are pretty indestructible, and you can put treats (frozen or fresh) or smear peanut butter inside to keep your dog occupied while you are out. Dental bones are great for cleaning your dog's teeth, but many don't last for very long with an intensive chewer; one that can is the Nylabone Dura Chew Wishbone, which is made of a type of plastic infused with flavours appealing to dogs. Get the large size and throw it away if it starts to splinter after a few weeks.

The Zogoflex Hurley and the Goughnut are both strong and float, so good for swimmers – and you'll get your money back on both if your Golden destroys them! For safety, the Goughnut (pictured) has a green exterior and red interior, so you can tell if your dog has penetrated the surface - as long as the green is showing, you can let your dog "goughnuts."

A natural hemp or cotton tug rope (pictured below) is another option, as the cotton rope acts like dental floss and helps with teeth cleaning. It is versatile and can be used for fetch games as well as chewing.

The First Few Days

Before you collect your puppy, let the breeder know what time you will arrive and ask him or her not to feed the pup for a couple of hours beforehand - unless you have a very long journey, in which case the puppy will need to eat something. He will be less likely to be car sick and should be hungry when he lands in his new home. (The same applies to an adult dog moving to a new home).

When you arrive, ask for an old towel or toy which has been with the pup's mother – you can leave one on an earlier visit to collect with the pup. Or take one with you and rub the mother with it to collect her scent and put this with the puppy for the first few days. It may help him to settle in. In the US, some puppies are flown to their new homes; you can still ask for a toy or towel.

Make sure you get copies of any health certificates relating to the parents. A good breeder will also have a Contract of Sale or Puppy Contract which outlines everyone's rights and responsibilities – see Chapter 4. Choosing a Puppy. It should also state that you can return the puppy if there are health issues within a certain time frame – although if you have picked your breeder carefully, it will hopefully not come to this. The breeder will give you details of worming and any vaccinations. Most good breeders supply information sheets and a puppy pack for new owners.

Find out exactly what the breeder is feeding and how much. You cannot suddenly switch a dog's diet; their digestive systems cannot cope with a sudden change. In the beginning, stick to whatever the puppy is used to. Again, good breeders will send some food home with the puppy.

The Journey Home

Bringing a new puppy home in a car can be a traumatic experience. Your puppy will be devastated at leaving his or her mother, brothers and sisters and a familiar environment. Everything will be strange and frightening and he or she may well whimper and whine - or even bark - on the way home. If you can, take somebody with you on that first journey – some breeders insist on having somebody there to hold and cuddle the pup to make his journey less traumatic. Under no circumstances have the puppy on your lap while driving. It is simply too dangerous - a Golden Retriever puppy is cute, lively and far too distracting.

Have an old towel between your travel companion and the pup as he may quite possibly urinate (the puppy, not the passenger!)

If you have to go along, then take a crate – either a purpose-made travel crate or a wire crate which he will use at home. Travel crates can be soft (like the one pictured) or hard plastic. If you buy a plastic one, make sure there is a good air flow through. Put a comfortable blanket in the bottom - preferably rubbed with the scent of the mother.

If you have a journey of more than a couple of hours, make sure that you take water and offer the puppy a drink en route. He may need to eliminate or have diarrhoea (hopefully, only due to nerves), but don't let him outside on to the ground in a strange place as he is not yet fully vaccinated. Cover the bottom of the crate with a waterproof material and put newspapers in half of it, so the pup can eliminate without staining the car seats.

Arriving Home

As soon as you arrive home, let your puppy into the garden or yard and when he 'performs,' praise him for his efforts. These first few days are critical in getting your puppy to feel safe and confident in his new surroundings. Spend time with your new arrival, talk to him often in a reassuring manner. Introduce him to his den and toys, slowly allow him to explore and show him around the house – once you have puppy-proofed it. (Photo of Mr Blue courtesy of Kelly Sisco, Show Me Goldens, Missouri, USA).

Golden puppies are extremely curious - and amusing, you might be surprised at their reactions to everyday objects. Puppies explore by sniffing and using their mouths, so don't scold for chewing. Instead, put objects you don't want chewed out of reach and replace them with chew toys. Golden Retriever puppies are particularly "mouthy" compared to some other breeds. This is because they were originally bred to carry things in their mouths, i.e. retrieve, so it's instinctive for them to want to use their mouths.

If you have other animals, introduce them slowly and in supervised sessions on neutral territory or outdoors where there is space so neither feels threatened - preferably once the pup has got used to his new surroundings, not as soon as you walk through the door. Gentleness and patience are the keys to these first few days, so don't over-face him. Have a special, gentle puppy voice and use his name often in a pleasant, encouraging manner. Never use his name to scold or he will associate it with bad things. The sound of his name should **always** make him want to pay attention to you as something good is going to happen - praise, food, playtime, and so on.

Resist the urge to pick the puppy up all the time – no matter how irresistible he is! Let him explore on his own legs, encouraging a little independence. One of the most important things at this stage is to ensure that your puppy has enough sleep – which is nearly all of the time - no matter how much you want to play with him or watch his antics when awake. (This lovely photo of a new-born pup and Mum courtesy of Jessica and Stephen Webb, HollyRoseFen Golden Retrievers, Lincolnshire, UK).

If you haven't decided what to call your new puppy yet, 'Shadow' might be a good suggestion, as he or she will follow you everywhere! Many puppies from different breeds do this, but Goldens like to stick close to their owners – both as puppies and adults. Our website receives many emails from worried new owners. Here are some of the most common concerns:

- 🐾 My puppy won't stop crying or whining

- 🐾 My puppy is shivering

- 🐾 My puppy won't eat

- 🐾 My puppy is very timid

- 🐾 My puppy follows me everywhere, she won't let me out of her sight

- 🐾 My puppy sleeps all the time, is this normal?

These behaviours are quite common at the beginning. They are just a young pup's reaction to leaving his mother and littermates and entering into a strange new world. It is normal for puppies to sleep most of the time, just like babies. It is also normal for some puppies to whine a lot during the first couple of days. A few puppies might not whine at all. If they are confident and have been very well socialised and partly housetrained by the breeder, settling in will be much easier.

Make your new pup as comfortable as possible, ensuring he has a warm (but not too hot), quiet den away from draughts, where he is not pestered by children or other pets. Handle him gently, while giving him plenty of time to sleep. During the first couple of nights try your best to ignore the pitiful cries, but you should still get up in the middle of the night to take him into the garden or yard. However, if you pick up or play with your pup every time he cries, he will learn that this behaviour gives him the reward of your attention.

A puppy will think of you as the new mother and it is quite normal for them to want to follow you everywhere, but after a few days start to leave your pup for short periods of a few minutes, gradually building up the time. A puppy unused to being left alone for short periods can grow up to have separation anxiety - see **Chapter 8. Canine Behaviour** for more information.

If your routine means you are normally out of the house for a few hours during the day, get your puppy on a Friday or Saturday so he has at least a couple of days to adjust to his new surroundings. A far better idea is to book time off work to help your puppy to settle in, if you can and, if you don't work, leave your diary free for the first couple of weeks. Helping a new pup to settle in is virtually a full-time job. This can be a frightening time for some puppies. Is your puppy shivering with cold or is it nerves? Avoid placing your pup under stress by making too many demands. Don't allow the kids to pester the pup and, until they have learned how to handle a dog, don't allow them to pick him up unsupervised, as they could inadvertently damage his delicate little body.

If your pup won't eat, spend time gently coaxing. If he leaves his food, take it away and try it later. Don't leave it down all of the time or he may get used to turning his nose up at it. The next time you put something down for him, he is more likely to be hungry. If your puppy is crying, it is probably for one of the following reasons:

- He is lonely
- He is hungry
- He wants attention from you
- He needs to go to the toilet

If it is none of these, then physically check him over to make sure he hasn't picked up an injury. Try not to fuss over him. If he whimpers, just reassure him with a quiet word. If he cries loudly and tries to get out of his allotted area, he probably needs to go to the toilet. Even if it is the middle of the night, get up (yes, sorry, this is best) and take him outside. Praise him if he goes to the toilet.

The strongest bonding period for a puppy is between eight and 12 weeks of age. The most important factors in bonding with your puppy are TIME spent with him and PATIENCE, even when he or she makes a mess in the house or chews something he shouldn't. Remember, your Golden pup is just a baby (dog) and it takes time to learn not to do these things. Spend time with your pup and you will have a loyal friend for life. Goldens are very focused on their humans and that emotional attachment may grow to become one of the most important aspects of your life – and certainly his.

Where Should the Puppy Sleep?

Where do you want your new puppy to sleep? You cannot simply allow him or her to wander freely around the house – at least not in the beginning. Ideally, he will be in a contained area, such as a pen or crate, at night. While it is not acceptable to shut a dog in a cage all day, you can keep your puppy in a crate at night until he or she is housetrained. Even then, some adult dogs still prefer to sleep in a crate.

You also have to consider whether you want the pup to permanently sleep in your bedroom or elsewhere. If it's the bedroom, do not allow him to jump on and off beds and/or couches or race up and down stairs until he has stopped growing, as this can cause joint damage.

 Some breeders recommend putting the puppy in a crate (or similar) on the floor next to your bed for the first two or three nights before moving him to the permanent sleeping place. Knowing you are close and being able to smell you will help overcome initial fears. He will probably still cry when you move him out of your bedroom, but that should soon stop, as he will have had those few days to get used to his new surroundings and feeling safe with you.

Very few eight-week-old puppies can go through the night without needing to wee (and sometimes poo); their bladders and self-control simply aren't up to it. To speed up housetraining, consider getting up half way through the night from Day One for the first week or so to let your pup outside for a wee. Just pick him up, take him outside with the minimum of fuss, praise the wee and put him back into the crate. After that, he should be able to last for around six hours, so set your alarm for an early morning call, and by the age of three months, a seven-hour stretch without accidents is realistic, if you've been vigilant with the daily housetraining. NOTE: While many breeders recommend getting up in the night, others are firmly against it, as they don't believe it speeds up housetraining! Ask your own breeder's advice on this one.

We don't recommend letting your new pup sleep on the bed. He will not be housetrained and also a puppy needs to learn his place in the household and have his own den. It's up to you whether you decide to let him on the bed when he's older – although do you really want to share your bed with a fully-grown 50-odd pound Golden Retriever that may well have collected mud, grass, burrs, weeds, insects, etc. while on his walks or swims? If you do allow your dog to sleep in the bedroom but not on the bed, be aware that it is not unusual for some Goldens - like many other types of dog – to snuffle, snore, fart and - if not in a crate - pad around the bedroom in the middle of the night and come up to the bed to check you are still there! None of this is conducive to a good night's sleep.

While it is not good to leave a dog alone all day, it is also not healthy to spend 24 hours a day together. He becomes too reliant on you and this increases the chances of separation anxiety when you do have to leave him. A Golden Retriever puppy used to being on his own every night is less likely to develop attachment issues, so consider this when deciding where he should sleep. Unlike previous dogs, our current dog sleeps in our bedroom (in his own basket) and also has separation anxiety. Any future dogs we have will sleep in a separate room from us after the first couple of nights – no matter how hard that is in the beginning when the puppy whimpers.

If you decide you definitely do want your pup to sleep in the bedroom from Day One, put him in a crate or similar with a soft blanket covering part of the crate initially. Put newspapers inside and set your alarm clock as very few pups are able to last the night without urinating.

··

Advice from the Breeders

We asked a number of breeders what essential advice they would give to new owners of Golden Retriever puppies, and if any surprises were in store for new owners. Here's what they said: Liz Spicer-Short, Priorschest Golden Retrievers, Dorset: "Watch them all the time. You will get very little else done, because they will be into something the moment you turn your back! They will explore everything, so try to make sure that they are not unsupervised for any length of time.

"Certain garden plants are poisonous to dogs, and too much plant material can obstruct their gut. Watch a new puppy on steps and around ponds. Their bones and joints are soft and immature and they can take surprisingly little exercise (whilst their brains think they can take more)." Photo courtesy of Liz.

Tim Hoke, Golden Meadows Golden Retrievers, California: "The biggest threat is the puppy coming

into contact with one of the major canine diseases. We always recommend that the new puppy have limited contact with the outside world until they have received their final vaccinations and rabies."

Claire Underwood, Bowcombe Golden Retrievers, Isle of Wight: "Don't allow your puppy to jump up and stand on its back legs, or go downstairs, jump off sofas etc. (these can be bad for hips). Be consistent about food, introduce new foods gradually and don't let your dog become obese. Be aware of dangerous things to chew, such as poisonous plants, and don't allow chocolate or grapes or raisins/sultanas. Don't allow your puppy to chew sticks or run after sticks." Pictured having a rest on a walk in the woods is Claire's handsome two-year-old Parsnip (Tribbson's Angel Delight), bred from show stock.

North Cornwall: "I think people are often unaware about how much puppies can chew. Really, it's best to treat them as if they were a human active toddler! There are so many hazardous things they can chew. Also for the first year, it's really not worth spending a lot of money on a bed. Old blankets or a piece of vet bed is perfect. Another thing which sometimes surprises new owners is how much puppies sleep! This is totally normal."

Richard and Suzanne Clear, Arunsglory Golden Retrievers, West Sussex: "When puppies leave their siblings and they are in new surroundings, new owners should be given something like a piece of blanket that's been shared by the mum, brothers and sisters, to sleep on for the first week at their new home. Young puppies just need constant love and attention."

Julian Pottage, Yorkbeach Golden Retrievers, Mid Glamorgan, Wales: "Mentally, imagine you have a small child coming to stay, a living being who will require regular interaction and supervision. Puppies tend to investigate by putting things in their mouth, so have a careful check for things lying around at a low level. My first puppy never chewed any wires, but I think that was because she thought they were mine, the pack leader's. As a young adult, she did eat the best part of a bar of chocolate once and quite a few raisins on another occasion – they do not always know what is good for them!"

Lesley Gunter, Moorvista, Derbyshire "A breeder should provide a handbook which includes a list of foods to avoid, such as chocolate, which can be poisonous to dogs. Golden Retriever puppies will usually chew toys pretty vigorously so care needs to be taken as they may eat the whole thing if not supervised. I use Nylabones and deer antler and Kongs as they are pretty much indestructible. One thing which surprises new owners about their puppies is their ability to eat just about anything – sometimes including their own poo and anyone else's!"

Stephen and Jessica Webb, HollyRoseFen Golden Retrievers, Lincolnshire: "Be prepared, have the crate set up as the pup's bedroom and have food and water bowls ready in place. Use the food the breeder gives you; there is less chance of a tummy upset. Never leave the pup unattended - everything is an adventure or a new sensation, including stones, slugs, snails, prohibited foods, dresses...the environment really! Have lot of toys ready, both hard and soft, and be prepared to play."

Karen Parsons, Arundel, West Sussex: "Dangers include young children, cleaning bottles, and stairs. Let the puppy have time out, allow space, but keep them involved in the family. New Golden Retriever puppies adapt quickly to their new family – if a problem occurs, it is usually the family members not the puppy causing the issue."

Karen Ireland, Trikiti Golden Retrievers, Hampshire: "Gosh, there are loads of potential dangers - from wiring to objects falling on them, but I usually advise my owners to keep their puppy confined in a fairly small area for quite a few weeks until they start to learn what they can touch and take notice of you telling them not to. How fast they grow is one thing that surprises some owners.

"Golden Retriever puppies don't look like pups for long, even though they seem to be pups till at least two...Some never grow out of puppyhood at all!" Photo of these five sleepy pups courtesy of Karen.

Sue Page, Dormansue Golden Retrievers, Surrey: "I tell my new owners that when they put their puppies to bed for the night in the kitchen not to run to them if they cry. I know that owners think I'm very hard, but if you run to your puppy the first night it knows that it only has to cry and you will be in with it. Before you know it you are sleeping down with your puppy every night. Most owners report back to me that it was heart-breaking the first night, but by the second night their puppy whimpered for a couple of minutes and then went straight to sleep.

"Dogs like rules as they want to do the right thing. So decide on the rules before you bring your little puppy home and stick to them. Remember that a puppy has no way of telling why it is allowed on the sofa on a dry day but yelled at when it comes in all wet and muddy and bounds on to the sofa the next day.

"I would say poisonous plants in the garden are one of the biggest hazards as a puppy will think nothing of chewing up a foxglove. Cables, especially in the lounge, are a hazard and when we have new puppies we just throw pillows over all the cables. For some reason a puppy doesn't seem to try and burrow underneath them. It doesn't look very pretty, but at least I know that my puppy is safe. I also make sure that new owners know not to feed things like chocolate or cooked bones to a puppy and they go away with a whole list of things never to give their puppy."

Jan Schick, Mildenhall Suffolk: "Essential advice would be to encourage new owners to think about what they are willing for their puppy to do before they take it home, e.g. is the puppy to be allowed upstairs at night? On the sofa? A specific toilet area in the garden? Also, to train the puppy with praise when it does as you wish and to ignore 'bad' behaviour. Scolding gives the dog attention and it might decide that 'naughty' action is worth 'scolding' attention. Dangers include electric wires and certain poisonous plants. Chocolate is also poisonous for dogs, so kind-hearted children willing to share need to be watched. As with children, under sink cleaners, etc. should be stored securely out of reach. Mostly I think new owners find their puppy's rapid growth surprising."

Lisa Mellor, Goodgrace Golden Retrievers, Essex, UK: "We provide a fairly comprehensive Puppy Guide for all our new owners that we hope sets out the main things they need to know and should take into consideration which may be a potential risk. These include the importance of giving puppy a few quiet days to settle themselves in their new surroundings before introducing them to one and all; and not over-exercising puppy, remembering that they are babies and need rest. They are still young and their soft bones are developing and so could be damaged if overdoing it. We advise a ratio of five minutes exercise per month of age (up to twice a day).

"Other than the clear dangers of not getting puppy vaccinated, the other advice we emphasize is the importance of socialising the puppy sufficiently. Socialising a puppy in the first few weeks and months of their lives and introducing them to as many new sights, sounds, people and experiences as possible is so important to ensure they are happy and confident, and do not develop behavioural problems because of poor ownership. Natural fearfulness increases in puppies from about five weeks, and the window of opportunity to experience new things without any fear closes at around 14 to 16 weeks. Probably the only feedback I can give about things that surprise new owners is that families comment on just how good the puppies are once they are home and how quickly they become part of the family. The surprise is probably that the puppies are too good to be true."

George and Val Coxwell, Revaliac Golden Retrievers, Devon: "Give a toy or cloth to the breeder so the puppy takes a smell home, and keep the puppy in contact with you as much as possible. Watch out for what they find to chew, particularly plants and plastic. Sometimes people are surprised by how loving Goldens are." Pictured is the Coxwell's six-month-old Millie (Cadover Firecrest of Revaliac), bred from working stock. George and Val will introduce Millie to their bloodline "to keep overall size in check, darken the colour and improve pigment" of their Revaliac Goldens.

Nicholas Lock, Bonsaviour Retrievers, Shropshire, added: "Make sure children never 'crowd' a puppy. Slowly introduce any older dogs. Keep all electrical wires out of puppy's reach. Make a specific area just for puppy to feel safe."

Wendy Pickup, Blenstone Golden Retrievers, Flintshire, Wales: "A couple of things which surprise new owners is how boisterous Golden Retriever puppies can be, and how they may already have a good idea of housetraining and already prefer to go outside to do their toilet."

Anna Cornelius-Jones, Mindieslodge Golden Retrievers, Dorset: "I always give my new owners a going home sheet with some pointers to be aware of for the first few nights/weeks. They may find their puppy will cry a lot of the first night after being separated from the rest of the litter. I send home a cloth with them with their mum and siblings' smell on and suggest that they put that in their bed with them, along with a decent-sized soft toy for them to snuggle in to. If they have another dog at home, they may find the puppy will try and cuddle in with them.

"A lot of patience is required for the first few weeks, not just for the puppy to get used to its new surroundings, but for the new owners to adjust to having a puppy about too. It's very much like having a very young child in the house and a lot of patience and understanding is needed. As with a child, anything you don't want chewed or eaten should be out of reach of the new puppy and careful attention given to anything they may get hold of and be seen to be eating. The garden can be quite a dangerous place for a new puppy and it is always a good idea if possible to section off an area where they can play safely and where no damage can be done."

Angie and Ray Gait, Sonodora Golden Retrievers, Hampshire: "The biggest surprise that new owners get is the need for constant supervision. Puppies are time consuming and you need eyes in the back of your head! Just like a baby or young child. However, the rewards are more than priceless!

"As KC Assured Breeders, we have to give extensive advice to all our puppy buyers before they have their puppy, and all dangers are covered in that. We also have our prospective puppy buyers over on several visits whilst the pups are with us, and all aspects of owning a puppy are discussed then. Inside and outside of the home should be puppy proof. Goldens are not for the house-proud, nor the gardener who has the finest manicured lawn and borders!"

Vaccinations and Worming

It is **always** a good idea to have your Golden Retriever checked out by a vet within a few days of picking him up. Some Puppy Contracts even stipulate that the dog should be examined by a vet within a certain time frame — often 48 hours. This is to everyone's benefit and, all being well, you are safe in the knowledge that, at least at the time of purchase, your puppy is healthy.

Keep your pup away from other dogs in the waiting room as he or she will not be fully protected against canine diseases until the vaccination schedule is complete. All puppies need these injections; very occasionally a pup has a reaction, but this is very rare and the advantages of immunisation far outweigh the disadvantages.

Vaccinations

An unimmunised puppy is at risk every time he meets other dogs as he has no protection against potentially fatal diseases — another point is that it is unlikely a pet insurer will cover an unvaccinated dog. It should be stressed that vaccinations are generally quite safe and side effects are uncommon. If your Golden Retriever is unlucky enough to be one of the **very few** that suffers an adverse reaction, here are the signs to look out for; a pup may exhibit one or more of these:

MILD REACTION - Sleepiness, irritability and not wanting to be touched. Sore or a small lump at the place where he was injected. Nasal discharge or sneezing. Puffy face and ears.

SEVERE REACTION - Anaphylactic shock. A sudden and quick reaction, usually before leaving the vet's, which causes breathing difficulties. Vomiting, diarrhoea, staggering and seizures.

A severe reaction is rare. There is a far greater risk of your Golden Retriever either being ill and/or spreading disease if he does not have the injections.

The usual schedule is for the pup to have his first vaccination at around eight weeks of age (before he leaves the breeder). This will protect him from a number of diseases in one shot. In the UK these are Distemper, Canine Parvovirus (Parvo), Infectious Canine Hepatitis (Adenovirus) and Kennel Cough (Bordetella). In the US this is known as DHPP. Puppies in the US also need vaccinating separately against Rabies. There are optional vaccinations for Coronavirus and - depending on where you live and if your dog is regularly around woods or forests - Lyme Disease. The puppy requires a second vaccination at 10 to 12 weeks.

Diseases such as Parvo and Kennel Cough are highly contagious and you should not let your new arrival mix with other dogs - unless they are your own and have already been vaccinated - until a week after his last vaccination, otherwise he will not be fully immunised. Parvovirus can also be transmitted by fox faeces.

The vaccination schedule for the USA is different, depending on which area you live in and what diseases are present. Full details can be found by typing *"AKC puppy shots"* into Google, which will take you to this page: http://www.akc.org/content/health/articles/puppy-shots-complete-guide

You shouldn't take your new puppy to places where unvaccinated dogs might have been, like the local park. This does not mean that your puppy should be isolated - far from it. This is an important time for socialisation. It is OK for the puppy to mix with another dog which you 100% know has been vaccinated and is up to date with its annual boosters. Perhaps invite a friend's dog round to play in your yard/garden to begin the socialisation process.

Once your puppy is fully immunised, you have a window of a few weeks when it's the best time to introduce him to as many new experiences - dogs, people, traffic, noises, other animals, etc. This critical period before the age of four and a half or five months is when he is at his most receptive. Socialisation should not stop at that age, but continue for the rest of your dog's life; but it is particularly important to socialise young puppies.

Currently, in the UK, your dog will currently need a booster injection every year of his life. The vet should give you a record card or send you a reminder, but it's also a good idea to keep a note of the date in your diary. Tests have shown that the Parvovirus vaccination gives most animals at least seven years of immunity, while the Distemper jab provides immunity for at least five to seven years and it is now believed that vaccinating every year can stress a dog's immune system. In the US, many vets now recommend that you take your dog for a 'titer' test once he has had his initial puppy vaccinations and one-year booster.

Titres (Titers in the USA)

Some breeders and dog owners feel very strongly that constantly vaccinating our dogs is having a detrimental effect on our pets' health. Although there is no scientific proof, some believe that over-vaccination may be contributing to the high number of Goldens dying early of cancer, particularly in the USA. Many vaccinations are now effective for several years, yet most vets still recommend annual "boosters."

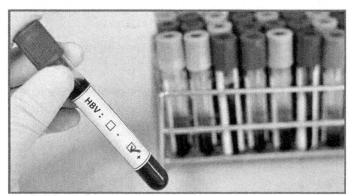

One alternative is titres. The thinking behind them is to avoid a dog having to have unnecessary annual vaccinations for certain diseases as he or she already has enough antibodies present. Still relatively new in the UK, they are more widespread among veterinary practices in the USA. One English vet we spoke to commented that a titre is only good for the day on which it is carried out, and that antibody levels may naturally drop off shortly afterwards, possibly leaving the animal at risk. He added that the dog would still need vaccinating against Leptospirosis. His claim is strongly refuted by advocates of titre testing.

To 'titre' is to take a blood sample from a dog (or cat) to determine whether he or she has enough antibodies to guarantee immunity against a particular disease, usually Parvovirus, Distemper and Adenovirus (Canine Hepatitis). If so, then an annual injection is not needed. Titering is not recommended for Leptospirosis, Bordetella or Lyme Disease, as these vaccines provide only short-term protection, and many US states also require proof of a Rabies vaccination.

The vet can test the blood at his or her clinic without sending off the sample, thereby keeping costs down for the owner. A titre for Parvovirus and Distemper currently costs around $100 or less in the US, and a titre test in the UK costs as little as £40. Titre levels are given as ratios and show how many times blood can be diluted before no antibodies are detected. So, if blood can be diluted 1,000 times and still show antibodies, the ratio would be 1:1000, which is a 'strong titre,' while a titre of 1:2 would be 'weak.' A strong (high) titre means that your dog has enough antibodies to fight off that specific disease and is immune from infection. A weak titre means that you and your vet should discuss revaccination - even then your dog might have some reserve forces known as 'memory cells' which will provide antibodies when needed. (If you are going on holiday and taking your dog to kennels, check whether the kennel accepts titre records; many don't).

One strong advocate of titres is Sue Page, of Dormansue Golden Retrievers, Surrey, who says: "I live in the UK, but I am extremely concerned about the risk of cancer. We can obviously look at what a dog eats, exercise etc., but I have particular concerns about all the chemicals we are showering our dogs with. Most people don't realise that there are tests you can do to ensure that you don't over-vaccinate or over-worm your dog. It is well known that, although very rare, all vaccinations have potential adverse reactions. These can range from mild problems such as cystitis to a severe autoimmune disease. There are also a lot of discussions going on as to whether the over-vaccination of dogs may be linked to the increased rates of cancers.

(Photo of this amusing trio courtesy of Sue).

"When my puppies go to their new homes I tell all my owners to follow their vet's advice about worming and vaccinating, as the last thing new owners require is to be at odds with their vets. However, a few owners do express concern about all the chemicals we are introducing into our puppies' lives and if they do, I explain how I try to give my dogs a chemical-free life, if possible, as adult dogs. All dogs must have their puppy vaccinations.

"Instead of giving my adult dogs their core vaccinations for Canine Distemper, Parvovirus and Adenovirus (Hepatitis) every three years, I just take my dogs down to the local vet and ask them to do something called a titre test, also known as a VacciCheck. They take a small amount of blood and send it to a lab and the lab checks for antibodies to the diseases. If they have antibodies to the diseases, there is no reason to give dogs a vaccination. If a puppy has its puppy vaccinations, it is now thought that the minimum duration of immunity is between seven and 15 years.

"However, you should note that there is a separate vaccination for Leptospirosis and Canine Parainfluenza, which is given annually. Leptospirosis is recommended by the BSAVA (British Small Animal Veterinary Association). Leptospirosis is more common in tropical areas of the world and not that common in England. In order to make a decision about whether to give this to your dog annually, you need to talk to your vet and do some research yourself so you can make an informed decision. It may be that Leptospirosis is a problem in your area. If you want to do some of your own research, then Ronald Schulz and Catherine O'Driscoll are some of the leading authorities on vaccinations and The Pet Welfare Alliance is also a good source of information."

Sue added: "We vaccinate our children up to about the age of 16. However, we don't vaccinate adults every one to three years, as it is deemed that the vaccinations they receive in childhood will cover them for a lifetime. This is what is being steadily proved for dogs and we are so lucky that we can titre test our dogs so we don't have to leave it to chance. "

The (UK) Kennel Club now includes titre testing information into its Assured Breeder Pack, but has yet to include it under its general information on vaccines on its website. The AKC discusses titering here: http://www.barkingbulletin.com/great-akc-wellness-plus-benefit and there is a further explanation at: www.embracepetinsurance.com/waterbowl/article/titer-testing

Worming

All puppies need worming (technically, deworming). A good breeder will give the puppies their first dose of worming medication at around two weeks old, then probably again at five and eight weeks before they leave the litter – or even more often. Get the details and inform your vet exactly what treatment, if any, your pup has already had. The main worms affecting puppies are roundworm and tapeworm. In certain areas of the US, the dreaded heartworm can also pose a risk. Roundworm can be transmitted from a puppy to humans – most often children - and can in severe cases cause blindness, or miscarriage in women, so it's important to keep up to date with worming. Worms in puppies are quite common; they are often picked up through their mother's milk. If you have children, get them into the habit of washing their hands after they have been in contact with the puppy – lack of hygiene is the reason why children are most susceptible. Most vets recommend worming a puppy once a month until he is six months old, and then around every two to three months.

In the US, dogs are given a monthly heartworm pill. It should be given every month when there is no heavy frost (as frost kills mosquitos that carry the disease); giving it all year round gives the best protection. The heartworm pill is by prescription only and deworms the dog monthly for heart worm, round, hook, and whip worm.

If your Golden Retriever is regularly out and about running through woods and fields, it is important to stick to a regular worming schedule, as he is more likely to pick up worms than one which spends less time in the Great Outdoors. Fleas can pass on tapeworms to dogs, but a puppy would not normally be treated unless it is known for certain he has fleas - and then only with caution. You need to know the weight of your Golden and then speak to your vet about the safest treatment to rid your puppy of the parasites.

It is not usually worth buying a cheap worming or flea treatment from a supermarket, as they are usually far less effective than more expensive vet-recommended preparations, such as **Drontal**.

Many people living in the US have contacted our website claiming the parasite treatment **Trifexis** has caused severe side effects, and even death, to their dogs. Although this evidence is only anecdotal, you might want consider avoiding Trifexis to be on the safe side - even if your vet recommends it.

Sue Page added: "It is a scientific fact that puppies are all born with worms and so breeders must worm their puppies. However, with my adult dogs I use a Company called Wormcount that will test the stools for worms, including heartworm and lungworm. I send samples of my dog's stools off every two to three months and, if they test positive I will worm them, and if negative I won't; 90% of the time my dogs test negative.

"This saves my dogs from having a monthly dose of spot on flea and wormer. Obviously, if they have fleas I will treat them, but as yet they never have. If anyone is interested you can get further details from www.wormcount.com or you can phone them on 01604 372382." (This is a UK number).

6. Crate Training and Housetraining

If you are unfamiliar with them, crates may seem like a cruel punishment for a lovable puppy. They are, however, becoming increasingly popular to help with housetraining (potty training), to give you and the puppy short breaks from each other and to keep the dog safe at night or when you are not there. Breeders, trainers, behaviourists and people who show dogs all use them and, as you will read, many Golden Retriever breeders believe they are also a valuable aid in helping to housetrain your dog.

Getting Your Dog Used to a Crate

If you decide to use a crate, then remember that it is not a prison to restrain the dog. It should only be used in a humane manner and time should be spent to make the puppy or adult dog feel like the crate is his own safe little haven. If used correctly and if time is spent getting the puppy used to the crate, it can be a godsend.

Crates may not be suitable for every dog. Goldens are not like hamsters or pet mice which can adapt to life in a cage; they thrive on being involved and living with others. Being caged all day is a miserable existence, and a crate should never be used as a means of confinement because you are out of the house all day. If the door is closed on the crate, your puppy must ALWAYS have access to water while inside.

If you do decide to use one - perhaps to put your dog in for short periods while you leave the house, or at night - the best place for it is in the corner of a room away from cold draughts or too much heat. And because Goldens like to be near their family, which is you and/or the other dogs, don't put the crate in a utility room or garage away from everybody else or the dog will feel lonely and isolated.

Dogs with thick coats like the Golden can overheat indoors. When you buy a crate, get a wire one (like the one pictured) which is robust and allows air to pass through, not a plastic one which may get very hot. If you cover the crate, don't cover it 100% or you will restrict the flow of air.

The crate should be large enough to allow your dog to stretch out flat on his side without being cramped, and he should be able to turn round easily and to sit up without hitting his head on the top. A fully-grown Golden will probably require a 42" crate. If you only intend buying one, get one of the larger sizes and divide it until your puppy grows into the full-sized crate.

Here is Midwest Pet Products sizing guide for crates, based on the anticipated adult weight of your dog: www.midwestpetproducts.com/midwestdogcrates/dog-crate-sizes.

You have a number of options when it comes to deciding where to put the crate. Perhaps consider leaving it in the kitchen or another room (preferably one with an easy-to-clean surface) where there are people during the day. If you have noisy children, you have to strike the balance between putting the crate somewhere where he won't feel isolated, yet is able to get some peace and quiet from the kids. You could then bring it into your bedroom for the first one or two nights until the puppy settles. Some breeders advise putting the crate right next to the bed for the first couple of nights or so – even raised up next to the bed, so the puppy doesn't feel alone. A couple of nights with broken sleep is worth it if it helps the young pup to settle in, as he or she will often then sleep thought the night quicker. After that, you could put the crate in a nearby place where the dog can hear or smell you at night-time - such as the landing - or you could leave it in the same place, e.g. the kitchen, 100% of the time.

It is only natural for any dog to whine in the beginning. He is not crying because he is in a cage. He would cry if he had the freedom of the room and he was alone - he is crying because he is separated from you. However, with patience and the right training, he will get used to it and some come to regard the crate as a favourite place. Some owners make the crate their dog's only bed, so he feels comfortable and safe in there. Crates aren't for every owner or every dog but, used correctly, they can:

- Create a canine den
- Be a useful housetraining tool
- Give you and the dog a bit of a break from each other
- Limit access to the rest of the house while your dog learns the household rules
- Be a safe way to transport your dog in a car

If you use a crate right from Day One, initially cover half of it with a blanket to help your puppy regard it as a den. He also needs bedding and it's a good idea to put a chew in as well. A large crate may allow your dog to eliminate at one end and sleep at the other, but this may slow down his housetraining. So, if you are buying a crate which will last for a fully grown Golden, get adjustable crate dividers – or make them yourself (or put a box inside) - to block part of it off while he is small so that he feels safe and secure, which he won't do in a very big crate. Pictured is a 42" crate.

You can order a purpose-made crate mat or a 'vet bed' to cover the bottom of the crate and then put some bedding on top. Vet beds are widely used by vets to make dogs feel warm, secure and cosy when receiving treatment, but they're just as good for using in the home. They are made from double-strength polyester with high fibre density to retain extra heat and allow air to permeate.

They also have drainage properties, so if your pup has an accident, he or she will stay dry, and they are a good choice for older dogs as the added heat is soothing for aging muscles and joints, and for any dogs recovering from surgery or treatment. Another added advantage of a vet bed is that you can wash it often and it shouldn't deteriorate. Bear in mind that a bored or lively Golden puppy is a little chew machine so, at this stage, don't spend a lot of money on a fluffy floor covering for the crate as it is likely to get destroyed.

Many breeders recommend **not** putting newspapers in one part of the crate, as this encourages the pup to soil the crate. If you have bought your puppy from a reputable breeder, she will probably already have started the housetraining process, and an eight-week-old pup should be able to last several hours without needing the toilet. It's then a case of setting your alarm clock to get up after five or six hours to let the pup out to do his or her business for the first week or so. You might not like it, but this will certainly speed up housetraining.

Once you've got your crate, you'll need to learn how to use it properly so that it becomes a safe, comfortable den for your dog. Here's a tried-and-tested method of getting your dog firstly to accept a crate, and then to actually want to spend time in there. Initially a pup might not be too happy about going inside, but he will be a lot easier to crate train than an adult dog which has got used to having the run of your house. These are the first steps:

1. Drop a few tasty puppy treats around and then inside the crate.
2. Put your puppy's favourite bedding or toy in there.
3. Keep the door open.
4. Feed your puppy's meals inside the crate. Again, keep the door open.

Place a chew or treat INSIDE the crate and close the door while your puppy is OUTSIDE the crate. He will be desperate to get in there! Open the door, let him in and praise him for going in. Fasten a long-lasting chew inside the crate and leave the door open. Let your puppy go inside to spend some time eating the chew.

IMPORTANT: Always remove your dog's collar before leaving him unattended in a crate. A collar can get caught in the wire mesh.

After a while, close the crate door and feed him some treats through the mesh while he is in there. At first just do it for a few seconds at a time, then gradually increase the time. If you do it too fast, he will become distressed. Slowly build up the amount of time he is in the crate. For the first few days, stay in the room, then gradually leave for a short time, first one minute, then three, then 10, 30 and so on.

Next Steps

5. Put your dog in his crate at regular intervals during the day - maximum two hours.
6. Don't crate only when you are leaving the house. Place the dog in the crate while you are home as well. Use it as a 'safe' zone.
7. By using the crate both when you are home and while you are gone, your dog becomes comfortable there and not worried that you won't come back, or that you are leaving him alone. This helps to prevent separation anxiety later in life.
8. Give him a chew and remove his collar, tags and anything else which could become caught in an opening or between the bars.
9. Make it very clear to any children that the crate is NOT a playhouse for them, but a 'special room' for the dog.
10. Although the crate is your dog's haven and safe place, it must not be off-limits to humans. You should be able to reach inside at any time.

The next point is important:

11. Do not let your dog immediately out of the crate if he barks or whines, or he will think that this is the key to opening the door. Wait until the barking or whining has stopped for at least 10 seconds before letting him out.

A puppy should not be left in a crate for long periods except at night time, and even then he has to get used to it first. Whether or not you decide to use a crate, the important thing to remember is that those first few days and weeks are a critical time for your puppy. Try and make him feel as safe and comfortable as you can. Bond with him, while at the same time gently and gradually introducing him to new experiences and other animals and humans.

A crate is one way of transporting your Golden in the car. Put the crate on the shady side of the interior and make sure it can't move around; put the seatbelt around it if necessary. If it's very sunny and the top of the crate is wire mesh, cover part of it so your dog has some shade and put the windows up and the air conditioning on. Never leave your Golden unattended in a vehicle; he can overheat very quickly - or be targeted by thieves.

Allowing your dog to roam freely inside the car is not a safe option, particularly if you - like me – are a bit of a 'lead foot' on the brake and accelerator! Don't let him put his head out of the window either, he can slip and hurt himself and the wind pressure can cause an ear infection or bits of dust, insects, etc. to fly into his eyes. Special travel crates are useful for the car, or for taking your dog to the vet's or a show. Choose one with holes or mesh in the side to allow free movement of air rather than a solid plastic one, in which your dog can soon overheat.

Alternatively, you can buy a metal grille to keep your dog or dogs confined to the back on the car.

Golden Breeders on Crates

Traditionally crates have been more popular in America than in the UK and the rest of Europe, but opinion is slowly changing and more owners are starting to use crates on both sides of the Atlantic. This is perhaps because people's perception of a crate is shifting from regarding it as a cage to thinking of it as a safe haven as well as a useful tool to help with housetraining and transportation, when used correctly.

Without exception, the breeders in this book believe that a crate should not be used for punishment or to imprison a dog all day while you are away from the house. This is cruel for any dog, but particularly a Golden, who was bred for the Great Outdoors, is extremely loyal and loves to be involved in your life. The keys to successful crate training are firstly to spend time enticing the dog into the crate so that he or she starts to enjoy spending time in there - most puppies will not initially like being in a crate and patience, along with the right techniques, are required. Secondly, never leave your Golden in there if he or she is distressed by it.

Several UK breeders have never used crates, including Nicholas Lock, of Bonsaviour Retrievers, Shropshire, who has bred Goldens for 10 years. Neither has Lisa Mellor, of Goodgrace Retrievers, who has 23 years' experience. Lisa added: "We don't use a crate and don't think this breed is suited to crating."

Sue Page, of Dormansue Golden Retrievers, Surrey says: "I don't use crates. But if new owners want to use crates, I am right behind them on this - as long as they don't use a crate for a punishment or leave the puppy locked in the crate for hours on end during the day."

Anna Cornelius-Jones, who has bred Mindieslodge Golden Retrievers in Dorset for 13 years: "I have not used a crate, but am not against it either. I always encourage new owners to do what they feel is best for them and their puppy. If they implement it at an early stage, there shouldn't be any

reason for any problems in getting the puppy used to a crate and it can give the new puppy the security of being in its own space where it sleeps and feels comfortable." (Photo of 13-year-old Candie courtesy of Anna).

Karen Parsons, of West Sussex: "I do not use a crate, but know many that do – they are useful to allow the puppy their own 'bedroom' and to allow for time-outs. Puppies also accept them as a safe place to be to allow them to relax and sleep, especially if there are children in the family."

George Coxwell, of Revaliac Golden Retrievers, Devon, has more than 30 years' experience with the breed and adds: "We only use a crate for illness."

Karen Ireland, of Trikiti Golden Retrievers, Hampshire (six years' breeding): "I bought a crate for Meg, but it was huge and I really didn't have anywhere suitable to put it, so never used it. I just made up a box complete with comfy blanket and a few stuffed toys, said "Goodnight", turned off the lights, went to bed and after a few moans, she slept like a baby. I don't class them as crates, but more like safe havens and if used correctly are a wonderful aid, but I certainly wouldn't leave any dog in there for very long; perhaps the odd hour for shopping, etc."

And now we hear from those who have used crates: Wendy Pickup, of Blenstone Golden Retrievers, Flintshire, Wales, who has bred Goldens for 26 years: "Crates are good to use one overnight, or during the day for a couple of hours at a time. Don't forget that a puppy needs to urinate every couple of hours and will wake up naturally at these times. If locked in a cage, he will have no choice but to urinate in his cage. My Number One tip is NEVER put a puppy or adult dog in a cage as a punishment – it is supposed to be a pleasant place to go, where the puppy can feel safe and secure."

Angie and Ray Gait, of Sonodora Golden Retrievers have also been breeding Goldens for more than a quarter of a century. Angie says: "Yes, I do use crates and recommend buyers to do the same. Pups should be left in crate overnight and when the owner is out during the day. The crate should become a pup's little safe haven, but never a punishment. Mine use crates until they can be trusted as regards chewing, etc. - usually round about nine months! I think they are fine in a crate up to four hours during the day. I don't sell pups to people who are out at work all day; someone needs to be a stay at home."

Dee Johnson, Johnsongrace Golden Retrievers, Cornwall (eight years' experience): "I normally use a crate for only about four weeks, really mainly for their own safety at night - and it helps with housetraining too." Claire Underwood, of Bowcombe Golden Retrievers, Isle of Wight, who started breeding Goldens more than 20 years ago, says: "The pups have open crates in their pen, so they are used to crates. They are great for travelling with young pups. I have never left a pup shut in a crate for longer than an hour."

Jan Schick, of Suffolk, is a relative newcomer to breeding, having produced her first litter three years ago: "I have only used a crate to keep a puppy safe at night when everyone is sleeping. In the daytime I have a puppy pen and use it when performing certain chores or when popping out to the shops. Again, it keeps the puppy safe from electric wires, etc. and is easily moved from room to room."

New breeders Lesley Gunter and Geoff Brown, of Moorvista, Derbyshire: "We do use a crate and our young bitch still sleeps in hers, though the door is open now. The key thing is to make the crate a place of safety and comfort for them and not somewhere to be put if they are being naughty or as a punishment. As long as the crate is big enough, I think it is OK to leave a puppy in it for two to three hours if you need to go out, and then overnight. I use a Kong toy to keep them occupied when they are put into the crate, and they then also associate the crate with nice things."

Julian Pottage, of Yorkbeach Golden Retrievers, Mid Glamorgan, Wales, who has nine years' breeding experience: "With my first Golden I did use a crate as well as a playpen. The latter is perhaps more useful because you can use it whether the puppy is tired or not. I do not think I left her in the crate for more than a couple of hours; less than one hour was more normal." Photo of seven-week-old Ted, courtesy of Julian.

Crates are much more widely used in the USA. Helen Dorrance, of Ducat Goldens, Texas, has bred Goldens for 42 years and says: "I do use crates, but like them for puppies who are older. I find that young female puppies especially tend to get bladder infections if they are crated for too long at too young an age. I prefer using exercise pens when they are young. I set up an exercise pen big enough so that they can have a bed and food and water at one end and a pee pad or litter box at the other end.

"I must confess though, there is nothing like a doggy door to speed up housetraining and they seem to learn that easily within a week. However, I do tell new puppy buyers that if they are not directly supervising their puppy, it is probably either eliminating where they don't want it to or chewing something they don't want chewed! Crates come in very handy if you are unable to watch your puppy at all times."

Tim Hoke, of Golden Meadows Retrievers, California, has 25 years' experience and agrees with Helen: "We strongly believe in crate training. As to duration, this depends on the age and time of day. Our puppies sleep eight hours at night in their crates. During the daytime, we have our pups take naps in their crates; a nap is usually one to two hours."

Kelly Sisco, of Show Me Goldens, has bred Goldens for four years and is a big fan of crates in the right situation: "Crate training is a must, even if you don't plan on keeping your puppy in a crate when they are bigger. Even if you're not planning on going on to show, your puppy must go to the vet at some point in its life. It is traumatic enough as it is, so teaching them that a crate is a good thing will help ease that experience.

"My dogs compete in nosework, rally, obedience and conformation. They must be comfortable in a crate in order to be at those events. We travel with our dogs as well. It is a lot easier in a hotel or a friend's/family member's house if you can put your dog into a crate."

Top 12 Housetraining Tips

How easy are Goldens to housetrain?

Well, the good news is that, according to our breeders, compared with many other breeds, the Golden is easy to housetrain. But the catch is that the dog is only as good as his or her owners. In other words, the speed and success of housetraining often depends largely on one factor: the time and effort you are prepared to put in - especially during the first couple of weeks. The more vigilant you are during the early days, the quicker your dog will be housetrained. It's as simple as that. Taking the advice in this chapter and being consistent with your routines and repetitions is the quickest way to toilet train (potty train) your Golden pup.

You have four big factors in your favour when it comes to housetraining:

1. Goldens are highly intelligent.

2. They are very eager to please their owners and love being praised.

3. Most would do anything for a treat.

4. A puppy's instinct is not to soil his or her own den.

From about the age of three weeks, a pup will leave his sleeping area to go to the toilet. Most good breeders will already have started the housebreaking process with their puppies, so when you pick up your little bundle of joy, all you have to do is ensure that you carry on the good work.

If you're starting from scratch when you bring your pup home, your new arrival thinks that the whole house is his den and may not realise that this is not the place to eliminate. Therefore you need to gently and persistently teach him that it is unacceptable to make a mess inside the home. Goldens, like all dogs, are creatures of routine - not only do they like the same things happening at the same times every day, but establishing a regular routine with your dog also helps to speed up obedience and toilet training.

Dogs are also very tactile creatures, so they will pick a toilet area which feels good under their paws. Many dogs like to go on grass - but this will do nothing to improve your lawn, so you should think carefully about what area to encourage your puppy to use. You may want to consider a small patch of gravel crushed into tiny pieces in your garden, or a corner of the garden or yard away from any attractive flower beds.

Some breeders advise against using puppy pads for any length of time as puppies like the softness of the pads, which can encourage them to eliminate on other soft areas - such as your carpets or bed. Although puppy pads are often more commonly used by people living in apartments, several breeders and owners do use puppy pads, alongside regularly taking the puppy outside to eliminate, and gradually reduce the area covered by the pads.

Follow these tips to speed up housetraining:

1. **Constant supervision** is essential for the first week or two if you are to housetrain your puppy quickly. This is why it is important to book the week or so off work when you bring

him home, if you can. Make sure you are there to take him outside regularly. If nobody is there, he will learn to urinate or poo(p) inside the house.

2. **Take your pup outside at the following times:**

   - As soon as he wakes – every time
   - Shortly after each feed
   - After a drink
   - When he gets excited
   - After exercise or play
   - Last thing at night
   - Initially every hour - whether or not he looks like he wants to go

You may think that the above list is an exaggeration, but it isn't! Housetraining a pup is almost a full-time job for the first few days. If you are serious about toilet training your puppy quickly, then clear your diary for a few days and keep your eyes firmly glued on your pup...learn to spot that expression or circling motion just before he makes a puddle - or worse – on your floor.

3. Take your pup to **the same place** every time, you may need to use a lead (leash) in the beginning - or tempt him there with a treat. Some say it is better to only pick him up and dump him there in an emergency, as it is better if he learns to take himself to the chosen toilet spot. Dogs naturally develop a preference for going in the same place or on the same surface. Take or lead him to the same patch every time so he learns this is his toilet area. **No pressure – be patient.** You must allow your distracted little darling time to wander around and have a good sniff before performing his duties – but do not leave him, stay around a short distance away. Sadly, puppies are not known for their powers of concentration; it may take a while for him to select the perfect bathroom!

4. **Housetraining is reward-based.** Give praise or a treat immediately after he has performed his duties in the chosen spot. Goldens love praise and learn quickly, and reward-based training is the most successful method for quick results.

5. **Share the responsibility.** It doesn't have to be the same person who takes the dog outside all the time. In fact it's easier if there are a couple of you, as housetraining is a very time-consuming business. Just make sure you stick to the same principles, command and patch of ground.

6. **Stick to the same routine.** Dogs understand and like routine. Sticking to the same one for mealtimes, short exercise sessions, play time, sleeping and toilet breaks will help to not only housetrain him quicker, but help him settle into his new home.

7. **Use the same word** or command when telling your puppy to go to the toilet – or while he is in the act. He will gradually associate this phrase or word with toileting and you will even be able to get him to eliminate on command after some weeks.

8. **Use your voice if you catch him in the act indoors.** A short sharp negative sound is best - NO! ACK! EH! - it doesn't matter, as long as it is loud enough to make him stop. Then start running enthusiastically towards your door, calling him into the garden and the chosen place and patiently wait until he has finished what he started indoors. It is no good scolding your dog if you find a puddle or unwanted gift in the house but don't see him do it; he won't know why you are cross with him. Only use the negative sound if you actually catch him in the act.

9. **No punishment.** Accidents will happen at the beginning, do not punish your Golden for them. He is a baby with a tiny bladder and bowels, and housetraining takes time - it is perfectly natural to have accidents early on. Remain calm and clean up the mess with a good strong-smelling cleaner to remove the odour, so he won't be tempted to use that spot again. Dogs have a very strong sense of smell; use a special spray from your vet or a hot solution of washing powder to completely eliminate the odour. Smacking or rubbing his nose in it can have the opposite effect - he will become afraid to do his business in your presence and may start going behind the couch or under the bed, rather than outside.

10. **Look for the signs.** These may be whining, sniffing the floor in a determined manner, circling and looking for a place to go, or walking uncomfortably - particularly at the rear end! Take him outside straight away, and try not to pick him up all the time. He has to learn to walk to the door himself when he needs to go outside. (Photo courtesy of Kelly Sisco, Show Me Goldens, USA).

11. **If you use puppy pads, only do so for a short time** or your puppy will get used to them.

12. **Use a crate at night-time** and for the first couple of weeks, set your alarm clock. An eight-week-old pup should be able to last five or six hours if the breeder has already started the process. Get up five hours after you go to bed and take the pup outside to eliminate. After a couple of days, gradually increase the time by 15 minutes. By the age of four or five months a Golden pup should be able to last eight hours without needing the toilet – provided you let him out last thing at night and first thing in the morning. Before then, you will have a lot of early mornings!

If using a crate, remember that during the day the door should not be closed until your pup is happy with being inside. At night-time it is acceptable to close the door. Consider keeping the pup close to you for the first two or three nights. He needs to believe that the crate is a safe place and not a trap or prison. If you don't want to use a crate, then section off an area inside one room or use a puppy pen to confine your pup at night.

And finally, one British breeder added this piece of advice: "If you are getting a puppy, invest in a good dressing gown and an umbrella!"

Breeders on Housetraining

Like many good breeders, Wendy Pickup, of Blenstone Golden Retrievers, Flintshire, provides new owners with extra information to take home which helps them to understand their puppy's needs. In her Notes For Buyers she says: "Your puppy has already started to ask to go out when she needs the toilet; in any case you will need to take her outside regularly. Typically, this would be every time she wakes up as well as after meals.

"Watch for the signs: searching the ground and sniffing is a good indication she needs to pass water. Puppies have relatively small bladders and may need to go out every two or three hours. Always choose the same place in the garden; remain with the puppy until she has performed and then give her plenty of praise. Remember, accidents will happen. If you catch your puppy in the act, simply take her outside and then praise her for her efforts. Never shout at or hit your puppy as this will cause confusion and is likely to make matters worse.

"During the times when puppy has no access to the garden, it is a good idea to place some newspaper on the floor. The newspaper could be moved nearer and nearer to the outside door until puppy realises to go to the door to ask to go out. Puppy training pads are also available from pet shops, although we find that puppies prefer to rip them up rather than to use them for their correct purpose!"

Dee Johnson, Cornwall: "Most of my puppies are 90% housetrained when they leave me at eight weeks. I always train them by teaching them a word to associate with it. So when they have a wee, I always say "Wee wee, good girl" or "Wee wee, good boy." Obviously I pass on the words I use to the new owners."

When asked how long it take to housetrain a Golden puppy, USA breeder Tim Hoke replied: "Depending on consistency of training, as young as three months and as old as eight months. Crate training is the easiest and most pain-free way to housetrain a puppy."

Fellow USA breeder Kelly Sisco added: "Goldens, in general, are pretty easy to potty train. Consistency is the key! With consistency and frequent potty breaks, it can usually be done within a month or so. By six months old, puppies should rarely be having accidents in the house. We give ours a treat immediately when they potty, as in before they even start kicking up the grass. We make a party of it and tell them they are the best, smartest dog in the whole wide world." Pictured with her feline friend is Kelly's four-year-old Lindy (Sky is the Limit for Lindy Zuligoldens).

Like a lot of good breeders, Karen Ireland starts the education early: "I start housetraining my pups as soon as they open their eyes and can move. I place a tray (rather like a large cat litter tray) with cat litter in right next to the whelping box and, no word of a lie, they use it!"

"They crawl out of the box and use the litter from around three weeks of age. I think they are amazing. By the time they leave me at around eight weeks, they are practically clean and trained to use a large 'stoned' area on my decked area. I send my new families off with a bag of used cat litter and tell them to scatter it in an area they want to use as a 'doggy toilet' and to take the pup when awake to that area (on a lead) and wait patiently until they do something, then praise like mad. I have had brilliant comments from all my new owners that housetraining was a synch."

Claire Underwood: "I would say mostly about three weeks, with night accidents up to about eight weeks (when pup is four months old). If the pups have been let out after eating they are easier to train once in their new home. My one tip would be always let the pup out straight after feeding." Richard and Suzanne Clear, Arunsglory Golden Retrievers, West Sussex: "In our experience, a puppy should be housetrained by around 12 to 15 weeks of age, barring the odd accident. All our puppies were going in a designated area before they left us at around nine weeks. You have to then be persistent and never let your guard down."

Liz Spicer-Short, Priorschest Golden Retrievers, Dorset: "They get the hang of it very quickly, providing you are on hand to take them out at every opportunity. They should have proper full control at four to five months of age. The one tip would be to establish a routine as quickly as you can; puppies thrive on routine. Don't use pads or newspaper at the door to start with, as you are effectively saying 'this is where you should go'. Get them outside and get a command such as 'Hurry up!' connected with the action. They want to please and will soon be going to the loo on command."

Breeders of eight years' standing, Stephen and Jessica Webb, of HollyroseFen Golden Retrievers, Lincolnshire: "We can easily train in four weeks. Crate train your puppy and use the crate overnight; pups rarely toilet in their beds. Initially take the puppy out every one to two hours, give lots of praise for success and try to ignore failure! If the pup has finished playing, eating, bathing or has just woken up, take him or her out straight away."

Wendy Pickup: "Speed of housetraining very much depends on the puppy, and how the litter has been brought up. I would say that at best it takes two weeks for a puppy to understand that he is supposed to go outside to the toilet – but a further six to eight weeks for him to learn how to ask to go outside. My tip is: whenever the puppy wakes up watch his behaviour – when he starts to sniff the floor and circle with purpose he needs to go out.

"Take the puppy to the door through which he is to go out, allow him outside and give PLENTY of praise when he performs. Wait outside with the puppy until he does perform – EVEN IN BAD WEATHER – YOU MUST BE THERE TO PRAISE HIM WHEN HE PERFORMS. Use the same routine every time." Pictured is Wendy's Mary (Blenstone Rainbow Mary) with her one-day-old litter.

Sue Page: "Housetraining a Golden Retriever puppy takes between four and four and a half months (from birth). Usually we get to four months and a puppy is more or less housetrained, but it takes the extra two weeks for it to be 99% reliable. However, if puppies get really excited, they can have accidents for months after this. I would say that no one can be with a puppy 100% of the time and not to beat yourself up when your puppy has an accident."

Jan Schick agrees: "I would say that most puppies are housetrained within four weeks from purchase at eight weeks old. I recommend that new owners put or show the puppy where to relieve itself immediately on waking and after eating. Always praise when the puppy uses the 'toilet' and never scold when mistakes are made." Lisa and Mark Mellor: "Most of our puppies are going outside to the toilet before they leave for their new homes at about eight weeks. Goldies are

instinctively a very clean breed and so if they can get outside, they will choose to do so. As the bladders of puppies aren't fully developed until three months of age, you would not expect a puppy to go all night without needing to go to the toilet – but in my experience they are housetrained by about three months latest, depending the effort of the new owners."

Shropshire breeder of 10 years Nicholas Lock, of Bonsaviour Golden Retrievers, adds: "Two to three months to housetrain. Buy and use chip shop wrapping paper for toilet training. It's a cheap alternative to puppy pads, and it's absorbent and hygienic." Pictured is Nicholas's Sam.

Anna Cornelius-Jones: "Goldens can be quite easy to train and they are always willing to learn, so a lot can be achieved in a relatively small amount of time. When housetraining, I advise new owners to be patient and not to scold too severely if an accident occurs. I encourage them to carry on with procedures I have started, i.e. using a tray and training liner along with making sure the puppy is put outside as soon as possible on waking and about 10 to 15 minutes after it has eaten. Hopefully, within a few months, they should know where to go and most will ask or show their new owner in some way that they need to go out."

As you have read, the details of housetraining may vary slightly from one breeder to another. The important thing as a new owner is to continue with the breeder's method, which your puppy has already part learned – and BE VIGILANT. Your Golden wants to learn and time spent housetraining during the first month will reap rewards with speedy results.

GENERAL HOUSETRAINING TIP: A trigger can be very effective to encourage your dog to perform his duties. Some people use a clicker or a bell - we used a word; well, two actually. Within a week or so I trained our puppy to urinate on the command of "Wee wee!" Think very carefully before choosing the word or phrase, as I often feel an idiot wandering around our garden last thing at night shouting "Max, WEE WEE!!" in an encouraging manner. (Although I'm not sure that the American expression "GO POTTY!!" sounds much better!

"How can you tell the dogs need to go out?"

7. Feeding a Golden Retriever

Golden Retrievers are not known for being fussy eaters. Most of them are highly motivated by food, which hardly touches the sides as they wolf it down. And it's true that many will chew almost anything that is put in front of them – as well as a lot that isn't – especially when young.

But to keep your dog's biological machine in good working order, it's important to supply the right fuel. Feeding the correct diet is an essential part of keeping your Golden fit and healthy.

The topic of feeding can be something of a minefield; owners are bombarded with endless choices as well as countless adverts from dog food companies, all claiming that theirs is best. There is not one food that will give every single dog the shiniest coat, the brightest eyes, the most energy, the best digestion, the least gas, the longest life and stop him from scratching or having skin problems.

Dogs are individuals, just like people, which means that you could feed a quality food to a group of dogs and find that most of them thrive on it, some do not so well, while a few might get an upset stomach or even an allergic reaction. The question is: "Which food is best for **my** Golden Retriever?"

If you have been given a recommended food from a breeder, rescue centre or previous owner, stick to this as long as your dog is doing well on it. A good breeder knows which food her dogs thrive on. If you do decide - for whatever reason - to change diet, then this must be done gradually. There are several things to be aware of when it comes to feeding:

1. Most Golden Retrievers are highly food motivated. Add to this their eagerness to please and you have a powerful training tool. You can use feeding time to reinforce a simple command on a daily basis.

2. However, many have no self-control when it comes to food, so it is up to you to control your dog's intake and keep the weight in check.

3. Some dogs have food sensitivities or allergies - more on this topic later.

4. Excess gas is not uncommon with dogs, and one of the main reasons for flatulence is the wrong diet.

5. Some dogs do not do well on diets with a high grain content.

6. There is anecdotal evidence that some Golden Retrievers thrive on a home-made or raw diet, particularly if they have been having skin issues with manufactured foods, but you need the time and money to stick to it.

7. Often, you get what you pay for with dog food, so a more expensive food is usually – but not always - more likely to provide better nutrition in terms of minerals, nutrients and high

quality meats. Cheap foods often contain a lot of grain; read the list of ingredients to find out. Dried foods (called 'kibble' in the US) tend to be less expensive than some other foods. They have improved a lot over the last few years and some of the best ones are now a good choice for a healthy, complete diet. Dried foods also contain the least fat and most preservatives. Foods such as Life's Abundance dry formulas do not contain any preservatives.

8. Sometimes elderly dogs may just get bored with their diet and go off their food. This does not necessarily mean that they are ill, simply that they have lost interest and a new food should be gradually introduced.

Our dog Max, who has inhalant allergies, is on a quality dried food which the manufacturers claim is 'hypoallergenic,' i.e. good for dogs with allergies. Max seems to do well on it, but not all dogs thrive on dried food. We tried several other foods first; it is a question of owners finding the best food for their dog. If you got your dog from a good breeder, they should be able to advise you.

Beware foods described as 'premium' or 'natural' or both, these terms are meaningless. Many manufacturers blithely use these words, but there are no official guidelines as to what they mean. However **"Complete and balanced"** IS a legal term and has to meet standards laid down by AAFCO (Association of American Feed Control Officials) in the USA.

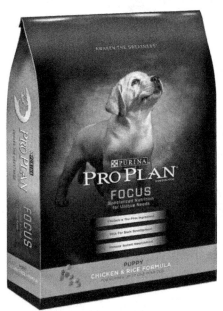

Always check the ingredients on any food sack, packet or tin to see what is listed first; this is the main ingredient and it should be meat or poultry, not grain. If you are in the USA, look for a dog food endorsed by AAFCO. In general, tinned foods are 60-70% water and often semi-moist foods contain a lot of artificial substances and sugar. Choosing the right food for your dog is important; it will influence his health, coat and sometimes even temperament.

There are three stages of your dog's life to consider when feeding: Puppy, Adult and Senior (also called Veteran). Some manufacturers also produce a Junior feed for adolescent dogs. Each represents a different physical stage of life and you need to choose the right food during each particular phase. (This does not necessarily mean that you have to feed Puppy, then Junior, then Adult then Senior food, some breeders switch their young dogs to Adult formulas fairly soon). Also, a pregnant female will require a special diet to cope with the extra demands on her body; this is especially important as she nears the latter stages of pregnancy.

Many owners feed their Goldens twice a day; this helps to stop a hungry dog gulping food down in a mad feeding frenzy, and reduces the risk of Bloat (see later section). Some owners of fussy eaters or older dogs who have gone off their food give two different meals each day to provide variety. One meal could be dried kibble, while the other might be home-made, with fresh meat, poultry and vegetables, or a tinned food. If you do this, make sure the two separate meals provide a balanced diet and that they are not too rich in protein – especially with young or old dogs.

We will not recommend one brand of dog food over another, but do have some general tips to help you choose what to feed. There is also some advice for owners of dogs with food allergies and intolerance. Food allergies are a growing problem in the canine world generally. Sufferers may itch, lick or chew their paws and/or legs, rub their face or get 'hot spots'. They may also get frequent ear infections as well as redness and swelling on their face. Switching to a grain-free diet can help to alleviate the symptoms, as your dog's digestive system does not have to work as hard. In the wild, a dog or wolf's staple diet would be meat with some vegetable matter from the stomach and intestines of the herbivores (plant-eating animals) that he ate – but no grains. Dogs do not digest corn or wheat (which are often staples of cheap commercial dog food) very efficiently. Grain-free diets still provide carbohydrates through fruits and vegetables, so a dog still gets all the necessary nutrients.

15 Top Tips for Feeding your Golden

1. If you choose a manufactured food, don't pick one where meat or poultry content is NOT the first item listed on the bag or tin. Foods with lots of cheap cereals or sugar are not the best choice.

2. Some dogs suffer from sensitive skin, 'hot spots' or allergies. A cheap food, often bulked up with grain, will only make this worse. If this is the case, bite the bullet and choose a high quality – usually more expensive – food, or consider a raw diet. You'll probably save money in vets' bills in the long run and your dog will be happier. A food described as 'hypoallergenic' on the sack means 'less likely to cause allergies.'

3. Consider feeding your Golden twice a day, rather than once. Smaller feeds are easier to digest, and reduce flatulence (gas) as well as the risk of Bloat. Puppies need to be fed more often; discuss exactly how often with your breeder.

4. Establish a feeding regime and stick to it. Dogs like routine. If you are feeding twice a day, feed once in the morning and then again at tea-time. Stick to the same times of day. Do not give the last feed too late, or your dog's body will not have chance to process or burn off the food before sleeping. He will also need a walk or letting out in the garden or yard after his second feed to allow him to empty his bowels. Feeding at the same times each day helps your dog establish a toilet regime.

5. Take away any uneaten food between meals. Most Goldens LOVE their food, but any dog can become fussy if food is available all day. Imagine if your dinner was left on the table for hours. Returning to the table two or three hours later would not be such a tempting prospect, but coming back for a fresh meal would be far more appetising. Also, when food is left all day, some dogs take the food for granted and lose their appetite. They start leaving food and you are at your wits' end trying to find something they will actually eat. Put the food bowl down twice a day and take it up after 20 minutes – even if there is some left. If he is healthy and hungry, he'll look forward to his next meal and soon stop leaving food. If a Golden Retriever does not eat anything for a couple of days, it could well be a sign that he is unwell.

6. Do not feed too many titbits (tidbits) and treats between meals. Extra weight will place extra strain on your Golden's joints and organs, have a detrimental effect on health and even lifespan. It also throws a balanced diet out of the window. Try to avoid feeding your dog from the table or your plate, as this encourages attention-seeking behaviour, begging and drooling.

7. Never give your dog cooked bones, as these can splinter and cause choking or intestinal problems. If your Golden is a gulper, avoid giving rawhide, as dogs who rush their food have a tendency to chew and swallow rawhide without first nibbling it down into smaller pieces.

8. If you switch to a new food, do the transition gradually. Unlike humans, dogs' digestive systems cannot handle sudden changes. Begin by gradually mixing some of the new food in with the old and increase the proportion so that after seven to eight days, all the food is the new one. The following ratios are recommended by Doctors Foster & Smith Inc: Days 1-3 add 25% of the new food, Days 4-6 add 50%, Days 7-9 add 75%, Day 10 feed 100% of the new food. By the way, if you stick to the identical brand, you can change flavours in one go.

9. NEVER feed the following items to your dog: grapes, raisins, chocolate, onions, Macadamia nuts, any fruits with seeds or stones, tomatoes, avocadoes, rhubarb, tea, coffee or alcohol. All of these are poisonous to dogs.

10. Check your dog's faeces (aka stools, poo or poop!) If his diet is suitable, the food should be easily digested and produce dark brown, firm stools. If your dog produces soft or light stools, or has a lot of gas or diarrhoea, then the diet may not suit him, so consult your vet or breeder for advice.

11. Feed your dog in stainless steel or ceramic dishes. Plastic bowls don't last as long and can also trigger an allergic reaction around the muzzle in some sensitive dogs. Ceramic bowls are best for keeping water cold.

12. If you have more than one dog, consider feeding them separately. Golden Retrievers normally get on very well with other pets, especially if introduced at an early age. But feeding dogs together can sometimes lead to food aggression from a dog either protecting his own food or trying to eat the food designated for another.

13. If you do feed leftovers, feed them INSTEAD of a balanced meal, not as well as - unless you are feeding a raw diet. High quality dog foods already provide all the nutrients, vitamins, minerals and calories that your dog needs. Feeding titbits or leftovers may be too rich for your Golden in addition to his regular diet and cause gas, scratching or other problems, such as obesity. You can feed your dog vegetables as a healthy low-calorie treat.

 Get your puppy used to eating raw carrots, pieces of apple, etc. as a treat and he will continue to enjoy them as an adult. If you wait until he's fully grown before introducing them, he may well turn his nose up.

14. Keep your dog's weight in check. Obesity can lead to the development of serious health issues, such as diabetes, high blood pressure and heart disease. Although weight varies from dog to dog, a good rule of thumb is that your Golden Retriever's tummy should be higher than his rib cage. If his belly is level or hangs down below it, he is overweight.

15. And finally, always make sure that your dog has access to clean, fresh water. Change the water and clean the bowl regularly – it gets slimy!

Many breeders feed their adult dogs twice a day, others feed just once, and yet others feed some dogs once a day and some dogs twice a day. As one US breeder put it: "They are not all made from the same cookie cutter." Start your dog on twice-daily feeds from four to six months old and, if he or she seems to be thriving on this regime, stick to it.

Types of Dog Food

We are what we eat. The right food is a very important part of a healthy lifestyle for dogs as well as humans. Here are the main options explained:

Dry dog food - also called kibble, is a popular and relatively inexpensive way of providing a balanced diet. It comes in a variety of flavours and with differing ingredients to suit the different stages of a dog's life. Cheap foods are often false economy, particularly if your Golden does not tolerate grain/cereal very well. You may also have to feed larger quantities to ensure he gets sufficient nutrients.

Canned food - another popular choice – and it's often very popular with dogs too. They love the taste and it generally comes in a variety of flavours. Canned food is often mixed with dry kibble, and

a small amount may be added to a dog that is on a dry food diet if he has lost interest in food. It tends to be more expensive than dried food and many owners don't like the mess. These days there are hundreds of options, some are very high quality and made from natural, organic ingredients and contain herbs and other beneficial ingredients.

A part-opened tin can sometimes smell when you open the fridge door. As with dry food, read the label closely. Generally, you get what you pay for and the origins of cheap canned dog food are often somewhat dubious. Some Goldens can suffer from diarrhoea or soft stools and/or gas with too much tinned or soft food.

Semi-Moist - These are commercial dog foods shaped like pork chops, salamis, bacon (pictured), burgers or other meaty foods and they are the least nutritional of all dog foods. They are full of sugars, artificial flavourings and colourings to help make them visually appealing. Goldens don't care two hoots what their food looks like, they only care how it smells and tastes; the shapes are designed to appeal to humans. While you may give your dog one as an occasional treat, they are not a diet in themselves and do NOT provide the nutrition your dog needs. Steer clear of them for regular feeding.

Freeze-Dried – (pictured) This is made by frozen food manufacturers for owners who like the convenience – this type of food keeps for six months to a year - or for those going on a trip with their dog. It says 'freeze-dried' on the packet and is highly palatable, but the freeze-drying process bumps up the cost. Freeze dried is one option if you are considering feeding a raw diet.

Home-Cooked - Some owners want the ability to be in complete control of their dog's diet, know exactly what their dog is eating and to be absolutely sure that his nutritional needs are being met. Feeding your dog a home-cooked diet is time consuming and expensive, and the difficult thing – as with the raw diet - is sticking to it once you have started out with the best of intentions. But many owners think the extra effort is worth the peace of mind.

If you decide to go ahead, you should spend the time to become proficient and learn about canine nutrition to ensure your dog gets all the vital nutrients.

What the Breeders Feed

We asked 21 Golden Retriever breeders what they feed their dogs. We are not recommending one brand over another, but the breeders' answers give an insight to what issues are important when considering food and why a particular brand has been chosen, starting in the UK:

Lisa and Mark Mellor, Goodgrace Retrievers, Essex: "We have tried a variety of foods and brands over the years and, when asked, we advise a complete dry food. The food is 'complete' in terms of nutrients, etc. and a dry food means that stools are firm and easy to pick up and not so smelly. Wet foods, on the other hand, mean looser stools. In terms of brand, again we have tried a variety and all we advise is to not purchase foods with colour additives. From a practical perspective, dry foods are easier to store in the house – you don't have smelly cans of dog food left over."

Dee Johnson, Johnsongrace Golden Retrievers, North Cornwall: "I think it's really down to giving a really good quality kibble to deal with food intolerances. I searched for years because of one of my girls getting colitis when she was younger. Then I moved her onto 'Gentle', which is cold-pressed and you only need to give them a small portion as there are no added fillers, etc. to fill them out. It has green-lipped mussels in and other really good ingredients and my dogs have such lovely coats and digestive systems. As far as raw goes, I think raw feeding is the 'in thing' for a lot of people as it sounds so much better for them, but I don't think it is any better- and bacteria such as E-coli, Salmonella, etc. are is a big risk with handling raw meats."

Wendy Pickup, Blenstone Golden Retrievers, Flintshire: "We feed Arden Grange, a complete food kibble. We soak the kibble, or moisten it at least. This is because the kibble swells when wet and, if eaten dry, we believe it may swell in the stomach and could cause bloat. The reason we choose to feed a complete food is that a lot of research and development has gone into producing these foods; the ingredients are balanced with the needs of the dog and there are many types within different ranges to suit different breeds and ages of dogs. It is also convenient for modern day living. Choose a good quality food; you pay for what you get."

Suffolk breeder Jan Schick: "I use a dry complete feed for my dogs so that I can be sure that they are receiving a properly balanced diet and I use different life stages of the same brand, i.e. mother and puppy programme, over five years, etc."

West Sussex breeder Karen Parsons: "I feed various types of Royal Canin dry food, depending on the individual dog and best type of food, e.g. sensitive stomach/age/puppy food. Dogs love raw food – it is good for them, but I will never feed them lamb bones as they splinter and get stuck in their throats." Pictured are Karen's Ruby, aged four, and Bodie, aged six. Both are bred from full working bloodlines

Anna Cornelius-Jones, Mindieslodge Golden Retrievers, Dorset: "I normally feed my puppies on a good low additive kibble, Arden Grange, until they go to their new owners. I have never fed them raw meat, but at present I have a new litter so am going to try it with these pups to see what benefits it may give. They will be fed the kibble too, which will be made into a porridge and when they are seven to eight weeks old, they will be introduced to it dry. I always advise new owners to stick to the diet they have been fed for the first few months and if they wish to change it later on, to introduce a new feed slowly to their regular meal times - otherwise it can cause stomach upsets."

Sue Page, Dormansue Golden Retrievers, Surrey: "I feed my dogs on James Wellbeloved. I put my last dog down at the age of 14 and a half and she was always fed on James Wellbeloved. I tried to feed my youngest dog on the raw food diet, but for some unknown reason she actually preferred James Wellbeloved! I totally understand that the raw food diet is much better than dried food, but to be honest a lot of households just can't afford to pay about £3 ($4+) a day - especially if they own several dogs. I don't therefore feed my puppies with raw food because the new owners may not be able to afford it when the dogs become adults and it would cost them £90 a month in food alone."

Karen Ireland, Trikiti Golden Retrievers, Hampshire: "Mine have never suffered from any food allergies, but when changing foods I always introduce them slowly over the course of about a week, otherwise this could cause upset tums. I feed my dogs a dry diet of kibble with a little watery gravy and any odd veggies mixed in. I have never used raw food because I know it does not contain all the vitamins they need. It also goes off too quickly for my liking - not that it would stay in the bowl very long! They have a lot of marrow bones, either filled ones from the pet shop or raw from the butcher's. They love them, they are good for the teeth and keep them quiet for hours - even after the middles have gone they gnaw away at them for weeks."

Another UK breeder added: "Goldens as a breed they seem to be prone to wet eczema -type skin patches. I have found that changing the food to one with a lower fat content helps. Since changing to Royal Canin Golden Retriever-specific food, I have had no skin problems with any of my dogs."

New Derbyshire breeder Lesley Gunter: "I feed Burns to all my dogs and they do very well on it. I feed my puppies entirely on Burns Puppy Food, first as a porridge and then gradually move to dry food. I wouldn't feed a raw diet, though I know people who do. I think there are hygiene issues and I have a grandson."

Julian Pottage, Yorkbeach Golden Retrievers, Mid Glamorgan, Wales: "In normal circumstances, I feed my dogs a natural holistic dry food. I have not tried raw food." Photo courtesy of Julian.

Claire Underwood, Bowcombe Golden Retrievers, Isle of Wight: "Raw food seems to be extremely good. I used to feed blocks of meat (you buy frozen), but I found this hard to manage and now feed a good dried food with low level of cereal. You should buy the appropriate food for the size of dog, especially

when still puppies, as you want their bones, etc. to develop at an appropriate rate."

Nicholas Lock: "We feed raw minced tripe, mixed with bran, vitamins and salmon fish oil. We find it regulates weight and gives dog all the nourishment needed naturally, and they have an excellent coat. The bran cleans the anal gland, and vitamins such as powdered seaweed are an excellent cleanser. We also feed ground eggshells for calcium (especially when whelping), and we add mashed vegetables to the feeds."

George and Val Coxwell, Revaliac Golden Retrievers, Devon: "Always give your dog the best food you can afford. We feed raw meat and biscuit, they do have the odd tin and we always cook the chicken. Puppies have raw beef mince, chicken, and rice pudding. The better you feed your dogs, the less money you spend at the vet's. In the end you actually save money, and in our experience that is a fact - proven over 40 years of breeding Golden Retrievers - with the dogs having a life well into double figures."

Another Golden Retriever breeder of more than 40 years' standing is Helen Dorrance, of Texas, who has some 'radical' advice for owners of dogs with allergies: "The biggest allergy/food sensitivity I see in Golden Retrievers is a chicken sensitivity. This can be manifested in several ways: itching, hot spots, hard-to-cure ear infections, full anal glands, pink feet, chewing feet or pulling out feathering - especially tail feathering. Unfortunately, chicken is in a lot of foods. It is best to scrutinize the ingredients and eschew anything (food or treats) that has chicken or chicken fat in it. Even a trace of chicken can set off the allergy. For instance, Purina Pro Plan Sensitive Skin and Stomach has salmon and rice as a base and almost all Goldens do well on it. However, Purina Pro Plan Beef and Rice and Salmon Performance seem fine on the surface, but contain an unspecified 'animal fat' and that seems to set off dogs' chicken allergies. There are, of course, several high-end, limited ingredient foods that would also suffice.

"A bit of a radical recommendation for Goldens prone to hot spots is to shave the dog down to the skin with a #10 blade. You eliminate the undercoat which traps the moisture that helps cause hot spots. It seems to help dogs with allergies in general - especially in the South where we have very short, mild winters with year-round pollination. You probably wouldn't need to shave dogs who live up North since they don't suffer from allergies the same way the southern dogs do.

"There has also been some research that says you should feed your puppy a protein source you don't intend to feed it as an adult. Apparently, when puppies are getting their vaccinations they can sometimes develop an immune response to their environment, including diet. Hence the recommendation to feed them a food you are unlikely to feed them as adults in case they develop a food sensitivity to their puppy diet." Pictured is Austin (Am/Can CH Ducat-Watermark G Force, owned by Pat Gibson), who won Best Veteran and a JAM at the 2010 GRCA National Specialty.

Kelly Sisco, Show Me Goldens, Missouri: "I feed Farmina. It's hard to get (I buy it by the truck load and have it shipped in) and not cheap, but such good food! I also cook for my dogs every Sunday and refrigerate it through the week. It is then put on top of their kibble. It is a mix of venison (we hunt) and vegetables."

Tim Hoke, Golden Meadows Retrievers, California: "We have been using Life's Abundance All Stage Dog Food for over 10 years. The company sources products from the US, it is made in small batches and is only available directly from the manufacturer, which means the food is at its peak efficiency when it arrives."

The Raw Diet

As you have read, most breeders involved in this book feed their dogs premium dried food. However, increasing numbers of dog owners and breeders are now considering a raw diet. Opinions are divided on the subject. There is anecdotal evidence that some dogs thrive on it, particularly those with food intolerances or allergies, although scientific proof is lagging behind. Claims made by fans of the raw diet include:

- Reduced symptoms of - or less likelihood of - allergies, and less scratching
- Better skin and coats
- Easier weight management
- Improved digestion
- Less doggie odour and flatulence
- Higher energy levels
- Reduced risk of bloat
- Helps fussy eaters
- Fresher breath and improved dental health
- Drier and less smelly stools, more like pellets
- Overall improvement in general health and less disease
- Most dogs love a raw diet

If your Golden is not doing well on a commercially-prepared dog food, or has skin issues, you might consider a raw diet. It emulates the way dogs ate before the existence of commercial dog foods, which may contain artificial preservatives and excessive protein and fillers – causing a reaction in some dogs. Dry, canned and other styles of processed food were mainly created as a means of convenience, but unfortunately this sometimes can affect a dog's health.

Some nutritionists believe that dogs fed raw whole foods tend to be healthier than those on other diets. They say there are inherent beneficial enzymes, vitamins, minerals and other qualities in meats, fruits, vegetables and grains in their natural forms that are denatured or destroyed when cooked. Many also believe dogs are less likely to have allergic reactions to the ingredients on this diet. Frozen food can be a valuable aid to the raw diet. The food is highly palatable, made from high quality ingredients and dogs usually wolf it down. The downsides are that not all pet food stores stock it, it can be expensive and you have to remember to defrost it.

Critics of a raw diet say that the risks of nutritional imbalance, intestinal problems and food-borne illnesses caused by handling and feeding raw meat outweigh any benefits. It is true that owners must pay strict attention to hygiene when preparing a raw diet and it may not be a suitable option if there are children in the household. The dog may also be more likely to ingest bacteria or parasites such as Salmonella, E. Coli and Ecchinococcus.

The View from one American Breeder

Karen Moore, of Icewind Goldens, New Jersey, USA, has taken a keen interest in canine nutrition over the last 35 years. She personally believes that there may be a general link between the high incidence of cancer in Goldens (particularly in the USA), as well as other health issues, and cheap dog food and talks of the horror of rendering plants where some dog foods are produced. Karen says: "The best diet you can feed your pet is a complete and balanced raw diet, meaning you can't just feed raw meat. Consumers are starting to become aware about dog food ingredients and I do see a trend of feeding our pets a more healthy diet. I believe that, as our pets' caregivers, we have an obligation to discover what our Goldens really need nutritionally and provide it for them.

"This is what we feed to our Goldens at Icewind: First, we had to find a company that had all the raw food we needed. Then the raw meat had to be antibiotic free, GMO free, no preservatives, it had to come from grass-fed animals, be USDA inspected with no growth hormones. Unfortunately, we could not find any pet stores that sold this kind of diet. But we did find something better - a family run company online and they would ship right to our home for free.

"We feed a complete and balanced diet of 80% raw meat, 10% bone and 10% organs which comes in either patties or large meat rolls. Also our dogs are fed on occasion raw venison, raw turkey necks, beef liver, raw chicken wings and backs. Dogs are carnivores, which means they eat meat as their main food source. They can eat vegetables, but veggies are not required for a nutritious dog diet." Photo, of Lanka and Karen's grandson, Mason, courtesy of Icewind Goldens.

"We did receive some resistance about feeding raw meat from some of our families taking their puppy home. Most people believe that dogs can survive on only pet store kibble due to the large dog food companies advertising, which place little value on your dog's health beyond their profits. So we came up with a compromise: raw complete freeze dried pet food. We found many brands, but all contained vegetable fillers. After searching, we did find one that only had 10 healthy ingredients, beef, beef tripe, ground beef bone, beef liver, beef heart, beef kidney, beef blood, beef fat, herring oil, and d-alpha tocopheryl (Vitamin E), plus it is a complete and balanced diet. The funny thing is we did receive feedback from some of our puppy families who mixed the raw freeze dried with kibble that their puppy would pick out just the freeze dried and leave the kibble. To me this shows how highly intelligent the Golden is!

"Next, I am a big believer in feeding raw goat milk as a super immune system builder. All our puppies are weaned this way, along with some complete raw meat. Our adults also receive raw goat milk a few times a week. The goat milk must be raw and not pasteurized because all the nutrients would be lost. Raw goat milk is commonly referred to as the universal milk of almost all mammals and is the most complete food known, according to the Journal of American Medicine. There are also many vitamins and minerals in raw goat milk, such as vitamin A, C, and D, calcium, electrolytes, trace elements, enzymes, omega 3 and 6 fatty acids, and magnesium, just to name a few. Raw goat milk is an incredible digestive aid; it also helps your dog obtain their daily moisture, which is very important.

"When needed, we feed organic plain canned pumpkin (not the pie filling) that has several benefits. Pumpkin is a fiber-rich food that also contains important vitamins and minerals, such as Vitamins A, E, and C, potassium and iron. But it is best used if you have a dog or puppy with diarrhea or constipation. In addition, our puppies are started on a nutritional supplement at five weeks old and continued for life. Since Goldens are prone to orthopedic problems, we feed a supplement that lubricates the joints and synthesizes new cartilage growth and tissue repair.

"One of our dogs' favorites is a raw beef marrow bone. Even an eight-week-old puppy will enjoy one. Dogs and puppies have a psychological and physical need to chew, and raw meat bones also have great dental health benefits. Even though you are feeding a healthy diet, there are other considerations to think about, such as obesity, stress, air pollution, sedentary lifestyle (a couch potato), overuse of vaccines or drugs from the vet, heartworm medication, flea and tick products."

There are two main types of raw diet, one involves feeding raw, meaty bones and the other is known as the BARF diet (*Biologically Appropriate Raw Food* or *Bones And Raw Food*), created by Dr Ian Billinghurst.

Raw Meaty Bones

This diet is:

- 🐾 Raw meaty bones or carcasses, if available, should form the bulk of the diet
- 🐾 Table scraps both cooked and raw, such as vegetables, can be fed
- 🐾 As with any diet, fresh water should be constantly available. **NOTE: Do NOT feed cooked bones, they can splinter**

Australian veterinarian Dr Tom Lonsdale is a leading proponent of the raw meaty bones diet. He believes the following foods are suitable:

- 🐾 Chicken and turkey carcasses, after the meat has been removed for human consumption
- 🐾 Poultry by-products, including heads, feet, necks and wings
- 🐾 Whole fish and fish heads
- 🐾 Sheep, calf, goat, and deer carcasses sawn into large pieces of meat and bone
- 🐾 Other by-products, e.g. pigs' trotters, pigs' heads, sheep heads, brisket, tail and rib bones
- 🐾 A certain amount of offal can be included in the diet, e.g. liver, lungs, trachea, hearts, tripe

He says that low-fat game animals, fish and poultry provide the best source of food for pet carnivores. If you feed meat from farm animals (cattle, sheep and pigs), avoid excessive fat and bones that are too large to be eaten.

Some of it will depend on what's available locally and how expensive it is. If you shop around you should be able to source a regular supply of suitable raw meaty bones at a reasonable price. Start with your local butcher or farm shop. When deciding what type of bones to feed your Golden Retriever, one point to bear in mind is that dogs are more likely to break their teeth when eating large knuckle bones and bones sawn lengthwise than when eating meat and bone together.

You'll also need to think about WHERE you are going to feed your dog. A dog takes some time to eat a raw bone and will push it around the floor, so the kitchen may not be the most suitable or hygienic place. Outside is one option, but what do you do when it's raining?

Establishing the right quantity to feed your Golden Retriever is a matter of trial and error. You will reach a decision based on your dog's activity levels, appetite and body condition. High activity and a big appetite show a need for increased food, and vice versa. A very approximate guide, based on raw meaty bones, for the average dog is 15%-20% of body weight per week, or 2%-3% a day. So, if your Golden weighs 30lb (just under 13.6kg), he or she will require 4.5lb-6lb (2-2.7kg) of carcasses or raw meaty bones weekly. Table scraps should be fed as an extra component of the diet. **These figures are only a rough guide** and relate to adult pets in a domestic environment.

Pregnant or lactating females and growing puppies may need much more food than adult animals of similar body weight. Dr Lonsdale says: "Wherever possible, feed the meat and bone ration in one large piece requiring much ripping, tearing and gnawing. This makes for contented pets with clean teeth. Wild carnivores feed at irregular intervals, in a domestic setting regularity works best and accordingly I suggest that you feed adult dogs and cats once daily. If you live in a hot climate I recommend that you feed pets in the evening to avoid attracting flies.

"I suggest that on one or two days each week your dog may be fasted - just like animals in the wild. On occasions you may run out of natural food. Don't be tempted to buy artificial food, fast your dog and stock up with natural food the next day. Puppies...sick or underweight dogs should not be fasted (unless on veterinary advice)."

Table scraps and some fruit and vegetable peelings can also be fed, but should not make up more than one-third of the diet. Liquidising cooked and uncooked scraps in a food mixer can make them easier to digest. **Things to Avoid:**

- 🐾 Excessive meat off the bone - not balanced
- 🐾 Excessive vegetables - not balanced
- 🐾 Small pieces of bone - can be swallowed whole and get stuck
- 🐾 Cooked bones - get stuck
- 🐾 Mineral and vitamin additives - create imbalance
- 🐾 Processed food - leads to dental and other diseases
- 🐾 Excessive starchy food - associated with bloat
- 🐾 Onions, garlic, chocolate, grapes, raisins, sultanas, currants - toxic to pets

- Fruit stones (pips) and corn cobs - get stuck
- Milk - associated with diarrhoea. Animals drink it whether thirsty or not and can get fat

Points of Concern

- Old dogs used to processed food may experience initial difficulty when changed on to a natural diet. Discuss the change with your vet first and then, if he or she agrees, switch your dog's diet over a period of a week to 10 days
- Raw meaty bones are not suitable for dogs with dental or jaw problems
- This diet may not be suitable if your dog gulps his food, as the bones can become lodged inside him, larger bones may prevent gulping
- The diet should be varied, any nutrients fed to excess can be harmful
- Liver is an excellent foodstuff, but should not be fed more than once weekly
- Other offal, e.g. ox stomachs, should not make up more than half of the diet
- Whole fish are an excellent source of food, but avoid feeding one species of fish constantly. Some species, e.g. carp, contain an enzyme which destroys thiamine (vitamin B1)
- If you have more than one dog, do not allow them to fight over the food, feed them separately if necessary
- Be prepared to monitor your dog while he eats the bones, especially in the beginning, and do not feed bones with sharp points. Take the bone off your dog before it becomes small enough to swallow
- Make sure that children do not disturb the dog when feeding or try to take the bone away
- Hygiene: Make sure the raw meaty bones are kept separate from human food and clean thoroughly any surface the uncooked meat or bones have touched. This is especially important if you have children. Feeding bowls are unnecessary, your dog will drag the bones across the floor, so feed them outside if you can, or on a floor that is easy to clean
- Puppies can and do eat diets of raw meaty bones, but you should consult the breeder or a vet before embarking on this diet with a young dog

You will need a regular supply of meaty bones - either locally or online - and you should buy in bulk to ensure a consistency of supply. For this you will need a large freezer. You can then parcel up the bones into daily portions. You can also feed frozen bones; some dogs will gnaw them straight away, others will wait for them to thaw. More information is available from the website www.rawmeatybones.com and I would strongly recommend discussing the matter with your breeder or vet first before switching to raw meaty bones.

The BARF diet

A variation of the raw meaty bones diet is the BARF created by Dr Ian Billinghurst, who owns the registered trademark 'Barf Diet'. A typical BARF diet is made up of 60%-75% of raw meaty bones (bones with about 50% meat, such as chicken neck, back and wings) and 25%-40% of fruit and vegetables, offal, meat, eggs or dairy foods. Bones must not be cooked or they can splinter inside the dog. There is a great deal of information on the BARF diet on the internet.

NOTE: Only start a raw diet if you have done your research and are sure you have the time and money to keep it going. There are numerous websites and canine forums with information on switching to a raw diet and everything it involves.

Food Allergies

Dog food allergies affect about one in 10 dogs. They are the third most common canine allergy for dogs after atopy (inhaled or contact allergies) and flea bite allergies. While there's no scientific evidence of links between specific breeds and food allergies, there is anecdotal evidence from owners that some Golden Retrievers can suffer a reaction to certain foods.

Food allergies affect males and females in equal measure as well as neutered and intact pets. They can start when your dog is five months or 12 years old - although the vast majority start when the dog is between two and six years old. It is not uncommon for dogs with food allergies to also have other types of allergies. If your dog is not well, how do you know if the problem lies with his food or not? Here are some common symptoms to look out for:

- Itchy skin (this is the most common). Your dog may lick or chew his paws or legs and rub his face with his paws or on the furniture, carpet, etc.
- Excessive scratching
- Ear infections
- Hot patches of skin – 'hot spots'
- Hair loss
- Redness and inflammation on the chin and face
- Recurring skin infections
- Increased bowel movements (maybe twice as often as usual)
- Skin infections that clear up with antibiotics but recur when the antibiotics run out

Allergies or Intolerance?

There's a difference between dog food *allergies* and dog food *intolerance*:

Typical reactions to allergies are skin problems and/or itching

Typical reactions to intolerance are diarrhoea and/or vomiting

Dog food intolerance can be compared to people who get diarrhoea or an upset stomach from eating spicy food. Both can be cured by a change to a diet specifically suited to the individual, although a food allergy may be harder to get to the root cause of. As they say in the canine world: "One dog's meat is another dog's poison." With dogs, certain ingredients are more likely to cause allergies than others. In order of the most common triggers across the canine world in general they are: **Beef, dairy products, chicken, wheat, eggs, corn, and soy.**

Unfortunately, these most common offenders are also the most common ingredients in dog foods! By the way, don't think if you put your dog on a rice and lamb kibble diet that it will automatically cure the problem. It might, but then again there's a fair chance it won't. The reason lamb and rice were thought to be less likely to cause allergies is simply because they were not traditionally included in dog food recipes - therefore fewer dogs had reactions to them.

It is also worth noting that a dog is allergic or sensitive to an **ingredient**, not to a particular brand of dog food, so it is very important to read the label on the sack or tin. If your Golden Retriever has a reaction to beef, for example, he will react to any food containing beef, regardless of how expensive it is or how well it has been prepared.

Symptoms of food allergies are well documented. Unfortunately, the problem is that these conditions may also be symptoms of other issues such as environmental or flea bite allergies, intestinal problems, mange and yeast or bacterial infections. You can have a blood test on your dog for food allergies, but many veterinarians now believe that this is not accurate enough.

The only way to completely cure a food allergy or intolerance is complete avoidance. This is not as easy as it sounds. First you have to be sure that your dog does have a food allergy, and then you have to discover which food is causing the reaction. Blood tests are not thought to be reliable and, as far as I am aware, the only true way to determine exactly what your dog is allergic to, is to start a food trial. If you don't or can't do this for the whole 12 weeks, then you could try a more amateurish approach, which is eliminating ingredients from your dog's diet one at a time by switching diets – remember to do this over a period of a week to 10 days.

A food trial is usually the option of last resort, due to the amount of time and attention that it requires. It is also called *'an exclusion diet'* and is the only truly accurate way of finding out if your dog has a food allergy and what is causing it. Before embarking on one, try switching dog food. A hypoallergenic dog food, either commercial or home-made, is a good place to start. There are a number of these on the market and they all have the word *'hypoallergenic'* in the name. Although usually more expensive, hypoallergenic dog food ingredients do not include common allergens such as wheat protein or soya, thereby minimising the risk of an allergic reaction. Many may have less common ingredients, such as venison, duck or types of fish. Here are some things to look for in a high quality food: meat or poultry as the first ingredient, vegetables, natural herbs such as rosemary or parsley, oils such as rapeseed (canola) or salmon.

There is anecdotal evidence that a raw diet can solve the problem, but only start raw feeding if you have the time, money and commitment to stick to it.

Here's what to avoid if your dog is showing signs of a food intolerance: corn, corn meal, corn gluten meal, meat or poultry by-products (as you don't know exactly what these are or how they have been handled), artificial preservatives (including BHA, BHT, Propyl Gallate, Ethoxyquin, Sodium Nitrite/Nitrate and TBHQBHA), artificial colours, sugars and sweeteners like corn syrup, sucrose and ammoniated glycyrrhizin, powdered cellulose, propylene glycol. If you can rule out all of these and you've tried switching diet without much success, then a food trial may be your only option.

Food Trials

Before you embark on one of these, you need to know that they are a real pain-in-the-you-know-what to monitor. You have to be incredibly vigilant and determined, so only start one if you 100% know you can see it through to the end, or you are wasting your time. It is important to keep a diary during a food trial to record any changes in your dog's symptoms, behaviour or habits.

A food trial involves feeding one specific food for 12 weeks, something the dog has never eaten before, such as rabbit and rice or venison and potato. Surprisingly, dogs are typically NOT allergic to foods they have never eaten before. The food should contain no added colouring, preservatives or flavourings.

There are a number of these commercial diets on the market, as well as specialised diets that have proteins and carbohydrates broken down into such small molecular sizes that they no longer trigger an allergic reaction. These are called *'limited antigen'* or *'hydrolysed protein'* diets.

Home-made diets are another option as you can strictly control the ingredients. The difficult thing is that this must be the **only thing** the dog eats during the trial. Any treats or snacks make the whole thing a waste of time. During the trial, you shouldn't allow your dog to roam freely, as you cannot control what he is eating or drinking when he is out of sight outdoors. Only the recommended diet must be fed. Do NOT give:

- Treats
- Rawhide (we do not recommend rawhide in any situation, it can get stuck in the dog)
- Pigs' ears
- Cows' hooves
- Flavoured medications (including heartworm treatments) or supplements
- Flavoured toothpastes
- Flavoured plastic toys

If you want to give a treat, use the recommended diet. (Tinned diets can be frozen in chunks or baked and then used as treats). If you have other dogs, either feed them all on the trial diet or feed the others in an entirely different location. If you have a cat, don't let the dog near the cat litter tray. And keep your dog out of the room when you are eating – not easy with a hungry Lab! But even small amounts of food dropped on the floor or licked off of a plate can ruin a food trial, meaning you'll have to start all over again.

Grain Intolerance

Although beef is the food most likely to cause allergies in the general dog population, there is plenty of anecdotal evidence to suggest that the ingredient most likely to cause a problem in some dogs is grain – just visit any internet forum to see some of the problems owners are experiencing with their dogs. 'Grain' is wheat or any other cultivated cereal crop. Some dogs also react to starch, which is found in grains and potatoes (also bread, pasta rice, etc)..

Some breeds (especially the Bully breeds, e.g. Bulldogs, Boxers, Bull Terriers and French Bulldogs) **can be prone to a build-up of yeast in the digestive system.** Foods that are high in grains and sugar can cause an increase in unhealthy bacteria and yeast in the stomach. This crowds out the good bacteria in the stomach and can cause toxins to occur that affect the immune system.

And when the immune system is not functioning properly the itchiness related to food allergies can cause secondary bacterial and yeast infections, which, in Goldens, may show as hot spots, ear infections, bladder infections, reddish or dark brown tear stains or other skin disorders. Symptoms of a yeast infection also include:

- Itchiness
- A musty smell
- Skin lesions or redness on the underside of the neck, the belly or paws

Although drugs such as antihistamines and steroids will temporarily help, they do not address the root cause. Wheat products are also known to produce flatulence in some Golden Retrievers, while corn products and feed fillers may cause skin rashes or irritations. Switching to a grain-free diet may help to get rid of yeast and bad bacteria in the digestive system. Introduce the new food over a week or so and be patient, it may take two to three months for symptoms to subside – but you will definitely know if it has worked after 12 weeks. Some owners also feed their dogs a daily spoonful of natural or live yoghurt, as this contains healthy bacteria and helps to balance the bacteria in your dog's digestive system - by the way, it works for humans too! Others have switched their dogs to a raw diet.

It is also worth noting that some of the symptoms of food allergies - particularly the scratching, licking, chewing and redness - can also be a sign of inhalant or contact (environmental) allergies, which are caused by a reaction to such triggers as pollen, grass or dust. Some dogs are also allergic to flea bites. See **Chapter 12. Skin and Allergies** for more details.

If you suspect your dog has a food allergy, the first port of call should be to the vet to discuss the best course of action. However, many vets' practices promote specific brands of dog food, which may or may not be the best for your dog. Don't buy anything without first checking every ingredient on the label. The website www.dogfoodadvisor.com provides useful information with star ratings for grain-free and hypoallergenic dogs' foods, or www.allaboutdogfood.co.uk if you are in the UK, or www.veterinarypartner.com/Content.plx?P=A&S=0&C=0&A=2499 for more details about canine food trials. We have no vested interest in these sites, but have found them to be good sources of unbiased information.

How Much Food?

This is another question I am often asked. The answer is … there is no easy answer! The correct amount of food for a dog depends on a number of factors:

- Breed
- Gender
- Age
- Natural energy levels
- Amount of daily exercise
- Health
- Environment
- Number of dogs in the house or kennel
- Quality of the food
- Whether your dog is working, competing, performing a service or simply a pet

Some breeds have a higher metabolic rate than others and energy levels vary tremendously from one dog to the next. Some Goldens are very energetic, while others are more laid-back. Generally, smaller dogs have faster metabolisms so require a higher amount of food per pound of body weight. Dogs that have been spayed may be more likely to put on weight. Growing puppies and young dogs need more food than senior dogs with a slower lifestyle.

Every dog is different; you can have two Golden Retrievers with different energy levels, body shapes and capacity for work or exercise. The energetic dog will burn off more calories. Maintaining a healthy body weight for dogs – and humans – is all about balancing what you take in with how much you burn off. If your dog is exercised a couple of times a day, is retrieving on shoots or competing in field trials or agility, or has regular play sessions with humans or other dogs, he will need more calories than a couch potato Goldie.

And certain health conditions such as an underactive thyroid, diabetes, arthritis or heart disease can lead to dogs putting on weight, so their food has to be adjusted accordingly. Just like us, a dog kept in a very cold environment will need more calories to keep warm than a dog in a warm climate, as they burn extra calories to keep themselves warm. Here's an interesting fact: a dog kept on his own is more likely to be overweight than a dog kept with other dogs, as he receives all of the food-based attention.

Manufacturers of cheaper foods usually recommend feeding more to your dog, as much of the food is made up of cereals, which are not doing much except bulking up the weight of the food – and possibly triggering allergies in your Golden. The daily recommended amount listed on the dog food sacks or tins is generally too high – after all, the more your dog eats, the more they sell! Because there are so many factors involved, there is no simple answer. However, below we have listed a broad guideline of the average number of **calories** a Golden Retriever with medium energy and activity levels needs. (These charts are not suitable for working dogs, as they require specialised high calorie diets during the season).

We feed our dog a dried hypoallergenic dog food made by James Wellbeloved in England. Here we list their recommended feeding amounts for dogs, listed in kilograms and grams. (28.3 grams=1 ounce, 1kg=2.2lb).

The number on the left is the dog's **adult weight** in kilograms. The numbers on the right are the amount of daily food that an average dog with average energy levels requires, measured in grams (divide this by 28.3 to get the amount in ounces). For example, a three-month-old Golden puppy which will grow into a 32kg (70.5lb) adult would require around 400 grams of food per day (14.1 ounces). As a very general rule of thumb, adult female Goldens may be expected to weigh 55lb to 65lb (25kg to 29.5kg), males 65lb to 75lb (29.5kg to 34kg), but it could be less with a lighter frame or more with a larger frame.

NOTE: The following Canine Feeding Chart gives only very general guidelines; your dog may need more or less than this. Use the chart as a guideline only and if your dog loses or gains weight, adjust meals accordingly.

PUPPY

Size type	Expected adult body weight	Daily serving in grams and ounces					
		2 mths	3 mths	4 mths	5 mths	6 mths	> 6 mths
LARGE	25kg	270g	350g	375g	375g	370g	Change to Large Breed Junior
	55lb	9.5oz	12.3oz	13.2oz	13.2oz	13oz	
	32kg	300g	400g	445g	450g	450g	
	70.5lb	10.6oz	14.1oz	15.7oz	15.9oz	15.9oz	
	40kg	355g	475g	525g	530g	530g	
	88lb	12.5oz	16.75oz	18.5oz	18.7oz	18.7oz	

JUNIOR

Size type	Expected adult body weight	Daily serving in grams and ounces						16 mths
		6 mths	7 mths	8 mths	10 mths	12 mths	14 mths	
LARGE	25kg 55lb	390g 13.75oz	380g 13.4oz	365g 12.9oz	330g 11.6oz	320g 11.3oz		Change to Large Breed Junior
	32kg 70.5lb	445g 15.7oz	435g 15.3oz	415g 14.6oz	380g 13.4oz	365g 12.9oz		
	40kg 88lb	555g 12.5oz	545g 16.75oz	530g 18.5oz	500g 18.7oz	460g 18.7oz	460g 18.7oz	

ADULT

Size type	Adult body weight	Daily serving in grams and ounces		
		High activity	Normal activity	Low activity
LARGE	25-40kg 55-88lb	380-535g 13.4-18.9oz	330-475g 11.6-16.75oz	285-410g 10-14.5oz

SENIOR

		Active	Normal
LARGE	25-40kg 55-88lb	345-495g 12.2-17.5oz	300-425g 10.6-15oz

Bloat (GDV, Gastric Dilation-Volvulus)

One reason that some owners feed their Goldens twice a day is to reduce the risk of canine bloat, particularly if their dogs are greedy gulpers. Canine bloat is a serious medical condition which requires urgent medical attention. Without it, the dog can die. In fact, it is one of the leading killers of dogs after cancer.

Bloat is known by several different names: twisted stomach, gastric torsion or Gastric Dilatation-Volvulus (GDV). It occurs mainly in larger breeds, particularly those with deep chests like Great Danes, Doberman Pinschers, Giant Schnauzers and Setters; however, the Golden Retriever can also be affected. Basically, bloat occurs when there is too much gas in the stomach. It is statistically more common in males than in females and dogs over seven years of age.

The causes are not fully understood, but there are some well-known risk factors. One is the dog taking in a lot of air while eating - either because he is greedy and gulping the food too fast, or stressed, e.g. in kennels where there might be food competition. A dog which is fed once daily and gorges himself could be at higher risk, and exercising straight after eating or after a big drink increases the risk (like colic in horses). Another potential cause is diet. Fermentable foodstuffs that produce a lot of gas can cause problems for the stomach if the gas is not burped or passed into the intestines. Bloat can occur with or without the stomach twisting (volvulus).

As the stomach swells with gas, it can rotate 90° to 360°. The twisting stomach traps air, food and water inside and the bloated organ stops blood flowing properly to veins in the abdomen, leading to low blood pressure, shock and even damage to internal organs.

Symptoms - Bloat is extremely painful and the dog will show signs of distress. He may stand uncomfortably or seem anxious for no apparent reason. A dog with bloat will often attempt to vomit every five to 30 minutes, but nothing is fetched up, except perhaps foam. Other signs include swelling of the abdomen (this will usually feel firm like a drum) – general weakness, difficulty breathing or rapid panting, drooling or excessive drinking. His behaviour will change and he may do some of the following: whine, pace up and down, look for a hiding place or lick the air.

Tips to Avoid Canine Bloat

❧ Some owners buy a frame for food bowls so they are at chest height for the dog, other experts believe dogs should be fed from the floor – do whichever slows your Golden down

❧ Buy a bowl with nobbles in (pictured) and moisten your dog's food – both of these will slow him down

❧ Feed twice a day rather than once

❧ Diet - avoid dog food with high fats or which use citric acid as a preservative, also avoid tiny pieces of kibble

❧ Don't let your dog drink too much water just before, during or after eating. Remove the water bowl just before mealtimes, but be sure to return it soon after

❧ Stress can possibly be a possible trigger, with nervous and aggressive dogs being more susceptible; maintain a peaceful environment for your dog, particularly around mealtimes

❧ IMPORTANT: Avoid vigorous exercise before or after eating, allow one hour either side of mealtimes before strenuous exercise

Bloat can kill a dog in less than one hour. If you suspect your Golden Retriever has bloat, get him into the car and off to the vet IMMEDIATELY. Even with treatment, mortality rates range from 10% to 60%. With surgery, this drops to 15% to 33%.

Overweight Dogs

It is far easier to regulate your Golden Retriever's weight and keep it at a healthy level than to try and slim down a voraciously hungry Golden Retriever when he becomes overweight. Golden Retrievers are often food obsessed and prone to putting on weight and, sadly, overweight and obese dogs are susceptible to a range of illnesses. According to James Howie, Veterinary Advisor to Lintbells, some of the main ones are:

Joint disease – excessive body weight may increase joint stress, which is a risk factor in joint degeneration (arthrosis), as is cruciate disease (knee ligament rupture). Joint disease tends to lead to a reduction in exercise that then increases the likelihood of weight gain which reduces exercise further. A vicious cycle is created. Overfeeding growing Golden Retrievers can lead to various problems, including the worsening of hip dysplasia. Weight management may be the only measure required to control clinical signs in some cases.

Heart and lung problems – fatty deposits within the chest cavity and excessive circulating fat play important roles in the development of cardio-respiratory and cardiovascular disease.

Diabetes – resistance to insulin has been shown to occur in overweight dogs, leading to a greater risk of diabetes mellitus.

Tumours – obesity increases the risk of mammary tumours in female dogs.

Liver disease – fat degeneration may result in liver insufficiency.

Reduced Lifespan - one of the most serious proven findings in obesity studies is that obesity in both humans and dogs reduces lifespan.

Exercise intolerance – this is also a common finding with overweight dogs, which can compound an obesity problem as fewer calories are burned off and are therefore stored, leading to further weight gain. Obesity also puts greater strain on the delicate respiratory system of Golden Retrievers, making breathing even more difficult for them.

Most Golden Retrievers are extremely loyal companions and very attached to their humans. However, beware of going too far in regarding your dog as a member of the family. It has been shown that dogs regarded as 'family members' (i.e. anthropomorphosis) by the owner are at greater risk of becoming overweight. This is because attention given to the dog often results in food being given as well.

The important thing to remember is that many of the problems associated with being overweight are reversible. Increasing exercise increases the calories burned, which in turn reduces weight. If you do put your dog on a diet, the reduced amount of food will also mean reduced nutrients, so he may need a supplement during this time.

Feeding Puppies

Feeding your Golden Retriever puppy the right diet is important to help his young body and bones grow strong and healthy. Puppyhood is a time of rapid growth and development, and puppies require different levels of nutrients to adult dogs. Initially, pups get all their nutrients from their mother's milk and then they are gradually weaned from three or four weeks of age.

Golden Retriever puppies should stay with their mothers and littermates until **at least** eight weeks old. During this time, the mother is still teaching her offspring some important rules about life. For the first few weeks after that, continue feeding the same puppy food and at the same times as the breeder. Dogs do not adapt to changes in their diet or feeding habits as easily as humans. If you live far away from the breeder, you might also want to consider taking a large container to fill with water at the breeder's house and mixing this water with your own tap water back home. Different types of water, e.g. moving from a soft water area to a hard water area or vice versa, can also upset a sensitive pup's stomach.

At home you can then slowly change his food based on information from the breeder and your vet —although some owners prefer to stick with the same food, as recommended by the breeder. This should be done very gradually by mixing in a little more of the new food each day over a period of seven to 10 days. If at any time your puppy starts being sick, has loose stools or is constipated, slow the rate at which you are switching him over. If he continues vomiting, seek veterinary advice as he may have a problem with the food you have chosen. Puppies who are vomiting or who have diarrhoea quickly dehydrate.

Because of their special nutritional needs, you should only give your puppy a food that is approved either just for puppies or for all life stages. If a feed is recommended for adult dogs only, it won't have enough protein, and the balance of calcium and other nutrients will not be right for a pup. Puppy food is very high in calories and nutritional supplements, so you want to switch to a junior or adult food once he leaves puppyhood, which is at about six months old. Feeding puppy food too long can result in obesity and orthopaedic problems. Getting the amount and type of food right for your pup is important. Feeding too much will cause him to put on excess pounds, and overweight puppies are more likely to grow into overweight adults. As a very broad guideline, Golden Retrievers normally mature (physically) into fully developed adults at around two years old, although some behave like giant puppies for much longer!

DON'T:

- Feed table scraps from the table. Your Golden will get used to begging for food, it will also affect a puppy's carefully balanced diet
- Feed food or uncooked meat that has gone off. Puppies have sensitive stomachs

DO:

- Regularly check the weight of your growing puppy to make sure he is within normal limits for his age. There are charts available on numerous websites, just type "puppy weight chart" into Google – you'll need to know the exact age and current weight of your puppy
- Take your puppy to the vet if he has diarrhoea or is vomiting for two days or more
- Remove his food after it has been down for 15 to 20 minutes. Food available 24/7 encourages fussy eaters

How Often?

Golden Retriever puppies have small stomachs but big appetites, so feed them small amounts on a frequent basis. Establishing a regular feeding routine with your puppy is good, as this will also help to toilet train him. Get him used to regular mealtimes and then let him outside to do his business straight away when he has finished. Puppies have fast metabolisms, so the results may be pretty quick! Don't leave food out for the puppy so that he can eat it whenever he wants, as you need to be there for the feeds because you want him and his body on a set schedule. Smaller meals are easier for him to digest and energy levels don't peak and fall so much with frequent feeds. There is some variation between recommendations, but as a general rule of thumb:

- Up to the age of three or four months, feed your puppy three or four times a day
- Then three times a day until he is four to six months old
- Twice a day until he is one year old
- Then once or twice a day for the rest of his life

 Goldens are very loving companions. If your dog is not responding well to a particular family member, a useful tactic is to get that person to feed the dog every day. The way to a Golden Retriever's heart is often through his or her stomach!

Feeding Seniors

Once your adolescent dog has switched to an adult diet he will be on this for several years. However, as a dog moves towards old age, his body has different requirements to those of a young dog. This is the time to consider switching to a senior diet. Dogs, generally, are living longer than they did 30 years ago – although this is not necessarily the case with Goldens. There are many factors that contribute to a longer life, including better immunisation and veterinary care, but one of the most important factors is better nutrition.

Generally a dog is considered to be 'older' or senior if he is in the last third of his normal life expectancy. Some owners of large breeds, such as Great Danes (with an average lifespan of nine years) switch their dogs from an adult to a senior diet when they are only six or seven years old. A Golden Retriever's lifespan is in the low double figures and when and if you switch depends on your individual dog, his or her energy levels and general health. Look for signs of your dog slowing down or having joint problems. If you wish to discuss it with your vet, you can describe any changes at your dog's annual vaccination appointment, rather than having the expense of a separate consultation.

As a dog ages his metabolism slows, his joints stiffen, his energy levels decrease and he needs less exercise, just as with humans. You may notice in middle or old age that your dog starts to put weight on. An adult diet may be too rich and have too many calories, so it may be the time to move to a senior diet. Having said that, some dogs stay on a normal adult diet all of their lives – although the amount is usually decreased and supplements added, e.g. for joints.

Even though he is older, keep his weight in check, as obesity in old age only puts more strain on his body - especially joints and organs - and makes any health problems even worse. Because of lower activity levels, many older dogs will gain weight and getting an older dog to slim down can be very difficult. It is much better not to let your Golden get too chunky than to put him on a diet. But if he is overweight, put in the effort to shed the extra pounds. This is one of the single most important things you can do to increase your Golden Retriever's quality AND length of life.

Other changes in canines are again similar to those in older humans and as well as stiff joints or arthritis, they may move more slowly and sleep more. Hearing and vision may not be so sharp and organs don't all work as efficiently as they used to; teeth may have become worn down. When this starts to happen, it is time to consider feeding your old friend a senior diet, which will take these changes into account. Specially formulated senior diets are lower in protein and calories but help to create a feeling of fullness.

Older dogs are more prone to develop constipation, so senior diets are often higher in fibre - at around 3% to 5%. Wheat bran can also be added to regular dog food to increase the amount of fibre - but do not try this if your Golden has a low tolerance or intolerance to grain. If your dog has poor kidney function, then a low phosphorus diet will help to lower the workload for the kidneys.

Ageing dogs have special dietary needs, some of which can be provided in the form of supplements, such as glucosamine and chondroitin, which help joints. Two popular joint supplements in the UK are GWF Joint Aid for dogs, used by several breeders, and Lintbell's Yumove. If your dog is not eating a complete balanced diet, then a vitamin/mineral supplement is recommended to prevent any deficiencies. Some owners also feed extra antioxidants to an older dog – ask your vet's advice on your next visit. Antioxidants are also found naturally in fruit and vegetables.

While some older dogs suffer from obesity, others have the opposite problem – they lose weight and are disinterested in food. If your old dog is getting thinner and not eating well, firstly get him checked out by the vet to rule out any possible diseases. If he gets the all-clear, your next challenge is to tempt him to eat. He may be having trouble with his teeth, so if he's on a dry food, try smaller kibble or moistening it with water or gravy.

Our dog loved his twice daily feeds until he recently got to the age of 10 when he suddenly lost interest in his food, which is a hypoallergenic kibble. We tried switching flavours within the same brand, but that didn't work. After a short while we mixed his daily feeds with a little gravy and a spoonful of tinned dog food – Bingo! He started wolfing it down again and was as lively as ever. At 12 he started getting some diarrhoea, so we switched again and now he is mainly on a chicken and rice diet with some senior kibble, which is working well.

Some dogs can tolerate a small amount of milk or eggs added to their food, and home-made diets of boiled rice, potatoes, vegetables and chicken or meat with the right vitamin and mineral supplements can also work well. See **Chapter 16. Caring for Golden Oldies** for more information on looking after an ageing Golden Retriever.

Reading Dog Food Labels

A NASA scientist would have a hard job understanding some manufacturers' labels, so it's no easy task for us lowly dog owners. Here are some things to look out for on the manufacturers' labels:

- 🐾 The ingredients are listed by weight and the top one should always be the main content, such as chicken or lamb. Don't pick one where grain is the first ingredient; it is a poor quality feed. Some dogs can develop grain intolerances or allergies, and often it is specifically wheat they have a reaction to

- 🐾 High on the list should be meat or poultry by-products, these are clean parts of slaughtered animals, not including meat. They include organs, blood and bone, but not hair, horns, teeth or hooves

- 🐾 Chicken meal (dehydrated chicken) has more protein than fresh chicken, which is 80% water. The same goes for beef, fish and lamb. So, if any of these meals are number one on the ingredient list, the food should contain enough protein

> **Ingredients:** Chicken, Chicken By-Product Meal, Corn Meal, Ground Whole Grain Sorghum, Brewers Rice, Ground Whole Grain Barley, Dried Beet Pulp, Chicken Fat (preserved with mixed Tocopherols, a source of Vitamin E), Chicken Flavor, Dried Egg Product, Fish Oil (preserved with mixed Tocopherols, a source of Vitamin E), Potassium Chloride, Salt, Flax Meal, Sodium Hexametaphosphate, Fructooligosaccharides, Choline Chloride, Minerals (Ferrous Sulfate, Zinc Oxide, Manganese Sulfate, Copper Sulfate, Manganous Oxide, Potassium Iodide, Cobalt Carbonate), DL-Methionine, Vitamins (Ascorbic Acid, Vitamin A Acetate, Calcium Pantothenate, Biotin, Thiamine Mononitrate (source of vitamin B1), Vitamin B12 Supplement, Niacin, Riboflavin Supplement (source of vitamin B2), Inositol, Pyridoxine Hydrochloride (source of vitamin B6), Vitamin D3 Supplement, Folic Acid), Calcium Carbonate, Vitamin E Supplement, Brewers Dried Yeast, Beta-Carotene, Rosemary Extract.

* A certain amount of flavourings can make a food more appetising for your dog. Choose a food with a specific flavouring, like *beef flavouring* rather than a general *meat flavouring*, where the origins are not so clear

* Guaranteed Analysis – This guarantees that your dog's food contains the labelled percentages of crude protein, fat, fibre and moisture. Keep in mind that wet and dry dog foods use different standards. (It does not list the digestibility of protein and fat and this can vary widely depending on their sources). While the Guaranteed Analysis is a start in understanding the food quality, be wary about relying on it too much. One pet food manufacturer made a mock product with a guaranteed analysis of 10% protein, 6.5% fat, 2.4% fibre, and 68% moisture (similar to what's on many canned pet food labels) – the ingredients were old leather boots, used motor oil, crushed coal and water!

Crude Protein (min)	32.25%
Lysine (min)	0.43%
Methionine (min)	0.49%
Crude Fat (min)	10.67%
Crude Fiber (max)	7.3%
Calcium (min)	0.50%
Calcium (max)	1.00%
Phosphorus (min)	0.44%
Salt (min)	0.01%
Salt (max)	0.51%

* Find a food that fits your dog's age, breed and size. Talk to your breeder, vet or visit an online Golden Retriever forum and ask other owners what they are feeding their dogs

* If your Golden has a food allergy or intolerance to wheat, check whether the food is gluten free; all wheat contains gluten

* Natural is best. Food labelled *'natural'* means that the ingredients have not been chemically altered, according to the FDA in the USA. However, there are no such guidelines governing foods labelled *'holistic'* – so check the ingredients and how it has been prepared

* In the USA, dog food that meets minimum nutrition requirements has a label that confirms this. It states: **"[food name] is formulated to meet the nutritional levels established by the AAFCO Dog Food Nutrient Profiles for [life stage(s)]"**

Even better, look for a food that meets the minimum nutritional requirements *'as fed'* to real pets in an AAFCO-defined feeding trial, then you know the food really delivers the nutrients that it is *'formulated'* to AAFCO feeding trials on real dogs are the gold standard. Brands that do costly feeding trials (including Nestlé and Hill's) indicate so on the package.

NOTE: Dog food labelled *'supplemental'* isn't complete and balanced. Unless you have a specific, vet-approved need for it, it's not something you want to feed your dog for an extended period of time. Check with your vet if in doubt.

If it all still looks a bit baffling, you might find the following websites, mentioned earlier, very useful. The first is www.dogfoodadvisor.com run by Mike Sagman. He has a medical background and analyses and rates hundreds of brands of dog food based on the listed ingredients and meat content. You might be surprised at some of his findings. The second is www.allaboutdogfood.co.uk run by UK canine nutritionist David Jackson.

To recap: no one food is right for every dog; you must decide on the best for yours. If you have a puppy, initially stick to the same food that the breeder has been feeding the litter, and only change diet later and gradually. Once you have decided on a food, monitor your puppy or adult. The best test of a food is how well your dog is doing on it.

If your Golden Retriever is happy and healthy, interested in life, has enough energy, is not too fat and not too thin, doesn't scratch a lot and has healthy-looking stools, then...

Congratulations, you've got it right!

8. Canine Behaviour

Just as with humans, a dog's personality is made up of a combination of temperament and character.

Temperament is the nature – or inherited characteristics - a dog is born with; a predisposition to act or react in a certain way. This is why getting your puppy from a good breeder is so important. Not only will he or she produce puppies from physically healthy dams and sires, but they will also look at the temperament of the dogs and only breed from those with good traits. You should also think carefully about what type of Golden Retriever you want: from working or show stock or a mixture of both.

Character is what develops through the dog's life and is formed by a combination of temperament and environment. How you treat your dog will have a huge effect on his or her personality and behaviour. Starting off on the right foot with good routines for your puppy is very important; so treat your dog well, spend time with him and make time for plenty of socialisation and exercise.

All dogs need different environments, scents and experiences to keep them stimulated and well-balanced. Golden Retrievers enjoy swimming and time spent off the lead (leash) running free.

Praise good behaviour, use positive methods and keep training short and fun. At the same time, all dogs should understand the "No" (or similar) command. Just as with children, a dog has to learn boundaries to adapt successfully and be content with his or her environment. Be consistent so your dog learns the guidelines quickly. All of these measures will help your dog grow into a happy, well-adjusted and well-behaved adult dog who is a delight to be with.

If you adopt a Golden Retriever from a rescue centre, you may need a little extra patience. These eager-to-please people-loving dogs may also arrive with some baggage. They have been abandoned by their previous owners for a variety of reasons - or perhaps forced to produce puppies in a puppy mill - and may very well still carry the scars of that trauma. They may feel nervous and insecure, they may be needy or aloof, and they may not know how to properly interact with a loving owner. Your time and patience is needed to teach these poor animals to trust again and to become happy in their new forever homes.

Understanding Canine Emotions

As pet lovers, we are all too keen to ascribe human characteristics to our dogs; this is called *anthropomorphism* – "the attribution of human characteristics to anything other than a human being." Most of us dog lovers are guilty of that, as we come to regard our pets as members of the family - and Goldies certainly regard themselves as members of the family. An example of anthropomorphism might be that the owner of a male dog might not want to have him neutered because he will "miss sex," as a human might if he or she were no longer able to have sex. This is simply not true. A male dog's impulse to mate is entirely governed by his hormones, not emotions. If he gets the scent of a bitch on heat, his hormones (which are just chemicals) tell him he has to mate with her. He does not stop to consider how attractive she is or whether she is 'the one' to produce his puppies. No, his reaction is entirely physical, he just wants to dive in there and get on with it!

It's the same with females. When they are on heat, a chemical impulse is triggered in their brain making them want to mate – with any male, they aren't at all fussy. So don't expect your little princess to be all coy when she is on heat, she is not waiting for Prince Charming to come along - the tramp down the road or any other scruffy pooch will do! It is entirely physical, not emotional.

Food is another issue – especially for many Goldens. A dog will not stop to count the calories of that lovely treat (you have to do that). No, he or she is driven by food and just thinks about getting the treat. Most non-fussy eaters will eat far too much, given the opportunity.

Golden Retrievers are very loving, incredibly loyal and extremely eager to please you, and if yours doesn't make you laugh from time to time, you must have had a humour by-pass. All of this adds up to one thing: an extremely endearing and loving family member that it's all too easy to reward - or spoil. It's fine to treat him like a member of the family - as long as you keep in mind that he is a dog and not a human. Understand his mind, patiently train him to learn his place in the household and that there are household rules he needs to learn – like not jumping on the couch when he's covered in mud - and you will be rewarded with a companion who is second to none and fits in beautifully with your family and lifestyle.

Dr Stanley Coren is a psychologist well known for his work on canine psychology and behaviour. He and other researchers believe that in many ways a dog's emotional development is equivalent to that of a young child. Dr Coren says: "Researchers have now come to believe that the mind of a dog is roughly equivalent to that of a human who is two to two-and-a-half years old. This conclusion holds for most mental abilities as well as emotions.

"Thus, we can look to human research to see what we might expect of our dogs. Just like a two-year-old child, our dogs clearly have emotions, but many fewer kinds of emotions than found in adult humans. At birth, a human infant only has an emotion that we might call excitement. This indicates how excited he is, ranging from very calm up to a state of frenzy. Within the first weeks of life the excitement state comes to take on a varying positive or a negative flavour, so we can now detect the general emotions of contentment and distress.

"In the next couple of months, disgust, fear, and anger become detectable in the infant. Joy often does not appear until the infant is nearly six months of age and it is followed by the emergence of shyness or suspicion. True affection, the sort that it makes sense to use the label "love" for, does not fully emerge until nine or ten months of age."

So, our Golden Retrievers can truly love us – but we knew that already!

According to Dr Coren, dogs can't feel shame, so if you are housetraining your puppy, don't expect him to be ashamed if he makes a mess in the house, he can't; he simply isn't capable of feeling shame. But he will not like it when you ignore him when he's behaving badly, and he will love it when you praise him for eliminating outdoors. He is simply responding to your reaction with his simplified range of emotions.

However, this story from one UK dog breeder gives us food for thought. She told us told us that when her Labrador has done something naughty, she is sent to the bathroom for a couple of minutes. She said: "Our breeding chocolate 'punishes' herself. If there is something she thinks she has done that will get her told off, she goes and sits in the bathroom – and you then have to hunt round the house to see if you can find what she thinks she has done!"

Dr Coren also believes that dogs cannot experience guilt, contempt or pride. I'm no psychology expert, but I'm not sure I agree. Take a Golden Retriever to a local dog show or obedience class, watch him perform and then maybe win a rosette and applause - is the dog's delight something akin to pride? Goldens can certainly experience joy. They love your attention and praise at home; is there a more joyful sight than your Golden running towards you, tail whirling round like a windmill, top lip pulled back to reveal a huge grin?

And if you want to see a happy dog, just watch a working Retriever out in the field. When they run through the dense undergrowth or dive into a stream and return with a present for you in the form of a deceased bird or small mammal - isn't there a hint of pride there?

Golden Retrievers can certainly show empathy - "the ability to understand and share the feelings of another" - and this is one reason why they make such excellent therapy and service dogs. Like many intelligent breeds, they can pick up on the mood and emotions of the owner.

One emotion that all dogs can experience is jealousy. It may display itself by possessive or aggressive behaviour over food or a toy, for example. An interesting article was published in the

PLOS (Public Library of Science) Journal in 2014 following an experiment into whether dogs get jealous. Building on research that shows that six-month old infants display jealousy, the scientists studied 36 dogs in their homes and video recorded their actions when their owners displayed affection to a realistic-looking stuffed canine (pictured).

Over three-quarters of the dogs were likely to push or touch the owner when they interacted with the decoy. The envious mutts were more than three times as likely to do this for interactions with the stuffed dog compared to when their owners gave their attention to other objects, including a book. Around a third tried to get between the owner and the plush toy, while a quarter of the put-upon pooches snapped at the dummy dog!

"Our study suggests not only that dogs do engage in what appear to be jealous behaviours, but also that they were seeking to break up the connection between the owner and a seeming rival," said Professor Christine Harris from University of California in San Diego.

The researchers believe that the dogs understood that the stuffed dog was real. The authors cite the fact that 86% of the dogs sniffed the toy's rear end during and after the experiment!

"We can't really speak of the dogs' subjective experiences, of course, but it looks as though they were motivated to protect an important social relationship. Many people have assumed that jealousy is a social construction of human beings - or that it's an emotion specifically tied to sexual and romantic relationships," said Professor Harris. "Our results challenge these ideas, showing that animals besides ourselves display strong distress whenever a rival usurps a loved one's affection."

Typical Golden Retriever Traits

Every dog is different, of course. But within the breeds, there are some similarities. Here are some typical Golden Retriever characteristics - some of them also apply to other breeds of dog, but put them all together and you have the blueprint for the Golden Retriever.

1. Compared with other breeds, Golden Retrievers may be too big and hairy for some dog lovers, but when it comes to natural temperament, they are second to none. Goldens are gentle, highly intelligent, affectionate, eager to please, biddable (trainable), adaptable, tolerant and devoted. They get along famously with humans, small and large, as well as other pets. Above all, they are loyal companions.

2. The Golden Retriever has a unique bond with humans and is able to fulfil many roles. Goldens make excellent working retrievers and excel in obedience and other competitions. They work as service (Assistance) and PAT (Pets As Therapy) dogs, helping a wide range of people, including people with vision, hearing or other physical disabilities, adults with epilepsy or diabetes, and autistic children; they visit hospitals, nursing homes and hospices to bring a little sunshine into people's lives.

3. The Golden Retriever was originally bred as a working gundog to retrieve game; many are still used for this purpose. Dogs bred from working lines often have a greater need for mental stimulation and higher exercise demands than other types of dog, such as those bred purely for companionship. Even if your Golden is a pet, he or she still has those natural instincts to some extent.

4. They have very soft mouths for retrieving - and can carry things very gently in their mouths.

5. Goldens have an instinctive love of water; it's in their genes. They have a hardy, double coat and cope well with cold water and snow.

6. They are tolerant and non-aggressive - provided they have been properly socialised. Goldens are known for getting along well with children - although young children and dogs should always be supervised – as well as other dogs and other pets.

7. Young Golden Retrievers can be extremely boisterous, jumping up and knocking things over, and some owners wonder what they have let themselves in for. They usually settle down by around two years of age.

8. They are one of the most popular of all dog breeds and make the most wonderful, loyal companions and family dogs - as long as they get enough physical and mental stimulation.

9. Golden Retrievers are highly intelligent dogs that enjoy being involved. They love to play both indoor and outdoor games and enjoy activities that challenge them, such as obedience events, field trials or retrieving on a shoot.

10. They do not make good guard dogs; they are too friendly. Many Goldens do not bark a lot.

11. Golden Retrievers love food and can be greedy; some can get possessive with their food. You have to monitor their diet and weight.

12. Goldens are very eager to please their owners; they are intelligent and love treats. All of this adds up to them being one of the easiest of all the breeds to train – provided you put the time in. They respond well to praise and treats, but are generally sensitive dogs and do not like rough handling or heavy-handed training.

13. The same goes for housetraining; a Golden Retriever can get the hang of it in a couple of weeks, provided you are extremely vigilant in the beginning.

14. Exercise varies from one Golden to another. Much depends on what bloodlines they come from and what they get used to as a puppy. They are, however, large dogs and the UK Kennel Club recommends "more than two hours per day." The AKC states: "Your Golden should never be allowed to run free." We strongly disagree with this; Goldens love to run free and swim and should be allowed to do so, once they have learned the recall.

15. Some Goldens are slow to mature, physically and mentally. A dog is usually regarded as a young adult by the age of about two years old – however, some Goldens remain young at heart throughout their lives. They are known for being enthusiastic, playful and having a sense of fun – and if yours doesn't make you laugh or even smile, you must have had a humour by-pass!

16. Goldens are happy to chill out and snuggle up with their owners after a good exercise session.

17. An under-exercised, under-stimulated Golden Retriever will display poor behaviour, as any dog would.

18. Golden Retrievers become very attached to their owners. They will steal your heart - OK, that's not very scientific, but ask anyone who owns one!

Cause and Effect

As you've read, treated well, socialised and trained, well-bred Golden Retrievers make devoted canine companions and excellent working and competitive dogs. They are affectionate and sociable, they love being around people or other dogs. Once you've had one, no other dog seems quite the same. But sometimes Golden Retrievers, just like other breeds, can develop behaviour problems. There are numerous reasons for this; every dog is an individual with his or her own temperament and environment, both of which influence the way he or she interacts with the world. Poor behaviour may result from a number of factors, including:

🐾 Poor breeding

🐾 Boredom, due to lack of exercise or mental challenges

🐾 Being left alone too long

🐾 Lack of socialisation

- Lack of training
- Being badly treated
- A change in living conditions
- Anxiety or insecurity
- Fear
- Being spoiled

Bad behaviour may show itself in a number of different ways, such as:

- Chewing or destructive behaviour
- Jumping up
- Constantly demanding attention
- Biting or nipping
- Growling
- Excessive barking
- Soiling or urinating inside the house
- Aggression towards other dogs

This chapter looks at some familiar behaviour problems. Although every dog is different, some common causes of unwanted behaviour are covered, along with tips to help improve the situation. The best way to avoid poor behaviour is to put in the time early on to socialise and train your dog, and nip any potential problems in the bud. If you are rehoming a dog, you'll need extra time and patience to help your new arrival unlearn some bad habits. NOTE: Further information on dealing with chewing and puppy biting are in **Chapter 10. Training.**

10 Ways to Avoid Bad Behaviour

Different dogs have different reasons for exhibiting bad behaviour. There is no simple cure for everything. Your best chance of ensuring your dog does not become badly behaved is to start out on the right foot and follow these simple guidelines:

1. **Buy from a good breeder**. They use their expertise to match suitable breeding pairs, taking into account factors such as good temperament, health and being "fit for function."
2. **Start socialisation right away**. We now realise the vital role that early socialisation plays in developing a well-rounded adult dog. It is essential to expose your dog to other people, places, animals and experiences as soon as possible. Give him a few days to settle in and then start – even if this means carrying him places until his vaccination schedule is complete. Lack of socialisation is one of the major causes of unwanted behaviour. Exposing your puppy to as many different things as possible goes a long way in helping a dog become a more stable, happy and trustworthy companion.

IMPORTANT: Socialisation does not end at puppyhood. Goldens are social creatures that thrive on sniffing, seeing, hearing and even licking. While the foundation for good behaviour is laid down during the first few months, good owners will reinforce social skills and training throughout a dog's life. Golden Retrievers love to be at the centre of the action and it is important that they learn when young that they are not also the centre of the universe. Socialisation helps them to learn their place in that universe and to become comfortable with it.

3. **Start training early** - you can't start too soon. Like babies, puppies have incredibly enquiring minds that can quickly absorb a lot of new information. You can start teaching your puppy to learn his own name as well as some simple commands a couple of days after you bring him home.

4. **Basic training should cover several areas**: housetraining, chew prevention, puppy biting, simple commands like 'sit', 'come', 'stay' and familiarising him with a collar or harness and lead. Adopt a gentle approach and keep training sessions short. Golden Retrievers are sensitive to you and your mood and do not respond well to harsh words or treatment. Start with five or 10 minutes a day and build up. Often the way a dog responds to his or her environment is a result of owner training and management – or lack of it. Puppy classes or adult dog obedience classes are a great way to start, but make sure you do your homework afterwards. Spend a few minutes each day reinforcing what you have both learned in class - owners need training as well as dogs!

5. **Reward your dog for good behaviour.** All behaviour training should be based on positive reinforcement; so praise and reward your dog when he does something good. Generally, Golden Retrievers live to please their owners, and this trait speeds up the training process. The main aim of training is to build a good understanding between you and your dog.

6. **Ignore bad behaviour**, no matter how hard this may be. If, for example, your dog is chewing his way through your shoes, the couch or toilet rolls or eating things he shouldn't, remove him from the situation and then ignore him. For some dogs even negative attention is some

attention. Or if he is constantly demanding your attention, ignore him. Remove yourself from the room so he learns that you give attention when you want to give it, **not** when he demands it. The more time you spend praising and rewarding good behaviour, while ignoring bad behaviour, the more likely he is to respond to you. If your pup is a chewer – and most are - make sure he has plenty of durable toys to keep him occupied. Goldens can chew their way through flimsy toys in no time.

7. **Take the time to learn what sort of temperament your dog has.** Is she by nature a nervous or confident girl? What was she like as a puppy, did she rush forward or hang back? Does she fight to get upright when on her back or is she happy to lie there? Is she a couch potato or a ball of fire? Your puppy's temperament will affect her behaviour and how she responds to the world around her. A timid Golden Retriever will certainly not respond well to a loud approach on your part, whereas an energetic, strong-willed one will require more patience and exercise.

8. **Exercise and stimulation.** A lack of either is another major reason for dogs behaving badly. Regular daily exercise, indoor or outdoor games and toys are all ways of stopping your dog from becoming bored or frustrated.

9. **Learn to leave your dog.** Just as leaving your dog alone for too long can lead to problems, so can being with him 100% of the time. The dog becomes over-reliant on you and then gets stressed when you leave; this is called *separation anxiety*. When your dog first arrives at your house, start by leaving him for a few minutes every day and gradually build it up so that after a few weeks you can leave him for up to four hours.

10. **Love your Golden Retriever – but don't spoil him,** however difficult that might be. You don't do your dog any favours by giving him too many treats, constantly responding to his demands for attention or allowing him to behave as he wants inside the house.

Separation Anxiety

It's not just dogs that experience separation anxiety - people do too. About 7% of adults and 4% of children suffer from this disorder. Typical symptoms for humans are:

- Distress at being separated from a loved one
- Fear of being left alone

Our canine companions aren't much different to us. When a dog leaves the litter, his owners become his new family or pack. It's estimated that as many as 10% to 15% of dogs suffer from separation anxiety. It is an exaggerated fear response caused by separation from their owner. Golden Retrievers are not particularly susceptible to separation anxiety as they tend to be more laid-back about separation than many other breeds, but some can suffer from it if they have not spent time away from their owners when young.

Separation anxiety is on the increase and recognised by behaviourists as the most common form of stress for dogs. Millions of dogs suffer from separation anxiety.

It can be equally distressing for the owner - I know because our dog, Max, suffers from this. He howls whenever we leave home without him. Fortunately his problem is only a mild one. If we return after only a short while, he's usually quiet. Although if we silently sneak back home and peek in through the letterbox, he's never asleep. Instead he's waiting by the door looking and listening for our return. It can be embarrassing.

Whenever I go to the Post Office, I tie him up outside and even though he can see me through the glass door, he still barks his head off - so loud that the people inside can't make themselves heard. Luckily the lady behind the counter is a dog lover and, despite the large **'GUIDE DOGS ONLY'** sign outside, she lets Max in. He promptly dashes through the door and sits down beside me, quiet as a mouse!

Tell-Tale Signs

Does your Golden Retriever do any of the following?

- Follow you from room to room – even the toilet - whenever you're home?
- Get anxious or stressed when you're getting ready to leave the house?
- Howl, whine or bark when you leave?
- Tear up paper or chew furniture or other objects?
- Dig, chew, or scratch at the carpet, doors or windows trying to join you?

- Soil or urinate inside the house, even though he is housetrained? (This **only** occurs when left alone)
- Exhibit restlessness - such as licking his coat excessively, pacing or circling?
- Greet you ecstatically every time you come home – even if you've only been out to empty the bins?
- Wait by the window or door until you return?
- Dislike spending time alone in the garden or yard?
- Refuses to eat or drink if you leave him?
- Howl or whine when one family member leaves - even though others are still in the room or car?

If so, he or she may suffer from separation anxiety. Fortunately, in many cases this can be cured.

Causes

Dogs are pack animals and being alone is not a natural state for them. Puppies should be patiently taught to get used to short periods of isolation slowly and in a structured way if they are to be comfortable with it. It is also important for them to have a den where they feel safe - this may be a crate or dog bed where the pup can sleep in peace and quiet. A puppy will emotionally latch on to his new owner, who has taken the place of his mother and siblings.

He will want to follow you everywhere initially and, although you want to shower him with love and attention, it's important to leave your new puppy alone for short periods in the beginning to avoid him becoming totally dependent on you. In our case, I was working from home when we got Max. With hindsight, we should have regularly left him alone for short periods more often in the critical first few weeks and months.

Adopted dogs may be particularly susceptible to separation anxiety. They may have been abandoned once already and fear it happening again.

There are several causes, one or more of which can trigger separation anxiety. These include:
- Not being left alone for short periods when young
- Poor socialisation with other dogs and people resulting in too much focus and dependence on you, his owner
- Boredom, Golden Retrievers are intelligent dogs and need physical and mental exercise
- Being left for too long by owners who are out of the house for much of the day
- Leaving a dog too long in a crate or confined space
- Being over-indulgent with your dog; giving him too much attention
- Making too much of a fuss when you leave and return to the house
- Mistreatment in the past, a dog from a rescue centre may have insecurities and feel anxious when left alone
- Wilful behaviour due to a lack of training

Symptoms are not commonly seen in middle-aged dogs, although dogs that develop symptoms when young may be at risk later on. Separation anxiety is, however, common in elderly dogs. Pets age and - like humans - their senses, such as hearing and sight, deteriorate. They become more dependent on their owners and may then become more anxious when they are separated from them - or even out of view.

It may be very flattering and cute that your dog wants to be with you all the time, but insecurity and separation anxiety are forms of panic, which is distressing for your Golden Retriever. If he shows any signs, help him to become more self-reliant and confident; he will be a happier dog.

So what can you do if your dog is showing signs of canine separation anxiety? Every dog is different, but here are some tried and tested techniques that have proved effective for some dogs.

12 Tips to Combat Separation Anxiety

1. After the first two or three days, practise leaving your new puppy or adult dog for short periods, starting with a minute or two and gradually lengthening the time you are out of sight.

2. Tire your Golden Retriever out before you leave him alone. Take him for a walk or play a game before leaving and, if you can, leave him with a view of the outside world, e.g. in a room with a patio door or low window.

3. Keep arrivals and departures low key and don't make a big fuss. For example, when I come home, Max is hysterically happy and runs round whimpering with a toy in his mouth. I make him sit and stay and then let him out into the garden without patting or acknowledging him. I pat him several minutes later.

4. Leave your dog a 'security blanket,' such as an old piece of clothing you have recently worn that still has your scent on it, or leave a radio on - not too loud - in the room with the dog. Avoid a heavy rock station! If it will be dark when you return, leave a lamp on a timer.

5. Associate your departure with something good. As you leave, give your dog a rubber toy, like a Kong, filled with a tasty treat, or a frozen treat. This may take his mind off your departure. (Some dogs may refuse to touch the treat until you return home).

6. If your dog is used to a crate, try crating him when you go out. Many dogs feel safe there, and being in a crate can also help to reduce destructiveness. Always take the collar off first. Pretend to leave the house, but listen for a few minutes. NEVER leave a dog in a crate with the door closed all day; two or three hours are long enough during the day.

Warning: if your dog starts to show major signs of distress, remove him from the crate immediately as he may injure himself.

7. Structure and routine can help to reduce anxiety in your dog. Carry out regular activities, such as feeding and exercising, at the same time every day.

8. Dogs read body language very well, many Goldens are intuitive. They may start to fret when they think you are going to leave them. One technique is to mimic your departure routine when you have no intention of leaving. So put your coat on, grab your car keys, go out of the door and return a few seconds later. Do this randomly and regularly and it may help to reduce your dog's stress levels when you do it for real.

9. Some dogs show anxiety in new places; get him better socialised and used to different environments, dogs and people.

10. However lovable your Golden Retriever is, if he is showing early signs of anxiety when separating from you, do not shower him with attention all the time when you are there. He will become too dependent on you.

11. If you have to leave the house for a few hours at a time, ask a neighbour or friend to call in - or drop the dog off with them.

12. Getting another dog to keep the first one company can help, but first ask yourself whether you have the time and money for two or more dogs. Can you afford double the vet's and food bills?

Sit-Stay-Down

Another technique for helping to reduce separation anxiety is to practise the common "sit-stay" or "down-stay" exercises using positive reinforcement. The goal is to be able to move briefly out of your dog's sight while he is in the "stay" position. Through this your dog learns that he can remain calmly and happily in one place while you go about your normal daily life.

You have to progress slowly with this. Get your dog to sit and stay and then walk away from him for five seconds, then 10, 20, a minute and so on. Reward your dog with a treat every time he stays calm.

Then move out of sight or out of the room for a few seconds, return and give him the treat if he is calm, gradually lengthen the time you are out of sight. If you're watching TV with your Golden Retriever snuggled up at your side and you get up for a snack, say "stay" and leave the room. When you come back, give him a treat or praise him quietly. It is a good idea to practise these techniques after exercise or when your dog is a little sleepy (but not exhausted), as he is likely to be more relaxed.

Canine separation anxiety is NOT the result of disobedience or lack of training. It's a psychological condition; your dog feels anxious and insecure.

NEVER punish your dog for showing signs of separation anxiety – even if he has chewed your best shoes. This will only make him worse.

NEVER leave your dog unattended in a crate for long periods or if he is frantic to get out, it can cause physical or mental harm. If you're thinking of leaving an animal all day in a crate while you are out of the house, get a rabbit or a hamster - not a dog.

Excessive Barking

Dogs, especially youngsters and adolescents, sometimes behave in ways you might not want them to, until they learn that this type of unwanted behaviour doesn't earn any rewards. Golden Retrievers are not usually excessive barkers – in fact, most of them don't bark very much - but any dog can bark a lot, until he learns not to.

Some puppies start off by being noisy from the outset, while others hardly bark at all until they reach adolescence or adulthood. Some may be triggered by other, noisier dogs in the household. On our website we get emails from dog owners worried that their young dogs are not barking enough. However, we get far more from owners whose dogs are barking too much! Some Goldens will bark if someone comes to the door – and then welcome them like best friends - while others remain quiet. However, they do not make good guard dogs, as they are friendly with everyone.

There can be a number of reasons a dog barks too much. He may be lonely, bored or demanding your attention. He may be possessive and over-protective and so barks (or howls) his head off when others are near you. He may have picked up the habit from other dogs. Excessive, habitual barking is a problem best corrected early on before it gets out of hand and drives you and your neighbours nuts.

The problem often develops during adolescence or early adulthood (before the age of two or three) as your dog becomes more confident. If your barking dog is an adolescent, he is probably still teething, so get him a good selection of hardy chews, and stuff a Kong toy with a treat or peanut butter to keep him occupied and gnawing. But give him these when he is quiet, not when he is barking.

Your behaviour can also encourage excessive barking. If your dog barks non-stop for several seconds or minutes and then you give him a treat to quieten him, he associates his barking with getting a nice treat. A better way to deal with it is to say in a firm voice: **"Quiet"** after he has made a few barks. When he stops, praise him and he will get the idea that what you want him to do is stop. The trick is to nip the bad behaviour in the bud before it becomes ingrained.

If he's barking to get your attention, ignore him. If that doesn't work, leave the room and don't allow him to follow you, so you deprive him of your attention. Do this as well if his barking and attention-seeking turns to nipping. Tell him to **"Stop"** in a firm voice - not shouting - remove your hand or leg and, if necessary, leave the room.

As humans, we can use our voice in many different ways: to express happiness or anger, to scold, to shout a warning, and so on. Dogs are the same; different barks and noises give out different messages. **Listen** to your dog and try and get an understanding of Golden Retriever language. Learn to recognise the difference between an alert bark, an excited bark, a demanding bark, a nervous, high pitched bark, an aggressive bark or a plain "I'm barking 'coz I can bark" bark!

If your dog is barking at other dogs, arm yourselves with lots of treats and spend time calming your dog down. When he or she starts to bark wildly at another dog - usually this happens when your dog is on a lead – distract your dog by letting them sniff a treat in your hand. Make your dog sit down and give a treat. Talk in a gentle manner and keep showing and giving your dog a treat for remaining calm and not barking. There are several videos on YouTube that show how to deal with this problem in the manner described here.

Speak and Shush!

Generally, Golden Retrievers are not good guard dogs, most of them couldn't care less if somebody breaks in and walks off with the family silver – they are more likely to approach the burglar for a treat or a pat. But if you do have a problem with excessive barking when somebody visits your home, the Speak and Shush technique is one way of getting a dog to quieten down.

If your Golden doesn't bark and you want him to, a slight variation of this method can also be used to get him to bark as a way of alerting you that someone is at the door.

When your dog barks at an arrival at your house, gently praise him after the first few barks. If he persists, gently tell him that that is enough. Like humans, some dogs can get carried away with the sound of their own voice, so try and discourage too much barking from the outset. The Speak and Shush technique teaches your dog or puppy to bark and be quiet on command. Get a friend to stand outside your front door and say "Speak" - or "Woof" or "Alert." This is the cue for your accomplice to knock or ring the bell – don't worry if you both feel like idiots, it will be worth the embarrassment!

When your dog barks, praise him profusely. You can even bark yourself in encouragement! After a few good barks, say "Shush" and then dangle a tasty treat in front of his nose. He will stop barking as soon as he sniffs the treat, because it is physically impossible for a dog to sniff and woof at the same time. Praise your dog again as he sniffs quietly and then give him the treat. Repeat this routine a few times a day and your Golden will quickly learn to bark whenever the doorbell rings and you ask him to speak. Eventually your dog will bark after your request but BEFORE the doorbell rings, meaning he has learned to bark on command. Even better, he will learn to anticipate the likelihood of getting a treat following your "Shush" request and will also be quiet on command.

With Speak and Shush training, progressively increase the length of required shush time before offering a treat - at first just a couple of seconds, then three, five, 10, 20, and so on. By alternating instructions to speak and shush, the dog is praised and rewarded for barking on request and also for stopping barking on request.

You need to have some treats at the ready, waiting for that rare bark. Wait until he barks - for whatever reason - then say "Speak" or whatever word you want to use, praise him and give him a treat. At this stage, he won't know why he is receiving the treat. Keep praising him every time he barks and give him a treat. After you've done this for several days, hold a treat in your hand in front

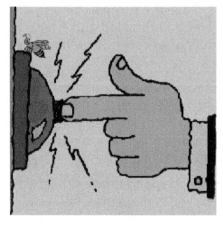

of his face and say "Speak." Your dog will probably still not know what to do, but will eventually get so frustrated at not getting the treat that he will bark. At which point, praise him and give him the treat. We trained our Golden Retriever to do this in a week or so and now he barks his head off when anybody comes to the door or whenever we give him the command: "Speak."

Always use your 'encouraging teacher voice' when training; speak softly when instructing your dog to Shush, and reinforce the Shush with whisper-praise. The more softly you speak, the more your dog will be likely to pay attention. Golden Retrievers respond very well to training when it is fun, short and reward-based.

Dealing with Aggression

Some breeds are more prone to aggression than others. Fortunately, this is a problem not often seen in Golden Retrievers. However, given certain situations, any dog can growl, bark or even bite. But ANY dog can be aggressive, given a certain set of circumstances.

Sometimes a dog learns unwanted behaviour from another dog or dogs, but often it is because the dog either feels insecure, or has become too territorial or protective of his food, owner or toys. By the way, puppy biting is not aggression; all puppies bite; they explore the world with their noses and mouths. But it is important to train your cute little pup not to bite, as he may cause injury if he continues as an adult.

Any dog can bite when under stress and, however unlikely it may seem, there are images on the internet of people who have been bitten by Golden Retrievers. There is an example of a Golden Retriever with food aggression (that gives Cesar Milan a nasty bite) at:
www.youtube.com/watch?v=RO1LoZTmLOY

Here are some different types of aggressive behaviour:

- ❉ Growling at you or other people
- ❉ Snarling or lunging at other dogs
- ❉ Growling or biting if you or another animal goes near his food
- ❉ Being possessive with toys
- ❉ Growling if you pet or show attention to another animal
- ❉ Marking territory by urinating inside the house
- ❉ Growling and chasing other small animals
- ❉ Growling and chasing cars, joggers or strangers
- ❉ Standing in your way, blocking your path
- ❉ Pulling and growling on the lead

Aggression is often due to the fact that the dog has not been properly socialised, and so feels threatened or challenged. Rather than being comfortable with new situations, other dogs or intrusions, he responds using "the best form of defence is attack" philosophy and displays aggressive behaviour to anything or anyone he perceives as a threat. As well as snarling, lunging, barking or biting, you should also look out for other physical signs, such as: raised hackles, top lip curled back to bare teeth, ears up and tail raised.

Golden Retrievers love your attention, but they can sometimes become possessive of you, their food or toys, which in itself can lead to bullying behaviour. Aggression may be caused by a lack of socialisation, an adolescent dog trying to see how far he can push the boundaries, nervousness, being spoiled by the owner, jealousy or even fear. This fear may come from a bad experience the dog has suffered or from lack of proper socialisation. Another form of fear-aggression is when a dog becomes over-protective/possessive of his owner, which can lead to barking and lunging at other dogs or humans.

An owner's treatment of a dog can be a further reason. If the owner has been too harsh with the dog, such as shouting, using physical violence or reprimanding the dog too often, this in turn causes poor behaviour. Aggression breeds aggression. Dogs can also become aggressive if they are consistently left alone, cooped up, under-fed or under-exercised. A bad experience with another dog or dogs can also be a cause.

Many dogs are more combative on the lead. This is because once on a lead, they cannot run away. Fight or flight. They know they can't escape, so they make themselves as frightening as possible and bark or growl to warn off the other dog or person. Train your dog from an early age to be comfortable walking on the lead. And socialisation is, of course vital – the first four to five months of a puppy's life is the critical time.

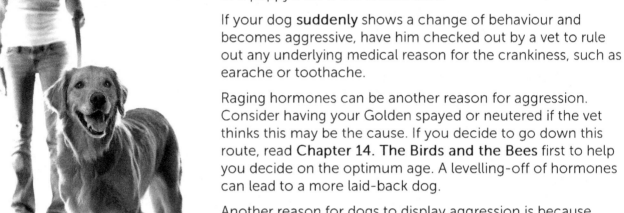

If your dog **suddenly** shows a change of behaviour and becomes aggressive, have him checked out by a vet to rule out any underlying medical reason for the crankiness, such as earache or toothache.

Raging hormones can be another reason for aggression. Consider having your Golden spayed or neutered if the vet thinks this may be the cause. If you decide to go down this route, read **Chapter 14. The Birds and the Bees** first to help you decide on the optimum age. A levelling-off of hormones can lead to a more laid-back dog.

Another reason for dogs to display aggression is because they have been spoiled by their owners and have come to believe that the world revolves around them. Not spoiling your dog and teaching him what is acceptable behaviour in the first place is the best preventative measure. Early training, especially during puppyhood and adolescence - before he or she develops unwanted habits - can save a lot of trouble in the future.

Professional dog trainers employ a variety of techniques with a dog that has become aggressive. Firstly they will look at the causes and then they almost always use reward-based methods to try and cure aggressive or fearful dogs. *Counter conditioning* is a positive training technique used by many professional trainers to help change a dog's aggressive behaviour towards other dogs. A typical example would be a dog that snarls, barks and lunges at other dogs while on the lead. It is the presence of other dogs that is triggering the dog to act in a fearful or anxious manner.

Every time the dog sees another dog, he or she is given a tasty treat to counter the aggression. With enough steady repetition, the dog starts to associate the presence of other dogs with a tasty treat. Properly and patiently done, the final result is a dog that calmly looks to the owner for the treat whenever he or she sees another dog while on the lead. Whenever you encounter a potentially aggressive situation, divert your Golden Retriever's attention by turning his head away from the other dog and towards you, so that he cannot make eye contact with the other dog.

Aggression Towards People

Desensitisation is the most common method of treating aggression. It starts by breaking down the triggers for the behaviour one small step at a time. The aim is to get the dog to associate pleasant things with the trigger, i.e. people or a specific person whom he previously feared or regarded as a threat. This is done through using positive reinforcement, such as praise or treats. Successful desensitisation takes time, patience and knowledge. If your dog is starting to growl at people, there are a couple of techniques you can try to break him of this bad habit before it develops into full-blown biting.

One method is to arrange for some friends to come round, one at a time. When they arrive at your house, get them to scatter kibble on the floor in front of them so that your dog associates the arrival of people with tasty treats. As they move into the house, and your dog eats the kibble, praise your dog for being a good boy or girl. Manage your dog's environment. Don't over-face him.

Most Golden Retrievers love children, but if yours is at all anxious around them, separate them or carefully supervise their time together in the beginning. Children typically react enthusiastically to dogs and some dogs may regard this as frightening or an invasion of their space.

Some dogs, particularly spoiled ones, may show aggression towards people other than the owner. Several people have written to our website on this topic and it usually involves a partner or husband. Often the dog is jealous of the attention the owner is giving to the other person, or it could be that the dog feels threatened by him. This is, however, more common with Toy breeds.

If it should arise with your Golden Retriever, the key is for the partner to gradually gain the trust of the dog. He or she should show that they are not a threat by speaking gently to the dog and giving treats for good behaviour. Avoid eye contact, as the dog may see this as a challenge. If the subject of the aggression lives in the house, then try letting this person give the dog his daily feeds. The way to a Golden Retriever's heart is often through his stomach.

A crate is also a useful tool for removing an aggressive dog from the situation for short periods of time, allowing him out gradually and praising good behaviour. As with any form of aggression, the key is to take steps to deal with it immediately.

In extreme cases, when a dog exhibits persistent bad behaviour that the owner is unable to correct, a canine professional may be the answer. However, this is not an inexpensive option. Far better to spend time training and socialising your dog as soon as you get him or her.

Coprophagia (Eating Faeces)

It is hard for us to understand why a dog would want to eat his or any other animal's faeces (stools, poop or poo, call it what you will), but it does happen. There is plenty of anecdotal evidence that some dogs love the stuff. Nobody fully understands why dogs do this, it may simply be an unpleasant behaviour trait or there could be an underlying reason.

It is also thought that the inhumane and useless housetraining technique of "sticking the dog's nose in it" when he has eliminated inside the house can also encourage coprophagia.

If your dog eats faeces from the cat litter tray - a problem several owners have contacted us about - the first thing to do is to place the litter tray somewhere where your dog can't get to it – but the cat can. Perhaps on a shelf or put a guard around it, small enough for the cat to get through, but not your Golden Retriever.

Our dog sometimes eats cow or horse manure when out in the countryside. He usually stops when we tell him to and he hasn't suffered any after effects – so far. But again, this is a very unpleasant habit as the offending material sticks to the fur around his mouth and has to be cleaned off.

Sometimes he rolls in the stuff and then has to be washed down. You may find that your Golden Retriever will roll in fox poo to cover the fox's scent. Try and avoid areas you know are frequented by foxes if you can, as their faeces can transmit several diseases, including Canine Parvovirus or worms – neither of these should pose a serious health risk if your dog is up to date with vaccinations and worming treatments.

Vets have found that canine diets with low levels of fibre and high levels of starch increase the likelihood of coprophagia. If your dog is exhibiting this behaviour, first check that the diet you are feeding is nutritionally complete.

Look at the first ingredient on the dog food packet or tin – is it corn or meat? Does he look underweight? Check that you are feeding the right amount. If there is no underlying medical reason, you will have to try and modify your dog's behaviour. Remove cat litter trays, clean up after your dog and do not allow him to eat his own faeces. If it's not there, he can't eat it.

One breeder told us of a dog which developed the habit after being allowed to soil his crate as a pup, caused by the owners not being vigilant in their housetraining. The puppy got used to eating his own faeces and then continued to do it as an adult, when it became quite a problem.

Don't reprimand the dog for eating faeces. A better technique is to cause a distraction while he is in the act and then remove the offending material.

NOTE: Coprophagia is sometimes seen in pups aged between six months to a year and often disappears after this age.

Important: This chapter provides just a general overview of canine behaviour. If your Golden Retriever exhibits persistent behavioural problems, particularly if he or she is aggressive towards people or other dogs, you should consider seeking help from a reputable canine behaviourist, such as those listed the Association of Professional Dog Trainers at http://www.apdt.co.uk (UK) or https://apdt.com (USA)

9. Exercise

One thing all dogs have in common – including every Golden Retriever ever born - is that they need daily exercise, and the best way for most owners to give them this is through regular walks. Some owners of working Retrievers regularly take part in shoots or hunts during the season, and agility, obedience, nosework and other canine competitions are a great way of allowing Goldens to burn off steam and fulfil their natural instinct for a challenge. Start regular exercise patterns early so your dog gets used to a regular routine; dogs love routine. Daily exercise helps to keep your dog content, healthy and free from disease. It:

- Strengthens respiratory and circulatory systems
- Helps get oxygen to tissue cells
- Wards off obesity
- Keeps muscles toned and joints flexible
- Aids digestion
- Releases endorphins which trigger positive feelings
- Helps to keep dogs mentally stimulated and socialised

How Much Exercise?

Goldens are generally regarded as having high exercise requirements, but there is no one-rule-fits-all solution. The UK Kennel Club recommends "More than two hours per day." However, the amount of exercise that each individual dog needs varies tremendously. It depends on a number of issues, including temperament, natural energy levels, your living conditions, whether your dog is kept with other dogs and, importantly, what he gets used to.

Another factor is whether your dog is bred from show or working stock. There are, of course, big variations from one individual dog to another, but often working Retrievers are happiest with more exercise and mental challenges than Golden Retrievers bred from show stock. After all, it makes sense. A dog whose parent was bred to run all day and be on the lookout for game is likely to have higher mental and physical energy demands than one bred to have a calmer nature for the show ring.

Working dogs are not usually couch potatoes. That's not to say Golden Retrievers don't love snuggling up on the couch with you; they most certainly do - they just need their exercise as well.

It is true to say that whichever Golden you choose, ALL of them require a fair amount of daily exercise. This breed is not small and was not bred as a companion dog; its origins are as a working dog - and all working dogs need daily physical and mental stimulation.

When we talk about "exercising" a Golden Retriever, most people think this means taking the dog out for a walk two or three times a day - and it does for most pet owners. However, there are other forms of exercise. Owners of working dogs or those that take part in competitions may train and exercise their dogs in short, high energy sessions. Owning more than one dog - or having friends with dogs - is a great way for your dog to get lots of exercise. A couple of dogs running round together will get far more exercise than a dog on his own.

Goldens are natural retrievers, i.e. they love fetching things back to you. As well as throwing a toy or ball for him to fetch, you can make it more interesting by hiding the object and training your dog to retrieve it - your dog will love the challenge. Playing in the garden or yard with toys or balls is also a great way to burn off steam (for both of you). If you play Frisbee, don't overdo it - especially with young, growing dogs, as this can lead to joint damage.

A fenced garden or yard is definitely an advantage, but should not be seen as a replacement for daily exercise away from the home, where a dog can experience new places, scents, other people and dogs. Your dog will enjoy going for walks on the lead (leash), but will enjoy it far more when he is allowed to run free. A Golden Retriever is never happier than when running around chasing a ball, following a scent or going for a swim.

If your dog is happy just to trot along besides you, then you need to devise some games to raise his heartbeat, build muscle and get him fit. As well as throwing a ball, you could arrange walks with other dogs, or invent some games which involve running. If you decide to go jogging with your Golden Retriever, build up the distance gradually. This loyal breed WILL want to keep up with you, regardless of how fit he is, and you don't want him to have a heart attack.

At the very least, you should devote a **minimum** of an hour a day to exercising your Golden - longer is preferable – spread over at least two sessions a day. You can hike or shoot with a fit Golden all day long and still not tire him out. If you don't think you have the time or energy levels for one to two hours of exercise a day, then consider getting a smaller companion breed with lower exercise needs.

The American Kennel Club (AKC) recommends that you **don't** let your Golden run free. I'm not sure who wrote that, but I am sure they have never owned a Golden Retriever! All the breeders involved in this book also let their dogs run free. The Golden was bred as a working dog and loves to follow his instincts to run free and swim. You must, however, make sure it is safe to let your dog off the lead, away from traffic and other hazards - and don't let your dog off the lead until he has learned the recall. Also, there are reports in both the UK and North America about dog attacks in public parks and dog parks. If you are at all worried about this, avoid popular dog walking areas and find woodlands, fields, beaches or open countryside where your dog can exercise safely.

Establish a Routine

Establish an exercise regime early in your dog's life. If possible, get him used to walks at the same

time every day, at a time that fits in with your daily routine. For example, take your dog out after his morning feed, then again in the afternoon and a toilet trip last thing at night. Golden Retrievers are instinctive swimmers and this is a great way for dogs to exercise; many veterinary practices now use water tanks, not only for remedial therapy, but also for canine recreation. (Photo courtesy of Angie and Ray Gait, Sonodora Golden Retrievers, Hampshire).

They will dash in and out of the water all day long if you'll let them, but remember that swimming is a lot more strenuous for a dog than walking or even running. Don't constantly throw that stick or ball into the water - your Golden Retriever will fetch it back until he drops; the same is true if he is following you on your cycle. Overstretching him could place a strain on his heart. He should exercise within his limits. We advise gently drying under your Golden's ear flaps after swimming to reduce the risk of ear infections.

Whatever routine you decide on, stick to it. If you begin by taking your dog out three times a day and then suddenly stop, he may become restless, attention-seeking and possibly destructive because he has been used to more exercise. Conversely, don't expect a dog used to very little exercise to suddenly go on day-long hikes; he will struggle. Golden Retrievers make suitable hiking or jogging companions, but they need to work up to longer sessions - and such strenuous activity is not at all suitable for puppies.

To those owners who say their dog is happy and getting enough exercise playing in the yard or garden, just show him his lead and see how he reacts. Do you think he is excited at the prospect of leaving the home and going for a walk? Of course he is. Nothing can compensate for interesting new scents, meeting other dogs, playing games, frolicking in the snow or going swimming.

Owning a Golden Retriever requires a big commitment from owners – you are looking at a lot of daily exercise for 10 or more years. Don't think that as your dog gets older he won't need exercising. Older dogs need exercise to keep their body, joints and systems functioning properly. They need a less strenuous regime – they are usually happier with more frequent shorter walks, but still enough to keep them physically and mentally active. Again, every dog is different, some are willing and able to keep on running to the end of their lives. Regular exercise can add months or even years to a dog's life.

The exception is if your old or sick dog is struggling – he will show you that he doesn't feel well enough to walk far by stopping and looking at you or sitting down and refusing to move.

Most Golden Retrievers love snow, but it can sometimes present problems with clumps of snow and ice building up on paws, ears, legs and tummy. Salt or de-icing products on roads and pathways can also cause irritation – particularly if he or she tries to lick it off - as they can contain chemicals that are poisonous to dogs. If your dog gets iced up, you can bathe paws and anywhere else affected in lukewarm (NOT HOT) water. If your dog spends a lot of time in snow, you might even invest in a pair of canine snow boots. These are highly effective in preventing snow and ice balls forming on paws – provided you can get the boots to stay on!

Mental Stimulation

Golden Retrievers are very intelligent. This is good news when it comes to training as they generally learn quickly. But the downside is that this intelligence needs to be fed. Without mental challenges, a dog can become bored, unresponsive, destructive, attention-seeking and/or needy. You should factor in play time with your dog – even gentle play time for old dogs. If your dog's behaviour deteriorates or he suddenly starts chewing things he's not supposed to or barking a lot, the first question you should ask yourself is: "Is he getting enough exercise?" Boredom through lack of exercise or mental stimulation - such being alone and staring at four walls a lot - leads to bad behaviour and it's why some Goldens end up in rescue centres, through no fault of their own. On the other hand, a Golden Retriever at the heart of the family getting plenty of daily exercise and stimulation is a happy dog and a loyal companion second to none.

Exercising Puppies

There are strict guidelines to stick to with puppies, as it is important not to over-exercise young pups. Their bones and joints are developing and cannot tolerate a great deal of stress, so playing Fetch or Frisbee for hours on end with your young Golden Retriever is not a good option. You'll end up with an injured dog and a pile of vet's bills.

We are often asked how much to exercise a pup. Just like babies, puppies have different temperaments and some will be livelier and need more exercise than others. The golden rule is to start slowly and build it up. The worst danger is a combination of over exercise and overweight when the puppy is growing.

Do not take him out of the yard or garden until he has completed his vaccinations and it is safe to do so – unless you carry him around to start the socialisation process. Then start with short walks on the lead every day. Puppies have enquiring minds. Get yours used to being outside the home environment and experiencing new situations as soon as possible. The general guideline is:

Five minutes of on-lead exercise per month of age

until the puppy is fully grown. That means a total of 15 minutes when he is three months (13 weeks old), 30 minutes when six months (26 weeks) old, and so on. Slowly increase the time as he gets used to being exercised and this will gradually build up his muscles and stamina. This may not sound like much exercise, but too much exercise early on places stress on young joints.

It is, however, OK for your young pup have free run of your garden or yard (once you have plugged any gaps in the fence), provided it has a soft surface such as grass, not concrete. He will take things at his own pace and stop to sniff or rest. If you have other dogs, restrict the time the pup is allowed to play with them, as he won't know when he's had enough. Once he is older, your dog can go out for much longer walks. And when your little pup has grown into a beautiful adult Golden Retriever with a skeleton capable of carrying him through a long and healthy life, it will have been worth all the effort.

A long, healthy life is best started slowly

Exercise Tips

* Golden Retrievers are intelligent and love a challenge. They like to use their brains, particularly working Goldens. Make time to play indoor and outdoor games - such as Fetch or Hide-The-Toy - regularly with your dog; even elderly Goldens like to play

- Don't strenuously exercise your dog straight after or within an hour of a meal as this can cause bloat, particularly in larger dogs. Canine bloat causes gases to build up quickly in the stomach, blowing it up like a balloon, which cuts off normal blood circulation to and from the heart. The dog can go into shock and then cardiac arrest within hours. If you suspect this is happening, get the dog to a vet immediately

- If you want your dog to fetch a ball, don't fetch it back yourself or he will never learn to retrieve! Train him when he's young by giving him praise or a treat when he brings the ball or toy back to your feet

- Do not throw a ball or toy repeatedly for a dog if he shows signs of over-exertion. Your Golden will fetch to please you and because it's great fun. Stop the activity after a while - no matter how much he begs you to throw it again

- If you throw a stick, try not to let your dog chew it to bits, as splinters can get lodged in the mouth – or worse

- The same goes for swimming, which is an exhausting exercise for a dog. Ensure he exercises within his limits; repeatedly retrieving from water may cause him to overstretch and get into difficulties. Gentle swimming is a good low-impact activity for older dogs

- Exercise older dogs more gently - especially in cold weather when it is harder to get their bodies moving. Have a cool-down period at the end of the exercise to reduce stiffness and soreness; it helps to remove lactic acids from the dog's body. Our 13-year-old loves a body rub

- Vary your exercise route – it will be more interesting for both of you

- If exercising off-lead at night, buy a battery-operated flashing collar for your dog

- Make sure your dog has constant access to fresh water. Dogs can't sweat much, they need to drink water to cool down

Admittedly, when it is pouring down with rain, freezing cold (or scorching hot), the last thing you want to do is to venture outdoors with your dog. But the lows are more than compensated for by the highs. Exercise helps you: bond with your dog, keep fit, see different places and meet new companions - both canine and human. In short, it enhances both your lives.

Socialisation

Your adult dog's character will depend largely on two things. The first is his temperament, which he is born with, and presumably one of the reasons you have chosen a Golden Retriever. (The importance of picking a good breeder who selects breeding stock based on temperament, physical characteristics and health cannot be over-emphasised).

The second factor is environment – or how you bring him up and treat him. In other words, it's a combination of **nature and nurture**. And one absolutely essential aspect of nurture is socialisation.

Scientists have come to realise the importance that socialisation plays in a dog's life. We also now know that there is a fairly small window which is the optimum time for socialisation - and this is up to the age of up to around four months. Most young animals, including dogs, are naturally able to get used to their everyday environment until they reach a certain age. When they reach this age, they become much more suspicious of things they haven't yet experienced. This is why it often takes longer to train an older dog.

The age-specific natural development allows a puppy to get comfortable with the normal sights, sounds, people and animals that will be a part of his life. It ensures that he doesn't spend his life jumping in fright or growling at every blowing leaf or bird in song. The suspicion that dogs develop in later puppyhood – after the critical window - also ensures that they do react with a healthy dose of caution to new things that could really be dangerous - Mother Nature is clever!

Socialisation means 'learning to be part of society', or 'integration'. When we talk about socialising puppies, it means helping them learn to be comfortable within a human society that includes many different types of people, environments, buildings, traffic, sights, noises, smells, animals, other dogs, etc.

Your Golden Retriever may already have a wonderful temperament, but he still needs socialising to avoid him thinking that the world is tiny and it revolves around him - which in turn leads to unwanted adult behaviour traits. Some young Goldens have a natural tendency to be very boisterous and good socialisation helps them to learn their place in society and become more relaxed adults. The ultimate goal of socialisation is to have a happy, well-adjusted dog that you can take anywhere. Socialisation will give your dog confidence and teach him not to be afraid of new experiences.

Ever seen a therapy or service Golden Retriever or a Guide Dog in action and noticed how incredibly well-adjusted to life they are? This is no coincidence. These dogs have been extensively socialised and are ready and able to deal in a calm manner with whatever situation they encounter. They are relaxed and comfortable in their own skin - just like you want your dog to be.

You have to start socialising your puppy as soon as you bring him home. Start by socialising him around the house and garden and, if it is safe, carry him out of the home environment (but do not put him on the floor or allow him to sniff other dogs until he's got the all-clear after his vaccinations). Regular socialisation should continue until your dog is around 18 months of age. After that, don't just forget about it. Socialisation isn't only for puppies, it should continue throughout your dog's life. As with any skill, if it is not practised, your dog will become less proficient at interacting with other people, animals, and environments.

Developing the Well-Rounded Adult Dog

Well-socialised puppies usually develop into safer, more relaxed and enjoyable adult dogs. This is because they're more comfortable in a wider variety of situations than poorly socialised canines. Dogs which have not been properly integrated are much more likely to react with fear or aggression to unfamiliar people, dogs and experiences.

Golden Retrievers who are relaxed about other dogs, honking horns, cats, farm animals, cyclists, veterinary examinations, traffic, crowds and noise are easier to live with than dogs who find these situations challenging or frightening. And if you are planning on showing your dog or taking part in canine competitions, get him used to the buzz of these events early on. Well-socialised dogs also live more relaxed, peaceful and happy lives than dogs which are constantly stressed by their environment. Socialisation isn't an "all or nothing" project. You can socialise a puppy a bit, a lot, or a whole lot. The wider the range of experiences you expose him to when young, the better his chances are of becoming a more relaxed adult. Don't over-face your little puppy. Socialisation should never be forced, but approached systematically and in a manner that builds confidence and curious interaction. If your pup finds a new experience frightening, take a step back, introduce him to the scary situation much more gradually, and make a big effort to do something he loves during the situation or right afterwards.

For example, if your puppy seems to be frightened by noise and vehicles at a busy road, a good method would be to go to a quiet road, sit with the dog away from - but within sight of - the traffic. Every time he looks towards the traffic say "YES" and reward him with a treat. If he is still stressed, you need to move further away. When your dog takes the food in a calm manner, he is becoming more relaxed and getting used to traffic sounds, so you can edge a bit nearer - but still just for short periods until he becomes totally relaxed. Keep each session short and positive.

Meeting Other Dogs

When you take your gorgeous and vulnerable little pup out with other dogs for the first few times, you are bound to be a little nervous. To start with, introduce your puppy to just one other dog – one which you know to be friendly, rather than taking him straight to the park where there are lots of dogs of all sizes racing around, which might frighten the life out of your timid little darling. Always make the initial introductions on neutral ground, so as not to trigger territorial behaviour. You want your Golden Retriever to approach other dogs with confidence, not fear.

From the first meeting, help both dogs experience good things when they're in each other's presence. Let them sniff each other briefly, which is normal canine greeting behaviour. As they do, talk to them in a happy, friendly tone of voice; never use a threatening tone.

Don't allow them to sniff each other for too long as this may escalate to an aggressive response. After a short time, get the attention of both dogs and give each a treat in return for obeying a simple command, such as "Sit" or "Stay." Continue with the "happy talk," food rewards and simple commands.

Of course, if you have more than one dog or a number of working Golden Retrievers, your puppy will learn to socialise within the pack. However, you should still spend time introducing him to new sights, sounds and animals. Here are some signs of fear to look out for when your dog interacts with other canines:

- 🐾 Running away
- 🐾 Freezing on the spot
- 🐾 Frantic/nervous behaviour, e.g. excessive sniffing, drinking or playing frenetically with a toy
- 🐾 A lowered body stance or crouching
- 🐾 Lying on his back with his paws in the air – this is a submissive gesture
- 🐾 Lowering of the head, or turning the head away

- Lips pulled back baring teeth and/or growling
- Hair raised on his back (hackles)
- Tail lifted in the air
- Ears high on the head

Some of these responses are normal. A pup may well crouch on the ground or roll on to his back to show other dogs he is not a threat. Try not to be over-protective, your puppy has to learn how to interact with other dogs, but if the situation looks like escalating into something more aggressive, calmly distract the dogs or remove your puppy – don't shout or shriek. The dogs will pick up on your fear and this in itself could trigger an unpleasant situation.

Another sign to look out for is eyeballing. In the canine world, staring a dog in the eyes is a challenge and may trigger an aggressive response. This is more relevant to adult dogs, as a young pup will soon be put in his place by bigger or older dogs; it is how they learn. The rule of thumb with puppy socialisation is to keep a close eye on your pup's reaction to whatever you expose him to so that you can tone things down if he seems at all frightened.

Always follow up a socialisation experience with praise, petting, a fun game or a special treat. One positive sign from a dog is the play bow, when he goes down on to his front elbows but keeps his backside up in the air. This is a sign that he is feeling friendly towards the other dog and wants to play.

Although Golden Retrievers are not naturally aggressive dogs, aggression is often grounded in fear, and a dog which mixes easily is less likely to be aggressive. Similarly, without frequent and new experiences, some Golden Retrievers can become timid and nervous when introduced to new experiences. Take your new dog everywhere you can. You want him to feel relaxed and calm in any situation, even noisy and crowded ones. Take treats with you and praise him when he reacts calmly to new situations. Once he has settled into your home, introduce him to your friends and teach him not to jump up. If you have young children, it is not only the dog that needs socialising! Youngsters also need training on how to act around dogs, so both parties learn to respect the other.

An excellent way of getting your new puppy to meet other dogs in a safe environment is at a puppy class. Ask around locally if any classes are being run. Some vets and dog trainers run classes for very junior pups who have had all their vaccinations. These help pups get used to other dogs of a similar age.

Breeders on Exercise

Helen Dorrance, Ducat Goldens, Texas: "The late Robyn Stirrat (Signature Golden Retrievers) gave me the following advice which has always held true: No forced exercise on young puppies, and if you do decide to run or bike with them, they should only trot one minute per month of age. In other words, eight-month-old puppies should only trot on leash for eight minutes a day. Year-old dogs would trot for 12 minutes a day, and so on. After the age of two years, dogs no longer have to be limited on how much exercise they get. Free running in the woods or country is fine for all ages since they can stop and start when they want and aren't forced to keep up with a human or other dogs."

Karen Moore, Icewind Goldens, New Jersey: "Goldens were developed as a sporting breed able to handle a full day of hunting, and exercise is very important for your Golden's health and wellbeing. I recommend a healthy adult has vigorous exercise twice a day for at least an hour each time. This will prevent stress, boredom, and behaviour problems. But for growing puppies, who need 18 hours of sleep a day, you should have short periods of free play without climbing stairs, jumping off the furniture or going for long hikes, which can cause bone problems."

Tim Hoke, of California, whose Golden Meadows Retrievers compete very successfully in the show ring, added: "Our dogs exercise for several hours a day, which includes walking, training and fetch."

Kelly Sisco, Show Me Goldens, Missouri, says: "My dogs are a rather lazy bunch. We live on 20 acres, where they have time to play every day and we take them down to swim in the pond. They are also happy to spend time napping inside. They do not require a ton of exercise, although we do make sure they do receive some for their health." Kelly obviously keeps her dogs fit, as they take part in "nosework, rally, obedience, conformation, lure coursing, pet therapy, a little bit of agility and our boy has done some hunt training."

Pictured is Kelly's two-year-old Cruise (Milagro De Oro King of Funy RN CGCA CGCU TKI).

Anna Cornelius-Jones, Mindieslodge Golden Retrievers, Dorset: "When you first get your puppy, exercise should be kept to a minimum. Also, for the first 12 months, stairs should be avoided as this can cause damage to their joints. Once they are fully grown then they are capable of going on longer walks. As you get to know your dog, you will know how much they can tolerate and what is too much."

Angie and Ray Gait, Sonodora Golden Retrievers, Hampshire : "Adult Goldies can take as much exercise as you wish; however it's the type of exercise that is important. An adult Golden should get about 45 minutes controlled walking and a good hour free run per day. None of this running by the side of a bike!" Sue Page, Dormansue Golden Retrievers, Surrey: "My dogs always get two 30-minute walks every single day and then about four times a week they get a one-hour walk on top of this."

Dee Johnson, Johnsongrace Golden Retrievers, North Cornwall: "We normally exercise ours between one and two hours a day. We have a big garden, so if they don't have a long walk, we play

some active game in the garden." Nicholas Lock, Bonsaviour Retrievers, Shropshire, adds: "Two hours for adults; two one-hour walks off-lead. Goldies have a lot of energy to burn off!"

Lesley Gunter, Moorvista Derbyshire: "I go for one long walk – usually mid-morning - for an hour to two hours. Obviously, this is only once a puppy is more than one year old. Retrievers need to be able to run freely, so the sooner a new owner lets them off the lead in a safe place, the better. A good breeder should give owners a chart showing them how much exercise for each month before one year old." (Pictured is Lesley's three-year-old Martha enjoying a splash on the West coast of Scotland. Martha is looking particularly pleased with herself, having recently won Best of Breed at Stoke Gundog Show).

Karen Parsons, Arundel, West Sussex: "A Golden will walk as much or as little as you want them to. Ours are 'working pets' and work all day on shoot days, but are still happy to go out and play the next day - although we tend to give them a rest that day and only have light exercise. When they are young you do not want to walk them too far until all their bones/muscles and tendons are strong."

Claire Underwood, Bowcombe Golden Retrievers, Isle of Wight: "Up to nine months old this is restricted to about ten minutes, slowly increasing to 15 to 20 minutes. After that, an hour's walk or two smaller walks. Twice a week we have a longer walk. My dogs run around on my farm in the morning and evening for about 45 minutes each time, so they exercise a lot." Liz Spicer-Short, Priorschest Golden Retrievers, Dorset: "Mine get between one and a half and three hours in three chunks - a decent walk in the morning, and afternoon and a shorter one at lunchtime."

Julian Pottage, Yorkbeach Golden Retrievers, Mid Glamorgan, Wales: "The intensity of exercise counts as well as the duration. Mine go out for at least 90 minutes a day and have some vigorous exercise - running or swimming - as part of it." Karen Ireland Trikiti Golden Retrievers, Hampshire: "I wish I had more time, but daily they have around one hour in the morning and one hour or more in the evening. They could do more, but are happy with this and generally settle down and sleep after each walk."

10. Training

Training a young dog is like bringing up a child. Put in the effort early on to teach them the guidelines and you will be rewarded with a well-adjusted, sociable individual who will be a joy to live with. Goldens are intelligent, extremely eager to please and love being with their humans. Most of them are greedy too! All of this adds up to one of the easiest breeds of all to train – unless you get a particularly stubborn individual! But only if you put in the time too. Goldens make wonderful companions, but let yours behave exactly how he wants and you may well finish up with a boisterous adult who rules your life. The secret of good training can be summed up quite simply:

Patience, Consistency, Praise and Reward

Goldens are eager to please and generally highly motivated by reward – both treats and praise, and this is a big bonus when it comes to training. Your dog WANTS to please you and enjoys learning. All you have to do is spend the time teaching your dog WHAT you want him to do, then repeat the actions so it becomes second nature.

 When training, try getting your pup used to a small piece of carrot or apple (like in the photo) as a healthy, low-calorie alternative to traditional dog treats.

Many owners would say that this breed has empathy (the ability to pick up on the feelings of others); they respond well to your encouragement and a positive atmosphere. They do not respond well to heavy-handed training methods. Goldens are known for their intelligence and are most certainly 'biddable', i.e. it is not difficult to teach them commands, provided you make it clear exactly what you want them to do; don't give conflicting signals. They and can be trained to a high level in a number of different fields.

Psychologist and canine expert Dr Stanley Coren has written a book called "The Intelligence of Dogs" in which he ranks the breeds. He surveyed dog trainers to compile the list and used "Understanding of New Commands" and "Obey First Command" as his standards of intelligence. He says there are three types of dog intelligence:

* Adaptive Intelligence (learning and problem-solving ability). This is specific to the individual animal and is measured by canine IQ tests

* Instinctive Intelligence. This is specific to the individual animal and is measured by canine IQ tests

* Working/Obedience Intelligence. This is breed-dependent

The brainboxes of the canine world are the 10 breeds ranked in the 'Brightest Dogs' section of his list. All dogs in this class:

* Understand New Commands with Fewer than Five Repetitions
* Obey a First Command 95% of the Time or Better

It will come as no surprise to anyone who has ever owned a Golden Retriever to know that the breed is in the top group, at Number Four. (The top 10 are, in order: Border Collie, Poodle, German Shepherd Dog, Golden Retriever, Doberman Pinscher, Shetland Sheepdog, Papillon, Rottweiler, Australian Cattle Dog).

By the author's own admission, the drawback of this rating scale is that it is heavily weighted towards obedience-related behavioural traits, which are often found in working dogs - like the Golden - rather than understanding or creativity, which is found in hunting dogs. As a result, some breeds, such as the Bully breeds (Bulldogs, French Bulldogs, Mastiffs, Bull Terriers, Pugs, etc). are ranked quite low on the list, due to their stubborn or independent nature.

Three golden rules when training a Golden Retriever are:

1. Training must be reward-based, not punishment based.

2. Keep sessions short or your dog will get bored.

3. Keep sessions fun, give your Golden a challenge and a chance to shine!

If you decide to enlist the help of a professional trainer, choose one registered with the Association of Professional Dog Trainers (APDT); you can find details at the back of the book. Make sure your chosen one uses positive reward-based training methods, as the old alpha-dominance theories have largely been discredited. When you train your dog, it should never be a battle of wills between you and him; it should be a positive learning experience for you both. Bawling at the top of your voice or smacking should play no part in training. Some Goldens may try to push the boundaries when they reach adolescence, as they come out of puppyhood and before they are mature adults. If you have a high spirited, high energy dog, you have to use your brain to think of ways that will make training challenging and to persuade your dog that what you want him to do is actually what he wants to do!

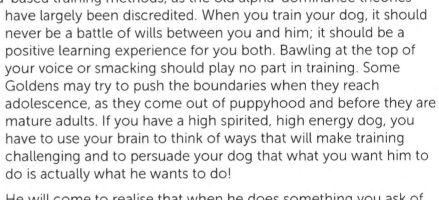

He will come to realise that when he does something you ask of him, something good is going to happen – treats, verbal praise, pats, play time, etc. You need to be firm with a strong-willed, stubborn or boisterous Golden, but all training should still be carried out using positive techniques.

Establishing the natural order of things is not something forced on a dog through shouting or violence; it is brought about by mutual consent and good training. Like most dogs, Goldens are happiest and behave best when they know and are comfortable with their place in the household. If you have adopted an older dog, you can still train him, but it will take a little longer to get rid of bad habits and instil good manners. Patience and persistence are the keys here.

Socialisation is a very important aspect of training. Your puppy's breeder should have already begun this process with the litter and then it's up to you to keep it going when the pup arrives home. Up to around 16 weeks' old pups can absorb a great deal of information, but they are also vulnerable to bad experiences. Pups who are not properly exposed to different people, other animals and situations can find them very frightening when they do finally encounter them later. They may react by cowering, urinating, barking, growling or biting. If they have positive experiences with people, noises, different situations and other animals before they turn 16 or 18 weeks of age, they are less likely to be afraid or to try to establish dominance later.

Don't just leave your dog at home in the early days, take him out and about with you, get him used to new people, places and noises. Dogs that miss out on being socialised can pay the price later.

One issue with many young Goldens is chewing. If you are not careful, some young pups and adolescents will chew through anything – including wires, phone chargers, remote controls, bedding, etc. And Goldens are not infrequent visitors to veterinary clinics to have 'foreign objects' removed from their stomachs. Train your young Golden only to chew the things you give him – so don't give him your old slippers, an old piece of carpet or anything that resembles something you don't want him to chew. Buy purpose-made long-lasting chew toys. Jumping up is another common issue. Goldens love everybody and are so enthusiastic about life, so it's often a natural reaction when they see somebody. You don't, however, want your fully-grown dog to jump up on grandma when he has just come back from a romp through the muddy woods and a swim in a dirty pond. Teach him while he is still small not to jump up!

12 Training Tips

1. Start training and socialising early. Like babies, puppies learn quickly and it's this learned behaviour that stays with them through adult life. Puppy training should start with a few minutes a day a few days after he has arrived home, even if he's only a few weeks old. The critical window is up to four months or so.

2. Your voice is a very important training tool. Your dog has to learn to understand your language and you have to understand him. Commands should be issued in a calm, authoritative voice - not shouted. Praise should be given in a happy, encouraging voice, accompanied by stroking or patting. If your dog has done something wrong, use a stern voice, not a harsh shriek. This applies even if your Golden Retriever is unresponsive at the beginning.

3. Avoid giving your dog commands you know you can't enforce. Every time you give a command that you don't enforce, he learns that commands are optional. One command equals one response. Give your dog only one command - twice maximum - then gently enforce it. Repeating commands or nagging will make him tune out, and teach him that the first few commands are a bluff. Telling your dog to "SIT, SIT, SIT, SIT!!!" is neither efficient nor effective. Give your dog a single "SIT" command, gently place him in the sitting position and then praise him.

4. Train your dog gently and humanely. Goldens are gentle by nature and do not respond well to being shouted at or hit. Keep training sessions short and upbeat so the whole experience is enjoyable for you and him. If obedience training is a bit of a bore, pep things up a bit by 'play training' by using constructive, non-adversarial games.

5. Begin your training around the house and garden or yard. How well your dog responds to you at home affects his behaviour away from the home as well. If he doesn't respond well at home, he certainly won't respond any better when he's out and about where there are 101 distractions, such as food scraps, other dogs, people, cats, interesting scents, etc.

6. Goldens LOVE their food and mealtimes are a great time to start training. Teach your dog to sit and stay at breakfast and dinnertime, rather than just putting the dish down and letting him dash over immediately. In the beginning, he won't know what you mean, so gently place him into the sit position while you say "Sit." Place a hand on his chest during the "Stay"

command - gradually letting go – and then give him the command to eat his dinner, followed by encouraging praise - he'll soon get the idea.

7. Use your dog's name often and in a positive manner. When you bring your pup or new dog home, use his name often so he gets used to the sound of it. He won't know what it means in the beginning, but it won't take him long to realise you're talking to him.

8. DON'T use his name when reprimanding, warning or punishing. He should trust that when he hears his name, good things happen. He should always respond to his name with enthusiasm, never hesitancy or fear. Use words such as "No," "Ack!" or "Bad Boy/Girl" in a stern (not shouted) voice instead. Some parents prefer not to use "No" with their dog, as they use it so often around the kids that it can confuse the pup! When a puppy is corrected by his mother, e.g. – if he bites her – she growls at him to warn him not to do it again. Using a short sharp sound like **"Ack!"** can work surprisingly well; it does for us.

9. Don't give your dog lots of attention (even negative attention) when he misbehaves. Dogs like attention. If yours gets lots when he jumps up on you, his bad behaviour is being reinforced. If he jumps up, push him away, use the command "No" or "Down" and then ignore him.

10. Timing is critical. When your puppy does something right, praise him immediately. If you wait a while he will have no idea what he has done right. Similarly, when he does something wrong, correct him straight away. For example, if he eliminates in the house, don't shout and certainly don't rub his nose in it; this will only make things worse. If you catch him in the act, use your "No" or "Ack" sound and immediately carry him out of the house. Then use the toilet command (whichever word you have chosen) and praise your pup or give him a treat when he performs. If your pup is constantly eliminating indoors, you are not keeping a close enough eye on him.

11. Give your dog attention when YOU want to – not when he wants it. When you are training, give your puppy lots of positive attention when he is good. But if he starts jumping up, nudging you constantly or barking to demand your attention, ignore him. Don't give in to his demands. Wait a while and pat him when you want and after he has stopped demanding your attention.

12. Start as you mean to go on. In other words, in terms of rules and training, treat your cute little pup as though he were a fully-grown Golden; introduce the rules you want him to live by as an adult. If you don't want your dog to take over your couch or bed or jump up at people when he is an adult, train him not to do it when he is small. You can't have one set of rules for a pup and one set for a fully-grown dog, he won't understand. Also make sure that everybody in the household sticks to the same set of rules. Your dog will never learn if one person lets him jump on the couch and another person doesn't.

Remember this simple phrase: **TREATS, NOT THREATS.**

Teaching Basic Commands

Sit - Teaching the Sit command to your Golden Retriever is relatively easy. Teaching a young pup to sit still for a few seconds is a bit more difficult! In the beginning you may want to put your protégé on a lead to hold his attention. Stand facing each other and hold a treat between your thumb and fingers just an inch or so above his head. Don't let your fingers and the treat get much further away or you might have trouble getting him to move his body into a sitting position. In fact, if your dog jumps up when you try to guide him into the Sit, you're probably holding your hand too far away from his nose. If your dog backs up, you can practise with a wall behind him.

As he reaches up to sniff it, move the treat upwards and back over the dog towards his tail at the same time as saying "Sit." Most dogs will track the treat with their eyes and follow it with their noses, causing their snouts to point straight up.

As his head moves up toward the treat, his rear end should automatically go down towards the floor. TaDa! (drum roll!)

As soon as he sits, say "Yes!" Give him the treat and tell your dog (s)he's a good boy or girl. Stroke and praise him for as long as he stays in the sitting position. If he jumps up on his back legs and paws you while you are moving the treat, be patient and start all over again. Another method is to put one hand on his chest and with your other hand, gently push down on his rear end until he is sitting, while saying "Sit." Give him a treat and praise, even though you have made him do it, he will eventually associate the position with the word 'sit'.

Once your dog catches on, leave the treat in your pocket (or have it in your other hand). Repeat the sequence, but this time your dog will just follow your empty hand. Say "Sit" and bring your empty hand in front of your dog's nose, holding your fingers as if you had a treat. Move your hand exactly as you did when you held the treat.

When your dog sits, say "Yes!" and then give him a treat from your other hand or your pocket.

Gradually lessen the amount of movement with your hand. First, say "Sit" then hold your hand eight to 10 inches above your dog's face and wait a moment. Most likely, he will sit. If he doesn't, help him by moving your hand back over his head, like you did before, but make a smaller movement this time. Then try again. Your goal is to eventually just say "Sit" without having to move or extend your hand at all.

Once your dog reliably sits on cue, you can ask him to sit whenever you meet and talk to people (admittedly, it may not work straight away, but it might help to calm him down a bit). The key is anticipation. Give your dog the cue before he gets too excited to hear you and before he starts jumping up on the person just arrived. Generously reward him the instant he sits. Say "Yes" and give treats every few seconds while he holds the Sit.

Whenever possible, ask the person you're greeting to help you out by walking away if your dog gets up from the sit and lunges or jumps towards him or her. With many consistent repetitions of this exercise, your dog will learn that lunging or jumping makes people go away, and polite sitting makes them stay and give him attention.

You can practise training your bouncy Golden not to jump up by arranging for a friend to come round, then for him or her to come in and out of the house several times. Each time, show the treat, give the Sit command (initially, don't ask your dog to hold the sit for any length of time), and then allow him to greet your friend. Ask your friend to reach down to pat your dog, rather than standing straight and encouraging the dog to jump up for a greeting.

If your dog is still jumping up, you can use a harness and lead inside the house to physically prevent him from jumping up at people, while still training him to sit when someone arrives. Treats and praise are the key. (You can also use the "Off" command - and reward with a treat for success - when you want your dog NOT to jump up at a person, or not to jump up on furniture).

'Sit' is a useful command and can be used in a number of different situations. For example, when you are putting his lead on, while you are preparing his meal, when he returned the ball you have just thrown, when he is jumping up, demanding attention or getting over-excited.

Come - This is another basic command that you can teach right from the beginning. Teaching your dog to come to you when you call (also known as 'the recall') is an important lesson. A dog who responds quickly and consistently can enjoy freedoms that other dogs cannot. Although you might spend more time teaching this command than any other, the benefits make it well worth the investment. Goldens love to run free, but you can't allow that in open spaces until your dog has learned the recall. (By the way, "Come" or a similar word is better than "Here" if you intend using the "Heel" command, as these words sound too similar).

Whether you're teaching a young puppy or an older Golden, the first step is always to establish that coming to you is the best thing he can do. Any time your dog comes to you whether you've called him or not, acknowledge that you appreciate it. You can do this with praise, affection, play or the magic bullet – treats! This consistent reinforcement ensures that your dog will continue to "check in" with you frequently.

1. Say your dog's name followed by the command "Come!" in an enthusiastic voice. You'll usually be more successful if you walk or run away from him while you call. Dogs find it hard to resist chasing after a running person, especially their owner.

2. He should run towards you. NOTE: Dogs tend to tune us out if we talk to them all the time. Whether you're training or out for an off-lead walk, refrain from constantly chattering to your dog - no matter how much of a brilliant conversationalist you are! If you're quiet much of the time, he is more likely to pay attention when you call him. When he does, praise him and give him a treat.

3. Often, especially outdoors, a young dog will start off running towards you but then get distracted and head off in another direction. Pre-empt this situation by praising your puppy and cheering him on when he starts to come to you and **before** he has a chance to get distracted.

Your praise will keep him focused so that he'll be more likely to come all the way to you. If he stops or turns away, you can give him feedback by saying "Uh-uh!" or "Hey!" in a different tone of voice (displeased or unpleasantly surprised). When he looks at you again, smile, call him and praise him as he approaches you.

Progress your dog's training in baby steps. If he's learned to come when called in your kitchen, you can't expect him to be able to do it straight away at the park or on the beach when he's surrounded by distractions. When you first try this outdoors, make sure there's no one around to distract your dog. It's a good idea to consider using a long training lead - or to do the training within a safe, fenced area. Only when your dog has mastered the recall in a number of locations and in the face of various distractions can you expect him to come to you regularly.

....

Down - There are a number of different ways to teach this command, which here means for the dog to lie down. (If you are teaching this command, then use the "Off" command to teach your dog not to jump up). This does not come naturally to a young pup, so it may take a little while for him to master the Down command. Don't make it a battle of wills and, although you may gently push him down, don't physically force him down against his will. This will be seen as you asserting dominance in an aggressive manner and your Golden will not like it.

1. Give the 'Sit' command.

2. When your dog sits, don't give him the treat immediately, but keep it in your closed hand. Slowly move your hand straight down toward the floor, between his front legs. As your dog's nose follows the treat, just like a magnet, his head will bend all the way down to the floor.

3. When the treat is on the floor between your dog's paws, start to move it away from him, like you're drawing a line along the floor. (The entire luring motion forms an L-shape).

4. At the same time say "Down" in a firm manner.

5. To continue to follow the treat, your dog will probably ease himself into the Down position. The instant his elbows touch the floor, say "Yes!" and immediately let him eat the treat. If your dog doesn't automatically stand up after eating the treat, just move a step or two away to encourage him to move out of the Down position. Then repeat the sequence above several times. Aim for two short sessions of five minutes or so per day.

If your dog's back end pops up when you try to lure him into a Down, quickly snatch the treat away. Then immediately ask your dog to sit and try again. It may help to let your dog nibble on the treat as you move it toward the floor. If you've tried to lure your dog into a Down, but he still seems confused or reluctant, try this trick:

1. Sit down on the floor with your legs straight out in front of you. Your dog should be at your side. Keeping your legs together and your feet on the floor, bend your knees to make a 'tent' shape.

2. Hold a treat right in front of your dog's nose. As he licks and sniffs the treat, slowly move it down to the floor and then underneath your legs. Continue to lure him until he has to crouch down to keep following the treat.

3. The instant his belly touches the floor, say "Yes!" and let him eat the treat. If your dog seems nervous about following the treat under your legs, make a trail of treats for him to eat along the way.

Some dogs find it easier to follow a treat into the Down from a standing position.

* Hold the treat right in front of your dog's nose, and then slowly move it straight down to the floor, right between his front paws. His nose will follow the treat

* If you let him lick the treat as you continue to hold it still on the floor, your dog will probably plop into the Down position

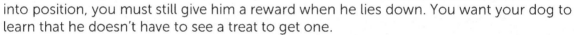
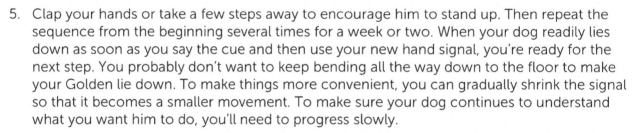

🐾 The moment he does, say "Yes!" and let him eat the treat (some dogs are reluctant to lie on a cold, hard surface. It may be easier to teach yours to lie down on a carpet). The next step is to introduce a hand signal. You'll still reward him with treats, though, so keep them nearby or hidden behind your back.

1. Start with your dog in a Sit

2. Say "Down"

3. Without a treat in your fingers, use the same hand motion you did before

4. As soon as your dog's elbows touch the floor, say "Yes!" and immediately get a treat to give him. Important: Even though you're not using a treat to lure your dog into position, you must still give him a reward when he lies down. You want your dog to learn that he doesn't have to see a treat to get one.

5. Clap your hands or take a few steps away to encourage him to stand up. Then repeat the sequence from the beginning several times for a week or two. When your dog readily lies down as soon as you say the cue and then use your new hand signal, you're ready for the next step. You probably don't want to keep bending all the way down to the floor to make your Golden lie down. To make things more convenient, you can gradually shrink the signal so that it becomes a smaller movement. To make sure your dog continues to understand what you want him to do, you'll need to progress slowly.

6. Repeat the hand signal, but instead of guiding your dog into the Down by moving your hand all the way to the floor, move it almost all the way down. Stop moving your hand when it's an inch or two above the floor. Practise the Down exercise for a day or two, using this slightly smaller hand signal. Then you can make your movement an inch or two smaller, stopping your hand three or four inches above the floor.

7. After practising for another couple of days, you can shrink the signal again. As you continue to gradually stop your hand signal farther and farther from the floor, you'll bend over less and less. Eventually, you won't have to bend over at all. You'll be able to stand up straight, say "Down," and then just point to the floor.

Your next job is a bit harder - it's to practise your dog's new skill in many different situations and locations so that he can lie down whenever and wherever you ask him to. Slowly increase the level of distraction; for example, first practise in calm places, like different rooms in your house or in your garden, when there's no one else around. Then increase the distractions; practise at home when family members are moving around, on walks and then at friends' houses, too.

....

Stay - This is a very useful command, but it's not so easy to teach a lively and distracted young Golden Retriever pup to stay still for any length of time. Here is a simple method to get your dog to stay; if you are training a young dog, don't ask him to stay for more than a few seconds at the beginning.

This requires some concentration from your dog, so pick a time when he's relaxed and well exercised, or just after a game or mealtimes - but not exhausted when he is too tired to concentrate.

1. Tell your dog to sit or lie down, but instead of giving a treat as soon as he hits the floor, hold off for one second. Then say "Yes!" in an enthusiastic voice and give him a treat. If your dog bounces up again instantly, have two treats ready. Feed one right away, before he has time to move; then say "Yes!" and feed the second treat.

2. You need a release word or phrase. It might be "Free!" or "Here!" or a word that you only use to release your dog from this command. Once you've given the treat, immediately give your release cue and encourage your dog to get up. Then repeat the exercise, perhaps up to a dozen times in one training session, gradually wait a tiny bit longer before releasing the treat. (You can delay the first treat for a moment if your dog bounces up).

3. A common mistake is to hold the treat high and then give the reward slowly. As your dog doesn't know the command yet, he sees the treat coming and gets up to meet the food. Instead, bring the treat toward your dog quickly - the best place to deliver it is right between his front paws. If you're working on a Sit-Stay, give the treat at chest height.

4. When your dog can stay for several seconds, start to add a little distance. At first, you'll walk backwards, because your Golden is more likely to get up to follow you if you turn away from him. Take one single step away, then step back towards your dog and say "Yes!" and give the treat. Give him the signal to get up immediately, even if five seconds haven't passed. The stay gets harder for your dog depending on how long it is, how far away you are, and what else is going on around him.

5. Trainer shorthand is **"distance, duration, distraction."** For best success in teaching a Stay, work on one factor at a time. Whenever you make one factor more difficult, such as distance, ease up on the others at first, then build them back up. So, when you take that first step back from your dog, adding distance, you should cut the duration of the stay.

6. Now your dog has mastered the Stay with you alone, move the training on so that he learns to do the same with distractions. Have someone walk into the room, or squeak a toy or bounce a ball once. A rock-solid stay is mostly a matter of working slowly and patiently to start with. Don't go too fast - the ideal scenario is that your Golden Retriever never breaks out of the Stay position until you release him.

If he does get up, take a breather and then give him a short refresher, starting at a point easier than whatever you were working on when he cracked. If you think he's tired or had enough, leave it for the day and come back later – just finish off on a positive note by giving one very easy command you know he will obey, followed by a treat reward.

Don't use the Stay command in situations where it is unpleasant for your dog. For instance, avoid telling him to stay as you close the door behind you on your way to work. Finally, don't use Stay to keep a dog in a scary situation.

Puppy Biting and Chewing

All Golden Retriever puppies spend a great deal of time chewing, playing, and investigating objects. And it's natural for them to explore the world with their mouths and needle-sharp teeth. We shouldn't be surprised that Goldens and other retrievers are known as being "mouthy" breeds, especially when young. After all, it's in their DNA; they were bred specifically to carry things in their mouths. When puppies play with people, they often bite, chew and mouthe on people's hands, limbs and clothing. Play biting is normal for puppies; they do it all the time with their littermates. They also bite moving targets with their sharp teeth; it's a great game.

But when they arrive in your home, they have to be taught that human skin is sensitive and body parts are not suitable biting material. Biting is not acceptable, not even from a puppy, and can be a real problem initially if you have children. When your puppy bites you or the kids, he is playing and investigating; he is NOT being aggressive. Even though Goldens are gentle dogs, puppy biting can develop into more aggressive rough play if not checked.

Make sure every time you have a play session, you have a soft toy nearby and when he starts to chew your hand or feet, clench your fingers (or toes!) to make it more difficult and distract him with a soft toy in your other hand. Keep the game interesting by moving the toy around or rolling it around in front of him. (He may be too young to fetch it back if you throw it). He may continue to chew you, but will eventually realise that the toy is far more interesting and lively than your boring hand.

If he becomes over-excited and too aggressive with the toy, if he growls a lot, stop playing with him and walk away. When you walk away, don't say anything or make eye or physical contact with your puppy. Simply ignore him, this is extremely effective and often works within a few days. If your pup is more persistent and tries to bite your legs as you walk away, thinking this is another fantastic game, stand still and ignore him. If he still persists, tell him "No!" in a very stern voice, then praise him when he lets go. If you have to physically remove him from your trouser leg or shoe, leave him alone in the room for a while and ignore his demands for attention if he starts barking.

Although you might find it quite cute and funny if your puppy bites your fingers or toes, it should be discouraged at all costs. You don't want your Golden Retriever doing this as an adolescent or adult, when he can inadvertently cause real injury.

Here are some tips to deal with puppy biting:

- Puppies growl and bite more when they are excited. Don't allow things to escalate, so remove your pup from the situation before he gets too excited by putting him in a crate or pen

- Don't put your hand or finger into your pup's mouth to nibble on; this promotes puppy biting

- Limit your children's play time with pup - and always supervise the sessions in the beginning. Teach them to gently play with and stroke your puppy, not to wind him up

- Don't let the kids (or adults) run round the house with the puppy chasing – this is an open invitation to nip at the ankles

- If your puppy does bite, remove him from the situation and people – never smack him

Tip Many Goldens are very sensitive and another method that can be very successful is to make a sharp cry of "Ouch!" when your pup bites your hand – even when it doesn't hurt. This worked very well for us. Your pup may well jump back in amazement, surprised that he has hurt you. Divert your attention from your puppy to your hand. He will probably try to get your attention or lick you as a way of saying sorry. Praise him for stopping biting and continue with the game. If he bites you again, repeat the process. A sensitive dog will soon stop biting you. You may also think about keeping the toys you use to play with your puppy separate from other toys. That way he will associate certain toys with having fun with you and will work harder to please you.

Goldens love playing and you can use this to your advantage by teaching your dog how to play nicely with you and the toy and then by using play time as a reward for good behaviour.

Why do puppies chew? As mentioned, Goldens, like babies, explore the world by putting things into their mouths. Secondly, puppy chewing is a normal part of the teething process. And thirdly, some pups, adolescents and adult dogs chew because they are bored – usually due to lack of exercise and/or mental stimulation.

If puppy chewing is a problem it is because your pup is chewing on something you don't want him to. So, the trick is to keep him, his mouth and sharp little teeth occupied with something he CAN chew on, such as a durable toy – see **Chapter 5. Bringing Your Puppy Home** for more information.

You might also consider freezing peanut butter and/or a liquid inside a Kong toy. Put the Kong into a mug, plug the small end with peanut butter and fill it with gravy before putting it into the freezer. (Don't leave the Kong and your Golden on your precious Oriental rug!).

This will keep your pup occupied for quite a long time. It is also worth considering giving the dog a frozen Kong when you leave the house if your dog suffers from separation anxiety. There are lots of doggie recipes for frozen Kongs online.

Clicker Training

Clicker training is a method of training that uses a sound - a click - to tell an animal when he does something right. The clicker is a tiny plastic box held in the palm of your hand, with a metal tongue that you push quickly to make the sound.

The clicker creates an efficient language between a human trainer and a trainee. First, a trainer teaches a dog that every time he hears the clicking sound, he gets a treat. Once the dog understands that clicks are always followed by treats, the click becomes a powerful reward.

When this happens, the trainer can use the click to mark the instant the animal performs the right behaviour. For example, if a trainer wants to teach a dog to sit, she'll click the instant his rump hits the floor and then deliver a tasty treat. With repetition, the dog learns that sitting earns rewards.

So, the 'click' takes on huge meaning. To the animal it means: "What I was doing the moment my trainer clicked, that's what she wants me to do." The clicker in animal training is like the winning buzzer on a game show that tells a contestant he's just won the money! Through the clicker, the trainer communicates precisely with the dog, and that speeds up training.

Although the clicker is ideal because it makes a unique, consistent sound, you do need a spare hand to hold it. For that reason, some trainers prefer to keep both hands free and instead use a one-syllable word like "Yes!" or "Good!" to mark the desired behaviour. In the steps below, you can substitute the word in place of the click to teach your pet what the sound means. It's easy to introduce the clicker to your Golden. Spend half an hour or so teaching him that the sound of the click means "Treat!" Here's how:

1. Sit and watch TV or read a book with your dog in the room. Have a container of treats within reach.

2. Place one treat in your hand and the clicker in the other. (If your dog smells the treat and tries to get it by pawing, sniffing, mouthing or barking at you, just close your hand around the treat and wait until he gives up and leaves you alone).

3. Click once and immediately open your hand to give your dog the treat. Put another treat in your closed hand and resume watching TV or reading. Ignore your dog.

4. Several minutes later, click again and offer another treat.

5. Continue to repeat the click-and-treat combination at varying intervals, sometimes after one minute, sometimes after five minutes. Make sure you vary the time so that your dog doesn't know exactly when the next click is coming. Eventually, he'll start to turn toward you and look expectantly when he hears the click - which means he understands that the sound of the clicker means a treat is coming his way.

If your dog runs away when he hears the click, you can make the sound softer by putting it in your pocket or wrapping a towel around your hand that's holding the clicker. You can also try using a different sound, like the click of a retractable pen or the word "Yes."

Clicker Training Basics

Once your dog seems to understand the connection between the click and the treat, you're ready to get started.

1. Click just once, right when your pet does what you want him to do. Think of it like pressing the shutter of a camera to take a picture of the behaviour.

2. Remember to follow every click with a treat. After you click, deliver the treat to your pet's mouth as quickly as possible.

3. It's fine to switch between practising two or three behaviours within a session, but work on one command at a time. For example, say you're teaching your Golden Retriever to sit, lie down and raise his paw. You can do 10 repetitions of sit and take a quick play break. Then do 10 repetitions of down, and take another quick break. Then do 10 repetitions of stay, and so on. Keep training sessions short and stop before you or your dog gets tired of the game.

4. End training sessions on a good note, when your dog has succeeded with what you're working on. If necessary, ask him to do something he can do well at the end of a session.

Collar and Lead Training

You have to train your dog to get used to a collar - or harness - and lead (leash), and then he has to learn to walk nicely on the lead. Teaching these manners can be challenging because many young

Goldens are very lively and don't necessarily want to walk at the same pace as you. All dogs will pull on a lead initially. This isn't because they want to show you who's boss, it's simply that they are excited to be outdoors and are forging ahead.

If you are worried about pulling on your young Golden's collar, you might prefer to use a body harness instead. Harnesses work well with some dogs, they take the pressure away from a dog's sensitive neck area and distribute it more evenly around the body. Harnesses with a chest ring for the lead can be effective for training. When your dog pulls, the harness turns him around.

Another option is to start your dog on a padded collar and then change to a harness once he has learned some lead etiquette – although padded collars can be quite heavy. Some dogs don't mind collars; some will try to fight them, while others will slump to the floor! You need to be patient and calm and proceed at a pace comfortable to him; don't fight your dog and don't force the collar on.

1. An adult Golden will require a collar one to one and a half inches wide (if you choose a flat, not rolled, collar) and normally 18 to 22 inches long. But for now, you need a small, lightweight one - not one he is going to grow into. You can buy one with clips to start with, just put it on and clip it together, rather than fiddling with buckles, which can be scary when he's wearing a collar for the first time. Stick to the principle of positive reward-based training and give a treat once the collar is on, not after you have taken it off. Then gradually increase the length of time you leave the collar on. IMPORTANT: If you leave your dog in a crate, or leave him alone in the house, take off the collar. He is not used to it and it may get caught on something, causing panic or injury to your dog.

2. Put the collar on when there are other things that will occupy him, like when he is going outside to be with you, or in the home when you are interacting with him. Or put it on at mealtimes or when you are doing some basic training. Don't put the collar on too tight, you want him to forget it's there. Some pups may react as if you've hung a two-ton weight around their necks, while others will be more compliant. If yours scratches the collar, get his attention by encouraging him to follow you or play with a toy to forget the irritation.

3. Once your puppy is happy wearing the collar, introduce the lead. An extending or retractable one is not really suitable for starting off with, as they are not very strong and no good for training him to walk close. Buy a fixed-length lead. Start off in the house or garden; don't try to go out and about straight away. Think of the lead as a safety device to stop him running off, not something to drag him around with. You want a dog that doesn't pull, so don't start by pulling him around; you don't want to get into a tug-of-war contest.

4. Attach the lead to the collar and give him a treat while you put it on. The minute it is attached, use the treats (instead of pulling on the lead) to lure him beside you, so that he gets used to walking with the collar and lead. As well as using treats you can also make good use of toys to do exactly the same thing - especially if your dog has a favourite. Walk around the house with the lead on and lure him forwards with the toy.

   It might feel a bit odd but it's a good way for your pup to develop a positive relationship with the collar and lead with the minimum of fuss. Act as though it's the most natural thing in the world for you to walk around the house with your dog on a lead – and just hope that the neighbours aren't watching! Some dogs react the moment you attach the lead and they feel some tension on it – a bit like when a horse is being broken in for the first time. Drop the lead and allow him to run round the house or yard, dragging it after him, but be careful he

doesn't get tangled and hurt himself. Try to make him forget about it by playing or starting a short fun training routine with treats. Treats are a huge distraction for most young Goldens. While he is concentrating on the new task, occasionally pick up the lead and call him to you. Do it gently and in an encouraging tone.

5.   The most important thing is not to yank on the lead. If it is gets tight, just lure him back beside you with a treat or a toy while walking. All you're doing is getting him to move around beside you. Remember to keep your hand down (the one holding the treat or toy) so your dog doesn't get the habit of jumping up at you. If you feel he is getting stressed when walking outside on a lead, try putting treats along the route you'll be taking to turn this into a rewarding game: good times are ahead... That way he learns to focus on what's ahead of him with curiosity and not fear.

Take collar and lead training slowly, give your pup time to process all this new information about the lead. Let him gain confidence in you, and then in the lead and himself. Some dogs can sit and decide not to move. If this happens, walk a few steps away, go down on one knee and encourage him to come to you using a treat, then walk off again.

For some pups, the collar and lead can be restricting and they will react with resistance. Some dogs are perfectly happy to walk alongside you off-lead, but behave differently when they have one on. Proceed in tiny steps if that is what your puppy is happy with, don't over face him, but stick at it if you are met with resistance. With training and patience, your puppy will learn to walk nicely on a lead; it is a question of when, not if.

Walking on a Lead

There are different methods, but we have found the following one to be successful for quick results. Initially, the lead should be kept fairly loose. Have a treat in your hand as you walk, it will encourage your dog to sniff the treat as he walks alongside. He will not pull ahead as he will want to remain near the treat.

Give him the command Walk or Heel and then proceed with the treat in your hand, keep giving him a treat every few steps initially, then gradually extend the time between treats. Eventually, you should be able to walk with your hand comfortably at your side, periodically (every minute or so) reaching into your pocket to grab a treat to reward your dog.

If your dog starts pulling ahead, first give him a warning, by saying 'No' or 'Steady', or a similar command. If he slows down, give him a treat. But if he continues to pull ahead so that your arm becomes fully extended, stop walking and ignore your dog. Wait for him to stop pulling and to look up at you. At this point reward him for good behaviour before carrying on your walk. Be sure to quickly reward him with treats and praise any time he doesn't pull and walks with you with the lead slack. If you have a lively young pup who is dashing all over the place on the lead, try starting training when he is already a little tired - after a play or exercise session – (but not exhausted).

 Another way is what dog trainer Victoria Stillwell describes as the Reverse Direction Technique. When your dog pulls, say "Let's Go!" in an encouraging manner, then turn away from him and walk off in the other direction, without jerking on the lead. When he is following you and the lead is slack, turn back and continue on your original way. It may take a few repetitions, but your words and body language will make it clear that pulling will not get your dog anywhere, whereas walking calmly by your side - or even slightly in front of you - on a loose lead will get him where he wants to go. There is an excellent video (in front of her beautiful house!) which shows Victoria demonstrating this technique and highlights just how easy it is with a dog that's easy to please. It only lasts three minutes and is well worth watching: https://positively.com/dog-behavior/basic-cues/loose-leash-walking.

....

Therapy Work

by Liz Spicer-Short

Goldens can be trained to a high level in several different fields, and one of these is therapy work. Liz Spicer-Short, of Priorschest Golden Retrievers, Dorset, UK, has bred Goldens for a quarter of a century. But her love affair with the breed goes back even further, to her childhood of more than 40 years ago. Here Liz takes us on a personal journey that illustrates the unique temperament of the Golden Retriever and why these dogs are so naturally suited to therapy and assistance work. She also gives an insight into raising her pups.

On my grandfather's 70th birthday he gave my sister and I £50 (about $70) each; a huge amount of money in the mid-1970s. I can't recall what Carrie did with her money, but I knew immediately - I wanted a Golden Retriever! We were moving house, so I had to wait a little over a year. Then, when I was nine years old, Honey came into our lives - and there has been a Golden there ever since.

Honey was a big male dog, square standing, with a handsome head and a kind heart. I remember him chewing Dad's newly-planted grapevine right down to the base and eating a dishcloth just before a 12-hour drive up to Scotland! But apart from that, he was a good friend, a loyal companion and great fun to have around. I am the eldest of four children, so growing up there were often lots of kids running around and he was always gentle and kind; a perfect family dog.

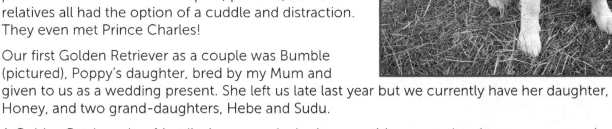

Skip forward 20 years or so. Due to my working shifts as a police officer, I didn't have a dog to call my own - but knew it was only a matter of time. My parents had Bella, then Poppy and her daughter, Lucky. My husband-to-be Rupert used to collect Poppy and Lucky from my parents and visit the local hospice; patients, staff and relatives all had the option of a cuddle and distraction. They even met Prince Charles!

Our first Golden Retriever as a couple was Bumble (pictured), Poppy's daughter, bred by my Mum and given to us as a wedding present. She left us late last year but we currently have her daughter, Honey, and two grand-daughters, Hebe and Sudu.

A Golden Retriever is a friendly, happy soul who loves nothing more than human company (and a muddy puddle!) - but a good therapy dog is made out of good raw material; it doesn't just happen. They need to be given lots of different, but positive, experiences, see lots of people, vehicles and situations, so that in the end they say, "I've never seen / done that before, but if you say it's OK, then I'll come with you."

That bond of trust takes time to build up and Pets As Therapy (PAT), the charity we work with, will not accept a dog for assessment until they are at least nine months old. When we lived in West Cork, Ireland, for a while, we were asked to go to a city centre hotel for a photo shoot as regular volunteers at the local hospice there. The car park was underground, and the lift had mirrors in it. Bumble did have a bit of a look, but walked in because she trusted us. There was then a massive marble-floored foyer but she took it all in her stride and was soon fast asleep on the carpet.

Puppies and young dogs need to gain experience, and a general training class is a good start. The one we go to follows the Kennel Club Good Citizen Scheme, from Puppy Foundation, through Bronze, Silver and Gold awards. It is a good start and any dog and handler that pass the Gold test can be rightly proud of themselves, it is a real achievement.

There are lots of establishments that are keen to have a Pets as Therapy dog visiting; at present we visit our local primary school and also a specialist college for children with learning difficulties and autism. The visits are structured, with one handler per dog - at the primary school a selected child reads out loud to us (one adult and one dog) for about twenty minutes, then has a hug and chat to the dog before going back to class. I sit on a beanbag with the child beside me, we each hold one side of the reading book and the spare hand is usually stroking the dog as we read!

At the specialist college the sessions are more structured around the child's specific needs - some benefit from quiet time, in which case the dog lies on the floor and has a brush and a stroke from the child. Other sessions are more physical, for instance based on the adventure playground or an impromptu obstacle course. The dogs won't have seen these before but they definitely know they are 'working' and rarely put a foot wrong. I am constantly humbled by what they achieve. It is not uncommon for a child to come to us having had a really challenging morning, spend half an hour with the dogs and go back to class much calmer and happier.

One thing to note is that the work really does challenge the dogs and they are often very tired after a visit. We make sure that they have breaks and they always have access to water. As a therapy dog handler, I make sure that the dogs are clean and that their nails are clipped short.

Most of the children at the schools we visit are keen to talk to the dogs, but it is important that the dogs do not take this for granted and they also need to accept the instruction to 'settle down' quietly beside us whilst we talk to someone. This is an instruction we use a lot at home - they learn that they haven't done anything wrong, but that there are times when they need to lie quietly without human interaction.

Another 'practice' we allow at home is that their front legs are allowed up on our laps only if instructed and for as long as we want and no longer. This is really useful when they visit a wheelchair user that wants to chat to them. Dogs cannot self-support this pose comfortably for

very long and should be allowed to get down as soon as they want to. They must not bark at or lick people whilst visiting and cannot 'give a paw' even if asked to by a child - if they did this to an elderly person with thin skin there is a chance of injury.

Although there is no way of objectively measuring the benefit of dog therapy, there is no doubt in my mind that it is a hugely positive activity. The dogs really enjoy it and over the years we have met some really lovely people through visiting.

(Stock photo of PAT Golden Retriever visiting boy in hospital).

As a Kennel Club Assured Breeder of Golden Retrievers, I know all my puppies from birth and the stud dog used is carefully selected both for temperament and soundness. Although an elbow score is not currently mandatory in the breed, vets are seeing more and more dogs with elbow dysplasia, and I will not breed from one of my girls or use a stud dog that has not had a clear (i.e. 0/0) elbow score. Whilst nothing in life is certain, you have more chance of ending up with a healthy, sound adult dog if you buy from health tested stock in the first place.

If you are thinking of buying a puppy it is really important to start your research early and accept that a puppy is not something you can buy 'off the shelf'. We prefer families to visit us and meet our dogs at home well before the pregnancy is even planned. We can talk through all aspects of dog ownership and they see how we care for, train and interact with our dogs. We don't have visitors here for a week before puppies are due or until the litter is four weeks old, then we invite the new owners to visit and choose which puppy they want to join their family. The pups are identified with individual coloured Velcro collars until they are microchipped at six and a half weeks old, and between seven and eight weeks old they go to their new homes.

We give our puppies the best upbringing we can, with lots of interaction and visitors. From about four weeks' old onwards, they spend their days in a large pen in our sitting room getting used to a variety of household noises, people and the older dogs being around, and then we take them back to a separate pen to sleep overnight. This way they get plenty of peace and quiet, but also get used to everyday life going on around them. I am sure that this approach sets them up well for being happy, adaptable dogs in the future and I always impress upon new owners that they need to give their puppy as many constructive experiences as possible. For instance, a dog who has never seen or heard a vacuum cleaner working might be quite genuinely terrified the first time he does, but if he has seen it regularly from an early age it won't be a problem.

Young dogs have a short attention span, so it is important not to overload them, and to make training fun and positive.

Breeders on Training

Sue Page, of Dormansue Golden Retrievers, Surrey, also has a therapy dog: "One of my dogs just loves being a PAT dog. PAT dogs have to go and sit with the people they are visiting. Daisy is so used to this that when we go down to our local vet's or even her dog classes, she just goes and sits with the person next to me as she thinks that is what is expected of her.

"Any dog used as a PAT dog can't paw people, as this would break an elderly person's skin and they also must not jump up. Daisy absolutely loves her visits to an elderly people's home and it enriches so many people's lives.

"My dogs both do agility during the summer and they have so much fun. It doesn't take them long to learn how to use the equipment, especially as they are rewarded with a small piece of cheese every time they get it right. The dogs always do much better than their owners at agility, as on a complicated course the owners often forget which piece of equipment their dog is supposed to go to next and point their dogs in totally the wrong direction! It's a great place to meet other dog owners and we all have such a laugh.

"They have also done a lot of obedience training and our club follows the Good Citizen Dog Training Scheme. It is fun to do and it is amazing the bad habits it corrects in owners. For instance, we are taught to ensure that our dogs never jump out of the back of a vehicle before they are commanded to do so."

Sue has lots of tips for new owners: "Golden Retrievers only ever want to please you, so they are very easy to obedience train. I tell all my new owners - and it is written into the sales contract - that they must take their dog to puppy socialisation classes. If you don't socialise your puppy when it is young with both people and dogs, then you can have a lifelong problem. It is now known that puppies learn the most from birth to 16 weeks of age, so it is vitally important that you allow your puppy to experience as many new things as possible during this time. You should give your puppy loads of reassurance when doing this.

"What the puppies take for granted at this stage in their lives will be what they will be happy with in their adult lives. It is sometimes fun for new owners to be thinking about this while waiting to take ownership of their new puppy. Whilst with me, they hear lots of household appliances and are visited by countless strangers as we work from home and everyone wants to see the puppies. When the puppies go to their new owners, they should be seeing things like horses, people with walking sticks, the beach, small children. If you don't have them in your household, go to the pub or basically do anything that you might expect them to be happy doing as adult dogs.

"Having lots of trips in the car is extremely important. I suggest to my owners that they start by putting their dogs in the car for no more than five minutes and take their dog for a lovely walk. This means that if a puppy is worrying about the car that you will be getting out again before the puppy really starts fretting. He quickly learns to associate the car with a joyful experience at the end of it. However, you must remember you need someone to hold the puppy for the first few weeks, as being put in the back of the car on its own is an extremely frightening experience."

We asked other breeders how easy Golden Retrievers are to train and if they had any tips to share. This is what they said, starting with the UK. Anna Cornelius-Jones: "Obedience training comes easy to most Goldens. I always encourage my new owners to attend some form of puppy and training classes early on. As this breed is renowned for wanting to please, they are very easy learners. Even if you have had dogs before or have another dog at home, your new puppy may not follow the rules and bad habits can be learnt.

"One thing that I find really useful is that, if when training your new puppy it doesn't seem to be 'getting it', then try something different. If you push too much with one discipline and they get bored, you may find that when you try again, they will resist what you are trying to teach them. Small sessions in small doses."

Claire Underwood: "Golden Retrievers are very responsive to obedience training. My tip would be go to puppy socialising; it teaches them when to 'leave' saying hello and when it is OK to say hello (to other dogs and to people). Don't let them get ahead of you, i.e. going out through doors or mugging you for their feeds, they can rule the roost and need to know you are in charge. They forget rules if not consistent."

Dee Johnson: "They are really easy to train and also very eager to please. Again, as with toilet training, I use certain words, which I use repeatedly when touching that toy. With Recall outside, I use food rewards. They pick it up so easily, but it's important to keep it up and train regularly." Wendy Pickup: "Goldens are generally easy to train, although they can be stubborn at times. My training tip is to use reward-based repetition - food or a favourite toy, whichever works best for the individual dog."

Nicholas Lock: "We use chopped fresh cooked liver to teach recall; they love it and it's a healthier option to chemical treats." Stephen and Jessica Webb: "Goldies are very easy to obedience train; they love to show their intelligence. We would advise all puppy owners to go to classes! There's no such thing as a bad dog, only bad owners."

Lisa Mellor: "Retrievers are always keen to be involved and engaged and so training, if handled correctly, is easy and straightforward. They are a smart breed and they are so keen to please - so both qualities you want and need. As far as tips go: start as you mean to go on (so, from a puppy) and be consistent. Use simple, one-word commands as it is much clearer, make training fun.

"Be happy and excited with them as they respond so much better – they want to please. And do give rewards, not all the time as otherwise it will always be expected, and it doesn't always have to be food treats." Photo of Cassie and pups, courtesy of Lisa

Jan Schick: "I have always found Golden Retrievers to be quick learners. They are so eager to please and the majority are treat-focused! A tip I give new owners is to establish the 'sit' command even before going to puppy training classes by saying 'sit' every time the puppy sits by itself. It soon learns to match the command with the action and it is such a useful skill i.e. a puppy cannot run if it is sitting and a puppy cannot jump up if it is sitting."

Lesley Gunter: "On the whole, they train really well. Goldens want to work and to please, and if you use positive training methods and are consistent with the training, they are a pleasure to train. They are usually greedy, so use tiny food treats each time a puppy does something you like, and they will soon get the message.

"I work with an obedience training school, so I would always advise people find a good local class. This is a great way to socialise a puppy, and to learn how to work with your dog and have fun whilst embedding some of the basic training exercises, such as walking to heel, stay, wait, recall and leave it. Key tips are: be consistent, all the family should use the same words and apply the same rules, such as where the dog is allowed to go in the house. Remember that your tone of voice is as important if not more important than the words you use. Teach your dog to be ignored – don't always give affection when they demand it, but on your terms. Retrievers can be quite demanding of attention, so this is really important. You are in charge!"

Julian Pottage: "As biddable dogs who like food, Goldens respond very well to reward-based training. Get a Golden puppy and you may find you have the star of the dog training class! My one tip is to go to a training class, no matter how many dogs you have had before. The distraction of having other puppies around does make a big difference." Karen Parsons: "These are such intelligent dogs, they train very easily. I recommend regular short training sessions, always finish on a good note and reward their skills."

George Coxwell: "Goldens train very well, as in all things the more time spent, the quicker they learn. However, I do feel some working lines respond better; I think some things are bred into the dog." Karen Ireland: "They are so easy to train. They live for food – any type, so if you want them to do anything, just have a treat in your hand and a clicker. Clickers are good too, show dogs what you want them to do, wait and if they respond, click, treat and praise. Repetition is the name of the game. They are very bright and pick up the tasks very quickly. My pups at five weeks old could sit, wait and come when called – chicken was the answer!"

Tim Hoke, USA: "Golden Retrievers are amazingly easy to train. It still amazes me that people pay us to train their puppies. We believe in both correction and reward. If the puppy makes a mistake, correct them as soon as possible, encourage them to behave correctly so you can reward them for appropriate behavior."

Kelly Sisco, USA: "My training tips are consistency and treats. I also recommend a puppy class to all of my puppy parents. Contrary to the old saying that old dogs can be taught new tricks - to sit, walk on a leash, down, recall, etc. – this is more difficult to do as dogs get older... so socialize that puppy early!"

Photo of two-year-old Benelli (Show Me Shootin' A Benelli CGCA CGCU RN) relaxing at home, courtesy of Kelly.

Helen Dorrance, USA: "Goldens are incredibly easy to train. Get a book on dog training and train your puppy for 10 to 15 minutes every day (with food treats) and you will be impressed with how much the puppy learns. Also make sure to properly socialize the puppy, which means you must take it off the premises by itself (no other companion dogs with it) for at least 20 minutes a week until it is four and a half months old. Puppy kindergarten classes are also very important. You can train a golden in a month to get a CD (Companion Dog) and in three months to get a novice agility title."

....

GENERAL NOTE: If your puppy is in a hyperactive mood or extremely tired, he is not likely to be very receptive to training.

CREDIT: With thanks to the American Society for the Prevention of Cruelty to Animals for assistance with parts of this chapter. The ASPCA has a great deal of good advice and training tips on **its website at:** www.aspca.org

....

11. Golden Retriever Health

When it comes to choosing and raising a dog, good health should always be a major consideration. Health has a major impact on quality of life. The first step is to select a puppy from a breeder who health screens her dogs and, secondly, to play your part in keeping your Goldie healthy throughout his or her life.

It is becoming increasingly evident that genetics can have a huge influence on a person's health and life expectancy – which is why so much time and money is currently being devoted to genetic research. A human is more likely to suffer from a hereditary illness if the gene - or genes - for that disorder is passed on from parents or grandparents. That person is said to have a 'predisposition' to the ailment if the gene(s) is in the family's bloodline. Well, the same is true of dogs.

There is not a single breed without the potential for some genetic weakness. For example, German Shepherd Dogs are more prone to hip problems than many other breeds, and 30% of Dalmatians have problems with their hearing. If you get a German Shepherd or a Dalmatian, your dog will not automatically suffer from these issues, but if he or she comes from unscreened parents, the dog will statistically be more likely to have them than a dog from a breed with no history of the complaint.

In other words, 'bad' genes can be inherited along with good ones.

You might have chosen your breeder based on the look of her dogs or maybe their ability to retrieve, but have you thought about the health of the puppy's parents and ancestors? Could they have passed on unhealthy genes to the puppy along with the good genes for all those features you are attracted to? **The way to reduce this risk is to health test.**

This is what The Golden Retriever Club (in the UK) says: "Golden retrievers are prone to several hereditary conditions – just to keep this in perspective with humans, the number is in the 100's. To try to control and eradicate these conditions, the British Veterinary Association (BVA), in conjunction with the Kennel Club (KC), have instigated three health schemes. Breeding stock are screened prior to mating and, although it is never possible to guarantee that clear parents will produce all-clear offspring, the likelihood is much increased:

"BVA/KC Eye Scheme - At present Goldens are examined for three eye conditions: Hereditary Cataract (HC), Progressive Retinal Atrophy (PRA) - now virtually eliminated in the UK – and Multifocal Retinal Dysplasia (MRD)."

"BVA/KC Hip Scheme - Under the BVA/KC scheme the dog's hips are X-rayed when the dog reaches a minimum of 12 months of age. The plates are then submitted to a specialist panel at the BVA who assess nine features of each hip, giving each feature a score."

"BVA/KC Elbow Scheme - This is the most recently introduced of the BVA schemes (March 1998). As it entails three x-rays of each elbow, some breeders feel that the risks outweigh the benefits.

"Elbow dysplasia is a multifactorial condition manifesting as a variety of developmental disorders of the elbow leading to osteoarthritis of the elbow joint.

"As the disease has a genetic component, screening should help breeders select suitable dogs for breeding. As with the hip scheme, the dog must be a minimum of 12 months of age before it is X-rayed for the scheme (hips and elbows are usually done at the same time) and the X-rays are sent off to be assessed by the BVA panel."

Anyone getting a Golden Retriever puppy is advised to check that the parents have the relevant certificates for hips, elbows and eyes. In the USA, these certificates will be issued by OFA (Orthopedic Foundation for Animals), or PennHIP. A small percentage of US Goldens are also are affected by a hereditary heart disease called Subvalvular Aortic Stenosis (SAS). Heart murmurs can be detected by a vet using a stethoscope and, if found, further tests are available. Look for the OFA all-clear certificate.

The Golden Retriever Club of America (GRCA) says: "The GRCA Code of Ethics requests that results from hip, elbow, eye, and heart examinations be placed in the public record on searchable databases, and the most widely used of such databases is provided by the Orthopedic Foundation for Animals at www.offa.org. Breeders often describe their dogs as "hip, elbow, eye, and heart certified" or as having "all their clearances" and these statements usually can be verified on the OFA website. Records can be accessed by searching using the dog's full registered name (with exact spelling) or registration number, and reputable breeders should not hesitate to provide you with this information."

'Hip scoring' and 'elbow scoring,' as the joint tests are called, are now an everyday part of producing healthy Golden Retriever puppies among responsible breeders. If you see a 'cheap' Golden or litter advertised, it is often because little or no screening has taken place. It's an indisputable fact; health tests cost money.

Golden Retrievers are also known to have a higher incidence of certain types of cancer than many other dog breeds. Although there is no genetic test for cancer, ask the breeder if there is any history of cancer in her bloodlines.

There is no 100% guarantee of perfect health for any dog - or human - but the chances of your dog suffering from an ailment the parents have successfully been screened for will be greatly reduced. That is true of hip and elbow dysplasia, which are caused by a combination of genes. And the good news is that health testing is helping to eradicate such diseases as PRA within the breed - see Eye Diseases later in this chapter for more detail.

So the best way of getting off to a good start is by choosing a puppy from health-tested parents. Of course, this may not be possible if you are taking on a dog from someone else or a rescue centre. If so, do try and get as much background health information as you can.

And be aware that just because the puppy and parents are registered with the Kennel Club (or AKC in the USA) and have pedigree certificates, it does not necessarily mean that they have passed any health tests. All a pedigree certificate guarantees is that the puppy's parents can be traced back several generations and the ancestors were all purebred Golden Retrievers. Many pedigree (purebred) dogs have indeed passed health tests, but prospective buyers should always find out **exactly** what health screening the sire and dam (mother and father) have undergone - ask to see original certificates - and what, if any, health guarantees the breeder is offering with the puppy.

Once you have your dog, much of the rest is up to you. Taking good care of him or her by feeding a quality food, monitoring your dog's weight, giving plenty of exercise, socialisation and stimulation, as well as regular grooming and check-overs will all help to keep your Goldie happy and healthy.

NOTE: This chapter is intended to be used as a medical encyclopaedia to help you to identify any potential issues and act on them promptly in the best interests of your dog. Read each section to see which ones are the most common health issues to affect Golden Retrievers in particular, and which are relevant to the dog population in general. **Your Golden Retriever will NOT get all of these ailments!**

....

Golden Retriever Insurance

Insurance is another point to consider for a new puppy or adult dog. The best time to get pet insurance is BEFORE you bring your Golden Retriever home and before any health issues develop. Don't wait until you need to seek veterinary help - bite the bullet and take out annual insurance. If you can afford it, take out life cover. This may be more expensive, but will cover your dog throughout his or her lifetime - including for chronic (recurring and/or long term) ailments, such as eye or joint problems, ear infections, and cancer.

Insuring a healthy puppy or adult dog is the only sure-fire way to ensure vets' bills are covered before anything unforeseen happens - and you'd be a rare owner if you didn't use your policy at least once during your dog's lifetime. According to the UK's Bought By Many, the Golden Retriever is somewhere in the middle when it comes to costs. The average monthly cost is £31.16 – although this varies based on a number of factors, including where you live – and compares with £7.43 for a Standard Poodle to £57.58 for a Boxer.

Bought By Many offers policies from insurers More Than at https://boughtbymany.com/offers/golden-retriever-insurance They get groups of single breed owners together, so you have to join the Golden Retriever Group, but it claims you'll get a 10% saving on normal insurance. We are not on commission - just trying to save you some money! There are numerous companies out there offering pet insurance. Read the small print and the amount of excess; a cheap policy may not always be the best long-term decision.

In the US, a good policy starts at around $35 per month, depending on where you live and how much excess you're willing to pay.

According to Pet Insurance Quotes in the USA, typical costs if your dog suffers from the following diseases are: Canine Cancer $5,000 to $20,000, Hip Dysplasia $4,000 to $6,000, Elbow Dysplasia $3,000 to $5,000, Cataracts $2,000 to $3,000. Full list here: www.petinsurancequotes.com/petinsurance/golden-retriever-dogs.html With advances in veterinary science, there is so much more vets can do to help an ailing dog - but at a cost. Surgical procedures can rack up bills of thousands of pounds or dollars. Pet Insurance Quotes rated insurance companies based on coverage, cost, customer satisfaction and the company itself and came up with a top dozen: 1. Healthy Paws, 2. Nationwide, 3. Petplan, 4. Pets Best, 5. Embrace, 6. Trupanion, 7. Figo, 8. Pets First, 9. ASPCA, 10. Pet Premium, 11. Pet Insurance, 12. 24PetWatch.

Of course if you make a claim, your monthly premium will increase, but if you have a decent insurance policy BEFORE a recurring health problem starts, your dog should continue to be covered if the ailment returns. You'll have to decide whether the insurance is worth the money. On the plus side, you'll have peace of mind if your devoted Golden Retriever falls ill and you'll know just how much to fork out every month.

Another point to consider is that dogs are at increasing risk of theft by criminals, including organised gangs. With the purchase price of puppies rising, dognapping more than quadrupled in the UK between 2010 and 2015, with around 50 dogs a day being stolen. Some 49% of dogs are snatched from owners' gardens and 13% from people's homes. Check that theft is included on the policy. Although nothing can ever replace your beloved companion, good insurance will ensure you are not out of pocket.

The information in this chapter is not written to frighten new owners, but to help you to recognise symptoms of the main conditions affecting Golden Retrievers and enable you to take prompt action, should the need arise. There are also a number of measures you can take to prevent or reduce the chances of certain physical and behavioural problems developing, including regular daily exercise, socialisation, a good diet and keeping their weight in check.

Three Golden Tips

1. **Buy a well-bred puppy** - A responsible breeder selects their stock based on:

   🐾 Temperament

   🐾 General health and DNA testing of the parents

🐾 Conformation (physical structure)

🐾 The ability to do a job (with working Retrievers in particular)

Although well-bred puppies are not cheap, believe it or not, committed Golden Retriever breeders are not in it for the money, often incurring high bills for health screening, veterinary fees, specialised food, etc. The main concern of a good breeder is to produce healthy puppies with good temperaments and instincts that are 'fit for function.'

Better to spend time beforehand choosing a good puppy than to spend a great deal of time and money later when your wonderful pet bought from an online advert or pet shop develops health problems due to poor breeding, not to mention the heartache that causes. **Chapter 4. Choosing a Puppy** has detailed information on how to find him or her and the questions to ask.

🐾 Don't buy from a pet shop - no reputable breeder allows her pups to end up in pet shops

🐾 Don't buy a puppy from a small ad on a general website

🐾 Don't buy a pup or adult dog unseen with a credit card - you are storing up trouble and expense for yourself. (If you have selected a reputable breeder located many states away in the USA and can't travel to see the puppy, make sure you ask lots of questions)

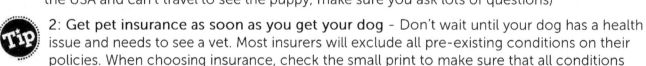

2: Get pet insurance as soon as you get your dog - Don't wait until your dog has a health issue and needs to see a vet. Most insurers will exclude all pre-existing conditions on their policies. When choosing insurance, check the small print to make sure that all conditions are covered and that if the problem is recurring, it will continue to be covered year after year. When working out costs, factor in the annual or monthly pet insurance fees and trips to a vet for check-ups, annual vaccinations, etc.

3: Find a good vet - Ask around your pet-owning friends, rather than just going to the first one you find. A vet that knows your dog from his or her puppy vaccinations and then right through their life is more likely to understand your dog and diagnose quickly and correctly

when something is wrong. If you visit a big veterinary practice, ask for the vet by name when you make an appointment. We all want our dogs to be healthy - so how can you tell if yours is? Well, here are some positive things to look for in a healthy Golden Retriever:

....

Signs of a Healthy Golden Retriever

1. **Eyes** - A healthy Golden Retriever's eyes are dark brown, sometimes medium brown, with dark rims. Paleness around the eyeball (conjunctiva) could be a sign of underlying problems. A red swelling in the corner of one or both eyes could be cherry eye. Sometimes the dog's third eyelid (the nictating membrane) is visible at the eye's inside corner - this is normal. There should be no thick, green or yellow discharge from the eyes. A cloudy eye could be a sign of cataracts.

2. **Nose** – A dog's nose is an indicator of health symptoms. Regardless of colour, it should normally be moist and cold to the touch as well as free from clear, watery secretions. Any yellow, green or foul smelling discharge is not normal - in younger dogs this can be a sign of canine distemper. The nose should preferably be black, although dark brown is acceptable.

   A pink nose or 'snow nose' may appear in winter due to a lack of Vitamin D, but the nose usually returns to a darker colour during summer. Some Golden Retrievers' noses turn pinkish with aging; this is because their bodies are producing less pigment and is not a cause for concern. (A 'Dudley nose,' more often seen in Labradors, is one where the nose, the area around the eyes and the feet lack any pigment from birth to old age and appear pink).

3. **Ears** – If you are choosing a puppy, gently clap your hands behind the pup (not so loud as to frighten him) to see if he reacts. If not, this may be a sign of deafness. Also, ear infections – sometimes known at "otitis" - can be a problem with some Goldens and other breeds with floppy ears. A pricked-up ear allows air to circulate, while a folded ear flap creates a warm, moist haven for mini horrors such as bacteria and mites. The ear flap can also trap dirt and dust and should be inspected during your regular grooming routine. An unpleasant smell, redness or inflammation are all signs of infection. Some wax inside the ear – usually brown or yellowy - is normal; lots of wax or crusty wax is not. Tell-tale signs of an infection are scratching the ears, rubbing them on the floor or furniture, or shaking the head a lot, often accompanied by an unpleasant smell.

4. **Mouth** – Gums should be a healthy pink or black colour, or a mixture. A change in colour can be an indicator of a health issue. Paleness or whiteness can be a sign of anaemia or lack of oxygen due to heart or breathing problems (this is hard to tell with black gums). Blue gums or tongue are a sign that your Goldie is not breathing properly. Red, inflamed gums can be a sign of gingivitis or other tooth disease. Again, your dog's breath should smell OK.

Young dogs will have sparkling white teeth, whereas older dogs will have darker teeth, but they should not have any hard white, yellow, green or brown bits.

5. **Coat and skin** – These are easy-to-monitor indicators of a healthy dog. A Golden Retriever has a dense double coat, and the outer waterproof layer of coat should look healthy, if somewhat coarse to the touch. Dandruff, bald spots, a dull lifeless coat, a discoloured or oily coat, or one that loses excessive hair, can all be signs that something is amiss. Skin should be smooth without redness. Normal skin pigment colour is black, but it can vary. If a puppy or adult dog is scratching, licking or biting himself a lot, he may have a condition that needs addressing before he makes it worse. Open sores, scales, scabs, red patches or growths can be a sign of a problem. Signs of fleas, ticks and other external parasites should be treated immediately. Check there are no small black specks, which may be fleas, on the coat or bedding.

6. **Weight** – It is a constant challenge for owners of some food-obsessed Golden Retrievers to keep them trim. A general rule of thumb is that your dog's stomach should be above the bottom of his rib cage when standing, and you should be able to feel his ribs beneath his coat without too much effort. Although show Golden Retrievers tend to be chunkier than their field counterparts, the rule still applies. If the stomach hangs below, the dog is overweight - or may have a pot belly, which can also be a symptom of other conditions.

7. **Temperature** – The normal temperature of a dog is 101°F to 102.5°F. (A human's is 98.6°F). Excited or exercising dogs may run a slightly higher temperature. Anything above 103°F or below 100°F should be checked out. The exceptions are female dogs about to give birth that will often have a temperature of 99°F. If you take your dog's temperature, make sure he or she is relaxed and *always* use a purpose-made canine thermometer, like the one pictured here for rectal use.

8. **Stools** - Poo, poop, business, faeces - call it what you will - it's the stuff that comes out of the less appealing end of your dog on a daily basis! It should be firm and brown, not runny, with no signs of worms or parasites. Watery stools or a dog not eliminating regularly are both signs of an upset stomach or other ailments. If it continues for a couple of days, consult your vet. If puppies have diarrhoea they need checking out much quicker as they can quickly dehydrate.

9. **Energy** – Golden Retrievers have fairly high energy levels. Your dog should have good amounts of energy with fluid and pain-free movements. Lack of energy or lethargy – if it is not the dog's normal character – could be a sign of an underlying problem.

10. **Smell** – There's no getting away from the fact that your Golden Retriever, with his long coat, almost certainly gives off a doggie odour (eau de dog!) This is perfectly normal - your Goldie should smell like a dog. However, if there is a musty, 'off' or generally unpleasant smell coming from his body, it could be a sign of a yeast infection. There can be a number of reasons for this; often the ears require attention or it can sometimes be an allergy to a certain food. Another reason for an unpleasant smell can be that one of the anal glands has become blocked and needs expressing, or squeezing - a job best left to the vet or groomer unless you know what you are doing! Whatever the cause, you need to get to the root of the problem as soon as possible before it develops into something more serious.

11. **Attitude** – A generally positive attitude is a sign of good health. Golden Retrievers are friendly, engaged and willing dogs, so symptoms of illness may include one or all of the following: a general lack of interest in his or her surroundings, tail not wagging, lethargy, not

eating food and sleeping a lot (more than normal). The important thing is to look out for any behaviour that is out of the ordinary for your individual dog.

So now you know some of the signs of a healthy dog – what are the signs of an unhealthy one? There are many different symptoms that can indicate your canine companion isn't feeling great. If you don't yet know your dog, his habits, temperament and behaviour patterns, then spend some time getting acquainted with him.

What are his normal character and temperament? Lively or calm, playful or serious, a joker or an introvert, bold or nervous, happy to be left alone or loves to be with people, a keen appetite or a fussy eater? How often does he empty his bowels, does he ever vomit? (Dogs will often eat grass to make themselves sick, this is perfectly normal and a natural way of cleansing the digestive system). You may think your Golden Retriever can't talk, **but he can!** If you really know your dog, his character and habits, then he CAN tell you when he's not well. He does this by changing his patterns.

Some symptoms are physical, some emotional and others are behavioural. It's important for you to be able to recognise these changes as soon as possible. Early treatment can be the key to keeping a simple problem from snowballing into something more serious. If you think your dog is unwell, it is useful to keep an accurate and detailed account of his symptoms to give to the vet, perhaps even take a video of him on your mobile phone. This will help the vet to correctly diagnose and effectively treat your dog.

Four Vital Signs of Illness

1. **Temperature** - A new-born puppy will have a temperature of 94-97ºF. This will reach the normal adult body temperature of 101ºF at about four weeks old. As stated, anything between 100ºF and 102.5ºF is regarded as normal for an adult dog. The temperature is normally taken via the rectum. If you do this, be very careful. It's easier if you get someone to hold your dog while you do this. Digital thermometers are a good choice, but **only use one specifically made for rectal use,** as normal glass thermometers can easily break off in the rectum. Ear thermometers are now available (pictured) - Walmart stocks them - making the task much easier, although they can be expensive and don't suit all dogs' ears. Remember that exercise or excitement can cause the temperature to rise by 2ºF to 3ºF when your dog is actually in good health, so wait until he is relaxed before taking his temperature. If it is above or below the norms and he seems off-colour, give your vet a call.

Ear Thermometer

2. **Respiratory Rate** - Another symptom of canine illness is a change in breathing patterns. This varies a lot depending on the size and weight of the dog. An adult dog will have a respiratory rate of 15-25 breaths per minute when resting. You can easily check this by counting your dog's breaths for a minute with a stopwatch handy. Don't do this if he is panting; it doesn't count.

3. **Heart Rate** - You can feel your Golden Retriever's heartbeat by placing your hand on his lower ribcage – just behind the elbow. Don't be alarmed if the heartbeat seems irregular compared to that of a human; it IS irregular in some dogs. Your dog will probably love the attention, so it should be quite easy to check his heartbeat. Just lay him on his side and bend his left front leg at the elbow, bring the elbow in to his chest and place your fingers on this area and count the beats.

   - Toy dogs have a heartbeat of up to 160 or 180 beats per minute
   - Small dogs have a normal rate of 90 to 140 beats per minute
   - Dogs weighing more than 30lb have a heart rate of 60 to 120 beats per minute; the larger the dog, the slower the normal heart rate
   - A young puppy has a heartbeat of around 220 beats per minute
   - An older dog has a slower heartbeat

4. **Behaviour Changes** - Classic symptoms of illness are any inexplicable behaviour changes. If there has NOT been a change in the household atmosphere, such as another new pet, a new baby, moving home, the absence of a family member or the loss of another dog, then the following symptoms may well be a sign that all is not well:

   - Depression
   - Anxiety and/or trembling
   - Falling or stumbling
   - Loss of appetite
   - Walking in circles
   - Being more vocal - grunting, whining and/or whimpering
   - Aggression – Golden Retrievers are normally extremely friendly
   - Tiredness - sleeping more than normal and/or not wanting to exercise
   - Abnormal posture

Your dog may normally show some of these signs, but if any of them appear for the first time or worse than usual, you need to keep him under close watch for a few hours or even days. Quite often he will return to normal of his own accord. Like humans, dogs have off-days too.

If he is showing any of the above symptoms, then don't over-exercise him, and avoid stressful situations and hot or cold places. Make sure he has access to clean water. There are many other signals of ill health, but these are four of the most important. Keep a record for your vet, if your dog does need professional medical attention, most vets will want to know:

WHEN the symptoms first appeared in your dog

WHETHER they are getting better or worse, and

HOW FREQUENT the symptoms are. Are they intermittent, continuous or increasing?

We have highlighted some of the indicators of good and poor health to help you monitor your dog's wellbeing. Getting to know his or her character, habits and temperament will go a long way towards spotting the early signs of ill health.

Hip Dysplasia

Hip Dysplasia (HD) - or Canine Hip Dysplasia (CHD) as it is also called - is the most common cause of hind leg lameness in dogs. Dysplasia means 'abnormal development,' and dogs with this condition develop painful degenerative arthritis of the hip joints. The hips are the uppermost joints on the rear legs of a dog, either side of the tail. HD is also the most common inherited orthopaedic problem seen in dogs. It can affect virtually all breeds, but is more common in large breeds, and one of these is the Golden Retriever, where the disease is well documented. America's OFA has tested more than 148,000 Golden Retrievers since 1974, and the BVA 14,000 in the UK. Although 'hip scoring' - the name given to the medical evaluation- is reducing the percentage of afflicted dogs, the Golden is still a breed known to be affected.

The UK's Golden Retriever Club explains the testing system: "Under the BVA/KC scheme the dog's hips are X-rayed when the dog reaches a minimum of 12 months of age. The plates are then submitted to a specialist panel at the BVA who assess nine features of each hip, giving each feature a score. The lower the score, the better the hips, so the range can be from 0 (clear) to 106 (badly dysplastic). The breed average is currently about 19. Dogs with 0:0 hips are very much the exception, rather than the rule. The parents' hip scores are shown on the puppy's registration as the score for each hip, e.g. 10:9 which would be 19, i.e. breed average."

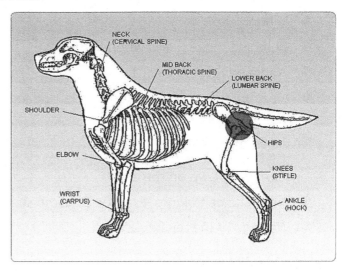

In the USA, the Golden Retriever has the 43rd highest hip scores out of 143 breeds tested by the OFA, with a median score of 10. This means that half of all Goldens in the USA have a hip score lower (better) than 10, and the other half are higher. NOTE: This is for each hip, so the combined score would be 20 if both hips scored 10. Dogs must be 24 months of age in the USA before they can receive their final hip certification.

The Golden Retriever Club of America recommends testing for hips, elbows, eyes and heart, and explains why it is so important to test breeding dogs: "All prospective puppy buyers want their new puppy to have the best possible chance for a long and healthy life, and regular veterinary care is important toward achieving that goal. But in addition, the risks for many significant health issues can be greatly reduced through careful breeding practices, beginning with certain screening examinations of the parents of a litter.

"Each breed (and mixed-bred dogs too) has its own particular hereditary problems, and Golden Retrievers are no exception. Failure to screen for these conditions before breeding results in taking unnecessary risks for genetic disease, and frequently leads to distress for the buyer and dog alike. Reputable breeders are expected to conduct screening examinations for these diseases on the parents of a litter, and to disclose the results to prospective puppy buyers."

What Exactly is Hip Dysplasia?

The hip is a ball and socket joint. Hip dysplasia is caused when the head of the femur (thigh bone) fits loosely into a shallow and poorly developed socket in the pelvis. Most dogs with dysplasia are born with normal hips, but due to their genetic make-up, and sometimes caused by or worsened by other factors, such as over-exercising young dogs, diet or obesity, the soft tissues that surround the joint develop abnormally.

The joint carrying the weight of the dog becomes loose and unstable, muscle growth lags behind normal growth and is often followed by degenerative joint disease, or osteoarthritis, which is the body's attempt to stabilise the loose hip joint. A dog with canine hip dysplasia often starts to show signs between five and 18 months old. Occasionally an affected dog will display no symptoms at all, while others may experience anything from mild discomfort to extreme pain. Early diagnosis gives a vet the best chance to tackle the problem, minimising the chance of arthritis developing. If your dog shows any of the following symptoms, it's time to get him to a vet:

- Lameness in the hind legs, particularly after exercise
- Difficulty or stiffness when getting up or climbing uphill
- A 'bunny hop' gait
- Dragging the rear end when getting up
- Waddling rear leg gait
- A painful reaction to stretching the hind legs, resulting in a short stride
- A side-to-side sway of the croup (area above the tail) with a tendency to tilt the hips down if you push down on the croup
- A reluctance to jump, exercise or climb stairs
- Wastage of the thigh muscle(s)

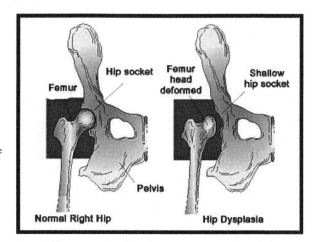

Causes and Triggers

While hip dysplasia is usually inherited, other factors can trigger or worsen the condition, including:

- Too much exercise, especially while the dog is still growing
- Extended periods without exercise
- Overfeeding, especially on a diet high in protein and calories
- Excess calcium, also usually due to overfeeding
- Obesity, which places excess stress on joints
- As with humans, damp or cold weather can worsen arthritic symptoms

Diet can play a role in the development of hip dysplasia. Feeding a high-calorie diet to growing dogs can trigger a predisposition to HD, as the rapid weight gain places increased stress on the hips. During their first year or so of life, it is particularly important that Golden Retriever puppies are fed a diet that contains the right amount of calories, minerals and protein, thereby reducing the risk of hip dysplasia. Ask your breeder or vet for advice.

Dogs that have a predisposition to the disease may have an increased chance of getting it if they are over-exercised at a young age. Young Golden Retrievers can be very lively and it's tempting to give them lots of exercise to help them burn off steam, but caution is required. Too much walking on hard surfaces, such as tarmac or concrete, as well as allowing a puppy to run up and down stairs frequently, can also trigger the condition in young dogs. See **Chapter 9. Exercise** for more information.

The key is moderate, low impact exercise for fast-growing young dogs. Activities that strengthen the gluteus muscles, such as running (preferably on grass) and swimming, are probably a good idea. Whereas high impact activities that apply a lot of force to the joint - such as jumping and catching Frisbees, are not recommended with young Goldies – however energetic they are. For more information, visit www.bva.co.uk/Canine-Health-Schemes/Hip-Scheme

Prevention and Treatment

The best way to avoid having to deal with hip dysplasia is by getting a dog from a dam and sire that have been 'hip scored' with low results. Hip scoring is playing a vital role in reducing the number of affected dogs in the breeding pool. Keeping your dog at a healthy weight and avoiding strenuous exercise, especially when young, can also help. A hip certificate will have a number written as 9:8 or 9/8, giving a total of 17 and indicating the score for each hip. (The section of BVA certificate, below right, shows a low combined hip score of 10).It is also far better if the dog has evenly matched hips, rather than a low score for one and a high score for the other. The Kennel Clubs advise breeders to only breed from dogs that score below the breed average. In the USA, dogs are given a rating - the equivalent BVA score is in brackets:

Excellent (0-4, with no hip higher than 3)

Good (5-10, with no hip higher than 6)

Fair (11-18)

Borderline (19-25)

Mild (26-35)

Moderate (36-50)

Severe (51-106)

Section C – TO BE COMPLETED BY SCRUTINEERS

CERTIFICATE OF SCORING

HIP JOINT	Score Range	Right	Left	
Norberg angle	0-6	0	1	
Subluxation	0-6	2	3	
Cranial acetabular edge	0-6	2	2	
Dorsal acetabular edge	0-6	—	—	
Cranial effective acetabular rim	0-6	—	—	
Acetabular fossa	0-6	—	—	
Caudal acetabular edge	0-5	—	—	
Femoral head/neck exostosis	0-6	—	—	
Femoral head recontouring	0-6	—	—	
TOTALS (max possible 53 per column)		4	6	10

 ALWAYS ask to see certificates for both dam and sire, whichever country you live in. If you are getting a puppy, you should ideally be looking for parents with below average hip scores (i.e. below or close to 10 for each hip). Avoid buying a puppy from parents with high scores.

There is no 100% guarantee that a puppy from low scoring parents will not develop hip dysplasia, as the condition is caused by a combination of genes, rather than just a single gene. However, the chances of it happening are significantly reduced. As with most conditions, early detection leads to a better outcome.

Treatment is geared towards preventing the hip joint getting worse as well as decreasing pain, and various medical and surgical treatments are now available to ease the dog's discomfort and restore some mobility. Treatment depends upon several factors, such as age, how bad the problem is and, sadly, sometimes how much money you can afford for treatment – another reason for taking out early insurance.

Management of the condition usually consists of restricting exercise, keeping body weight down and then managing pain with analgesics and anti-inflammatory drugs. As with humans, cortisone injections may sometimes be used to reduce inflammation and swelling. Cortisone can be injected directly into the affected hip to provide almost immediate relief for a tender, swollen joint. In severe cases, surgery may be an option.

Elbow Dysplasia

Elbow Dysplasia (ED) is abnormal development of the elbow; it affects many breeds and is thought to be on the increase in the canine population. It is more commonly seen in medium to large fast-growing breeds, and the Golden Retriever is one of these, with about one in 10 being affected in the UK and one in nine in the USA, according to OFA statistics. (A dog's elbows are at the top of his or her front legs).

ED often starts in puppyhood, often at four to 10 months, although it can be later. It causes arthritis, which is painful, affects the dog for the rest of his life and is difficult to treat. There are a number of causes, but the biggest one is thought to be genetic, (45% to 71% of the chance of the disease occurring - Guthrie and Pidduck 1990). Dogs who show no symptoms can still be carriers of the disease. Other factors such as rate of growth, diet and level of exercise may influence the severity of the disease in an individual dog, but they cannot prevent it or reduce the potential of the dog to pass it on to offspring.

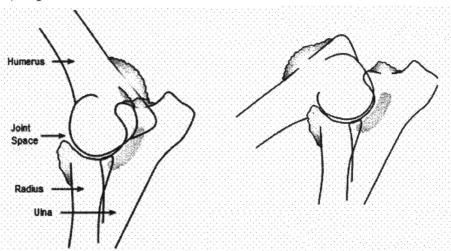

The shaded areas on the left (extended elbow) and right (flexed elbow) show the changes to bone and cartilage as a result of elbow dysplasia. Image courtesy of the BVA.

Many bones in a new-born puppy are not a single piece of bone, but several different pieces with cartilage in between. This is especially true of long limb bones. As the puppy grows, the cartilage changes into bone and several pieces of bone fuse together forming one entire bone (as in the diagram). For instance the ulna, a bone in the forearm, starts out as four pieces that eventually fuse into one bone. Some parts of the joint may have abnormal development, resulting in an uneven joint surface, inflammation, lameness and arthritis. It eventually causes elbow arthritis associated with joint stiffness (reduced range of motion) and lameness.

The most notable symptom is a limp. Your dog may hold his leg out away from his body while walking, or even lift a front leg completely, putting no weight on it. Signs may be noted as early as four months old and many dogs will go through a period between six months and a year old when symptoms will be at their worst. After this, some may show less severe symptoms. As yet there is no DNA test for Elbow Dysplasia. Vets can often diagnose the condition in young dogs well before they are old enough to be elbow scored; most dogs with diagnosed ED are never scored. Elbow score results are graded from zero (best) to three (worst). **Prospective owners should look for a 0/0 elbow score from a puppy's parents.**

Again there is no 100% guarantee because, as yet, there is no DNA test. This also means there is no way to identify breeding dogs that carry the genes for the ED, but who display no signs of it themselves. It is, however, a very good start to buy a puppy from zero-rated parents. For more info, visit www.bva.co.uk/canine-health-schemes/elbow-scheme

Treatment - Treatment varies depending on the exact cause of the condition. A young dog is usually placed on a regular, low-impact exercise programme - swimming can be good. Owners must carefully manage their dog's diet and weight. Oral or injected medication such as non-steroidal anti-inflammatory drugs (NSAIDS) may be necessary to make him more comfortable; they are prescribed to reduce pain and inflammation.

After the age of 12 to 18 months, sometimes a dog's lameness becomes less severe and some individuals function very well. In most cases, degenerative joint disease (arthritis) occurs as the dog gets older, regardless of the type of treatment. In some severe cases, a dog can be effectively helped with surgery.

If you live in the UK, visit the Kennel Club's **MyKC** online at www.thekennelclub.org.uk/our-resources/mykc where you can see the health results of your puppies' parents, and whether any pups have been affected by ED or any other hereditary disease.

Eye Conditions

Hereditary Cataracts (HC)

Cataracts occur when the lens of one or both eyes becomes cloudy, which prevents light passing through on to the retina at the back of the eye. This results in poor vision and, as the cataract covers more of the lens, can eventually lead to blindness in one or both eyes. Cataracts occur in many breeds. The type that most commonly affects the Golden Retriever is Juvenile Cataracts (JC), also known as Juvenile Hereditary Cataracts (JHC), where the defective gene is passed down from one or other parent. They usually develop when the dog is between one and three years of age.

The puppy or young dog's eyesight is not badly affected in many cases of Juvenile Cataracts. The dog still sees basic shapes, but they may be slightly blurry and if the puppy's cataracts are small, they can be watched and may not need any treatment. They are often "benign," i.e. they won't go away, but won't progress either. However, a dog with JC cannot get a CLEAR eye certificate and should not be bred. If you are buying a puppy, you should ask to see the parents' **current annual eye test certificates,** which show that the dog was clear on the day he or she was tested – although they do not guarantee that the dog will not develop cataracts in the future. All breeding stock should be tested annually.

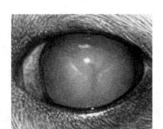 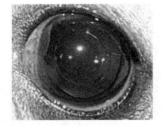

Left: eye with cataracts. Right: same eye with artificial lens

Some puppies born with (congenital) cataracts can improve as they mature. That's because the lens inside the puppy's eye grows along with the dog. When the area of cloudiness on the lens remains the same size, by the time the puppy becomes an adult, the affected portion of the lens is relatively small. By adulthood, many dogs born with cataracts are able to compensate and see "around" the cloudiness.

There are also non-hereditary cataracts. Just as with humans, cataracts can also develop later in a dog's life or old age when the body starts to deteriorate. In dogs aged six or older they are known as known as Senile or Late Onset Cataracts, and they are much less common in elderly dogs than in elderly humans. Other causes of cataracts are diabetes mellitus, trauma/injury, infection or toxins. Cataracts can affect the entire lens or a localised area. They may develop rapidly over weeks or slowly over years and can occur in one eye before the other.

Diagnosis and Treatment

Often no treatment is required for Juvenile Cataracts. However, you should always get them checked out by a vet straight away. And if your dog develops cataracts later in life, they are often progressive and require prompt treatment. You might notice a white film across your dog's eye(s), or that his pupils have changed colour, or the middle of the pupil may have a white spot or area. Try shining a flashlight at your dog's eyes or taking a picture with flash, you should see a coloured reflection in your dog's eyes. If you see something grey or dull white, it may be a cataract. Hereditary and late onset cataracts can also be diagnosed when the owner notices their dog bumping into furniture.

If you think your dog may have cataracts, it is important to get him to a vet as soon as possible. The vet will refer your dog to a specialist who will carry out the same eye exam that is done for breeding stock. The process is painless and simple, drops are put into the eyes and after a few minutes the dog is taken into a dark room for examination and diagnosis. Early removal of more serious cataracts can restore vision and provide a dramatic improvement in the quality of your dog's life. The only treatment for **severe** canine cataracts is surgery (unless the cataracts are caused by another condition like diabetes). Despite what you may have heard, laser surgery does not exist for canine cataracts, neither is there any proven medical treatment other than surgery.

Surgery is not cheap, it can cost thousands of pounds or dollars, but it is almost always (85%-90%+) successful. The dog has to have a general anaesthetic and the procedure is similar to small incision cataract surgery in people. An artificial lens is often implanted in the dog's eye to replace the cataract lens. (Dogs can see without an artificial lens, but the image will not be in focus). Once a cataract is removed, it does not recur.

After the procedure, the dog usually stays at the surgery overnight so the professionals can monitor him. Once back home, he will have to wear a protective Elizabethan collar, or E collar, for about one to two weeks while his eye is healing. The next part is important: you have to keep him quiet

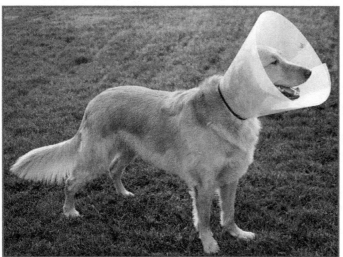

and calm (not always easy with a lively Golden!) You'll also have to give him eye drops, perhaps four times a day for the first week and then less frequently after that.

The success of cataract surgery depends very much on the owner doing all the right things. But all the effort will be worth it when your dog regains his sight.

There is some scientific evidence that a small percentage of dogs that undergo cataract removal may later develop glaucoma. Discuss the severity of cataract(s) and all options thoroughly with your vet or ophthalmic specialist.

PRA (Progressive Retinal Atrophy)

PRA is the name for several progressive diseases that lead to blindness. First recognised at the beginning of the 20th century in Gordon Setters, this inherited condition has been documented in over 100 breeds. Golden Retrievers, Cocker Spaniels and Poodles are all recognised as being among the breeds that can be affected by the disease. According to The Golden Retriever Club, PRA has been "virtually eliminated" in the UK. It is thought to affect 1% or less of all Goldens in the USA.

The University of California, Davis School of Veterinary Medicine states: "Golden Retrievers are affected by more than one form of PRA, with mutations in three distinct genes having been identified. Two of such mutations are known as GR_PRA1 and GR_PRA2.

"GR_PRA1 results from a mutation in the SLC4A3 gene and accounts for over 60% of diagnosed Golden Retrievers. GR_PRA2 results from a mutation in the TTC8 gene and accounts for 30% of Golden Retrievers diagnosed with PRA. Both mutations are autosomal recessive, **thus two copies of the same affected gene must be present for the disease to be observed** and both males and females are equally affected. Presence of one copy of each affected gene in the same dog will not cause blindness. Clinical signs of GR_PRA1 appear around six years of age. Clinical symptoms of GR-PRA2 appear around four years of age."

A dog which has DNA tested as a CARRIER will not show signs of PRA but could pass it on and, if bred, should only be mated with a CLEAR dog. Tested dogs get one of three results:

CLEAR - free from disease

CARRIER - has the gene, is unaffected by it, but could pass the disease on to offspring

AFFECTED - has inherited the disease and could develop PRA

Ideally, only dogs tested CLEAR should be used for breeding. However, if bred, a CARRIER should only ever be mated with a CLEAR dog or bitch. The gene is 'Autosomal Recessive;' and these are all possible outcomes – **they are the same for all the other hereditary diseases caused by autosomal recessive traits:**

Parent clear + parent clear = pups clear

Parent clear + parent carrier = 50% will carry the disease, 50% will be clear

Parent clear + parent affected = 100% will be carriers

Parent carrier + parent clear = 50% will carry disease, 50% will be clear

Parent carrier + parent carrier = 25% clear, 25% affected and 50% carry disease

Parent carrier + parent affected = 50% affected and 50% carry disease

Parent affected + parent clear = 100% will carry disease

Parent affected + parent carrier = 50% affected and 50% carry disease

Parent affected + parent affected = 100% affected

Golden Retrievers born with normal eyesight can develop PRA any time from as early as one year old to middle age. It causes cells in the retina at the back of the eye to degenerate and die, even though the cells seem to develop normally early in life. A dog's rod cells operate in low light levels and are the first to lose normal function, and so the first sign of PRA is night blindness. Then the cone cells gradually lose their normal function in full light situations. Most affected dogs will eventually go blind.

If your dog has PRA, you may first notice that he lacks confidence in low light; he is perhaps reluctant to go down stairs or along a dark hallway. If you look closely into his eyes, you may see the pupils dilating (becoming bigger) and/or the reflection of greenish light from the back of his eyes. As the condition worsens, he might then start bumping into things, first at night and then in the daytime too. The condition is not painful and the eyes often appear normal - without redness, tearing or squinting. The lenses may become opaque or cloudy in some dogs.

Sadly, there is no cure, but NOT breeding from affected dogs is slowly eradicating the disease among Goldens. A small group of vets in the USA have prescribed an antioxidant supplement to slow down the disease. The average dog takes less than a year from diagnosis to total blindness, however, they claim that dogs provided with the supplement have gone more than three years since diagnosis without complete vision loss. Although promising, these results have been met with some scepticism from the wider veterinary community.

While eyesight is extremely important to dogs, their other senses are more highly developed than in humans and they do not rely as much as we do on our eyes, and PRA develops slowly, giving the dog time to adjust to his changing situation. Many blind dogs live happy lives with a little extra help from their owners.

Golden Retriever Pigmentary Uveitis (GRPU)

This awful disease is spreading in the USA and becoming a cause for concern. First seen in the Northeastern United States in the early 1990s, not much is known about it and, as yet, there is no test for GRPU. Veterinary ophthalmologists in the USA recommend annual eye tests for **all** Goldens (not just breeding stock), right through to old age. The condition is very rare in the UK.

"Uveitis" means intraocular (inside the eye) inflammation, similar to arthritis. And just as arthritis can be caused by many things, so can uveitis. Sadly, there is no cure and the condition often leads to blindness if not detected early.

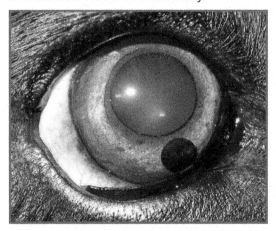

Symptoms (a dog may show one or more of these) are: redness of the conjunctiva (the clear, moist membrane that coats the inner surfaces of the eyelids and outer surface of the eye), the iris changing colour, squinting, a narrowing or abnormal shape of the pupil, sensitivity to light (photophobia), cloudiness of the eye and low pressure inside the eye. Another sign is "iris cysts" (like the one pictured), which appear as small black floating spots at the front of the eye. Not all dogs with iris cysts will develop GRPU, and not all dogs with GRPU have iris cysts. However, if either eye has iris cysts, this is a red flag and a risk factor for GRPU.

Scientists think there may be a genetic link, but have not yet identified the gene or genes responsible. One reason the disease is spreading so quickly is that often Golden Retrievers do not show signs until they are around eight or nine years old – usually after they have finished breeding. Usually both eyes are affected and the dog arrives at the vet's aged between eight and 10 years with cloudy or red eyes and a relatively recent loss of some vision. In fact, the condition has been present for many years. If GRPU is advanced and the eyes are blind with glaucoma, then the only option is to remove both eyes. Dr Terri L. McCalla DVM, of Washington-based Animal Eye Care, has spent some time researching the disease and is emerging as an authority. She says: "A recent study of GRPU in three Midwestern states revealed a prevalence of 5.5% in all Golden Retrievers examined by a veterinary ophthalmologist; indeed, in dogs examined that were at least 8 years of age, the prevalence was 9.9%. Treatment of GRPU depends on the stage of disease. It is the author's opinion that if affected dogs are identified in the early stage of the disease and placed on lifetime treatment and examined regularly by an ophthalmologist, they will not progress to the middle and late stages of the disease and their vision is saved."

For more information read Dr McCalla's article at: http://animaleyecare.net/diseases/grpu, Dr Wendy Townsend's study results at www.ncbi.nlm.nih.gov/pubmed/24134580 or the GRCA's excellent fact sheet at www.grca.org/about-the-breed/health-research/experts-answer-pigmentary-uveitis-questions

Glaucoma

Glaucoma is a condition which puts pressure on the eye, and if the condition becomes chronic or continues without treatment, it will eventually cause permanent damage to the optic nerve, resulting in blindness. It is not very common in Goldens and when it does occur, it is usually associated with Pigmentary Uveitis.

A normal eye contains a fluid called aqueous humour to maintain its shape, and the body is constantly adding and removing fluid from inside of the eye to maintain the pressure inside the eye at the proper level. Glaucoma occurs when the pressure inside the eyeball becomes higher than normal. Just as high blood pressure can damage the heart, excessive pressure inside the eye can damage the eye's internal structures. Unless glaucoma is treated quickly, temporary loss of vision or even total blindness can result.

The cornea and lens inside the eye are living tissues, but they have no blood vessels to supply the oxygen and nutrition they need; these are delivered through the aqueous humour. In glaucoma, the increased pressure is most frequently caused by this fluid not being able to properly drain away from the eye. Fluid is constantly being produced and if an equal amount does not leave the globe, then the pressure starts to rise, similar to a water balloon. As more water is added the balloon stretches more and more. The balloon will eventually burst, but the eye is stronger so this does not happen. Instead the eye's internal structures are damaged irreparably. Primary glaucoma is normally inherited (not a common issue with Golden Retrievers) and secondary glaucoma is caused by another problem, such as a wound to the eye or GRPU.

Symptoms - With primary glaucoma, both eyes are rarely affected equally or at the same time, it usually starts in one eye several months or even years before it affects the second one. Glaucoma is a serious disease and it's important for an owner to be able to immediately recognise initial symptoms. If treatment is not started within a few days - or even hours in some cases - of the pressure increasing, the dog will probably lose sight in that eye. Here are the early signs:

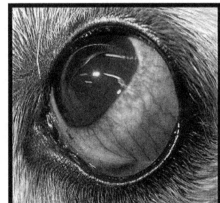

- 🐾 Pain

- 🐾 The whites of an eye look bloodshot

- 🐾 A dilated pupil or one pupil looks bigger than the other

- 🐾 Rapid blinking

- Cloudiness in the cornea at the front of the eye

- Loss of appetite, which may be due to headaches

- Change in attitude, less willing to play, etc.

Most dogs will not display all of these signs at first, perhaps just one or two. A dog rubbing his eye with his paw, against the furniture or carpet or your leg is a common - and often unnoticed- early sign. Some dogs will also seem to flutter the eyelids or squint with one eye. The pupil of the affected eye will usually dilate (get bigger) in the early stages of glaucoma. It may still react to all bright light, but it will do so very slowly. Remember that glaucoma, even primary glaucoma, will usually only initially affect one of the eyes.

If the pupil in one eye is larger than in the other, something is definitely wrong and it could be glaucoma. If you suspect your dog has the condition, get him to the vet as soon as possible, i.e. **immediately,** not the day after, this is a medical emergency. The vet will carry out a manual examination and test your dog's eye pressure using a tonometer on the surface of the eye. There is still a fair chance that the dog may lose sight in this eye, but a much better chance of saving the second eye with the knowledge and preventative measures learned from early intervention. Treatment will revolve around reducing the pressure within the affected eye, draining the aqueous humour and providing pain relief, as this can be a painful condition for your dog. There are also surgical options for the long-term control of glaucoma. As yet it cannot be cured.

Multifocal Retinal Dysplasia (MRD)

The retina is the delicate transparent membrane at the back of the eye that is made up of several layers. For dogs (or humans) to see, light passes through the lens on to the retina – similar to light passing through a lens and on to the film at the back of a pre-digital camera. This is processed as an image when it is 'developed' – i.e. relayed to the central nervous system via the optic nerve. Retinal dysplasia occurs when the cells and layers of retinal tissue do not develop properly and start to separate from the underlying membrane.

Affected puppies may have no symptoms, while more severely affected dogs may display generally poor eyesight, a reluctance to walk into dark areas, bumping into things or a sudden loss of vision. MRD can be diagnosed in a puppy by a vet using an ophthalmoscope, although signs may sometimes not appear until the pup is six months of age. If MRD is present, the vet sees one of the following symptoms:

- Folds in the retina that look like grey streaks

- Rosettes on the retina that show up as grey patches

- Increased reflectivity of the tapetal (coloured area) of the retina

As yet there is no cure for this disease, but many dogs do learn to successfully adapt to their lack of vision as their hearing and sense of smell are far more highly developed than those of humans. If you are buying a puppy, ask to see **current annual eye certificates** for both parents and ask the breeder if there is any history of Multifocal Retinal Dysplasia in her bloodlines. If you want more in-depth information about eye conditions affecting Goldens and tests available, read the BVA leaflet here:
www.bva.co.uk/uploadedFiles/Content/Canine_Health_Schemes/Eye_Leaflet(1).pdf

Entropion

This is a condition in which the edge of the lower eyelid rolls inward, causing the dog's eyelashes and fur to rub the surface of the eyeball, or cornea. In rare cases the upper lid can also be affected, and one or both eyes may be involved. This painful condition is thought to be hereditary and is more commonly found in dog breeds with wrinkled faces -such as the Bulldog - although other affected breeds include the Golden Retriever and Poodle.

The affected dog will scratch at his painful eye with his paws and this can lead to further injury. If your dog is to suffer from entropion, he will usually show signs at or before his first birthday. You will notice that his eyes are red and inflamed and they will produce tears. He will probably squint.

The tears typically start off clear and can progress to a thick yellow or green mucus. If the entropion causes corneal ulcers, you might also notice a milky-white colour develop. This is caused by increased fluid that affects the clarity of the cornea. For your poor dog, the irritation is constant. Imagine how painful and uncomfortable it would be if you had permanent hairs touching your eyes. It makes my eyes water just thinking about it.

It's important to get your dog to the vet as soon as you suspect entropion before he scratches his cornea and worsens the problem. The condition can cause scarring around the eyes or other issues that can affect a dog's vision if left untreated.

A vet will make the diagnosis after a painless and relatively simple inspection of your dog's eyes. But before he or she can diagnose entropion, they will have to rule out other issues, such as allergies, which might also be making your dog's eyes red and itchy.

In young dogs, some vets may delay surgery and treat the condition with medication until the dog's face is fully formed to avoid having to repeat the procedure at a later date. In mild cases, the vet may successfully prescribe eye drops, ointment or other medication.

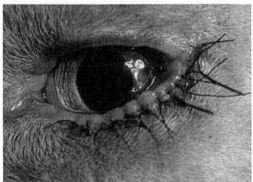

However, the most common treatment for more severe cases is a fairly straightforward surgical procedure – a 'nip and tuck' - to pin back the lower eyelid. Discuss the severity of the condition and all the options before proceeding to surgery.

For anyone with a dog suffering from entropion, there is an interesting post-surgery diary with photos of a Bulldog with the condition, which gives an insight into the condition and recovery at: www.bulldogsworld.com/health-and-medical/post-operative-pictures-and-daily-recovery-log-entropion-surgery

A disorder which can affect older Goldens is **eyelid tumours**. These need examining by a vet as soon as you notice one. Although they are usually benign (harmless) they can sometimes spread, so it is best to have them removed while they are still small.

....

Eyelash Disorders

Distichiasis, trichiasis and **ectopic cilia** are canine eyelash disorders that can affect any breed, although some are more susceptible than others. Distichiasis is an eyelash that grows from an abnormal spot on the eyelid, trichiasis is ingrowing eyelashes and ectopic cilia are single or multiple hairs that grow through the inside of the eyelid ('cilia' are eyelashes).

With distichiasis (also called distichia), small eyelashes abnormally grow on the inner surface or the very edge of the eyelid, and both upper and lower eyelids may be affected. The affected eye becomes red, inflamed, and may develop a discharge. The dog will typically squint or blink a lot, just like a human with a hair or other foreign matter in the eye. The dog will often rub his eye against furniture, other objects or the carpet. In severe cases, the cornea can become ulcerated and it looks blue. If left, the condition usually worsens and severe ulcerations and infections develop, which can lead to blindness. The dog can make the condition worse by scratching or rubbing his eyes.

One US breeder added: "The eyelashes frequently seem to come and go. It is recommended that you don't breed a dog with distichia to another dog with distichia. There are some severe cases where the hairs have to be plucked, but in general the extra eyelashes fall out and aren't always present from one exam to another."

Treatment usually involves electro- or cryo-epilation where a needle is inserted into the hair follicle emitting an ultra-fast electric current which produces heat to destroy the stem cells responsible for hair growth. This procedure may need to be repeated after several months because all of the abnormal hairs may not have developed at the time of the first treatment -although this is not common with dogs older than three years.

Sometimes surgery may be required and here the lid is split to remove the areas where the abnormal hairs grow. Both treatments require anaesthesia and usually result in a full recovery. After surgery, the eyelids are swollen for several days and the eyelid margins turn pink. Usually they return to their normal colour within four months. Antibiotic eye drops are often used following surgery to prevent infections. All three conditions are straightforward to diagnose.

Dry Eye (Keratoconjunctivitis sicca)

KCS is the technical term for a fairly common condition known as 'dry eye' which can affect any breed of dog, although Goldens are not particularly prone to it. It is caused by not enough tears being produced. With insufficient tears, a dog's eyes can become irritated and the conjunctiva appears red. It's estimated that as many as one in five dogs can suffer from dry eye at one time or another in their lives.

The eyes typically develop a thick, yellowy discharge. Infections are common as tears also have anti-bacterial and cleansing properties, and inadequate lubrication allows dust, pollen and other debris to accumulate. The nerves of these glands may also become damaged.

In many cases the reason for dry eye is not known, other times it may be caused by injuries to the tear glands, eye infections, reactions to drugs, an immune reaction or even the gland of the third eyelid being surgically removed by mistake. Left untreated, the dog will suffer painful and chronic eye infections, and repeated irritation of the cornea results in severe scarring, and ulcers may develop which can lead to blindness.

Treatment usually involves drugs; cyclosporine, ophthalmic ointment or drops are the most common. In some cases, another eye preparation – Tacrolimus - is also used and may be effective when cyclosporine is not. Sometimes artificial tear solutions are also prescribed. In very severe cases, an operation can be performed to transplant a salivary duct into the upper eyelid, causing saliva to drain into and lubricate the eye. This procedure is rarely used, but is an option.

Heart Problems

Heart issues are relatively common among the canine population in general. Heart failure, or **congestive heart failure (CHF)**, occurs when the heart is not able to pump blood around the dog's body properly.

The heart is a mechanical pump. It receives blood in one half and forces it through the lungs, then the other half pumps the blood through the entire body. Subvalvular Aortic Stenosis (SAS) is the most common congenital heart disease in Golden Retrievers. Goldens can also be affected by the less common TVD Tricuspid Valve Dysplasia (TVD).

Other forms of heart failure in dogs in general are Degenerative Valvular Disease (DVD) and Dilated Cardiomyopathy (DCM), also known as an enlarged heart). Some dogs can also suffer from Pulmonic Stenosis, which is a congenital narrowing in the region of the pulmonary valve. However, most dogs don't require any medical treatment. Smaller breeds more often suffer from Mitral Valve Disease.

In people, heart disease usually involves the arteries that supply blood to the heart muscle becoming hardened over time, causing the heart muscles to receive less blood than they need. Starved of oxygen, the result is often a heart attack.

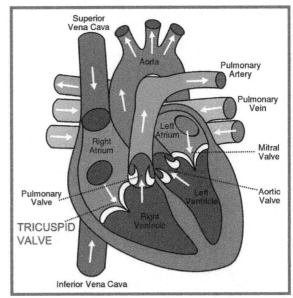

In dogs, hardening of the arteries (arteriosclerosis) and heart attacks are very rare. However, heart disease is quite common, and in dogs it is often seen as heart failure, which means that the muscles 'give out.' This is usually caused by one chamber or side of the heart being required to do more than it is physically able to do. It may be that excessive force is required to pump the blood through an area and over time the muscles fail. Unlike a heart attack in humans, heart failure in a dog is a slow insidious process that occurs over months or even years. Once symptoms are noted, they will usually worsen over time until the dog requires treatment.

Symptoms of a Heart Condition

- Tiredness
- Decreased activity levels
- Restlessness, pacing around instead of settling down to sleep
- Intermittent coughing - especially during exertion or excitement. This tends to occur at night, sometimes about two hours after the dog goes to bed or when he wakes up in the morning. This coughing is an attempt to clear the lungs

As the condition worsens, other symptoms may appear:

- Lack of appetite
- Rapid breathing
- Abdominal swelling (due to fluid)
- Noticeable loss of weight

- Fainting (syncope)
- Paleness

Diagnosis and Treatment - If your dog is exhibiting a range of the above symptoms, the vet may suspect congestive heart failure. He will carry out tests to make sure; these may include listening to the heart, chest X-rays, blood tests, electrocardiogram (a record of your dog's heartbeat) or an echocardiogram.

If the heart problem is due to an enlarged heart (DCM) or valve disease, the condition cannot be reversed. Instead, treatment focuses on managing the symptoms with various medications, which may change over time as the condition worsens. The vet may also prescribe a special low salt diet for your dog, as sodium (found in salt) determines the amount of water in the blood. The amount of exercise will also have to be controlled. There is some evidence that vitamin and other supplements may be beneficial; discuss this with your vet.

The prognosis for dogs with congestive heart failure depends on the cause and severity, as well as their response to treatment. Sadly, CHF is progressive, so your dog can never recover from the condition. But once diagnosed, he can live a longer, more comfortable life with the right medication and regular check-ups.

Heart Murmurs

Heart murmurs are not uncommon in dogs. Our dog was diagnosed with a Grade 2 murmur several years ago and, of course, your heart sinks when the vet gives you the terrible news. But once the shock is over, it's important to realise that there are several different severities of the condition and, at its mildest, it is no great cause for concern.

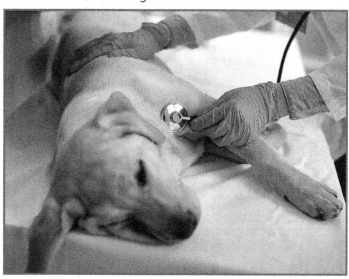

Our dog is 13 now and fit, although he's slowed down a bit. He still has no signs of the heart murmur (except through the vet's stethoscope). However, we are always on alert for a dry, racking cough, which is a sign of Mitral Valve Disease. So far it hasn't happened, touch wood.

Literally, a heart murmur is a specific sound heard through a stethoscope, it results from the blood flowing faster than normal within the heart itself or in one of the two major arteries. Instead of the normal 'lubb dupp' noise, an additional sound can be heard that can vary from a mild 'pshhh' to a loud 'whoosh'. The different grades are:

- **Grade 1** - barely audible
- **Grade 2** - soft, but easily heard with a stethoscope
- **Grade 3** - intermediate loudness; most murmurs which are related to the mechanics of blood circulation are at least grade III
- **Grade 4** - loud murmur that radiates widely, often including opposite side of chest
- **Grades 5 and Grade 6** - very loud, audible with stethoscope barely touching the chest; the vibration is also strong enough to be felt through the animal's chest wall

Murmurs are caused by a number of factors; it may be a problem with the heart valves or could be due to some other condition, such as hyperthyroidism, anaemia or heartworm. In puppies, there are two major types of heart murmurs, and they will probably be detected by your vet at the first or second vaccinations. The most common type is called an innocent 'flow murmur'. This type of murmur is soft - typically Grade 2 or less - and is not caused by underlying heart disease. An innocent flow murmur typically disappears by four to five months of age.

However, if a puppy has a loud murmur - Grade 3 or louder - or if the heart murmur is still easily heard with a stethoscope after four or five months of age, the likelihood of the puppy having an underlying heart problem becomes much higher. The thought of a puppy having congenital heart disease is worrying, but it is important to remember that the disease will not affect all puppies' life expectancy or quality of life. A heart murmur can also develop suddenly in an adult dog with no prior history of the problem. This is typically due to heart disease that develops with age.

In toy and small breeds, a heart murmur may develop in middle-aged to older dogs due to an age-related thickening and degeneration of one of the valves in the heart, the mitral valve. This thickening of the valve prevents it from closing properly and as a result it starts to leak, this is known as mitral valve disease. The more common type of heart disease affecting larger dog breeds in middle age is Dilated Cardiomyopathy (DCM).

Subvalvular Aortic Stenosis (SAS)

SAS occurs when there is a narrowing (stenosis) caused by a ridge of abnormal tissue that restricts blood flow from the heart to the aorta. This narrowing is classified as Mild, Moderate or Severe. Sadly, dogs with the Severe form of the disease often die before the age of five years, and even seemingly healthy dogs can die suddenly of SAS. This is partly because dogs may show no clear signs of the illness, and also owners often don't recognise symptoms as a cause for concern.

Typical symptoms, when present, are:
- Exercise intolerance
- Difficulty breathing
- Weakness
- Fainting (especially when excited)
- In extreme cases, sudden death

In 2014 researchers identified a gene mutation responsible for SAS after studying thousands of Newfoundlands. Only one parent needs to carry the mutation to pass it to the puppies, and not all dogs with the mutation develop the disease. If SAS is detected, it is often after a heart murmur has been discovered by a vet who then runs a series of diagnostic tests. According to Purina Pro Club, the median survival age for dogs receiving treatment is 19 months, and for those dogs receiving medical therapy (consisting of beta blockers to help slow the heart) it is 56 months. Dogs with mild to moderate cases of SAS typically live much longer, possibly having normal lifespans - although this has yet to be confirmed by hard scientific evidence.

The Golden Retriever Club of America www.grca.org states: "A small percentage of Goldens are affected with a hereditary heart disease called subvalvular aortic stenosis. While this is not common in the breed, it can be serious, so all prospective breeding dogs should be examined over the age of

12 months by a board-certified veterinary cardiologist. If a murmur is detected through auscultation (listening with a stethoscope), additional diagnostic tests are available and may be recommended. Normal cardiac exams should be certified by the OFA, and dogs with hereditary heart disease generally should not be bred."

Tricuspid Valve Dysplasia (TVD)

This is a heart condition where blood doesn't flow as it should though the heart, either due to the valves not closing enough to stop the blood flow when they are supposed to, or valves becoming too narrow and restricting the flow of blood. TVD testing is not a mandatory requirement by the Kennel Clubs in the UK or USA, although some USA breeders do test for it.

The heart valves are there to make sure that blood only flows in one direction. If the valve and cords do not develop properly while the embryonic puppy is in the mother's womb, the puppy may be born with TVD - where a defective tricuspid valve causes the atrium to be dilated and the ventricle to enlarge. Over time, this overload raises pressures on the arteries and causes blood to pool in the body.

Although TVD is a hereditary congenital disorder - i.e. dogs are born with it - many puppies with the condition do not show any symptoms and often appear healthy for quite some time. The condition might first be discovered by a cardiac murmur at an annual check-up at the vet's, or a dog may suddenly develop one or more of the symptoms associated with congestive heart failure or SAS, which are:

- Loud breathing/panting
- Exercise intolerance
- Fainting
- Fluid or swelling in the abdomen
- Body extremities cool to the touch

A dog with a mild problem and little blood regurgitation, i.e. backflow, can live a normal lifespan, provided certain precautions are taken, such as not over-exerting the dog and avoiding prolonged exercise and extreme cold conditions. Dogs more severely affected might have a lifespan of just a few months after symptoms of congestive heart failure develop.

An echocardiogram (cardiac ultrasound) is the best way of diagnosing TVD. An X-ray usually reveals an enlarged right side of the heart. A small number of vets perform replacement valve surgery, but it is extremely expensive and not widely practised.

Hypothyroidism

Hypothyroidism is a common hormonal disorder in dogs and is due to an under-active thyroid gland. The gland (located on either side of the windpipe in the dog's throat) does not produce enough of the hormone thyroid, which controls the speed of the metabolism. Dogs with very low thyroid levels have a slow metabolic rate. It occurs mainly in dogs over the age of five. Some Golden Retrievers are regarded as at low to medium risk of contracting hypothyroidism.

It usually occurs most frequently in larger, middle-aged dogs of either gender. The symptoms are often non-specific and quite gradual in onset, and they may vary depending on breed and age. Most forms of hypothyroidism are diagnosed with a blood test and the OFA provides a registry for thyroid screening in the USA.

Common Symptoms - These have been listed in order, with the most common ones being at the top of the list:

- High blood cholesterol
- Lethargy
- Hair loss
- Weight gain or obesity
- Dry coat or excessive shedding
- Hyper pigmentation or darkening of the skin, seen in 25% of cases
- Intolerance to cold, seen in 15% of dogs with the condition

Treatment - Although hypothyroidism is a type of auto-immune disease and cannot be prevented, symptoms can usually be easily diagnosed and treated. Most affected dogs can be well-managed on thyroid hormone replacement therapy tablets. The dog is placed on a daily dose of a synthetic thyroid hormone called thyroxine (levothyroxine). The dog is usually given a standard dose for his weight and then blood samples are taken periodically to monitor him and the dose is adjusted accordingly. Depending upon your dog's preferences and needs, the medication can be given in different forms, such as a solid tablet, in liquid form, or a gel that can be rubbed into your dog's ears. Once treatment has started, he will be on it for the rest of his life.

In some less common situations, surgery may be required to remove part or all of the thyroid gland. Another treatment is radioiodine, where radioactive iodine is used to kill the overactive cells of the thyroid. While this is considered one of the most effective treatments, not all dogs are suitable for the procedure and lengthy hospitalisation is often required. Happily, once the diagnosis has been made and treatment has started, whichever treatment your dog undergoes, the majority of symptoms disappear.

NOTE: **Hyper**thyroidism (as opposed to **hypo**thyroidism) is caused by the thyroid gland producing **too much** thyroid hormone. It is quite rare in dogs, more often seen in cats. A common symptom is the dog being ravenously hungry, but losing weight.

··

Epilepsy

Epilepsy means repeated seizures (also called fits or convulsions) due to abnormal electrical activity in the brain. It can affect any breed of dog and in fact affects around four or five dogs in every 100.

If seizures happen because of a problem somewhere else in the body, such as heart disease (which stops oxygen reaching the brain), this is not epilepsy. Affected dogs behave normally between seizures. In some cases, the gap between seizures is relatively constant, in others it can be very irregular with several seizures occurring over a

short period of time, but with long intervals between 'clusters' of seizures.

Some forms of epilepsy are inherited and some breed experts believe there may be a genetic link for epilepsy in Golden Retrievers, but, as yet, there is no scientific evidence to back this up. A study carried out in Sweden (Heske et al. 2014), based on data from insurance companies on 35 breeds, found that the Boxer emerged as the breed most likely to be affected by epilepsy, and the Golden Retriever was around the middle of the list at 16th. The results are at: www.instituteofcaninebiology.org/blog/epilepsy-incidence-and-mortality-in-35-dog-breeds.

There are a number of reasons why a Golden may develop epilepsy, and some are age-dependent. In dogs under one year old, triggers may include birth defects, such as water on the brain (Hydrocephalus), inflammatory diseases, infections, metabolic or autoimmune problems, or trauma. In dogs aged between one and five years, many of these causes may apply, along with toxic exposure or sensitivity to drugs or vaccinations. With older dogs, blood clots, high blood pressure or strokes are additional causes. The most common form of epilepsy in dogs is known as **Idiopathic Epilepsy,** which means that there is no detectable injury, disease or abnormality.

Anyone who has witnessed their dog having a seizure knows how frightening it can be. Seizures are not uncommon, and many dogs only ever have one. If your dog has had more than one seizure, it may be that he or she is epileptic. The good news is that, just as with people, there are medications to control seizures in dogs, allowing them to live relatively normal lives with normal lifespans.

Symptoms

Some dogs seem to know when they are about to have a seizure and may behave in a certain way. You will come to recognise these signs as meaning that an episode is likely. Often dogs just seek out their owner's company and come to sit beside them when a seizure is about to start.

There are two main types of seizure: **Petit Mal,** which is the lesser of the two and may involve facial twitching, staring into space with a fixed glaze and/or upward eye movement, sometimes accompanied by urination. **Grand Mal** is more often what we think of when we talk about a seizure: most dogs become stiff, fall onto their side and make running movements with their legs. Sometimes they will cry out and may lose control of their bowels or bladder. Once the seizure starts, the dog is unconscious – he cannot hear or respond to you. While it is distressing to watch, **the dog is not in any pain,** even if he or she is howling.

Most seizures last between one and three minutes - it is worth making a note of the time the seizure starts and ends – or record it on your phone because it often seems that it goes on for a lot longer than it actually does. If you are not sure whether or not your dog has had a seizure, look on YouTube, where there are many videos of dogs having epileptic seizures.

Afterwards dogs behave in different ways. Some just get up and carry on with what they were doing, while others appear dazed and confused for up to 24 hours afterwards. Most commonly, dogs will be disorientated for only 10 to 15 minutes before returning to their old self. They often have a set pattern of behaviour that they follow - for example going for a drink of water or asking to go outside to the toilet. If your dog has had more than one seizure, you may well start to notice a pattern of behaviour which is typically repeated.

Most seizures occur while the dog is relaxed and resting quietly. It is very rare for one to occur while exercising. They often occur in the evening or at night. In a few dogs, seizures seem to be triggered by particular events or stress. It is common for a pattern to develop and, should your dog suffer from epilepsy, you will gradually recognise this as specific to your dog.

The most important thing is to **stay calm**. Remember that your dog is unconscious during the seizure and is not in pain or distressed. It is likely to be more distressing for you than for him. Make sure that he is not in a position to injure himself, for example by falling down the stairs, but otherwise do not try to interfere with him. Never try to put your hand inside his mouth during a seizure or you are very likely to get bitten.

It is very rare for dogs to injure themselves during a seizure. Occasionally they may bite their tongue and there may appear to be a lot of blood, but it's unlikely to be serious; your dog will not swallow his tongue. If it goes on for a very long time (more than 10 minutes), his body temperature will rise, which can cause damage to other organs such as the liver and kidneys and brain. In very extreme cases, some dogs may be left in a coma after severe seizures.

Repeated seizures can cause damage to the brain. The damage caused is cumulative and after a lot of seizures there may be enough brain damage to cause early senility (with loss of learned behaviour and housetraining or behavioural changes).

When Should I Contact the Vet?

Generally, if your dog has a seizure lasting more than five minutes, or is having more than two or three a day, you should contact your vet. When your dog starts fitting, make a note of the time. If he comes out of it within five minutes, allow him time to recover quietly before contacting your vet. It is far better for him to recover quietly at home rather than be bundled into the car and carted off to the vet right away. However, if your dog does not come out of the seizure within five minutes, or has repeated seizures close together, contact your vet immediately, as he or she will want to see your dog as soon as possible. If this is his first seizure, your vet may ask you to bring him in for a check-up and some routine blood tests. Always call your vet's practice before setting off to be sure that there is someone there who can help when you arrive.

There are many things other than epilepsy that cause seizures in dogs. When your vet first examines your dog, he or she will not know whether your dog has epilepsy or another illness. It's unlikely that the vet will see your dog during a seizure, so it is **vital** that you're able to describe in some detail just what happens. Your vet may need to run a range of tests to ensure that there is no other cause of the seizures. These may include blood tests, possibly X-rays, and maybe even a scan (MRI) of your dog's brain. If no other cause can be found, then a diagnosis of epilepsy may be made.

If your Golden Retriever already has epilepsy, remember these key points:

- Don't change or stop any medication without consulting your vet
- See your vet at least once a year for follow-up visits
- Be sceptical of 'magic cure' treatments

Treatment

It is not usually possible to remove the cause of the seizures, so your vet will use medication to control them. Treatment will not cure the disease, but it will manage the signs – even a well-controlled epileptic may have occasional seizures. As yet there is no cure for epilepsy, so don't be tempted with 'instant cures' from the internet.

There are many drugs used in the control of epilepsy in people, but very few of these are suitable for long-term use in a dog. Two of the most common are Phenobarbital and Potassium Bromide (some dogs can have negative results with Phenobarbital). There are also a number of holistic remedies advertised, but we have no experience of them or any idea if any are effective. Other factors which have proved useful in some cases are avoiding dog food containing preservatives, adding vitamins, minerals and /or enzymes to the diet and ensuring drinking water is free of fluoride.

Many epileptic dogs require a combination of one or more types of drug to achieve the most effective control of their seizures. Treatment is decided on an individual basis and it may take some time to find the best combination and dose of drugs for your pet. You need patience when managing an epileptic pet. It is important that medication is given at the same time each day.

Once your dog has been on treatment for a while, he will become dependent on the levels of drug in his blood at all times to control seizures. If you miss a dose of treatment, blood levels can drop and this may be enough to trigger a seizure. Each epileptic dog is an individual and a treatment plan will be designed specifically for him. It will be based on the severity and frequency of the seizures and how he responds to different medications.

Keep a record of events in your dog's life, note down dates and times of episodes and record when you have given medication. Each time you visit your vet, take this diary along with you so he or she can see how your dog has been since his last check-up. If seizures are becoming more frequent, it may be necessary to change the medication. The success or otherwise of treatment may depend on YOU keeping a close eye on your Golden Retriever to see if there are any physical or behavioural changes.

It is not common for epileptic dogs to stop having seizures altogether. However, provided your dog is checked regularly by your vet to make sure that the drugs are not causing any side effects, **there is a good chance that he will live a full and happy life.**

Remember, live **with** epilepsy not **for** epilepsy. With the proper medical treatment, most epileptic dogs have far more good days than bad ones. Enjoy all those good days.

Thanks to www.canineepilepsy.co.uk for assistance with this article. If your Golden Retriever has epilepsy, we recommend reading this excellent website to gain a greater understanding of the illness.

Canine Diabetes

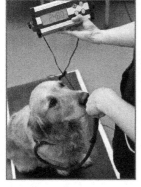

Diabetes can affect dogs of all breeds, sizes and both genders, as well as obese dogs. There are two types: *diabetes mellitus* and *diabetes insipidus.* Diabetes mellitus (sugar diabetes) is the most common form and affects one in 500 dogs. Because most Goldens love their food, it can be a battle to keep them at an ideal weight. But next time your Goldie pleads for an extra treat with his beautiful big brown eyes, remember that that the threat of diabetes in middle-aged and older overweight dogs is very real.

Diabetes is now treatable and need not shorten a dog's lifespan or interfere greatly with his quality of life. Due to advances in veterinary science, diabetic dogs undergoing treatment now have the same life expectancy as non-diabetic dogs of the same age and gender.

However, if left untreated, the disease can lead to cataracts, increasing weakness in the legs (neuropathy), other ailments and even death. In dogs, diabetes is typically seen anywhere between the ages of four to 14, with a peak at seven to nine years. Both males and females can develop it; unspayed females have a slightly higher risk. The typical canine diabetes sufferer is middle-aged, female and overweight, but there are also juvenile cases.

Diabetes insipidus is caused by a lack of vasopressin, a hormone that controls the kidneys' absorption of water. *Diabetes mellitus* occurs when the dog's body does not produce enough insulin and cannot successfully process sugars. Dogs, like us, get their energy by converting the food they eat into sugars, mainly glucose. This glucose travels in the dog's bloodstream and individual cells then remove some of that glucose from the blood to use for energy. The substance that allows the cells to take glucose from the blood is a protein called *insulin.*

Insulin is created by beta cells that are located in the pancreas, next to the stomach. Almost all diabetic dogs have Type 1 diabetes; their pancreas does not produce any insulin. Without it, the cells have no way to use the glucose that is in the bloodstream, so the cells 'starve' while the glucose level in the blood rises. Your vet will use blood samples and urine samples to check glucose concentrations in order to diagnose diabetes. Early treatment helps to prevent further complications developing.

Symptoms of Diabetes Mellitus

- 🐾 Extreme thirst
- 🐾 Excessive urination
- 🐾 Weight loss
- 🐾 Increased appetite
- 🐾 Coat in poor condition
- 🐾 Lethargy
- 🐾 Vision problems due to cataracts

Some diabetic dogs go blind. Cataracts may develop due to high blood glucose levels causing water to build up in the eyes' lenses. This leads to swelling, rupture of the lens fibres and the development of cataracts. In many cases, the cataracts can be surgically removed to bring sight back to the dog. However, some dogs may stay blind even after the cataracts are gone, and some cataracts simply cannot be removed. Blind dogs are often able to get around surprisingly well, particularly in a familiar home.

Treatment and Exercise

Treatment starts with the right diet. Your vet will prescribe meals low in fat and sugars. He will also recommend medication. Many cases of canine diabetes can be successfully treated with a combination of diet and medication, while more severe cases may require insulin injections. In the newly-diagnosed dog, insulin therapy begins at home.

Normally, after a week of treatment, you return to the vet for a series of blood sugar tests over a 12-14 hour period to see when the blood glucose peaks and when it hits its lows. Adjustments are then made to the dosage and timing of the injections. Your vet will explain how to prepare and inject the insulin. You may be asked to collect urine samples using a test strip of paper that indicates the glucose levels in urine.

If your dog is already having insulin injections, beware of a 'miracle cure' offered on some internet sites. It does not exist. There is no diet nor vitamin supplement which can reduce your dog's dependence on insulin injections, because vitamins and minerals cannot do what insulin does in the dog's body. If you think that your dog needs a supplement, discuss it with your vet first to make sure that it does not interfere with any other medication.

Managing your dog's diabetes also means managing his activity level. Exercise burns up blood glucose the same way that insulin does. If your dog is on insulin, any active exercise on top of the insulin might cause him to have a severe low blood glucose episode, called 'hypoglycaemia.' Keep your dog on a reasonably consistent exercise routine. Your usual insulin dose will take that amount of exercise into account. If you plan to take your dog out for some demanding exercise, such as running round with other dogs, you may need to reduce his usual insulin dose.

Tips

- You can usually buy specially formulated diabetes dog food from your vet

- You should feed the same type and amount of food at the same time every day

- Most vets recommend twice-a-day feeding for diabetic pets (it's OK if your dog prefers to eat more often). If you have other pets, they should also be on a twice-a-day feeding schedule, so that the diabetic dog cannot eat from their bowls.

- Help your dog to achieve the best possible blood glucose control by not feeding him table scraps or treats between meals

- Watch for signs that your dog is starting to drink more water than usual. Call the vet if you see this happening, as it may mean that the insulin dose needs adjusting

Remember these simple points:

Food raises blood glucose - Insulin and exercise lower blood glucose - Keep them in balance

For more information on canine diabetes visit **www.caninediabetes.org**

Canine Cancer

This is the biggest single killer and will claim the lives of one in four dogs, regardless of breed. It is the cause of nearly half the deaths of all dogs aged 10 years and older, according to the American Veterinary Medical Association. There is evidence Golden Retrievers are more prone to cancer than other breeds – particularly in the USA.

In the 1980s, the Golden Retriever was not considered a breed with a high risk of cancer and dogs regularly lived to 13 years of age. But by the end of the 1990s, cancer rates within the breed had rocketed. The 1998-99 Golden Retriever Club of America National Health Survey studied cause of death for 427 Goldens and found that 292 of them (68%) were affected by some form of cancer. Read the full report here: www.grca.org/wp-content/uploads/2015/08/healthsurvey1.pdf. Today the life expectancy of a Golden is closer to eight to 11 or 12 years.

One experienced US breeder said: "The current biggest health threat to Golden Retrievers is the cancer issue. They are considered the number one cancer breed (surpassing Boxers and other breeds). Some veterinarians even call them the "Cancer Retriever breed." They are most prone to Hemangiosarcoma (cancer of the blood vessels) and many of the current cancer research is done with Goldens. It is in every line, very difficult to avoid and can cause sudden death at early ages."

The UK's Animal Cancer Trust states: "Golden Retrievers are affected by a number of different cancer types, including lymphoma, haemangiosarcoma and mast cell tumours, although there are several other tumours that occur relatively commonly in this breed."

In her research article "Breed-Predispositions to Cancer in Pedigree Dogs", Jane M. Dobson, of the Department of Veterinary Medicine, University of Cambridge, UK, found that of 927 Golden Retrievers studied, 360 – or 38.8% - died of cancer. The most common types of cancer were: mast cell (skin), lymphoma (lymph glands), oral melanoma (mouth), fibrosarcoma (bones), and histiocytic tumours. Read the article here: www.hindawi.com/journals/isrn/2013/941275/

The USA's Morris Animal Foundation launched the Golden Retriever Lifetime Study to look at why so many Goldens are dying of cancer and other diseases. The biggest study of its kind, some 3,000 dogs were enrolled between 2012 and 2015 and Golden lovers around the world are now eagerly awaiting the results.

Symptoms

Early detection is critical, and some things to look out for are:

- Swellings anywhere on the body, neck, legs or paws
- Lumps in a dog's armpit or under the jaw
- Sores that don't heal
- Weight loss
- Laboured breathing
- Changes in exercise or stamina level

- Change in bowel or bladder habits
- Increased drinking or urination
- Bad breath, which can be a sign of oral cancer
- Nosebleeds, which can be a sign of hemangiosarcoma
- Poor appetite, difficulty swallowing or excessive drooling
- Vomiting

Mast cell tumours (MCTs), also called mastocytomas, are one of the most common types of cancer and found on or under the skin, showing as raised, round masses. They often affect older dogs, although dogs of all ages can be affected. Malignant mast cell tumours can spread to the lymph nodes, spleen, liver and bone marrow if left untreated. If the tumour is spotted early and completely surgically removed, the dog often has an excellent prognosis. Dogs that are tumour-free after six months are unlikely to have a recurrence.

If your dog has been spayed or neutered, there is some evidence that the risk of certain cancers decreases.* These cancers include uterine and breast/mammary cancer in females, and testicular cancer in males (if the dog was neutered before he was six months old). Along with controlling the pet population, spaying is especially important because mammary cancer in female dogs is fatal in about 50% of all cases.

* Recent studies show that some dogs may have a higher risk of certain cancers after neutering.

Diagnosis and Treatment

Just because your dog has a skin growth doesn't mean that it's cancerous. As with humans, tumours may be benign (harmless) or malignant (harmful). Your vet will probably confirm the tumour using X-rays, blood tests and possibly ultrasounds. He or she will then decide whether it is **benign** (harmless) or **malignant** (harmful) via a biopsy in which a tissue sample is taken and examined under a microscope.

If your dog is diagnosed with cancer, there is hope. Advances in veterinary medicine and technology offer various treatment options, including chemotherapy, radiation and surgery. Unlike with humans, a dog's hair will not fall out with chemotherapy. Canine cancer is growing at an ever-increasing rate, and one of the difficulties is that your dog cannot tell you when a cancer is developing. However, if cancers can be detected early enough through a physical or behavioural change, they often respond well to treatment.

Over recent years, we have all become more aware of the risk factors for human cancer. Responding to these by changing our habits is having a significant impact on human health. For example, stopping smoking, protecting ourselves from over-exposure to strong sunlight and eating a healthy, balanced diet all help to reduce cancer rates.

We know to keep a close eye on ourselves, go for regular health checks and report any lumps and bumps to our doctors as soon as they appear. Increased cancer awareness is definitely improving human health. The same is true with your dog.

The success of treatment will depend on the type of cancer, the treatment used and how early the tumour is found. The sooner treatment begins, the greater the chances of success.

Reducing the Risk

One of the best things you can do for your dog is to keep a close eye on him for any tell-tale signs. This shouldn't be too difficult and can be done as part of your regular handling and weekly grooming session. If you notice any new bumps, for example, monitor them over a period of days to see if there is a change in their appearance or size. If there is, then make an appointment to see your vet as soon as possible. It might only be a cyst, but better to be safe than sorry.

While it is impossible to completely prevent cancer from occurring, the following points may help to reduce the risk:

- 🐾 Feed a healthy diet with little or, preferably, no preservatives
- 🐾 Consider adding a dietary supplement, such as antioxidants, Vitamins, A, C, E, beta carotene, lycopene or selenium, or coconut oil – check compatibility with any other treatments

- Don't let your Golden get overweight
- Give pure, filtered or bottled water (fluoride-free) for drinking
- Regular daily exercise
- Keep your dog away from chemicals, pesticides, cleaning products, etc. around the garden and home
- Avoid passive smoking
- Consider using natural flea remedies (check they are working) and avoid unnecessary vaccinations
- If your dog has light skin, don't leave him in the blazing sunshine for extended periods
- Check your dog regularly for lumps and bumps and any other physical or behavioural changes
- Talk to your vet about spaying and castration – the pros and cons and the optimum age

- If you are buying a puppy, ask whether there is a history of cancer among the parents and grandparents

Research into earlier diagnosis and improved treatments is being conducted at veterinary schools and companies all over the world. Advances in biology are producing a steady flow of new tests and treatments which are now becoming available to improve survival rates and canine cancer care.

If your dog is diagnosed with cancer, do not despair, there are many options and new, improved treatments are constantly being introduced.

Disclaimer: The author is not a vet. This chapter is intended to give owners an indication of some of the medical conditions that may affect their dog or dogs and the symptoms to look out for. If you have any concerns regarding the health of your dog, our advice is always the same: consult a veterinarian.

12. Skin and Allergies

Allergies are a growing problem among the canine population in general. Visit any busy vet's clinic these days – especially in spring and summer – and it's likely that one or more of the dogs is there because of some type of sensitivity. Experts are not sure why. It may have something to do with the way we breed or feed our dogs, but as yet there is no hard scientific evidence to support either theory.

There is anecdotal evidence that some Goldens can be more likely than other breeds to develop the allergic skin condition Canine Atopic Dermatitis, which can be caused by a number of different things. There is also a hereditary condition known as Golden Retriever Ichthyosis.

Skin conditions, allergies and intolerances are on the increase in dogs as well as humans. How many children did you hear of having asthma or a peanut allergy when you were at school? Not too many, I'll bet, yet allergies and adverse reactions are now relatively common – and it's the same with dogs. This is a complicated topic and a whole book could be written on this subject alone.

While many dogs have no problems at all, some suffer from sensitive skin, allergies, yeast infections and/or skin disorders, causing them to scratch, bite or lick themselves excessively on the paws and other areas. Symptoms may vary from mild itchiness to a severe reaction.

Current thinking is that a predisposition to skin issues and allergies can sometimes be inherited – Golden Retriever Ichthyosis is one such example. The Golden Retriever breeders involved in this book mostly said that their dogs have had few or no problems – however, they are all 'Approved Breeders' or 'Breeders of Merit' and choose their breeding stock very carefully. If you haven't already bought your puppy, one question to ask the breeder is if either of the parents suffers from allergies, itchiness or intolerances. Another fairly common condition with floppy-eared dogs in general is ear infections – more about these later.

One UK breeder added: "One of my dogs developed skin sensitivity, which the vet told me can emerge around three years old, probably to pollen from crops. I have found that Goldies can get 'hot spots' if they have had a flea bite or similar and will lick it, which quickly becomes a sore. Check their skin if you see a wet patch or a patch that they are excessively licking and biting."

As with humans, the skin is the dog's largest organ. It acts as the protective barrier between your dog's internal organs and the outside world; it also regulates temperature and provides the sense of touch. Surprisingly, a dog's skin is actually thinner than ours, and it is made up of three layers:

1. **Epidermis** or outer layer, the one that bears the brunt of your dog's contact with the outside world.

2. **Dermis** is the extremely tough layer mostly made up of collagen, a strong and fibrous protein. This is where blood vessels deliver nutrients and oxygen to the skin, and it also acts

as your dog's thermostat by allowing his body to release or retain heat, depending on the outside temperature and your dog's activity level.

3. **Subcutis** is a dense layer of fatty tissue that allows your dog's skin to move independently from the muscle layers below it, as well as providing insulation and support for the skin.

FACT: In humans, allergies often trigger a reaction within the respiratory system, causing us to wheeze or sneeze - whereas allergies or hypersensitivities in a dog often cause a reaction in his or her **skin.**

Skin can be affected from the **outside** by fleas, parasites, or inhaled or contact allergies triggered by grass, pollen, man-made chemicals, dust, mould etc. These environmental allergies are especially common in some Terriers as well as the Miniature Schnauzer, Bulldog and certain other breeds. They are also thought to be more common than average in Goldens.

Skin can be affected from the **inside** by things that your dog eats or drinks. Like all dogs, a Golden Retriever can suffer from food allergies or intolerances as well as environmental allergies. Across the dog population in general, environmental allergies are more common than food allergies.

Canine skin disorders are a complex subject. Some Goldens can run through fields, swim through dirty water, dig holes and roll around in the grass (and far more unpleasant stuff) with no after-effects at all. Others may have less contact with the countryside and have an excellent diet, but still experience severe itching.

Skin problems may be the result of one or more of a wide range of causes - and the list of potential remedies and treatments is even longer. It's by no means possible to cover all of them in detail in this chapter. The aim here is to give a broad outline of some of the ailments most likely to affect Golden Retrievers and how to deal with them. We have also included remedies tried with some success by ourselves (we have a dog with skin issues) and other owners of affected dogs, as well as advice from a holistic specialist.

This information is not intended to take the place of professional help. We are not animal health experts and you should always contact your vet as soon as your dog appears physically unwell or uncomfortable. This is particularly true with skin conditions:

If a vet can find the source of the problem early on, there is more chance of successfully treating it before it has chance to develop into a more serious condition with secondary issues.

There is anecdotal evidence that switching to a raw diet or raw meaty bones diet can significantly help some canines with skin issues. See **Chapter 7. Feeding a Golden** for more information. Certainly, the quality of your dog's diet can affect his health.

One of the difficulties with skin ailments is that the exact cause is often difficult to diagnose, as the symptoms may also be common to other issues. If environmental allergies are involved, some specific tests are available costing hundreds of pounds or dollars. You will have to take your vet's advice on this as the tests are not always conclusive and, if the answer is pollen or dust, it is extremely difficult to keep your dog away from the triggers while still having a normal life - unless you and your Golden spend all your time in a spotlessly clean city apartment or show home (which is, quite frankly, highly unlikely!) It is often a question of managing a skin condition, related to the environment, rather than curing it.

Skin issues and allergies often develop in adolescence or early adulthood, which may be anything from a few months to two or three years old. Our dog Max was perfectly normal until he reached two when he began scratching, triggered by environmental allergies - most likely pollen. He's now 12 and over the years he's been on various different remedies which have all worked for a time. As Max's allergies are seasonal, he normally does not have any medication between October and March. But come spring and as sure as daffodils are daffodils, he starts scratching again. We now think we have the solution to keep it under control – read more later in this chapter – and Max lives a happy, normal life.

Tip Another issue reported by some owners is food allergy or intolerance (there is a difference) – often to grain; although one of our experienced breeders has also noted an intolerance to chicken in some Goldens. Allergies and their treatment can cause a lot of stress for dogs and owners alike. The number one piece of advice is that if you suspect your Golden Retriever has an allergy or skin problem, try to **deal with it right away** - either via your vet or natural remedies – before the all-too-familiar scenario kicks in and it develops into a chronic (long term) condition.

Whatever the cause, before a vet can diagnose the problem you have to be prepared to tell him or her all about your dog's diet, exercise regime, habits, medical history and local environment. He or she will then carry out a thorough physical examination, possibly followed by further tests, before a course of treatment or new diet can be prescribed.

Ichthyosis

Golden Retrievers, Jack Russell Terriers and Bulldogs are known to be affected by this skin disease – fortunately Goldens have only a mild form of the condition. It was first recognised in the 1990s and gets its name named from *ichthys*, the Greek word for fish, as the dog's skin has a fish-scale appearance. Breeders sometimes refer to it as "puppy dandruff." The disorder is inherited; it is autosomal recessive, which means that both parents must carry a copy of the faulty gene for their puppies to inherit the disorder.

A DNA test is now available for ichthyosis. According to the Antagene laboratory: "More than 50% of Golden Retrievers in Europe are carriers of the genetic mutation responsible for Ichthyosis." (A Carrier does not necessarily show signs of the condition, but can pass it on to puppies if bred with an Affected dog or another Carrier).

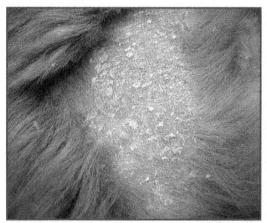

A University of Pennsylvania study of 46 Golden Retrievers diagnosed with ichthyosis from January 2004 to January 2007 found that all the dogs had mild to moderate dry scaling with variable dark patches on their abdomens. They had large, loose scales ranging in colour from soft white to grey. "The dogs looked like walking snow globes," says Elizabeth Mauldin, D.V.M., associate professor of pathology and dermatology at the University of Pennsylvania School of Veterinary Medicine.

The 46 dogs consisted of 25 females and 21 males. Some 22 dogs had skin lesions when they were younger than one year of age; three dogs developed the disorder between one and two years of age; and 13 dogs were older than two. The age of onset was unknown for eight dogs.

Symptoms - Dandruff on the back and belly, usually seen between the ages of one and 18 months. The skin looks dirty and scaly, and becomes dry, rough and with a hyperpigmentation (dark patches). Special shampoos can be used to prevent infections occurring.

Treatment – Your vet will first have to make a correct diagnosis; ichthyosis can sometimes be mistaken for seborrhoea, another skin disease which causes excessive dandruff, or parasites. There is no cure for ichthyosis, but mild cases can be managed by bathing the dog in a special shampoo and moisturising the skin.

....

Types of Allergies

Canine Atopic Dermatitis (cAD) or *Canine Dermatitis* means inflammation of a dog's skin and it can be triggered by numerous things, but the most common by far is allergies. An allergy is an exaggerated response to something in the environment.

In response to these allergens, a dog's immune system overreacts and produces a protein called IgE which triggers the release of compounds called histamines that cause irritation and inflammation. (This is why people and dogs with hay fever and similar allergies may be prescribed **antihistamines**). Vets estimate that one in four dogs in their clinics is there due to some kind of allergy. Typical symptoms are:

- Chewing on paws
- Rubbing the face on the carpet
- Scratching the body – stomach, etc.
- Scratching or biting the anus
- Itchy ears, head shaking
- Hair loss
- Mutilated skin with sore or discoloured patches or hot spots

A Golden Retriever who is allergic to something will show it through skin problems and itching; your vet may call this *'pruritus'*. It may seem logical that if a dog is allergic to something he inhales, like certain pollen grains, his nose will run; if he's allergic to something he eats, he may vomit, or if allergic to an insect bite, he may develop a swelling. But in practice this is seldom the case.

The skin is the organ that is often affected by allergies, causing a mild to severe itching sensation over the body and maybe a chronic ear infection. Dogs with allergies often chew their feet until they are sore and red. You may see yours rubbing his face on the carpet or couch or scratching his belly and flanks. Because the ear glands produce too much wax in response to the allergy, ear infections can occur, with bacteria and yeast - which is a fungus - often thriving in the excessive wax and debris.

But your Golden Retriever doesn't have to suffer from allergies to get ear infections, the lack of air flow under the floppy ears make the breed prone to the condition. (By the way, if your dog does develop a yeast infection and you switch to a grain-free diet, avoid those which are potato-based, as these contain high levels of starch).

US holistic vet Dr Jodie Gruenstern highlights the effect that diet can have on allergies: "Grains and other starches have a negative impact on gut health, creating insulin resistance and inflammation. It's estimated that up to 80% of the immune system resides within the gastrointestinal system;

building a healthy gut supports a more appropriate immune response. The importance of choosing fresh proteins and healthy fats over processed, starchy diets (such as kibble) can't be overemphasized."

An allergic dog may cause skin lesions or 'hot spots' by constant chewing and scratching. Sometimes he will lose hair, which can be patchy, leaving a mottled appearance. The skin itself may be dry and crusty, reddened, swollen or oily, depending on the dog. It is very common to get secondary bacterial skin infections due to these self-inflicted wounds. An allergic dog's body is reacting to molecules called allergens. These may come from:

- Grass, tree or plant pollens
- Foods or food additives, such as specific meats, grains, preservatives or colourings
- Milk products
- Fabrics, such as wool or nylon
- Rubber and/or plastics (e.g. plastic food bowl)
- House dust and/or dust mites
- Mould
- Flea bites
- Chemical products used around the house

These allergens may be **inhaled** as the dog breathes, **ingested** as the dog eats or caused by **contact** with the dog's body when he walks or rolls. However they arrive, they all cause the immune system to produce the IgE protein. This in turn causes various irritating body chemicals (otherwise known as hormones), such as histamine, to be released. In dogs these chemical reactions and cell types occur in sizeable amounts only within the skin, hence the scratching.

Inhalant Allergies (Atopy)

The most common allergies in dogs are inhalant and seasonal - at least at first; some allergies may develop and worsen. Substances which can cause an allergic reaction in dogs are similar to those causing problems for humans. Dogs of all breeds can suffer from them. A clue to diagnosing these allergies is to look at the timing of the reaction. Does it happen all year round? If so, this may be mould, dust or some other trigger which is permanently in the environment. If the reaction is seasonal, then pollens may well be the culprit. A diagnosis can be made by one of three methods of **allergy testing.**

The most common is a blood test that checks for antibodies caused by antigens in the dog's blood, and there are two standard tests: a RAST test (radioallergosorbent) and an ELISA test (enzyme-linked immunosorbent assay). According to the Veterinary and Aquatic Services Department of Drs. Foster and Smith, they are very similar, but many vets feel that the ELISA test gives more accurate results.

The other type of testing is intradermal skin testing where a small amount of antigen is injected into the skin of the animal and after a short period of time, the area around the injection site is inspected to see if the dog has had an allergic reaction. This method has been more widely used in the USA than the UK to date. Here is a link to an article written by the owner of a Boxer dog with severe inhalant allergies: www.allergydogcentral.com/2011/06/30/dog-allergy-testing-and-allergy-shots

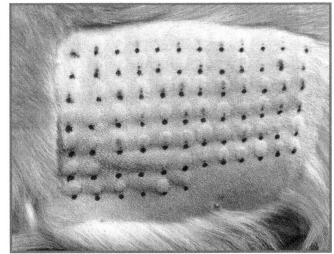

This photo shows a Golden which has undergone intradermal skin testing. In this particular case, the dog has been tested for more than 70 different allergens, which is a lot. In all likelihood, your dog would be tested for fewer. The injections are in kits. If you consider this option, ask the vet or specialist how many allergens are in the kit.

Intradermal skin testing is regarded as 'the gold standard' of allergy testing for atopy. The dog is sedated and an area on his side is shaved down to the skin. A small amount of antigen is injected into the dog's skin on this shaved area. This is done in a specific pattern and order. After a short time the shaved area is examined to detect which antigens, if any, have created a reaction. It may look pretty drastic, but reactions – the visible round bumps -are only temporary and the fur grows back.

Intradermal skin testing works best when done during the season when the allergies are at their worst. The good news is that it is not necessarily much more expensive than blood testing and after a while the dog is none the worse for the ordeal. The procedure is normally carried out by a veterinary dermatologist or a vet with some dermatological experience, and dogs need to be clear of steroids and antihistamines for around six weeks beforehand.

While allergy testing is not particularly expensive, the intradermal method usually requires your dog to be sedated. And there's also no point doing it if you are not going to go along with the recommended method of treatment afterwards - which is immunotherapy, or 'hyposensitisation', and this can be an expensive and lengthy process. It consists of a series of injections made specifically for your dog and administered over months (or even years) to make him more tolerant of specific allergens. Vets in the US claim that success rates can be as high as 75%.

But before you get to the stage of considering allergy testing, your vet will have had to rule out other potential causes, such as fleas or mites, fungal, yeast or bacterial infections and hypothyroidism. Due to the time and cost involved in skin testing, vets treat most mild cases of allergies with a combination of avoidance, fatty acids, tablets, and sometimes steroid injections for flare-ups. Many owners of dogs with allergies also look for natural alternatives as long-term use of steroids, for example, can cause other health issues.

Environmental or Contact Irritations

These are a direct reaction to something the dog physically comes into contact with. It could be as simple as grass, specific plants, dust or other animals. If the trigger is grass or other outdoor materials, the allergies are often seasonal. The dog may require treatment (often tablets, shampoo or localised cortisone spray) for spring and summer, but be perfectly fine with no medication for the other half of the year. This is the case with our dog – although he also has inhalant allergies.

 Let's face it, it is impossible for a Golden Retriever to avoid the Great Outdoors. So, if you suspect yours may have outdoor contact allergies, get him to stand in a tray or large bowl of water on your return from a walk – or hose him down underneath. Washing his feet and

under his belly will reduce his scratching and biting by reducing the allergens to a tolerable level.

Other possible triggers include dry carpet shampoos, caustic irritants, new carpets, cement dust, washing powders or fabric conditioners. If you wash your dog's bedding or if he sleeps on your bed, use a fragrance-free, if possible, hypoallergenic, laundry detergent and avoid fabric conditioner. The irritation may be restricted to the part of the dog - such as the underneath of the paws or belly - which has touched the offending object. Symptoms are skin irritation - either a general problem or specific hotspots - itching (pruritus) and sometimes hair loss. Readers sometimes report to us that their dog will incessantly lick one part of the body, often the paws, anus, belly or back.

Our dog went through a phase of jumping round like he had been stung like a bee to frantically lick and bite his anus; it made our eyes water just to watch it! A swift trip to the vet resulted in a steroid injection and a cortisone spray which we applied directly to the anus and quickly solved the problem. If he occasionally (every couple of years) has a flare up, we use the spray for a day or so and it clears it up. This type of spray can be very effective if the itchy area is small, but no good for spraying all over a dog's body.

···

Flea Bite Allergies (FAD, Flea Allergy Dermatitis)

This is an extremely common canine allergy and can affect all breeds. To compound the problem, many dogs with flea allergies also have inhalant allergies. FAD is typically seasonal, worse during summer and autumn – peak time for fleas - and in warmer climates where fleas are prevalent.

This type of allergy is not to the flea itself, but to proteins in flea saliva, which are deposited under the dog's skin when an adult flea feeds on the dog's blood. Just one bite to an allergic Golden will cause intense and long-lasting itching. Fleas typically don't stay on the dog except for the minutes to hours when they are feeding, which is why owners often don't see live fleas on their dog, unless there is a severe flea infestation.

The first clues that your Golden may suffer from FAD are itching and hair loss in the area from the middle of the back to the base of the tail and down the rear legs (known to vets as 'the flea triangle'). Intradermal or specialised blood tests can confirm a flea allergy, followed by hyposensitisation treatment. Flea bite allergies can only be totally prevented by keeping all fleas away from the dog.

Various flea prevention treatments are available, and it's important to keep up to date with preventative treatments – see the section on **Parasites**. If you suspect your dog may be allergic to fleas, consult your vet for the proper diagnosis and medication.

One UK Golden breeder said: "Some Goldens are afflicted for life with skin allergies; often due to fleas. We find ordinary Dettol dabbed on sore spots is good. It also stops them licking."

Diet and Food Allergies

Food is the third most common cause of allergies in dogs. Cheap dog foods bulked up with grains and other ingredients can cause problems. If you feed your dog a dry commercial dog food, make sure that it's high quality, preferably hypoallergenic, and that the first ingredient listed on the sack is meat or poultry, not grain (although some Goldens can have a sensitivity to chicken).

Without the correct food, a dog's whole body - not just his skin and coat - will continually be under stress and this manifests itself in a number of ways. The symptoms of food allergies are similar to those of most allergies:

- Itchy skin affecting primarily the face, feet, ears, forelegs, armpits and anus
- Excessive scratching
- Chronic or recurring ear infections
- Hair loss
- Hot spots
- Skin infections that clear up with antibiotics, but return after the antibiotics have finished
- Often increased bowel movements, maybe twice as many as normal

The bodily process which occurs when an animal has a reaction to a particular food agent is not very well understood, but the veterinary profession does know how to diagnose and treat food allergies. As many other problems can cause similar symptoms (and also the fact that many sufferers also have other allergies), it is important that any other problems are identified and treated before food allergies are diagnosed.

Atopy, FAD, intestinal parasite hypersensitivities, sarcoptic mange and yeast or bacterial infections can all cause similar symptoms. This can be an anxious time for owners as vets try one thing after another to get to the bottom of the allergy. The normal method for diagnosing a food allergy is elimination. Once all other causes have been ruled out or treated, then a food trial is the next step – and that's no picnic for owners either - see **Chapter 7. Feeding a Golden** for more information. As with other allergies, dogs may have short-term relief by taking fatty acids, antihistamines and/or steroids, but removing the offending items from the diet is the only permanent solution.

Acute Moist Dermatitis (Hot Spots)

Acute moist dermatitis or 'hot spots' are not uncommon. A hot spot can appear suddenly and is a raw, inflamed and often bleeding area of skin. The area becomes moist and painful and begins spreading due to continual licking and chewing. Hot spots can become large, red, irritated lesions in a short space of time. The cause is often a local reaction to an insect bite; fleas, ticks, biting flies and even mosquitoes have been known to cause acute moist dermatitis. Other causes include:

- Allergies - inhalant allergies and food allergies
- Mites
- Ear infections
- Poor grooming
- Burs or plant awns
- Anal gland disease
- A dirty coat due to inadequate grooming
- Hip dysplasia or other types of arthritis and degenerative joint disease

The good news is that, once diagnosed and with the right treatment, hot spots disappear as soon as they appeared. The underlying cause should be identified and treated, if possible. Check with your vet before treating your Golden Retriever for fleas and ticks at the same time as other medical treatment (such as anti-inflammatory medications and/or antibiotics), as he or she will probably advise you to wait.

Treatments may come in the form of injections, tablets or creams – or your dog might need a combination of them. Your vet will probably clip and clean the affected area to help the effectiveness of any spray or ointment and your hapless dog might also have to wear an E-collar until the condition subsides, but usually this does not take long.

Parasites

Demodectic Mange (Demodex)

Demodectic mange is also known as Demodex, red mange, follicular mange or puppy mange. It is caused by the tiny torpedo-shaped mite Demodex canis – pictured - which can only be seen through a microscope. The mites actually live inside the hair follicles on the bodies of virtually every adult dog - and most humans - without causing any harm or irritation. In humans, the mites are found in the skin, eyelids and the creases of the nose ...try not to think about that!

The Demodex mite spends its entire life on the host dog. Eggs hatch and mature from larvae to nymphs to adults in 20 to 35 days and the mites are transferred directly from the mother to the puppies within the first week of life by direct physical contact. Demodectic mange is not a disease of poorly kept animals or dirty kennels. It is generally a disease of young dogs with inadequate or poorly developed immune systems (or older dogs suffering from a suppressed immune system).

Vets currently believe that virtually every mother carries and transfers mites to her puppies and most are immune to the mites' effects, but a few puppies are not and they develop full-blown mange. They may have a few (less than five) isolated lesions and this is known as localised mange – often around the head; this happens in around 90% of cases. But in the other 10% of cases, it develops into generalised mange which covers the entire body or region of the body. This is most likely to develop in puppies with parents that have suffered from mange. Most lesions in either form develop after four months of age. It can also develop around the time when females have their first heat cycle and may be due to a slight dip in the bitch's immune system.

Symptoms – Bald patches are usually the first sign, usually accompanied by crusty, red skin which sometimes appears greasy or wet. Usually hair loss begins around the muzzle, eyes and other areas on the head. The lesions may or may not itch. In localised mange, a few circular crusty areas appear, most frequently on the head and front legs of three to six-month-old puppies. Most will self-heal as the puppies become older and develop their own immunity, but a persistent problem needs treatment, as you don't want generalised mange to develop.

With generalised mange there are bald patches over the entire coat, including the head, neck, body, legs, and feet. The skin on the head, side and back is crusty, often inflamed and oozing a clear fluid. The skin itself will often be oily to touch and there is usually a secondary bacterial infection. Some puppies can become quite ill and develop a fever, lose their appetites and become lethargic. If you suspect your puppy has generalised demodectic mange, get him to a vet straight away.

There is also a condition called pododermatitis, when mange affects a puppy's paws. It can cause bacterial infections and be very uncomfortable, even painful. The symptoms of this mange include hair loss on the paws, swelling of the paws (especially around the nail beds) and red/hot/inflamed areas which are often infected. Treatment is always recommended, and it can take several rounds to clear it up.

Diagnosis and Treatment – The vet will normally diagnose demodectic mange after he or she has taken a skin scraping. As these mites are present on every dog, they do not necessarily mean the dog has mange. Only when the mite is coupled with lesions will the vet diagnose mange. Treatment usually involves topical (on the skin) medication and sometimes tablets. In 90% of cases, localised demodectic mange resolves itself as the puppy grows.

If the dog has just one or two lesions, these can usually be successfully treated using specific creams and spot treatments. With the more serious generalised demodectic mange, treatment can be lengthy and expensive. The vet might prescribe an anti-parasitic dip every two weeks. Owners should always wear rubber gloves when treating their dog, and it should be applied in an area with adequate ventilation. It should also be noted that **some dogs can react to these dips,** so check with your vet as to whether it will be suitable. Most severe cases need six to 14 dips every two weeks. After the first three or four dips, your vet will probably take another skin scraping to check the mites have gone. Dips continue for one month after the mites have disappeared, but dogs shouldn't be considered cured until a year after their last treatment.

Other options include the heartworm treatment Ivermectin. This isn't approved by the FDA for treating mange, but is often used to do so. It is usually given orally every one to two days, or by injection, and can be very effective. **Again, some dogs react badly to it.** Another drug is Interceptor (Milbemycin oxime), which can be expensive as it has to be given daily. However, it is effective on up to 80% of the dogs who did not respond to dips – but should be given with caution to pups under 21 weeks of age.

Adult dogs that have the generalised condition may have underlying skin infections, so antibiotics are often given for the first several weeks of treatment. They might also have immune system issues, and because the mite flourishes on dogs with suppressed immune systems, you should try to get to the root cause of the problem, especially if your Golden Retriever is older when he or she develops demodectic mange.

Adult dogs that have recurring or persistent cases of demodectic mange should not be bred.

Sarcoptic Mange (Scabies)

Also known as canine scabies, this is caused by the parasite *Sarcoptes scabiei*, and is often far worse than Demodex. It is also highly contagious.

This microscopic mite can cause a range of skin problems, the most common of which is hair loss and severe itching. The mites can infect other animals such as foxes, cats and even humans, but prefer to live their short lives on dogs. Fortunately, there are several good treatments for this mange and the disease can be easily controlled.

In cool, moist environments, the mites live for up to 22 days. At normal room temperature they live from two to six days, preferring to live on parts of the dog with less hair. These are the areas you may see him scratching, although it can spread throughout the body in severe cases.

Diagnosing canine scabies can be somewhat difficult, and it is often mistaken for inhalant allergies. Symptoms are intense scratching, a skin rash, crusty scabs and hair loss (alopecia). Once diagnosed, there are a number of effective treatments, including selamectin (Revolution), an on-the-skin solution applied once a month which also provides heartworm prevention, flea control and some tick protection. Various Frontline products are also effective – check with your vet for the correct one.

Because your dog does not have to come into direct contact with an infected dog to catch scabies, it is difficult to completely protect him. Groomers, veterinary clinics, parks and boarding kennels are all places where a dog can catch scabies; symptoms will usually arrive two to six weeks later. Foxes and their environment can also transmit the mite, so you might want to consider keeping your Golden away from areas where you know foxes are active.

Fleas

When you see your dog scratching and biting, your first thought is probably: "He's got fleas!" and you may well be right. Fleas don't fly, but they do have very strong back legs and they will take any opportunity to jump from the ground or another animal into your Golden Retriever's lovely warm coat. You can sometimes see the fleas if you part your dog's fur.

And for every flea that you see on your dog, there is the awful prospect of hundreds of eggs and larvae in your home or kennel. So if your dog is unlucky enough to catch fleas, you'll have to treat your environment as well as your dog in order to completely get rid of them.

The best form of cure is prevention. Vets recommend giving dogs a preventative flea treatment every four to eight weeks. This may vary depending on your climate, the season - fleas do not breed as quickly in the cold - and how much time your dog spends outdoors. Once-a-month topical insecticides - like Frontline and Advantix - are the most commonly used flea prevention products on the market. You part the skin and apply drops of the liquid on to a small area on your dog's back, usually near the neck. Some kill fleas and ticks, and others just kill fleas - check the details.

It is worth spending the money on a quality treatment, as cheaper brands may not rid your Golden completely of fleas, ticks and other parasites. Sprays, dips, shampoos and collars are other options, as are tablets and injections in certain cases, such as before your dog goes into boarding kennels or has surgery. Incidentally, a flea bite is different from a flea bite allergy.

NOTE: There is considerable anecdotal evidence from dog owners of various breeds that the US flea and worm tablet *Trifexis* can cause severe side effects in some dogs. You may wish to read owners' comments at: www.max-the-schnauzer.com/trifexis-side-effects-in-schnauzers.html

Ticks

A tick is not an insect, but a member of the arachnid family, like the spider. There are over 850 types of them, divided into two types: hard shelled and soft shelled. Ticks don't have wings - they can't fly, they crawl. They have a sensor called Haller's organ which detects smell, heat and humidity to

help them locate food, which in some cases is a Golden Retriever. Ticks' diets consists of one thing and one thing only – blood! They climb up onto tall grass and, when they sense an animal is close, crawl on.

Ticks can pass on a number of diseases to animals and humans, the most well-known of which is **Lyme Disease**, a serious condition which causes lameness and other problems. Dogs which spend a lot of time outdoors in high risk areas, such as woods, can have a vaccination against Lyme Disease.

If you do find a tick on your Golden Retriever's coat and are not sure how to get it out, have it removed by a vet or other expert. Inexpertly pulling it out yourself and leaving a bit of the tick behind can be detrimental to your dog's health. Prevention treatment is similar to that for fleas. If your dog has particularly sensitive skin, he might do better with a natural flea or tick remedy - but check it provides the right level of protection first.

....

Heartworm

Heartworm is a serious and potentially fatal disease affecting pets in North America and many other parts of the world (but not the UK). Foot-long heartworms live in the heart, lungs and associated blood vessels of affected pets, causing severe lung disease, heart failure and damage to other organs in the body.

The dog is a natural host for heartworms, which means that heartworms living inside the dog mature into adults, mate and produce offspring. If untreated, their numbers can increase; dogs have been known to harbour several hundred worms in their bodies. Severe heartworm disease causes lasting damage to the heart, lungs and arteries, and can affect the dog's health and quality of life long after the parasites are gone. For this reason, prevention is by far the best option and treatment - when needed - should be administered as early as possible.

The mosquito (pictured) plays an essential role in the heartworm life cycle. When a mosquito bites and takes a blood meal from an infected animal, it picks up baby worms which develop and mature into 'infective stage' larvae over a period of 10 to 14 days. Then, when the infected mosquito bites another dog, cat or susceptible wild animal, the infective larvae are deposited onto the surface of the animal's skin and enter the new host through the mosquito's bite wound.

Once inside a new host, it takes approximately six months for the larvae to develop into adult heartworms. Once mature, heartworms can live for five to seven years in a dog. In the early stages of the disease, many dogs show few or no symptoms. The longer the infection persists, the more likely symptoms will develop. These include:

- A mild persistent cough
- Reluctance to exercise
- Tiredness after moderate activity
- Decreased appetite
- Weight loss

As the disease progresses, dogs may develop heart failure and a swollen belly due to excess fluid in the abdomen. Dogs with large numbers of heartworms can develop sudden blockages of blood flow within the heart leading to the life-threatening caval syndrome. This is marked by a sudden onset of laboured breathing, pale gums and dark, bloody or coffee-coloured urine. Without prompt surgical removal of the heartworm blockage, few dogs survive.

Although more common in south eastern US, heartworm disease has been diagnosed in all 50 states. Because infected mosquitoes can fly indoors, even dogs which spend much time inside the home are at risk. For that reason, the American Heartworm Society recommends that you get your dog tested every year and give your dog heartworm preventive treatment for 12 months of the year.

Thanks to the American Heartworm Society for assistance with the section.

Ringworm

This is not actually a worm, but a fungus and is most commonly seen in puppies and young dogs. It is highly infectious and often found on the face, ears, paws or tail. The ringworm fungus is most prevalent in hot, humid climates but, surprisingly, most cases occur in autumn and winter. Ringworm infections in dogs are not that common; in one study of dogs with active skin problems, less than 3% had ringworm.

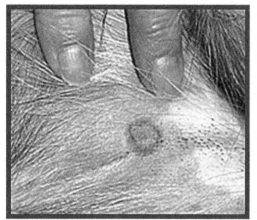

Ringworm is transmitted by spores in the soil and by contact with the infected hair of dogs and cats, which can be typically found on carpets, brushes, combs, toys and furniture. Spores from infected animals can be shed into the environment and live for over 18 months; fortunately most healthy adult dogs have some resistance and never develop symptoms. The fungi live in dead skin, hairs and nails - and the head and legs are the most common areas affected.

Tell-tale signs are bald patches with a roughly circular shape (pictured). Ringworm is relatively easy to treat with fungicidal shampoos or antibiotics from a vet. Humans can catch ringworm from pets, and vice versa. Children are especially susceptible, as are adults with suppressed immune systems and those undergoing chemotherapy.

Hygiene is extremely important. If your dog has ringworm, wear gloves when handling him and wash your hands well afterwards. And if a member of your family catches ringworm, make sure they use separate towels from everyone else or the fungus may spread. As a teenager I caught ringworm from horses at stables where I worked at weekends - much to my mother's horror - and was treated like a leper by the rest of the family until it had cleared up!

Bacterial infection (Pyoderma)

Pyoderma literally means 'pus in the skin' (yuk!) and fortunately this condition is not contagious. Early signs of this bacterial infection are itchy red spots filled with yellow pus, similar to pimples or spots in humans. They can sometimes develop into red, ulcerated skin with dry and crusty patches.

Pyoderma is caused by several things: a broken skin surface, a skin wound due to chronic exposure to moisture, altered skin bacteria, or impaired blood flow to the skin. Dogs have a higher risk of developing an infection when they have a fungal infection or an endocrine (hormone gland) disease such as hyperthyroidism, or have allergies to fleas, food or parasites.

Pyoderma is often secondary to allergic dermatitis and develops in the sores on the skin which happen as a result of scratching. Puppies often develop 'puppy pyoderma' in thinly-haired areas such as the groin and underarms. Fleas, ticks, yeast or fungal skin infections, thyroid disease, hormonal imbalances, heredity and some medications can increase the risk. If you notice symptoms, get your dog to the vet quickly before the condition develops from *superficial pyoderma* into *severe pyoderma*, which is very unpleasant and takes a lot longer to treat.

Bacterial infection, no matter how bad it may look, usually responds well to medical treatment, which is generally done on an outpatient basis. Superficial pyoderma will usually be treated with a two to six-week course of antibiotic tablets or ointment. Severe or recurring pyoderma looks awful, causes your dog some distress and can take months of treatment to completely cure. Medicated shampoos and regular bathing, as instructed by your vet, are also part of the treatment. It's also important to ensure your dog has clean, dry, padded bedding.

Interdigital Cysts

These are not common in Goldens, but can affect any breed – Bulldogs are particularly prone to them. If you've ever noticed a fleshy red lump between your dog's toes that looks like an ulcerated sore or a hairless bump, then it was probably an interdigital cyst (interdigital furuncle). These can be very difficult to get rid of since they are not the primary issue, but often a sign of some other condition. They are sometimes associated with obesity - but even slim dogs can suffer from them.

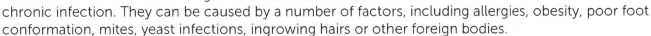

Actually these are not cysts, but the result of *furunculosis*, a condition of the skin which clogs hair follicles and creates chronic infection. They can be caused by a number of factors, including allergies, obesity, poor foot conformation, mites, yeast infections, ingrowing hairs or other foreign bodies.

These nasty-looking bumps are painful for your dog, will probably cause him to limp and can be a nightmare to get rid of. Vets might recommend a whole range of treatments to get to the root cause of the problem. It can be extremely expensive if your dog is having a barrage of tests or biopsies and even then you are not guaranteed to find the underlying cause. The first thing he or she will probably do is put your dog in an E-collar to stop him licking the affected area, which will never recover properly as long as he's constantly licking it. This again is stressful for your dog. Here are some remedies your vet may suggest:

* Antibiotics and/or steroids and/or mite killers
* Soaking his feet in Epsom salts twice daily to unclog the hair follicles
* Testing him for allergies or thyroid problems
* Starting a food trial if food allergies are suspected
* Shampooing his feet
* Cleaning between his toes with medicated (benzoyl peroxide) wipes
* Reducing the dog's weight
* A referral to a veterinary dermatologist
* Surgery

If you suspect your Golden Retriever has an interdigital cyst, take him to the vet for a correct diagnosis and then discuss the various options. A course of antibiotics may be suggested initially, along with switching to a hypoallergenic diet if a food allergy is suspected. If the condition persists, many owners get discouraged, especially when treatment may continue for many weeks.

Before you resort to any drastic action, first try soaking the affected paw in Epsom salts for five or 10 minutes twice a day for up to a month until they have completely disappeared. (You will know after a week if they are having any effect). After the soaking, clean the area with medicated wipes, which are antiseptic and control inflammation. In the US these are sold under the brand name Stridex pads in the skin care section of any grocery, or from the pharmacy. If you think the cause may be an environmental allergy, wash your dog's paws and under his belly when you return from a walk, this will help to remove pollen and other allergens. (Some owners have also reported adding human athlete's foot powder to the salts or athlete's foot cream to the dog's paw after bathing).

Canine Acne

This is not uncommon and - just as with humans - generally affects teenagers, often between five and eight months of age with dogs. Acne occurs when oil glands become blocked causing bacterial infection, and these glands are most active in teenagers. Acne is not a major health problem as most of it will clear up once the dog becomes an adult, but it can recur. Typical signs are pimples, blackheads or whiteheads around the muzzle, chest or groin. If the area is irritated, then there may some bleeding or pus that can be expressed from these blemishes.

Hormonal Imbalances

These occur in dogs of all breeds. They are often difficult to diagnose and occur when a dog is producing either too much (hyper) or too little (hypo) of a particular hormone. One visual sign is often hair loss on both sides of the dog's body. The condition is not usually itchy. Hormone imbalances can be serious as they are often indicators that glands which affect the dog internally are not working properly. However, some types can be diagnosed by special blood tests and treated effectively.

....

Ear Infections

The Golden Retriever's long, floppy ears mean that the breed can be susceptible to ear infections. Infection of the external ear canal (outer ear infection) is called otitis externa and is one of the most common types seen. However, the fact that your dog has recurring ear infections does not necessarily mean that his ears are the source of the problem – although they might be.

One common reason for them in Golden Retrievers is moisture in the ear canal, which in turn allows bacteria to flourish there. But some dogs with chronic or recurring ear infections have inhalant or food allergies or low thyroid function (hypothyroidism). Sometimes the ears are the first sign of allergy. The underlying problem must be treated or the dog will continue to have long term ear infections.

Tell-tale signs include your dog shaking his head, scratching or rubbing his ears a lot, or an unpleasant smell coming from the ears. If you look inside the ears, you may notice a reddy brown or yellow discharge, it may also be red and inflamed with a lot of wax. Sometimes a dog may appear depressed or irritable; ear infections are painful. In chronic cases, the inside of his ears may become crusty or thickened. Dogs can have ear problems for many different reasons, including:

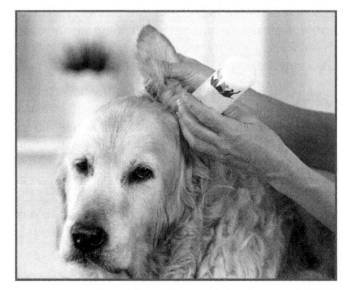

- ❧ Allergies, such as environmental or food allergies
- ❧ Ear mites or other parasites
- ❧ Bacteria or yeast infections
- ❧ Injury, often due to excessive scratching
- ❧ Hormonal abnormalities, e.g. hypothyroidism
- ❧ The ear anatomy and environment, e.g. excess moisture

Hereditary or immune conditions and tumours

In reality, many Golden Retrievers have ear infections due to the structure of the ear. Breeds that have pricked up ears have far few problems because Nature's design allows air to circulate inside the ear, keeping them cool and healthy. However, the Golden's long, floppy ears often prevent sufficient air flow inside the ear. This can lead to bacterial or yeast infections - particularly if there is moisture inside. These warm, damp and dark areas under the ear flaps provide an ideal breeding ground for bacteria.

Treatment depends on the cause and what – if any - other conditions your dog may have. Antibiotics are used for bacterial infections and antifungals for yeast infections. Glucocorticoids, such as dexamethasone, are often included in these medications to reduce the inflammation in the ear. Your vet may also flush out and clean the ear with special drops, something you may have to do daily at home until the infection clears.

It can be difficult to get medication into the lower (horizontal) part of the ear. The best method is to hold the dog's ear flap with one hand and put the ointment or drops in with the other, if possible tilting the dog's head away from you so the liquid flows downwards **with gravity.** Make sure you then hold the ear flap down and massage the medication into the horizontal canal before letting go of your dog, as the first thing he will do is shake his head – and if the ointment or drops aren't massaged in, they will fly out.

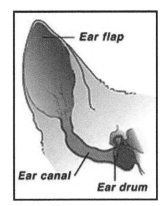

Nearly all ear infections can be successfully managed if properly diagnosed and treated. But if an underlying problem remains undiscovered, the outcome will be less favourable. Deep ear infections can damage or rupture the eardrum, causing an internal ear infection and even permanent hearing loss. Closing of the ear canal (*hyperplasia* or *stenosis)* is another sign of severe infection. Most extreme cases of hyperplasia will eventually require surgery as a last resort; the most common procedure is called a 'lateral ear resection'. This is an **extremely** painful procedure for the dog and should only be considered as a last resort.

To avoid or alleviate recurring ear infections, check your dog's ears and clean them regularly. After swimming, care should be taken to ensure the inside of the ear is thoroughly dry afterwards – as well as after bathing at home if you do bath your dog. There is more information on how to clean your dog's ears in **Chapter 13. Grooming.**

If your dog appears to be in pain, has smelly ears, or if his ear canals look inflamed, contact the vet straight away. If you can nip the first infection in the bud, there is a chance it will not return. If your dog has a ruptured or weakened eardrum, ear cleansers and medications could do more harm than good. Early treatment is the best way of preventing a recurrence.

NOTE: When cleaning your dog's ears, be very careful not to put anything too far down inside. Visit YouTube to see videos of how to correctly clean without damaging them. DO NOT use cotton buds, these are too small and can damage the ear.

Some Allergy Treatments

Treatments and success rates vary tremendously from dog to dog and from one allergy to another, which is why it is so important to consult a vet at the outset. Earlier diagnosis is more likely to lead to a successful treatment. Some owners whose dogs have recurring skin issues find that a course of antibiotics or steroids works wonders for their dog's sore skin and itching. However, the scratching starts all over again shortly after the treatment stops.

Food allergies require patience, a change of diet and maybe even a food trial, and the specific trigger is notoriously difficult to isolate – unless you are lucky and hit on the culprit straight away. With inhalant and contact allergies, blood and skin tests are available, followed by hyposensitisation treatment. However, this is not inexpensive and in some cases the specific trigger for many dogs remains unknown. So the reality for many owners of Golden Retrievers with allergies is that they manage the ailment with various medications and practices, rather than curing it completely.

Our Personal Experience

After corresponding with numerous other dog owners and consulting our vet, Graham, over the last decade, it seems that our experiences with allergies are not uncommon. This is borne out by the many owners who have contacted our website about their pet's allergy or sensitivities. According to Graham, more and more dogs are appearing in his waiting room every spring with various types of allergies. The root cause still remains to be seen.

Our dog was perfectly fine until he was about two years old when he began to scratch a lot. He scratched more in spring and summer, which meant that his allergies were almost certainly inhalant or contact-based and related to pollens, grasses or other outdoor triggers. One option was for Max to have a barrage of tests to discover exactly what he was allergic to. We decided not to do this, not because of the cost, but because our vet said it was highly likely that he was allergic to pollens. If

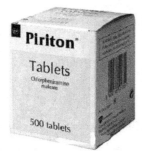

we had confirmed an allergy to pollens, we were not going to stop taking him outside for walks, and at that time hyposensitisation was not well known, so the vet treated him on the basis of seasonal inhalant or contact allergies, probably related to pollen.

As already mentioned, it's beneficial to have a shallow bath or hose outside and to rinse the dog's paws and underbelly after a walk in the countryside. This is something our vet does with his own dogs and has found that the scratching reduces as a result.

Regarding medications, Max was at first put on to a tiny dose of Piriton (pictured), an inexpensive antihistamine sold in the millions for hay fever sufferers (human and canine), and for the first few springs and summers, this worked well.

Allergies can often change and the dog can also build up a tolerance to a treatment, which is why they can be so difficult to treat. This has been the case with Max over the years. The symptoms change from season to season, although the main ones remain and they are: general scratching, paw biting and ear infections. A couple of years ago Max started nibbling his paws for the first time - a habit he persists with - although not to the extent that they become red and raw. Over the years we have tried a number of treatments, all of which have worked for a while, before he comes off the medication in autumn for six months when plants and grasses mostly stop growing outdoors. He manages perfectly fine the rest of the year without any treatment at all.

If we were starting again from scratch, knowing what we know now, I would certainly investigate a raw diet, if necessary in combination with holistic remedies. Our dog is now 12, we feed him a high quality hypoallergenic dry food. His allergies are manageable, he loves his food, still has plenty energy (although he sleeps a lot more) and is otherwise healthy, and so we are reluctant to make such a big change at this point in his life.

One season Max was put on a short course of steroids. These worked very well for five months, but steroids are not a long-term solution, as prolonged use can cause Cushing's Disease and other problems. Another spring Max was prescribed a non-steroid daily tablet called Atopica, sold in the

UK only through vets. The active ingredient is **cyclosporine**, which suppresses the immune system. Some dogs can get side effects, although Max didn't, and holistic practitioners believe that it is harmful to the dog. This treatment was expensive (around £1 or US$1.30 a day), but initially extremely effective – so much so that we thought we had cured the problem completely. However, after a couple of seasons on cyclosporine he developed a tolerance to the drug and started scratching again.

A few years ago he went back on the antihistamine Piriton, a higher dose than when he was two years old, and this worked very well again. One advantage of this drug is that is it manufactured by the million for dogs and is therefore very inexpensive.

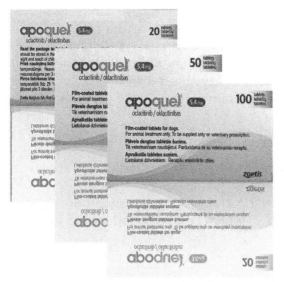

In 2013 the FDA approved **Apoquel** (oclacitinib) to control itching and inflammation in allergic dogs. In some quarters it has been hailed a **'wonder drug'** for canine allergies. In fact it has proved so popular in the UK and North America that in 2014-15 there was a shortage of supply, with the manufacturers not being able to produce it fast enough.

We have tried it with excellent results. There was some tweaking at the beginning to get the daily dose right, but it really has proved effective for us. Like clockwork last spring Max suddenly started scratching like crazy - just as he does every spring. We got him into the vet pretty smartish, where he had a single steroid injection to control the itching until the Apoquel kicked in. He went on a double dose of Apoquel for two weeks and continued throughout the summer on a normal, single dose. Of course, he still scratches – all dogs do – but I would say it completely controls that frantic scratching followed by hot spots. For a Golden Retriever weighing 30kg (66lb) a typical dosage would be one 16mg tablet per day. This currently costs around £2 (US$2.60) per day; you can buy the tablets cheaper online, but you have to produce a prescription from your vet.

Most vets recommend adding fish oils (which contain Omega-3 fatty acids) to a daily feed to keep your dog's skin and coat healthy all year round – whether or not he has problems. We add a liquid supplement called Lintbells' Yumega Itchy Dog, which contains Omegas 3 and 6, to one of Max's two daily feeds all year round and this definitely seems to help his skin. In the past when the scratching got particularly bad, we bathed him in an antiseborrhoeic shampoo (called Malaseb) twice a week for a limited time. This also helped, although this has not been necessary since he started on the Apoquel.

The main point is that most allergies are manageable. They may change throughout the life of the dog and you may have to alter the treatment. Max may have allergies, but he wouldn't miss his walks for anything and, all in all, he is one contented canine. We've compiled some anecdotal evidence from our website from owners of dogs with various allergies. Here are some of their suggestions:

Bathing - bathing your dog using shampoos that break down the oils which plug the hair follicles. These shampoos contain antiseborrhoeic ingredients such as benzoyl peroxide, salicylic acid, sulphur or tar. One example is Sulfoxydex shampoo, which can be followed by a cream rinse such as Episoothe Rinse afterwards to prevent the skin from drying out.

Dabbing – Using an astringent such as witch hazel or alcohop on affected areas. We have heard of zinc oxide cream being used to some effect. In the human world, this is rubbed on to mild skin abrasions and acts as a protective coating. It can help the healing of chapped skin and nappy rash in babies. Zinc oxide works as a mild astringent and has some antiseptic properties and is safe to use on dogs, *as long as you do not allow the dog to lick it off*.

Daily supplements - Vitamin E, vitamin A, zinc and omega oils all help to make a dog's skin healthy. Feed a daily supplement which contains some of these, such as fish oil, which provides omega.

Here are some specific remedies from owners. We are not endorsing them, we're just passing on the information. Check with your vet before trying any new remedies.

A medicated shampoo with natural tea tree oil has been suggested. Some owners have reported that switching to a fish-based diet has helped lessen scratching, while others have suggested home-cooked food is best, if you have the time to prepare the food. Another reader said: "My eight-month-old dog also had a contact dermatitis around his neck and chest. I was surprised how extensive it was. The vet recommended twice-a-week baths with an oatmeal shampoo. I also applied organic coconut oil daily for a few weeks and this completely cured the dermatitis. I put a capsule of fish oil with his food once a day and continue to give him twice-weekly baths. His skin is great now."

Several owners have tried coconut oil with some success. Here is an article on the benefits of coconut oils and fish oils, check with your vet first:
www.cocotherapy.com/fishoilsvsvirginoil_coconutoil.htm

Another reader added a teaspoonful of canola (rapeseed) oil in her dog's food every other day, shampooed the carpets and switched laundry detergent, all of which helped to reduce her dog's scratching.

Breeders on Allergies

To put skin issues in context, by far the majority of the Golden Retriever breeders involved in this book have not had any problems with their dogs and allergies – although they do choose their breeding stock with care. Many stressed the importance of feeding a high quality diet. Here are their experiences:

Helen Dorrance, of Ducat Goldens, Texas, has more than 42 years' experience and during that time has produced more than 50 Golden Retriever champions. She said: "The biggest allergy/food sensitivity I see in Golden Retrievers is a chicken sensitivity. The sensitivity can be manifested in several ways: itching, hot spots, hard to cure ear infections, full anal glands, pink feet, chewing feet or pulling out feathering - especially tail feathering. (Photo of the handsome, healthy Oliver courtesy of Helen).

"Unfortunately, chicken is in a lot of foods. It is best to scrutinize the ingredients and eschew anything (food or treats) that has chicken or chicken fat in it. Even a trace of chicken can set off the allergy. For instance, Purina Pro Plan Sensitive Skin and Stomach has salmon and rice as a base and almost all Goldens do well on it.

However, Purina Pro Plan Beef and Rice and Salmon Performance seem fine on the surface, but contain an unspecified 'animal fat' and that seems to set off dogs' chicken allergies. There are, of course, several high-end, limited ingredient foods that would also suffice. A bit of a radical recommendation for Goldens prone to hot spots is to shave the dog down to the skin with a No. 10 blade! You eliminate the undercoat which traps the moisture that helps to cause hot spots. It seems to help dogs with allergies in general - especially in the south where we have very short, mild winters with year round pollination. You probably wouldn't need to shave dogs who live up north since they don't suffer from allergies the same way the southern dogs do.

"There has also been some research that says you should feed your puppy a protein source you don't intend to feed it as an adult. Apparently, when puppies are getting their vaccinations they can sometimes develop an immune response to their environment, including diet. Hence the recommendation to feed them a food you are unlikely to feed them as adults in case they develop a food sensitivity to their puppy diet."

Tim Hoke, Golden Meadows Golden Retrievers, California: "The biggest current issue with skin seems to be coming out of Europe. The issue is Ichthyosis, a condition in which the skin has a 'fish scale'-like look and texture; it also causes excessive dandruff." (Photo of puppy courtesy of Tim).

Julian Pottage, Yorkbeach Golden Retrievers, Mid Glamorgan, Wales: "None of our owners have reported food sensitivities. A very few puppies have had dry skin, which a diet rich in fish or fish oils works well for." Liz Spicer-Short, Priorschest Golden Retrievers, Dorset, UK: "As a breed they seem to be prone to wet eczema-type skin patches. I have found that changing the food to one with a lower fat content helps. Since changing to Royal Canin Golden Retriever specific food I have had no skin problems with any of my dogs."

Dee Johnson, of Johnsongrace Golden Retrievers, North Cornwall, agrees: "I think with food intolerances, it is really down to giving a really good quality kibble. I searched for years because of one of my girls getting colitis when she was younger. Then I moved her onto 'Gentle,' which is cold-pressed and you only need to give a small portion as there are no added fillers etc. to fill them up. It contains green-lipped mussels and other really good ingredients, and my dogs have such lovely coats and digestive systems." Another breeder added: "Skin issues can occur in Golden Retrievers if they are fed a poor diet or bathed too often."

Anna Cornelius-Jones, Mindieslodge Golden Retrievers, Dorset: "I have never had any skin issues or allergies when the puppies have been in my care, until they have gone to their new owners. Some pups have sometimes had mild skin problems, which has been put down to bedding and detergents used to wash their bedding in."

A UK breeder with more than two decades' experience added that she had had experience of eczema, but that use of a standard skin cream, such as Sudocreme, had quickly cleared it up. Another UK breeder added: "One of my own dogs has an allergic skin reaction every May/June with sore patches which spreads rapidly. Obviously, quick veterinary treatment is called for, but this year I have taken all walks away from the neighbouring agricultural fields and with only two more weeks to go of the 'danger time', her skin has remained fine so far. So, again, trying to find the trigger for these allergies is paramount so that hopefully they can be avoided."

The Holistic Approach

As canine allergies become increasingly common, more and more owners of dogs with allergies and sensitivities are looking towards natural foods and remedies to help deal with the issues. Others are finding that their dog does well for a time with injections or medication, but then the symptoms slowly start to reappear. A holistic practitioner looks at finding the root cause of the problem and treating that, rather than just treating the symptoms.

Dr Sara Skiwski is a holistic vet working in California. She writes here about canine environmental allergies: "Here in California, with our mild weather and no hard freeze in Winter, environmental allergens can build up and cause nearly year-round issues for our beloved pets. Also seasonal allergies, when left unaddressed, can lead to year-round allergies. Unlike humans, whose allergy symptoms seem to affect mostly the respiratory tract, seasonal allergies in dogs often take the form of skin irritation/inflammation. "Allergic reactions are produced by the immune system. The way the immune system functions is a result of both genetics and the environment: Nature versus Nurture. Let's look at a typical case. A puppy starts showing mild seasonal allergy symptoms, for instance a red tummy and mild itching in Spring. Off to the vet!

"The treatment prescribed is symptomatic to provide relief, such as a topical spray. The next year when the weather warms up, the patient is back again - same symptoms but more severe this time. This time the dog has very itchy skin. Again, the treatment is symptomatic - antibiotics, topical spray (hopefully no steroids), until the symptoms resolve with the season change. Fast forward to another Spring...on the third year, the patient is back again but this time the symptoms last longer, (not just Spring but also through most of Summer and into Fall). By Year Five, all the symptoms are significantly worse and are occurring year round. This is what happens with seasonal environmental allergies. The more your pet is exposed to the allergens they are sensitive to, the more the immune system over-reacts and the more intense and long-lasting the allergic response becomes. What to do?

"In my practice, I like to address the potential root cause at the very first sign of an allergic response, which is normally seen between the ages of six to nine months old. I do this to circumvent the escalating response year after year. Since the allergen load your environmentally-sensitive dog is most susceptible to is much heavier outdoors, I recommend two essential steps in managing the condition. They are vigilance in foot care as well as fur care.

"What does this mean? A wipe down of feet and fur, especially the tummy, to remove any pollens or allergens is key. This can be done with a damp cloth, but my favorite method is to get a spray bottle filled with Witch Hazel and spray these areas. First, spray the feet then wipe them off with a cloth, and then spray and wipe down the tummy and sides. This is best done right after the pup has been outside playing or walking. This will help keep your pet from tracking the environmental allergens into the home and into their beds. If the feet end up still being itchy, I suggest adding foot soaks in Epsom salts."

Dr Skiwski also stresses the importance of keeping the immune system healthy by avoiding unnecessary vaccinations or drugs: "The vaccine stimulates the immune system, which is the last thing your pet with seasonal environmental allergies needs. I also will move the pet to an anti-inflammatory diet. Foods that create or worsen inflammation are high in carbohydrates. An allergic pet's diet should be very low in carbohydrates, especially grains. Research has shown that 'leaky gut,' or dysbiosis, is a root cause of immune system overreactions in both dog and cats (and some humans). Feed a diet that is not processed, or minimally processed; one that doesn't have grain and takes a little longer to get absorbed and assimilated through the gut. Slowing the assimilation assures that there are not large spikes of nutrients and proteins that come into the body all at once and overtax the pancreas and liver, creating inflammation.

"A lot of commercial diets are too high in grains and carbohydrates. These foods create inflammation which overtaxes the body and leads not just to skin inflammation, but also to other inflammatory conditions, such as colitis, pancreatitis, arthritis, inflammatory bowel disease and ear infections. Also, these diets are too low in protein, which is needed to make blood. This causes a decreased blood reserve in the body and in some of these animals this can lead to the skin not being properly nourished, starting a cycle of chronic skin infections which produce more itching."

After looking at diet, check that your dog is free from fleas and then these are some of Dr Skiwski's suggested supplements:

- ✓ **Raw (Unpasteurised) Local Honey** - an alkaline-forming food containing natural vitamins, enzymes, powerful antioxidants and other important natural nutrients, which are destroyed during the heating and pasteurisation processes. Raw honey has anti-viral, anti-bacterial and anti-fungal properties. It promotes body and digestive health, is a powerful antioxidant, strengthens the immune system, eliminates allergies, and is an excellent remedy for skin wounds and all types of infections. Bees collect pollen from local plants and their honey often acts as an immune booster for dogs living in the locality.

  Dr Skiwski says: "It may seem odd that straight exposure to pollen often triggers allergies, but that exposure to pollen in the honey usually has the opposite effect. But this is typically what we see. In honey, the allergens are delivered in small, manageable doses and the effect over time is very much like that from undergoing a whole series of allergy immunology injections."

- ✓ **Mushrooms** - make sure you choose the non-poisonous ones! Dogs don't like the taste, so you may have to mask it with another food. Medicinal mushrooms are used to treat and prevent a wide array of illnesses through their use as immune stimulants and modulators, and antioxidants. The most well-known and researched are reishi, maitake, cordyceps, blazei, split-gill, turkey tail and shiitake. The mushrooms stabilise mast cells in the body, which have the histamines attached to them. Histamine is what causes much of the inflammation, redness and irritation in allergies. By helping to control histamine production, the mushrooms can moderate the effects of inflammation and even help prevent allergies in the first place.

WARNING! Mushrooms can interact with some over-the-counter and prescription drugs, so do your research as well as checking with your vet first.

- ✓ **Stinging Nettles** - contain biologically active compounds that reduce inflammation. Nettles have the ability to reduce the amount of histamine the body produces in response to an allergen. Nettle tea or extract can help with itching. Nettles not only help directly to decrease the itch, but also work overtime to desensitise the body to allergens, helping to reprogramme the immune system.

- ✓ **Quercetin** – is an over-the-counter supplement with anti-inflammatory properties. It is a strong antioxidant and reduces the body's production of histamines.

- ✓ **Omega-3 Fatty Acids** - these help decrease inflammation throughout the body. Adding them into the diet of all pets - particularly those struggling with seasonal environmental allergies – is very beneficial. If your dog has more itching along the top of their back and on their sides, add in a fish oil supplement. Fish oil helps to decrease the itch and heal skin lesions. The best sources of Omega 3s are krill oil, salmon oil, tuna oil, anchovy oil and other fish body oils, as well as raw organic egg yolks. If using an oil alone, it is important to give a vitamin B complex supplement.

✓ **Coconut Oil** - contains lauric acid, which helps decrease the production of yeast, a common opportunistic infection. Using a fish body oil combined with coconut oil before inflammation flares up can help moderate or even suppress your dog's inflammatory response.

Dr Skiwski adds: "Above are but a few of the over-the-counter remedies I like. In non-responsive cases, Chinese herbs can be used to work with the body to help to decrease the allergy threshold even more than with diet and supplements alone. Most of the animals I work with are on a program of Chinese herbs, diet change and acupuncture. So, the next time Fido is showing symptoms of seasonal allergies, consider rethinking your strategy to treat the root cause instead of the symptom."

With thanks to Dr Sara Skiwski, of the Western Dragon Integrated Veterinary Services, San Jose, California, for her kind permission to use her writings as the basis for this section.

Photo of Belle (Southvalley Cracking Lass) aged three years, courtesy of Nicholas Lock and Elaine Griffiths, Bonsaviour Retrievers, Shropshire, UK

This chapter has only just touched on the complex subject of skin disorders. As you can see, the causes and treatments are many and varied. One thing is true, whatever the condition, if your Golden Retriever has a skin issue, seek a professional diagnosis <u>as soon as possible</u> before attempting to treat it yourself and before the condition becomes entrenched. Early diagnosis and treatment can sometimes nip the problem in the bud.

Some skin conditions cannot be completely cured, but they can be successfully managed, allowing your dog to live a happy, pain-free life. If you haven't got your puppy yet, ask the breeder if there is a history of skin issues or allergies/food intolerances in her bloodlines. Once you have your dog, remember that good quality diet and attention to cleanliness and grooming can go a long way in preventing and managing canine skin problems and ear infections.

13. Grooming

Golden Retrievers have many advantages over other breeds: they are highly intelligent and willing to please, they get along with everybody, are non-aggressive towards other dogs, they love children and the elderly, they can work as therapy or assistance dogs and are one of the easiest breeds to obedience train and housetrain. They also look fantastic with their luxurious golden coat. These are just a few of their outstanding qualities.

However, there is a price to pay for everything - and with the Golden it's grooming! These dogs are definitely high maintenance when it comes to keeping them clean and tidy. And this is definitely not a breed for the super house-proud. Goldens love running free outdoors, they are instinctive swimmers, and they are drawn to mud like metal to a magnet, which has earned them the nickname of 'swamp collies' among certain devotees of working dogs! Some Goldens are also great diggers. All of this means, not surprisingly, that they often arrive home in less than pristine condition.

They can also shed for Europe – or America.

If your dog is often running free outdoors, it's a good idea to have an outside tap so you can hose him down before coming indoors. And a utility room or other small room with a hard surface where you can clean him up before entering the rest of the house is also an advantage.

Most Golden Retrievers have a double coat, with a soft, dense undercoat that keeps the dog warm in winter, and when he is swimming in freezing cold water. The outer coat is coarser, water-repellent and wavy. All Goldens have the trademark 'feathering' which can start to show as early as three months old. The feathering is visible on the tail, back of the forelegs and thighs and the front of the neck. Puppies change from being fluffy little bundles to dogs with a stunning flowing coat over a period of a year and a bit. By about 18 months most Goldens will have their full adult coats. The AKC describes the Golden Retriever coat as: "Rich, lustrous golden of various shades."

There is no getting away from the fact that Goldens do shed a lot. But exactly how much and when depends on a number of factors, such as bloodlines, skin condition, diet, gender, whether your dog has been neutered or spayed, and temperature of the environment (a dog kept in a centrally heated house will normally shed for longer than a working dog kept in an outdoor kennel, where the seasons are more evident). Some Goldens have a naturally thicker coat than others – show-type Retrievers generally have more coat than working Retrievers. Some dogs shed predominantly twice a year – usually spring and autumn (fall), while others shed all year round. The bottom line is that if a Golden is the dog for you, then you have to be prepared to groom the dog regularly – and also be prepared for some mess around the house.

No dogs should be bathed too often as they can lose some of their natural coat oils, but your Golden will require a bath from time to time to stop him getting smelly. He will probably also need trimming occasionally to stop him getting matted when his coat thickens. You can do this yourself or take him to the groomer's two or three times a year.

Grooming doesn't just mean giving your Golden Retriever a quick tickle with a brush a couple of times a week. There are other facets to grooming that play a part in keeping your dog clean and skin-related issues at bay. Time spent grooming is also time spent bonding with your dog; this physical and emotional inter-reliance brings us closer to our pets. Routine grooming sessions also allow you to examine your Golden's coat, skin, ears, teeth, eyes, paws and nails for signs of problems. Although puppies require fairly minimal brushing, it's important to get yours used to being handled and groomed from an early age; a stubborn adult Golden will not take too kindly to being handled if he is not used to it.

Other benefits of regular brushing are that it removes dead hair and skin, stimulates blood circulation and spreads natural oils throughout the coat, helping to keep it in good condition. If brushed regularly, a Golden Retriever only needs a bath (unless he has a skin condition or is being shown) when he is covered in mud, fox poo, cow manure or any other unmentionable substances that Golden Retrievers enjoy rolling in - and even eating! If you do notice an unpleasant smell - in addition to any normal gassy emissions - and he hasn't been rolling in the aforementioned organic matter, then your dog could have a yeast infection that may require a visit to the vet.

Many owners use a pin brush or bristle brush, comb and undercoat rake to groom their Golden. Another method of removing dead hair and cutting down on hair shed around the house is to use a grooming tool called a Furminator (pictured, above), which thins out the dense undercoat and removes dead hair. But use this only occasionally – not every day – and carefully on the undercoat. If you buy one, make sure it is the 'Long Hair' version.

It is not suitable for all Golden Retrievers; occasionally, a dog may develop bare patches or simply dislike the Furminator. This may be because he or she has a finer coat or sensitive skin, so try a

softer brush or a grooming glove, such as a hound glove (pictured). Also, some owners prefer not to use a Furminator as, although designed to remove the dense undercoat, they say it can break up the top coat on their dog. They are not for every dog, but worth a try, due to their effectiveness. You can just brush your dog, or another method is to gently squirt the coat with a fine spray of water to prevent the hairs from breaking. Then rub with a hound glove to remove loose and dead hair, and finally use a bristle brush to remove all the remaining loose hair. Bristle brushes can be expensive, but they last forever.

If your Golden is resisting your grooming efforts, take him out of his 'comfort zone' by placing him on a table or bench - make sure he can't jump off. You'd be surprised what a difference this can make once he is out of his normal environment - i.e. floor level - and at your level, where you can more easily control him. A few things to look out for when grooming are:

Acne - Little red pimples on a dog's face and chin means he has got acne. A dog can get acne at any age, not just as an adolescent. Plastic bowls can also trigger the condition, which is why stainless steel ones are often better. Daily washing followed by an application of an antibiotic cream is usually enough to get rid of the problem; if it persists it will mean a visit to your vet.

Dry skin - A dog's skin can dry out, especially with artificial heat in the winter months. If you spot any dry patches, for example on the inner thighs or armpits, or a cracked nose, massage a little petroleum jelly or baby oil on to the dry patch.

Eyes - These should be clean and clear. Cloudy eyes, particularly in an older dog, could be early signs of cataracts. Red or swollen tissue in the corner of the eye could be a symptom of cherry eye, which can affect dogs of all breeds. Ingrowing eyelashes is another issue which causes red, watery eyes. If your dog has an issue, you can start by gently bathing the eye(s) with warm water and cotton wool - but never use anything sharp; your dog can suddenly jump forwards or backwards, causing injury. If the eye is red or watering for a few days or more, get it checked out by a vet.

....

Breeders on Grooming

We start with the USA breeders: Tim Hoke, California: "We groom the dogs every two weeks, i.e. shampoo, nails, teeth cleaning, and we brush the dogs daily. A Golden Retriever sheds all day, every day." Kelly Sisco, Missouri: "They shed a lot. They go to the groomer's once a month, then they get baths at home as frequently as needed (with a pond and a farm, it's frequent!). All four of my adults are therapy certified and they also have to get a bath before each therapy visit."

Helen Dorrance, Texas, is unusual in that she shaves her Golden Retrievers: "Goldens should be bathed and groomed once a week; they shed 24/7. If you don't like to vacuum, once again have your dog shaved and you will get respite for at least a couple of months as the dog grows back its hair. Many people would say why get a Golden Retriever if you are just going to shave it? To me, if the hair on the floor means you want to return your dog or buy a doodle (which needs to be shaved every six weeks) instead, then just shave your Golden."

UK breeders: Anna Cornelius-Jones: "Unfortunately, Goldens are quite renowned for moulting and at times can do it in abundance. I groom mine on a regular basis every week so that it reduces the shed and also gets rid of any doggy smells from the undercoat. They also go to the groomers at least three times a year.

"There are always times in between where they have a home bath, as Goldens do love water - so if they find a muddy puddle out on a walk, this becomes a necessity once home. In the summer, we always have a paddling pool out for them to swim and lay in as well."

Dee Johnson: "I only bath mine when they really need it. Because I have five Goldens, we find they shed a lot, particularly twice a year. We can fill up our vacuum cleaner to the brim in one vacuuming! I groom all of mine between one and two times a week. I also do all my own trimming, etc." Liz Spicer-Short: "I groom mine four or five times a week and bath when necessary - when they've rolled in something unmentionable!"

Julian Pottage: "I never bath mine. I am very lucky to have a dog-friendly beach nearby – and I do not show them. Most of the time grooming is about twice a week. When they are moulting, however, it is twice a day! Most of the time they hardly shed at all, but when they do (roughly midweek between seasons) they shed a lot. People tell me that the males shed less." Richard and Suzanne Clear: "We groom ours once every two days and bath every six weeks. They shed a lot."

Karen Ireland: "I groom my dogs at least once a week, usually with a sturdy comb. I very rarely bathe them, but they do go swimming whenever I can get them to our local shoreline and yes, they shed something wicked. Late spring/early summer is the worst; no end of brushing/combing gets rid of the surplus hair and I spend hours daily vacuuming. It is a good job I love them, as this part is quite hard work."

Stephen and Jessica Webb: "Retrievers do shed! Grooming helps considerably; every two to three days is good. All dogs and owners benefit from the dog being bathed. Some owners take this on themselves, others use professional dog groomers." Photo courtesy of Stephen and Jessica.

Jan Schick: "I bath my dogs approximately once every four to six months, but more frequently if they manage to roll in their favourite 'Eau de Reynard' (fox poo!). They moult copiously and they would happily be groomed every hour on the hour! I actually groom them once every one or two days."

Wendy Pickup: "We bath whenever necessary - three times a year is a good general guide, and every week if the dog is attending a weekly dog show. We bath entire males usually twice a year, entire females depend on the gap between their seasons – they tend to shed for two months prior to each season, and their new coat may take two to three months to grow in again. Neutered dogs or bitches may shed a small amount continually."

Sue Page: "Goldies have such a love of water and rolling in unmentionables that you never have to have a rota where you bath a dog every say three months. You bath your Goldie when he needs it. Grooming is very important. Some Golden Retrievers have a double coat and they need grooming once or twice a week. Goldies with a single coat can probably be groomed every two weeks. However, when they moult you should groom them every day, paying particular attention to behind the ears."

Karen Parsons (working retrievers): "They go to the dog groomer's once a quarter. Ours do not shed much, just spring and autumn." Lesley Gunter and Geoff Brown: "Ours get washed with a hose after most walks to clean their feet and undersides. They swim regularly in the river, and we bath them properly every three to four months, more if we're showing them."

Claire Underwood: "They shed all the time, but with two major moults. I groom once a week, although the Kennel Club recommends twice a week. Keep feet and feathers trimmed to make it easier to keep clean. When their coat becomes thick, I trim areas to prevent matting. My dogs bathe themselves regularly in my stream and water troughs. I use a special shampoo on my itchy dog."

Ear Cleaning

It is not uncommon for some Golden Retrievers to suffer from ear infections. Breeds with pricked-up ears suffer far fewer ear infections than those with floppy ears which hang down, like the Golden Retriever. This is because an upright ear allows air to circulate inside, whereas covered inner ears are generally warm, dark and moist, making them a haven for bacteria and yeast. This can lead to recurring infections and, in severe cases, the dog going deaf or even needing a surgical operation.

Goldens love swimming, which can also cause ear infections if the area under the ear flap remains wet for long periods. The wetness, combined with the warmth of an enclosed space, is an ideal breeding ground for bacteria. A good habit to get into is to towel dry under the ear flaps after your dog has been swimming. Keep an eye out for redness or inflammation of the ear flap or inner ear, or a build-up of dark wax, and if your Golden has particularly hairy ears, the hair inside the ear flap should be regularly plucked to allow air to circulate more freely.

Some owners with susceptible dogs bathe the inner ear with cotton wool and warm water or a veterinary ear cleaner as part of their regular grooming routine. Whether or not your dog has issues, it is good practice to check his or her ears and eyes regularly.

 Never put anything sharp or narrow - like a cotton bud – inside your dog's ears, as you can cause damage.

Typical signs of an ear infection are: your dog shaking his head a lot, scratching his ears, rubbing his ears on the carpet or ground, and/or an unpleasant smell coming from the ears, which is a sign of a yeast infection. If your dog exhibits any of these signs, consult your vet ASAP, as simple routine cleaning won't solve the problem, and **ear infections are notoriously difficult to get rid of** once your dog's had one. The secret is to keep your dog's ears clean, dry and free from too much hair right from puppyhood and hope that he never gets one.

One method of cleaning your Golden's ears is to get a good quality ear cleaning solution from your vet's or local pet/grooming supply shop. Then squeeze the cleaner into your Golden's ear canal and rub the ear at the base next to the skull. Allow your dog to shake his or her head and use a cotton ball to gently wipe out any dirt and waxy build up inside the ear canal.

Method Two is to use a baby wipe and gently wipe away any dirt and waxy build up. In both cases it is important to only clean as far down the ear canal as you can see to avoid damaging the eardrum. The first method is preferred if you are also bathing your dog, as it will remove any unwanted water that may have got down into the ears during the bath. See **Chapter 12. Skin and Allergies** for more information on ear infections.

Nail Trimming

If your Golden Retriever is regularly exercised on grass or other soft surfaces, his nails may not be getting worn down sufficiently, so they may have to be clipped or filed. Nails should be kept short for the paws to remain healthy. Long nails interfere with the dog's gait, making walking awkward or painful and they can also break easily, usually at the base of the nail where blood vessels and nerves are located.

Get your dog used to having his paws inspected from puppyhood; it's also a good opportunity to check for other problems, such as cracked pads or interdigital cysts. (These are swellings between the toes, often due to a bacterial infection). Be prepared: many dogs dislike having their nails trimmed, so it requires patience and persistence on your part.

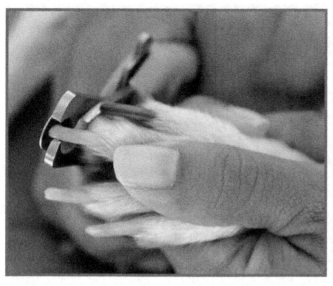

To trim your dog's nails, use a specially designed clipper. Most have safety guards to prevent you cutting the nails too short. Do it before they get too long; if you can hear the nails clicking on the floor, they're too long. You want to trim only the ends, before 'the quick,' which is a blood vessel inside the nail. You can see where the quick ends on a white nail, but not on a dark nail.

Clip only the hook-like part of the nail that turns down. Start trimming gently, a nail or two at a time, and your dog will learn that you're not going to hurt him. If you accidentally cut the quick, stop the bleeding with some styptic powder.

Another option is to file your dog's nails with a nail grinder tool. Some dogs may have tough nails that are hard to trim and this may be less stressful for your dog, with less chance of pain or bleeding. The grinder is like an electric nail file and only removes a small amount of nail at a time. Some owners prefer to use one as it is harder to cut the quick, and many dogs prefer them to a clipper. However, you have to introduce your Golden gradually to the grinder - they often don't like the noise or vibration at first. If you find it impossible to clip your dog's nails, or you are at all worried about doing it, take him to a vet or a groomer - and ask him or her to squeeze your dog's anal sacs while he's there!

And while we're discussing the less appealing end of your Golden Retriever, let's dive straight in and talk about anal sacs. Sometimes called scent glands, these are a pair of glands located inside your dog's anus that give off a scent when he has a bowel movement. You won't want to hear this, but problems with impacted anal glands are not uncommon in dogs! When a dog passes firm stools, the glands normally empty themselves, but soft poo(p) or diarrhoea can mean that not enough pressure is exerted to empty the glands, causing discomfort to the dog. If they become infected, this results in swelling and pain. In extreme cases one or both anal glands can be removed.

If your dog drags himself along on his rear end - 'scooting' - or tries to lick or scratch his anus, he could well have impacted anal glands that need squeezing, also called expressing - either by you if you know how to do it, your vet or a groomer. (He might also have worms). Either way, it pays to keep an eye on both ends of your dog!

Bathing Your Golden Retriever

If you groom your Golden Retriever every week, you shouldn't need to bathe him very often – unless, as mentioned, he's been rolling in something smelly. If your dog regularly returns from his daily walks covered in mud, hose him down before allowing him back into the house. This is perfectly acceptable; a Golden Retriever's coat is designed to cope with water. But do not regularly use shampoos or other products (unless advised to do so by a vet), as a dog needs to keep his coat naturally oily and general shampoos rid the coat of its natural oils.

Never use human shampoos on your Golden as these will only irritate his skin. A dog's skin has a different pH to that of a human. If you do occasionally use a shampoo on your Golden Retriever, use one specially medicated for dogs - such as Malaseb or similar. It is expensive, but lasts a long time. There is also a wide range of shampoos for dogs containing natural organic ingredients.

If a Golden Retriever is left in a dirty condition, this can cause irritation, leading to skin issues, scratching and/or excessive shedding. It's all a question of getting the balance right, and this will to some extent depend on how much outdoor exercise your Golden gets, what sort of areas he's running in, how often he swims and what his natural skin condition is like.

Teeth Cleaning

Veterinary studies show that by the age of signs of gum disease. Symptoms include yellow and brown build-up of tartar along the gum line, red inflamed gums and persistent bad breath.

You can give your dog a daily dental treat, such as Dentastix or Nylabone, or regularly give him a large raw bone (but not chicken, as this splinters) to help with dental hygiene, but you should also brush your Golden's teeth every now and again if you think he may be developing a problem.

Take things slowly in the beginning and give your dog lots of praise. Golden Retrievers love your attention (and food) and many will start looking forward to teeth brushing sessions - especially if they like the flavour of the toothpaste! Use a pet toothpaste, as the human variety can upset a canine's stomach. The real benefit comes from the actual action of the brush on the teeth, and various brushes, sponges and pads are available - the choice depends on factors such as the health of your dog's gums, the size of his mouth and how good you are at teeth cleaning.

Get your dog used to the toothpaste by letting him lick some off your finger when he is young. If he doesn't like the flavour, try a different one. Continue this until he looks forward to licking the paste - it might be instant or take days.

Put a small amount on your finger and gently rub it on one of the big canine teeth at the front of his mouth. Then get him used to the toothbrush or dental sponge - praise him when he licks it - for several days. The next step is to actually start brushing.

Lift his upper lip gently and place the brush at a 45° angle to the gum line. Gently move the brush backwards and forwards. Start just with his front teeth and then gradually do a few more. You don't need to brush the inside of his teeth as his tongue keeps them relatively free of plaque. With a bit of encouragement and patience, it can become an enjoyable, bonding experience for you both.

As you can see, grooming isn't just about brushing your Golden Retriever a couple of times a week. Goldens do require a bit of extra care when it comes to grooming and keeping them (and the house) clean; it's all part of the bargain when you decide to get this exceptional breed.

14. The Birds and the Bees

Judging by the number of questions our website receives from owners who ask about the canine reproductive cycle and breeding their dogs, there is a lot of confusion about the doggy facts of life out there.

Some owners want to know whether they should breed their dog, while others ask if and at what age they should have their dog neutered – this term can refer to both the spaying of females and the castration of males.

Owners of females often ask when she will come on heat, how long this will last and how often it will occur. Sometimes they want to know how you can tell if a female is pregnant or how long a pregnancy lasts. So here, in a nutshell, is a chapter on the facts of life as far as Golden Retrievers are concerned.

....

Females and Heat

Just like all other mammal females, including humans, a female Golden Retriever has a menstrual cycle - or to be more accurate, an oestrus cycle. This is the period of time when she is ready (and willing!) for mating and is more commonly called *heat* or being *on heat*, *in heat* or *in season*.

A female Golden Retriever has her first cycle from about six to nine months old. However, there are some bloodlines with longer spans between heat cycles and the female may not have her first heat until she is 10 months to one year old, occasionally even as late as 18 months old.

She will generally come on heat every six to nine months, although some bitches may only have one cycle per year. The timescale also becomes more erratic with old age in unspayed females. It can also be irregular with young dogs.

On average, the heat cycle will lasts around 21 days, but can be anything from seven to 10 days up to four weeks. Within this period there will be several days in the middle of the cycle that will be the optimum time for her to get pregnant. This phase is called the *oestrus*. The third phase, called *dioestrus*, begins immediately following oestrus. During this time, her body will produce hormones whether or not she is pregnant. Her body thinks and acts like she is pregnant. All the hormones are present; only the puppies are missing. This can sometimes lead to what is known as a 'false pregnancy'.

Good breeders wait until a female is fully health tested, has had one or two heat cycles and is at least 18 months old before mating. Females should not be used for breeding too early; pregnancy draws on the calcium reserves needed for their own growing bones. If bred too early, she may break down structurally and have more health issues in later life. Good breeders also limit the number of litters from each female, as breeding can take a lot out of them.

To protect females from overbreeding, the UK's Kennel Club introduced Breeding Restrictions in 2012. Now it will not register a litter from any bitch:

1. That has already had four litters.

2. If she is less than one year old at the time of mating.

3. If she is eight years or older when she whelps (gives birth).

4. If the litter is the result of any mating between father and daughter, mother and son or brother and sister.

5. If she has already had two C-Sections (Caesarean Sections).

Breeders then spend considerable time researching a suitable mate. The Kennel Club's Mate Select programme at www.thekennelclub.org.uk/services/public/mateselect is an excellent tool for UK breeders. It enables them to check the health test results of a potential mate, and also gives a figure for the Coefficient of Inbreeding, to ensure that the dog they are thinking of mating theirs with is not too closely related, which in turn can lead to unhealthy puppies.

The Golden Retriever Club of America (GRCA) Code of Ethics stipulates that dogs selected for breeding should be of good health and temperament, and includes the paragraph that they should: "Be in overall good health, and be physically and mentally mature (which is generally not until two years of age)."

The US equivalent of Mate Select is the K9 programme at www.k9data.com, which is used by responsible breeders to check the Coefficient of prospective mates.

Heat

While a female dog is on heat, she produces hormones that attract male dogs. Because dogs have a sense of smell thousands of times stronger than ours, your girl on heat is a magnet for all the males in the neighbourhood. It is believed that they can detect the scent of a female on heat up to two miles away! They may congregate around your house or follow you around the park (if you are brave or foolish enough to venture out there while she is in season), waiting for their chance to prove their manhood – or mutthood in their case.

Don't expect your precious little princess to be fussy. Her hormones are raging when she is on heat and, during her most fertile days, she is ready, able and ... VERY willing! As she approaches the optimum time for mating, you may notice her tail bending slightly to one side. She will also start to urinate more frequently. This is her signal to all those virile male dogs out there that she is ready for mating.

Although breeding requires specialised knowledge on the part of the owner, it does not stop a female on heat from being extremely interested in attention from any old mutt! To avoid an unwanted pregnancy you must keep a close eye on your female and not allow her to freely wander where she may come into contact with other dogs when she is on heat- and that includes the garden, unless it is 100% dog proof.

It is amazing the lengths some entire (uncastrated) males will go to impregnate a female on heat. Travelling great distances to follow her scent, jumping over barriers, digging under fences, chewing through doors or walls and sneaking through hedges are just some of the tactics employed by canine Casanovas on the loose. Some dogs living in the same house as a bitch in season have even been known to mate with her through the bars of a crate! If you do have an entire male, you need to physically keep him in a separate place, perhaps with an understanding friend, outdoor kennel or even boarding kennels. The desire to mate is all-consuming and can be accompanied by howling or 'marking' (urinating) indoors from a frustrated male.

Avoid taking your female out in public places while she is in season, and certainly don't let her run free if you are away from home and may encounter other dogs. During this time you can compensate for these restrictions by playing more indoor or garden games to keep her mentally and physically active.

You can buy a spray which masks the natural oestrus scent of your female. Marketed under such attractive names as "Bitch Spray," these will lessen the scent, but not eliminate it. They might be useful for reducing the amount of unwanted attention, but are not a complete deterrent. There is, however, no canine contraceptive and the only sure-fire way of preventing your female from becoming pregnant is spaying. (There is a "morning after pill" – actually a series of oestrogen tablets or an injection - which some vets may administer, but reported side effects are severe, including Pyometra, bone marrow suppression and infertility).

The first visual sign of heat that you may notice is that her vulva (external sex organ, or pink bit under her tail) becomes swollen, which she will lick to keep herself clear. She will then bleed; this is sometimes called spotting. It will be a light red or brown at the beginning of the heat cycle, turning more watery later.

Some females can bleed quite heavily; this is normal. But if you have any concerns, contact your vet to be on the safe side. She may also start to 'mate' with your leg, other dogs or objects. These are all normal signs of heat.

Some females naturally want to keep themselves clean by licking; others don't. If your girl leaves an unwanted trail around the house, cover anything you don't want stained. You might also consider using disposable doggy diapers/nappies or reusable sanitary pants (pictured). Unlike women, female dogs do not go through the menopause and can have puppies even when they are quite old. A litter for an elderly female (older than seven years) is not advisable as it can result in complications – for both mother and pups.

Neutering - Pros and Cons

Once a straightforward subject, this is currently a hot topic in the dog world. Dogs which are kept purely as pets – i.e. not for showing or working – have often been spayed or neutered. There is also the very real life-threatening risk of Pyometra in unspayed middle - aged females. However, there is mounting scientific evidence that Golden Retrievers should not be spayed or neutered at least until they are through puberty, regardless of what your vet might advise. Armed with the facts, it is for each individual owner to decide what is best for their dog.

A major argument for neutering of both sexes is that there is already too much indiscriminate breeding of dogs in the world. As you will read in **Chapter 15. Golden Retriever Rescue**, it is estimated that 1,000 dogs are put to sleep **every hour** in the USA alone. It is for this reason that rescue organisations in North America, the UK and Australia neuter all dogs that they rehome. Some areas in the United States, e.g. LA, have even adopted a compulsory sterilisation policy:

www.avma.org/Advocacy/StateAndLocal/Pages/sr-spay-neuter-laws.aspx aimed at "reducing and eventually eliminating the thousands of euthanizations conducted in Los Angeles' animal shelters every year." The RSPCA, along with most UK vets, also promotes the benefits of neutering: www.rspca.org.uk/adviceandwelfare/pets/general/neutering. It is estimated that more than half of all dogs in the UK are spayed or castrated. Another point is that you may not have a choice. Some Puppy Contracts from KC and AKC breeders may stipulate that, except in special circumstances, you agree to neuter the dog as a Condition of Sale.

The other side of the coin is that there is recent scientific evidence that neutering – and especially early neutering - can have a detrimental effect on the health of dogs, and Golden Retrievers are particularly badly affected. In 2013, the University of California, Davis School of Veterinary Medicine published a study revealing that neutered Golden Retrievers appear to be at a higher risk of joint disorders and cancers compared with sexually intact dogs of the same breed. Read the news report online here: http://www.aaha.org/blog/NewStat/post/2014/07/17/785809/UC-Davis-study-neutering-golden-retrievers-Labradors.aspx.

The full original report, called "Neutering Dogs: Effects on Joint Disorders and Cancers in Golden Retrievers," by Gretel Torres de la Riva, Benjamin L. Hart , Thomas B. Farver, Anita M. Oberbauer, Locksley L. McV. Messam, Neil Willits, Lynette A. Hart can be read at: http://journals.plos.org/plosone/article?id=10.1371/journal.pone.0055937

A follow-up study involving male and female Golden Retrievers (with around a 5% incidence of joint disorders in intact dogs) found that Goldens that had been neutered before six months of age were four or five times more likely to have joint problems. The same study looked at cancer in Golden Retrievers. Intact females had a 3% rate of cancer, while females spayed up to eight years old were three to four times more likely to get cancer. Neutering male Goldens had "relatively minor effects." http://journals.plos.org/plosone/article?id=10.1371/journal.pone.0102241

Many vets and rescue organisations advise spaying or castrating puppies at just a few months old. However, in light of this scientific evidence, you may want to consider whether you spay a female Golden, or at least wait until she is four years of age, given the increased joint and cancer risks. If you have a male and decide to neuter him, you would be well advised to wait until he is fully grown.

···

Spaying

Spaying is the term traditionally used to describe the sterilisation of a female dog so that she cannot become pregnant. This is normally done by a procedure called an 'ovariohysterectomy' and involves the removal of the ovaries and uterus (womb). Although this is a routine operation, it is major abdominal surgery and she has to be anaesthetised.

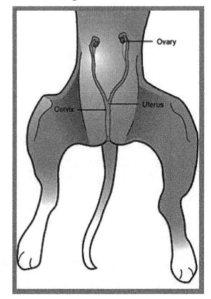

One less invasive option offered by some vets is an 'ovariectomy', which removes the ovaries, but leaves the womb intact. It requires only a small incision and can even be carried out by laparoscopy (keyhole surgery). The dog is anaesthetised for a shorter time and there is less risk of infection or excess bleeding during surgery. One major reason often given for not opting for an ovariectomy is that the female still runs the risk of the life-threatening disease Pyometra (infection of the uterus or womb) later in life. However, there is currently little or no scientific evidence of females that have undergone an ovariectomy contracting Pyometra at a later date.

If a female is spayed before her first heat cycle, she will have an almost zero risk of mammary cancer (the equivalent of breast cancer in women). Even after the first heat, spaying reduces the risk of this cancer by 92%. Some vets claim that the risk of mammary cancer in unspayed female dogs can be as high as one in four. Your vet may encourage you to have your dog spayed while she is still a puppy. However, as you have just read, there is increasing scientific evidence that early spaying has a detrimental effect on later health in Goldens.

If you do wish to have your dog spayed, our advice is to wait until she is 18 months or older; and there is emerging evidence that is it better to wait until a female is at least four years old. Personally, we would consider spaying a female Golden at that age to reduce the risk of her later contacting Pyometra, which is a serious threat for unspayed middle-aged bitches. Spaying is a much more serious operation for females than neutering is for males. It involves an internal abdominal operation, whereas the neutering procedure is carried out on the male's testicles, which are outside his abdomen. As with any major procedure, there are pros and cons.

For:

- Spaying prevents infections, cancer and other diseases of the uterus and ovaries

- A spayed bitch will have a greatly reduced risk of mammary cancer

- Spaying eliminates the risk of Pyometra, which results from hormonal changes in the female's reproductive tract and affects many unspayed middle-aged females

- It reduces hormonal changes that can interfere with the treatment of diseases like diabetes or epilepsy

- Spaying can reduce behaviour problems, such as roaming, aggression towards other dogs, anxiety or fear (not all canine experts agree with this)

- You don't have to guard your female against unwanted attention from males as she will no longer have heat cycles

- You no longer have to cope with any potential mess caused by bleeding inside the house during heat cycles

- A University of Georgia study involving 40,000 death records from the Veterinary Medical Database from 1984-2004, found that sterilised dogs lived on average 1.5 years longer: http://journals.plos.org/plosone/article?id=10.1371/journal.pone.0061082 A spayed dog does not contribute to the pet overpopulation problem

Against:

- There is scientific evidence that spaying Golden Retrievers before six months of age can greatly increase the chance of joint problems developing

- A further study by the same scientists indicated that the risk of cancer after spaying increased by 300% to 400%

- Complications can occur, including an abnormal reaction to the anaesthetic, bleeding, stitches breaking and infections; **these are not common**

- Occasionally there can be long-term effects connected to hormonal changes. These include weight gain or less stamina, which can occur years after spaying

- Older females may suffer some urinary incontinence, but it only affects a few spayed females - discuss with your vet

- Cost. This can range from £100 to £300 in the UK (approximately $150-$500 at a vet's practice in the USA, or around $50 at a low cost clinic, for those that qualify)

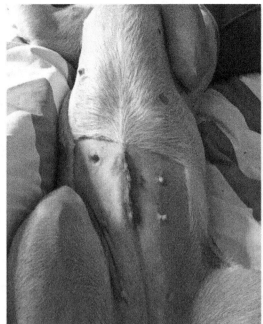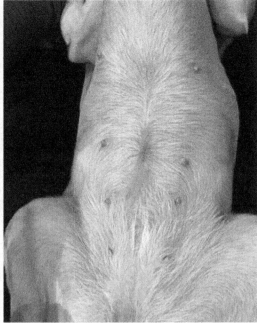

These photographs are reproduced courtesy of Guy Bunce and Chloe Spencer, of Dizzywaltz Labrador Retrievers, Berkshire, England. The one on the left shows four-year-old Disney shortly after spaying (ovariohysterectomy). The one on the right shows Disney a few weeks later.

Neutering

Neutering male dogs involves castration; the removal of the testicles. This can be a difficult decision for some owners, as it causes a drop in the pet's testosterone levels, which some humans – men in particular! - feel affects the quality of their dog's life. Fortunately, dogs do not think like people and male dogs do not miss their testicles or the loss of sex.

Unless you specifically want to breed, work or show your dog, or he has a special job, neutering is recommended by animal rescue organisations and vets. Even then, Golden Retrievers working in service or for charities are routinely neutered and this does not impair their ability to perform their duties. There are countless unwanted puppies, many of which are destroyed. There is also the problem of a lack of knowledge from the owners of some breeding dogs, resulting in the production of poor puppies with congenital health or temperament problems.

Technically, neutering can be carried out at any age over eight weeks, provided both testicles have descended. However, recent research is definitely coming down on the side of waiting until the dog is at least one year old. Surgery is relatively straightforward, and much less of a major operation for a male than spaying is for a female. Complications are less common and less severe than with spaying. Although he will feel tender afterwards, your dog should return to his normal self within a couple of days. Dogs neutered before puberty tend to grow a little larger than dogs done later. This is because testosterone is involved in the process that stops growth, so the bones grow for longer without testosterone.

When he comes out of surgery, his scrotum (the sacs that held the testicles) will be swollen and it may look like nothing has been done. But it is normal for these to slowly shrink in the days following surgery. Here are the main pros and cons:

For:

❧ Behaviour problems such as aggression and wandering off are reduced (again, some experts disagree with this)

Incision   Testicles

- Unwanted sexual behaviour, such as mounting people or objects, is usually reduced or eliminated

- Testicular problems such as infections, cancer and torsion (painful rotation of the testicle) are eradicated

- Prostate disease, common in older male dogs, is less likely to occur

- A submissive entire (un-neutered) male dog may be targeted by other dogs. After he has been neutered, he will no longer produce testosterone and so will not be regarded as much of a threat by the other males, so he is less likely to be bullied

- A neutered dog is not fathering unwanted puppies

Against:

- A major scientific study seems to show that Goldens neutered before six months of age are four to five times more likely to have joint problems

- As with any surgery, there can be bleeding afterwards, you should keep an eye on him for any blood loss after the operation. Infections can also occur, generally caused by the dog licking the wound, so try and prevent him doing this. If he persists, use an Elizabethan collar (E-collar). In the **vast majority** of cases, these problems do not occur

- Some dogs' coats may be affected (this also applies to spaying); supplementing the diet with fish oil can compensate for this

- Cost - this starts at around £80 in the UK (in the USA this might cost upwards from $100 at a private veterinary clinic, or from $50 at a low cost or Humane Society clinic)

Two other phrases you may hear when discussing this subject are 'tubal ligation' or 'vasectomy'. Many veterinary papers have been written on these topics, but as yet, not many vets offer them as options, possibly because they have not been trained to carry out these procedures at vet school. The first is the tying of a female's Fallopian tubes and the second is the clamping shut of the sperm ducts from the male's testicles. In both procedures, the dog continues to produce hormones (unlike with spaying and neutering), but is unable to get pregnant or father puppies. With further data on the positive effects of hormones, these operations could become more common in the future – although vets will first have to learn these new techniques.

Myths

Here are some common myths about neutering and spaying:

Neutering or spaying will spoil the dog's character - There is no evidence that any of the positive characteristics of your dog will be altered. He or she will be just as loving, playful and loyal. Neutering may reduce aggression or roaming, especially in male dogs, because they are no longer competing to mate with a female.

A female needs to have at least one litter - There is no proven physical or mental benefit to a female having a litter.

Mating is natural and necessary - We tend to ascribe human emotions to our dogs, but they do not think emotionally about sex or having and raising a family. Unlike humans, their desire to mate or breed is entirely physical, triggered by the chemicals called hormones within their body. Without these hormones – i.e. after neutering or spaying – the desire disappears or is greatly reduced.

Male dogs will behave better if they can mate - This is simply not true; sex does not make a dog behave better. In fact, it can have the opposite effect. Having mated once, a male may show an increased interest in females. He may also consider his status elevated, which may make him harder to control or call back.

....

Pregnancy

A canine pregnancy will normally last for 58 to 65 days, regardless of the size or breed of the dog. Sometimes pregnancy is referred to as the *'gestation period.'*

It's a good idea to take a female for a pre-natal check-up after mating. The vet should answer any questions about type of food, supplements and extra care needed, as well as informing the owner about any physical changes likely to occur in your female.

There is a blood test available that measures levels of *relaxin*. This is a hormone produced by the ovary and the developing placenta, and pregnancy can be detected by monitoring relaxin levels as early as three weeks after mating. The levels are high throughout pregnancy and then decline rapidly after the female has given birth.

A vet can usually see the puppies using Ultrasound from around the same time. X-rays carried out five or more weeks into the pregnancy give the breeder a good idea of the number of puppies. They can also help to give the vet more information, which is particularly useful if the bitch has had previous whelping problems. Here are some of the signs of pregnancy:

* After mating, many females become more affectionate. (However, some will become uncharacteristically irritable and maybe even a little aggressive)

* The female may produce a slight clear discharge from her vagina about one month after mating

* Three or four weeks after mating, a few females experience morning sickness – if this is the case, feed little and often. She may seem more tired than usual

* She may seem slightly depressed and/or show a drop in appetite. These signs can also mean there are other problems, so you should consult your vet

* Her teats (nipples) will become more prominent, pink and erect 25 to 30 days into the pregnancy. Later on, you may notice a fluid coming from them

* After about 35 days, or seven weeks, her body weight will noticeably increase

* Many pregnant females' appetite will increase in the second half of pregnancy

* Her abdomen will become noticeably larger from around day 40, although first-time mums and females carrying few puppies may not show as much

- Her nesting instincts will kick in as the delivery date approaches. She may seem restless or scratch her bed or the floor

- During the last week of pregnancy, females often start to look for a safe place for whelping. Some seem to become confused, wanting to be with their owners and at the same time wanting to prepare their nest. Even if the female is having a C-section, she should still be allowed to nest in a whelping box with layers of newspaper, which she will scratch and dig as the time approaches

If your female becomes pregnant – either by design or accident - your first step should be to consult a vet.

Litter Size

According to the breeders involved in this book, this varies considerably from one Golden Retriever to another, but the breed often has medium to large litters. An average might be around eight puppies, but it could be far fewer or as many as 15.

False Pregnancies

As many as 50% or more of intact (unspayed) females may display signs of a false pregnancy. In the wild it was common for female dogs to have false pregnancies and to lactate (produce milk). This female would then nourish puppies if their own mother died.

False pregnancies occur 60 to 80 days after the female was in heat - about the time she would have given birth – and are generally nothing to worry about for an owner. The exact cause is unknown, however, hormonal imbalances are thought to play an important role. Some dogs have shown symptoms within three to four days of spaying; these include:

- Making a nest

- Mothering or adopting toys and other objects

- Producing milk (lactating)

- Appetite fluctuations

- Barking or whining a lot

- Restlessness, depression or anxiety

- Swollen abdomen

- She might even appear to go into labour

Try not to touch your dog's nipples, as touch will stimulate further milk production. If she is licking herself repeatedly, she may need an E-collar to minimise stimulation. To help reduce and eliminate milk production, you can apply cool compresses to the nipples

Under no circumstances should you restrict your Golden Retriever's water supply to try and prevent her from producing milk. This is dangerous as she can become dehydrated.

Some unspayed bitches may have a false pregnancy with each heat cycle. Spaying during a false pregnancy may actually prolong the condition, so better to wait until it is over to have her spayed. False pregnancy is not a disease, but an exaggerated response to normal hormonal changes. Owners should be reassured that even if left untreated, the condition almost always resolves itself.

However, if your Golden Retriever appears physically ill or the behavioural changes are severe enough to worry you, visit your vet. He or she may prescribe tranquilisers to relieve anxiety, or diuretics to reduce milk production and relieve fluid retention. In rare cases, hormone treatment may be necessary. Generally, dogs experiencing false pregnancies do not have serious long-term problems, as the behaviour disappears when the hormones return to their normal levels in two to three weeks.

One exception is **Pyometra**, a disease mainly affecting unspayed middle-aged females, caused by a hormonal abnormality. Pyometra follows a heat cycle in which fertilisation did not occur and the dog typically starts showing symptoms within two to four months. Commonly referred to as 'pyo', there are 'open' and 'closed' forms of the disease. Open pyo is usually easy to identify with a smelly discharge, so prompt treatment is easy. Closed pyo is often harder to identify and you may not even notice anything until your girl becomes feverish and lethargic. When this happens, it is very serious and time is of the essence. Typically, vets will recommend immediate spaying in an effort to save the bitch's life.

Signs of Pyometra are excessive drinking and urination, with the female trying to lick a white discharge from her vagina. She may also have a slight temperature. If the condition becomes severe, her back legs will become weak, possibly to the point where she can no longer get up without help. Pyometra is serious if bacteria take a hold, and in extreme cases it can be fatal. It is also relatively common and needs to be dealt with promptly by a vet, who will give the dog intravenous fluids and antibiotics for several days. In most cases this is followed by spaying.

Should I Breed From My Golden Retriever?

The short and simple answer is: Unless you know exactly what you are doing or seek expert help, **NO, leave it to the experts.** You need specialist knowledge to successfully breed healthy Goldens with good temperaments that conform to the Breed Standard. But the rising cost of puppies and increasing number of dog owners is tempting more people to consider breeding their dogs.

Prices for Golden Retriever puppies vary from area to area so it's hard to give an exact figure. A straw poll among breeders involved in this book reveal that you can expect to pay from around £900 up to about £1,200 in the UK for a fully health-tested pet from a Kennel Club Assured Breeder, depending on where you live on the country. If a pup has show or field trial champion ancestors, expect to pay more. In the USA, prices range considerably from state to state, but $2,000 upwards would not be out of the ordinary for an AKC-registered fully health-tested pet; more for a pup with show prospects.

(The photo shows a litter of seven-week-old puppies from working lines bred by UK breeder Karen Parsons, of Arundel, West Sussex).

You can't just put any two dogs together and expect perfect, healthy puppies every time; ethical and successful breeding is much more scientific and time-consuming than that. Inexperience can result in poor

specimens of the breed or tragic consequences, with the loss of pups - or even the mother. Sometimes a C-section (Caesarean section) may be necessary. In the UK, all C-sections have to be registered with the Kennel Club. These are carried out when the mother is unable to birth the pups naturally – and timing is critical. Too early and the pups may be underdeveloped or the mother can bleed to death; too late and the pups can die.

A major study published in 2010 carried out jointly by the BSAVA (British Small Animal Veterinary Association) and the UK's Kennel Club looked at 13,141 bitches from 151 breeds and the incidence of C-Sections over a 10-year period. The resulting report at http://bit.ly/2cV6MF3 revealed that some 17.7% (one in every 5.6) of Golden Retrievers involved in the study had to have C-Sections. And since 2012, the UK's Kennel Club will no longer register puppies from a female who has had more than two C-Sections, "except for scientifically proven welfare reasons and in such cases normally provided that the application is made prior to mating."

Breeding healthy Goldens to type is a complex, expensive and time-consuming business when all the fees, DNA and health tests, care, nutrition and medical expenses have been taken into account.

Experienced UK breeder Sue Page, of Dormansue Golden Retrievers, Surrey, says: "A first-time breeder doesn't know where to look for a suitable stud dog. So many people think that their neighbour's lovely Golden Retriever would be a wonderful sire for the litter. Hey, stop there! Firstly, the stud and your own dog have to have all the correct health certificates in place. Secondly, you should breed for the betterment of the breed and, thirdly, mating isn't always quite as easy as you think it should be. You need to know what tests you should carry out in order to know exactly when to mate a dog.

"When we register dogs with the Kennel Club we have a choice whether we endorse the Registration with 'Progeny Not Eligible for Registration.' This doesn't stop an owner breeding from their dog, but it does mean they can't register the litter with the Kennel Club. This is very useful because if an owner wants to breed and register the litter with the Kennel Club, then they have to come back to the breeder and we can ensure that the owner is pointed in the right direction. I will always try and do as much as I can to help and I am very proud that one of my owners is now an established breeder herself."

Even when you have taken every precaution, Mother Nature can still throw a curve ball and things can still go wrong.

Sue tells a very sad tale: "My dog, Jemima, was pregnant with her second litter of puppies. I had bred Jemima myself, so she was very special. She was in first stage labour for three days and so we took her to a vet to have a Caesarean, which is usually very straightforward and Mum and puppies go home within a few hours of the operation."

(Pictured, standing, is Jemima, aged three, with her first litter aged five weeks. Next to her is her mother, Pandy, aged five).

"When she got home, Jemima had a strange limp on one of her back legs and was in extreme pain. I phoned the vet who said to bring her straight back, but she was so distressed that I said we would collect some painkillers instead as I didn't want to move her. Later we found that she was also having extreme difficulty emptying her bladder. Eventually, she went to a veterinary hospital where they confirmed that there was a problem with her bladder.

"They taught me to express the bladder. You have to bend down and squeeze it, like like getting air out of a small rugby ball, and it takes a lot of effort. I carried on doing this for eight weeks, but it was obvious that she wouldn't regain the use of her bladder. I was doing this about 12 times a day and hurt myself internally, which meant I could no longer continue.

"All the puppies survived, even though we had to hand-rear them a lot of the time, as Jem was too weak to feed them. In the end we had to have Jem put to sleep and I was beside myself with grief. I blamed myself because if I hadn't bred her in the first place, the bladder damage wouldn't have happened during the Caesarean. It took me several years to get back to breeding after this."

Breeding Costs

Here's an idea of what to consider if you are seriously thinking about breeding - and doing it properly:

- Hip and elbow scoring and annual eye test for the parent(s)
- Pre-mate tests
- Stud fees
- Pregnancy – ultrasound scan, worming, extra food and supplements for the mother
- Equipment – whelping box, vet bed, thermometer, feeding bottles, heat mat, hibiscrub, etc.
- Birth – vet's fees, possible C-Section if the mother can't whelp naturally
- Puppies – vaccinations and worming, puppy food, coloured collars
- Kennel Club or AKC registration

And these are just the basics! Even without a C-Section, these four-figure costs are considerable and swallow up a large chunk of any profit you thought you might make. And if there is a problem with the mother, birth or puppies and you rack up vet's bills, you can actually make a loss on a litter.

Ask Yourself This...

1. Did I get my Golden Retriever from a good, ethical breeder? Dogs sold in pet stores and on general sales websites are seldom good specimens and can be unhealthy.

2. Are my dog and his or her close relatives free from health issues? Joint or eye issues are just some of the illnesses Golden pups can inherit. Are you 100% sure your breeding dog is free from them all? Also, an unhealthy female is also more likely to have trouble with pregnancy and whelping.

3. Does my dog have a good temperament? Does he or she socialise well with people and other animals? Dogs with poor temperaments should not be bred, regardless of how good they look.

4. Do I understand COI and its implications? Coefficient of Inbreeding measures the common ancestors of a dam and sire and indicates the probability of how genetically similar they are. Breeding from too closely-related dogs can result in health issues for the offspring.

5. Does my dog conform to the Breed Standard as laid down by the Kennel Club or AKC? Do not breed from a Golden Retriever that is not an excellent specimen, hoping that somehow the puppies will turn out better. They won't. Talk with experienced breeders and ask them for an honest assessment of your dog.

6. Is my female at least in her second heat cycle? Breeders often prefer to wait a little longer, until their female is at least two years old and physically mature, when they are able to carry a litter to term and are robust and mature enough to whelp and care for a litter. Also, some health tests cannot be finalised until a dog is two years old. Even then, not all females are suitable. Some are simply poor mothers who don't care for their puppies; others don't produce enough milk - which means you have to do it.

7. Am I financially able to provide good veterinary care for the mother and puppies, particularly

if complications occur? If you are not prepared to make a significant financial commitment to a litter, then don't breed your dog. A single litter can easily cost you thousands of pounds or dollars - and what if you only get a couple of puppies?

Have I got the indoor space? Mother and pups will need their own space in your home which will become messy as new-born pups do not come into this world housetrained (potty trained). It should also be warm and draught-free. (This photo shows Willow's six-day-old pups at "The Milk Bar!" Courtesy of Angie and Ray Gait, of Sonodora Golden Retrievers, Hampshire, UK).

8. Can I cope with lots of puppies at once? Some Goldens may have large litters of more than a dozen pups.

9. Can I devote the time to breeding? Caring for mother and young pups is a 24/7 job in the beginning and involves many sleepless nights. During the day, you cannot simply go off to work or leave the house with the mother and young pups unattended. It is not uncommon for a dam to be unable or unwilling to provide milk for her puppies, particularly when a C-section is involved as it may take up to 72 hours for the anesthesia to completely wear off. In which case, you have to tube feed the puppies every couple of hours throughout the day and night. Breeding is a huge tie.

10. Am I confident enough in my breeding programme to offer a puppy health warranty?

11. Will I be able to find good homes for all the pups and be prepared to take them back if necessary? Good breeders do not let their precious puppies go to any old home. They often have a waiting list before the litter is born.

You may have the most wonderful Golden Retriever in the world, but only enter the world of canine breeding if you have the right knowledge and motivation. Don't do it just for the money or the cute factor – or to show the kids 'The Miracle of Birth!' Breeding poor examples only brings heartache to owners in the long run when health or temperament issues develop.

Having said all of that, good Golden Retriever breeders are made, not born. Like any expert, they do their research and learn their trade over several years. If you're serious, spend time researching the breed and its genetics and make sure you are going into it for the right reasons and not just for the money - ask yourself how you intend to improve the breed.

A great way of learning about breeding Golden Retrievers is to find a mentor; someone who somebody who is already successfully breeding Golden Retrievers. By 'successful' we mean somebody who is producing healthy, handsome puppies with good temperaments, not someone who is making lots of money churning out poor quality puppies.

(Pictured is Daisy-May's "Vino" litter – all named after wines! The pups all had dark stripes until they were 48 hours old. They were bred by Dee Johnson, of Johnsongrace Golden Retrievers, North Cornwall, UK).

Talk to the breeder you got your pup from, visit dog shows and make contact with established breeders or look at the Kennel Club or AKC website for details of breeders near you. Contact the UK's Golden Retriever Club https://thegoldenretrieverclub.co.uk or the Golden Retriever Club of America (USA) www.grca.org and ask them to help find a suitable person who is willing to help you get started.

One book which a couple of our breeders have recommended is **Book of the Bitch** by J. M. Evans and Kay White, which is useful for reference.

Committed Golden Retriever breeders aren't in it for the cash. They use their skills and knowledge to produce healthy pups with good temperaments that conform to the Breed Standard and ultimately improve the breed.

Our advice is: when it comes to breeding Golden Retrievers, leave it to the experts or seek expert advice.

Pictured is Daisy-May's "Vino" litter aged five weeks. As you can see, the stripes are long gone! Photo courtesy of Dee Johnson.

15. Golden Retriever Rescue

Not everybody who is thinking of getting a Golden Retriever gets one as a puppy from a breeder. Some people prefer to adopt a dog from a rescue organisation. What could be kinder and more rewarding than giving a poor, abandoned dog a happy and loving home for the rest of his life?

Not much really; adoption saves lives and gives unfortunate dogs a second chance of happiness. The problem of homeless dogs is truly depressing. It's a big issue in Britain, but even worse in the US, where the sheer numbers in kill shelters is hard to comprehend. Randy Grim states in "Don't Dump The Dog" that 1,000 dogs are being put to sleep every hour in the States.

According to Jo-Anne Cousins, former Executive Director at IDOG, who has spent many years involved in US canine rescue, the situations leading to a dog ending up in rescue can often be summed up in one phrase: 'Unrealistic expectations.'

She said: "In many situations, dog ownership was something that the family went into without fully understanding the time, money and commitment to exercise and training that it takes to raise a dog. While they may have spent hours on the internet pouring over cute puppy photos, they probably didn't read any puppy training books or look into actual costs of regular vet care, training and boarding."

That lack of thought was highlighted in a story that appeared in the Press in my Yorkshire home town. A woman went shopping on Christmas Eve in a local retail centre. She returned home £700 (over $900) poorer with a puppy she had bought on impulse. The pup was in a rescue centre two days later.

Common reasons for a dog being put into rescue include:

- A change in family circumstance, such as divorce or a new baby
- A change in work patterns
- Moving home
- The dog develops health issues

Often, the 'unrealistic expectations' come home to roost and the dog is given up for rescue because:

- He has too much energy, needs too much exercise, knocks the kids over and/or jumps on people - young Goldens are boisterous and sometimes lack co-ordination
- He is growling and/or nipping. All puppies bite, it is their way of exploring the world; they have to be trained not to bite the things (such as humans) that they are not supposed to bite
- He chews or eats things he shouldn't
- He makes a mess in the house - housetraining requires time and patience from the owner

- He needs a lot more exercise and attention than the owner is able or prepared to give. Golden Retrievers are not small dogs and require a lot of time and commitment from the owner – especially in the beginning

- He costs too much to keep - the cost of feeding a Golden, vets' bills, etc. are not insignificant

There is, however, a ray of sunshine for some of these dogs. Every year many thousands of people in the UK, North America and countries all around the world adopt a rescue dog and the story often has a happy ending.

The Dog's Point of View...

If you are serious about adopting a Golden Retriever, then you should do so with the right motives and with your eyes wide open. If you're expecting a perfect dog, you could be in for a shock. Rescue dogs can and do become wonderful companions, but a lot of it depends on you.

Golden Retrievers are people-loving dogs. Sometimes those that have ended up in rescue centres are traumatised. Some may have health problems. They don't understand why they have been abandoned, neglected or badly treated by their beloved owners and may arrive at your home with 'baggage' of their own until they adjust to being part of a loving family again. This may take time. Patience is the key to help the dog to adjust to his or her new surroundings and family and to learn to love and trust again. Ask yourself a few questions before you take the plunge and fill in the adoption forms:

- Are you prepared to accept and deal with any problems - such as bad behaviour, chewing, aggression, timidity, jumping up or eliminating in the house - which a rescue dog may initially display when arriving in your home?

- How much time are you willing to spend with your new dog to help him integrate back into normal family life?

- Can you take time off work to be at home and help the dog settle in at the beginning?

- Are you prepared to take on a new addition to your family that may live for another decade?

- Are you prepared to stick with the dog even if he or she develops health issues later?

Think about the implications before rescuing a dog - try and look at it from the dog's point of view. What could be worse for the unlucky dog than to be abandoned again if things don't work out between you?

Other Considerations

Adopting a rescue dog is a big commitment for all involved. It is not a cheap way of getting a Golden Retriever and shouldn't be viewed as such. It could cost you several hundred pounds - or dollars. You'll have adoption fees to pay and often vaccination and veterinary bills as well as worm and flea medication and spaying or neutering. Make sure you're aware of the full cost before committing.

Although Golden Retrievers are known for being faithful and loving companions, some in rescue shelters or foster homes have been badly treated or had difficult lives, and these dogs need plenty of time to rehabilitate. Some may have initial problems with housetraining, others may need socialisation with people and/or other dogs. And if you are serious about adopting, you may have to wait a while until a suitable dog comes up. One way of finding out if you, your family and home are suitable is to volunteer to become a foster home for one of the rescue centres. Fosters offer temporary homes until a forever home becomes available. It's a shorter-term arrangement, but still requires commitment and patience.

Another point to consider is that it's not just the dogs that are screened - you'll also have to undergo a screening by the rescue organisation. Rescue groups and shelters have to make sure that prospective adopters are suitable and they have thought through everything very carefully before making such a big decision. They also want to match you with the right dog - putting a lively young Golden with an elderly couple might not be the perfect match. It would be a tragedy for the dog if things did not work out.

Most rescue groups will ask a raft of personal questions - some of which may seem intrusive. If you are serious about adopting, you will have to answer them. Here are some of the details required on a typical adoption form:

- Name, address and details, including ages, of all people living in your home
- Size of your garden (if you have one) and height of the fence around it
- Extensive details of any other pets
- Your work hours and amount of time you spend away from the home each day
- Type of property you live in
- Whether you have any previous experience with Golden Retrievers
- Your reasons for wanting to adopt a Golden Retriever
- If you have ever previously given up a dog for adoption
- Whether you have any experience dealing with canine behaviour or health issues
- Details of your vet
- If you are prepared for aggression/destructive behaviour/chewing/fear and timidity/soiling inside the house/medical issues
- Whether you agree to insure your dog
- Whether you are prepared for the financial costs of dog ownership
- Whether you are willing to housetrain and obedience train the dog
- Your views on dog training methods classes
- Where your dog will sleep at night
- Whether you are prepared to accept a Golden Retriever cross
- Details of two personal referees

If you work away from the home, it is useful to know that as a general rule of thumb, UK rescue organisations will not place dogs in homes where they will be left alone for more than four or five hours at a stretch. After you've filled in the adoption form, a chat with a representative from the charity usually follows. There will also be an inspection visit to your home - and your vet may even be vetted!

If all goes well, you will be approved to adopt and it's then just a question of waiting for the right match to come along. When he or she does, a meeting will be arranged with the dog for all family members, you pay the adoption fee and become the proud new owner of a Golden Retriever. It might seem like a lot of red tape, but the rescue groups have to be as sure as they can that you will provide a loving, forever home for the unfortunate dog. It would be terrible if things didn't work out and the dog had to be placed back in rescue again.

All rescue organisations will neuter the dog or, if he or she is too young, specify in the adoption contract that the dog must be neutered and may not be used for breeding. Many rescue organisations have a lifetime rescue back-up policy, which means that if things don't work out, the dog must be returned to them.

Rescue Organisations

Rescue organisations are often run by volunteers who give up their time to help dogs in distress. They often have a network of foster homes, where a Golden Retriever is placed until a permanent new home can be found. Foster homes are better than shelters, as Goldens thrive on human contact. Fostering helps to keep the dog socialised, and the people who foster are able to give sufficient attention to the individual dog in their care.

There are also online Golden Retriever forums where people sometimes post information about a dog that needs a new home. Even if you can't or don't want to offer a permanent home, there are other ways that you can help these worthy organisations, such as by short-term fostering or helping to raise money.

UK - There is a range of regional Golden Retriever rescue organisations in the UK. If no website is given, visit this Kennel club page for details): www.thekennelclub.org.uk/services/public/findarescue/Default.aspx?breed=2047 and The Golden Retriever Club has a Rescue page that lists all of the regional GR clubs and rescue contacts at https://thegoldenretrieverclub.co.uk/rescue-page

Berkshire Downs & Chilterns Golden Retriever Club Rescue, www.bdcgrc.org.uk/index.asp?ID=25

Golden Retriever Club of Northumbria Rescue

Golden Retriever Club of Scotland Rescue Scotland

Golden Retriever Rescue Cymru www.goldenretrieverrescuecymru.co.uk

Midland Golden Retriever Club Rescue

North West Golden Retriever Rescue www.retrieverrescue.net

North West Golden Retriever Club, Lancashire, Cheshire, Merseyside, Greater Manchester, North Wales www.nwgrc.co.uk

South Western Golden Retriever Club Rescue, Dorset

Southern Golden Retriever Rescue, Kent, Surrey, East and West Sussex, Hampshire, Greater London www.southerngoldenretrieverrescue.org.uk

There's also a number of general adoption websites with Golden Retrievers and Golden Retriever crosses for rehoming: www.oldies.org.uk www.dogsblog.com/category/golden-retriever

www.rspca.org.uk/findapet/rehomeapet

USA

The Golden Retriever Club of America National Rescue Committee co-ordinates and networks services for nearly 100 local Golden Retriever organisations. This page has all the details: www.grca-nrc.org/localrescues.html

And US-wide **Rescue Me** has a Facebook page dedicated to Golden Retrievers and Golden crosses that need new homes; just type '**Rescue Me! Golden Retriever Rescue**' into a Facebook search. There are also general websites, such as www.petfinder.com, www.aspca.org/adopt-pet and www.adoptapet.com

This is by no means an exhaustive list, but it does cover some of the main organisations involved. If you do visit these websites, you cannot presume that the descriptions are 100% accurate. They are given in good faith, but ideas of what constitutes a 'lively' dog may vary. Some dogs advertised may have other breeds in their genetic make-up. It does not mean that these are necessarily worse dogs, but if you are attracted to the Golden Retriever for its temperament and other assets, make sure you are looking at a Golden Retriever.

DON'T get a dog from eBay, Craig's List, Gumtree or any of the other general advertising websites that sell golf clubs, jewellery, old cars, washing machines, etc. You might think you are getting a bargain dog, but in the long run you may well pay the price. If the dog had been well bred and properly cared for, he or she would not be advertised on such websites - or sold in pet shops. You may be storing up a whole load of trouble for yourselves in terms of health and/or behaviour issues, due to poor breeding and environment.

If you haven't been put off with all of the above... Congratulations, you may be just the family or person that poor homeless Golden Retriever is looking for!

If you can't spare the time to adopt - and adoption means forever - you might want to consider fostering. Or you could help by becoming a home inspector or fundraiser to help keep these very worthy rescue groups providing such a wonderful service. However you decide to get involved, Good Luck!

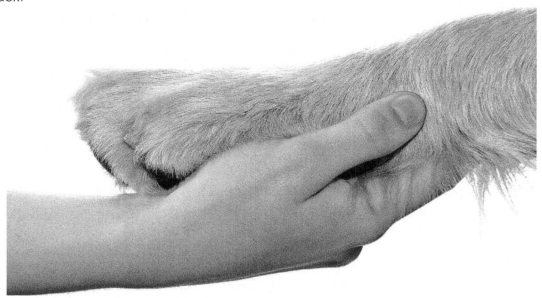

Saving one dog will not change the world,
But it will change the world for one dog

16. Caring for Golden Oldies

If your Golden Retriever has been well looked after and has suffered no serious diseases, he or she may well live to double figures. A good lifespan is 12 to 14 years, and a handful of Goldens will live even longer. Lifespan is influenced by genetics and also by owners, in terms of how you feed, exercise and generally look after your dog.

If your Golden does reach a ripe old age, at some point before the end, he or she will start to feel the effects of ageing. After having got up at the crack of dawn when your dog was a puppy, you may find that he now likes to sleep in longer in the morning. Physically, joints will probably become stiffer and organs - such as heart, liver and kidneys - may not function as effectively. On the mental side - just as with humans - your dog's memory, ability to learn and awareness will start to dim.

Your faithful companion might become a bit stubborn, grumpier or a little less tolerant of lively dogs and children. He may start waking up or wandering about the house in the middle of the night, taking forever to sniff a blade of grass, or seeking out your company more often. He might even have the odd "accident" inside the house.

You may also notice that he doesn't see or hear as well as he used to. On the other hand, your old friend might not be hard of hearing at all. He might have developed that affliction common to many older dogs - ours included - of 'selective hearing.' Our 13-year-old Max has bionic hearing when it comes to the word "Dinnertime" whispered from 20 yards, yet these days seems strangely unable to hear the commands "Stay" or "Here" when we are right in front of him!

You can help ease your mature dog gracefully into old age by keeping an eye on him, noticing the changes and taking action to help as much as possible. This might involve a visit to the vet for supplements and/or medications, modifying your dog's environment, changing his or her diet and slowly reducing the amount of daily exercise. Much depends on the individual dog. Just as with humans, a Golden Retriever of ideal weight that has been physically and mentally active all of his life is likely to age slower than an overweight, under-stimulated couch potato.

Keeping older Goldens at that optimum weight can be challenging as they age. Some become more obsessed with food, even though they are getting less exercise. Also, their metabolisms slow down, making it easier to put on the pounds unless their daily calories are reduced. At the same time, extra weight places additional, unwanted stress on joints and organs, making them have to work harder than they should.

We normally talk about dogs being old when they reach the last third of their lives. This varies greatly from dog to dog and bloodline to bloodline. Some Golden Retrievers may start to show signs of ageing at seven or eight years old, while others may remain fit in mind and body for much longer. Several owners have told us that their dogs are showing few signs of ageing at 10 or 11 years old. Competitively, a Golden Retriever is classed as a 'Veteran' at seven years old in the show ring and eight years old in Working Tests (although many don't act their age!)

Physical and Mental Signs of Ageing

If your Golden Retriever is in or approaching the last third of his life, here are some signs that his body is feeling its age:

❧ He has generally slowed down and no longer seems as keen to go out on his walks – or if he does want to go, he doesn't want to go as far. He is happy pottering and sniffing (and often takes forever to inspect a single clump of grass!) Some are less keen to go outside in bad weather

❧ He gets up from lying down more slowly and he goes up and down stairs more slowly. He can no longer jump on to the couch or bed. These are all signs that his joints are stiffening, often due to arthritis

❧ He is getting grey hairs, particularly around the muzzle

❧ He has put on a bit of weight

❧ He may have the occasional 'accident' (incontinence) inside the house

❧ He urinates more frequently

❧ He drinks more water

❧ He has bouts of constipation or diarrhoea

❧ The foot pads thicken and nails may become more brittle

❧ One or more lumps or fatty deposits (lipomas) develop on his body. Our Max developed two small bumps on top of his head aged 10 and we took him straight to the vet, who performed an operation to remove them. They were benign (harmless), but you should always get them checked out ASAP in case they are an early form of cancer, they can also grow quite rapidly, even if benign. They often appear on the chest, flanks or armpit

❧ He can't regulate his body temperature as he used to and so feels the cold and heat more

❧ He doesn't hear as well as he used to

❧ His eyesight may deteriorate – if his eyes appear cloudy he may be developing cataracts and you should see your vet as soon as you notice the signs. Just as with humans, most older dogs live quite well with failing eyesight

❧ He has bad breath (halitosis), which could be a sign of dental or gum disease. If so, brush his teeth regularly and give him a daily dental stick, such as Dentastix or similar. If the bad breath persists, get him checked out by a vet

❧ If he's inactive he may develop callouses on the elbows, especially if he lies down on hard surfaces – this is more common with large dogs than small ones

It's not just your dog's body that deteriorates; his mind does too. It's often part of the normal ageing process. Your dog may display some, all or none of these signs of Canine Cognitive Dysfunction:

❧ His sleep patterns change; an older dog may be more restless at night and sleepy during the day. He may start wandering around the house at odd times, causing you sleepless nights

❧ He barks more, sometimes at nothing or open spaces

❧ He stares at objects, such as walls, or wanders aimlessly around the house or garden

- He displays increased anxiety, separation anxiety or aggression; although aggression is more common with some other breeds and most ageing Goldens remain gentle souls

- He forgets or ignores commands or habits he once knew well, such as coming when called and sometimes toilet training

- Some dogs may become more clingy and dependent, often resulting in separation anxiety. He may seek reassurance that you are near him as his faculties fade and he becomes a bit less confident and independent. Others may become a bit disengaged and less interested in human contact

Understanding the changes happening to your dog and acting on them compassionately and effectively will help ease your dog's passage through his or her senior years. Your dog has given you so much pleasure over the years, now he or she needs you to give that bit of extra care for a happy, healthy old age. You can also help your Golden Retriever to stay mentally active by playing gentle games and getting new toys to stimulate interest.

Changing Habits

As dogs age they need fewer calories and less protein, so many owners switch to a food specially formulated for older dogs. These are labelled 'Senior,' 'Ageing' or 'Mature.' Check the labelling; some are specifically for dogs aged over eight, others may be for 10 or 12-year-olds. If you are not sure if a senior diet is necessary for your Golden, talk to your vet the next time you are there. Remember, if you do change brand, switch the food gradually over a week or so. Unlike with humans, a dog's digestive system cannot cope with sudden changes of diet.

Consider feeding your old dog a supplement, such as Omega-3 fatty acids for the brain and coat, or one to help joints. Our dog gets a squirt of Yumega Omega 3 and half a scoop of Joint Aid in one of his daily feeds. There are also medications and homeopathic remedies, such as melatonin which has natural sedative properties, to help relieve anxiety. Check with your vet before introducing anything new.

Our dog used to be very sensitive to loud noises and the lead up to Bonfire Night was a nightmare. (This is November 5th in the UK, a cause for celebration, but a worry if you have animals as there are countless firework displays and loud bangs). However, since his hearing has deteriorated, he is actually far more relaxed, as loud noises are muffled and no longer frightening to him.

If your Golden Oldie has started to ignore your verbal commands when out on a walk – either through 'switching off' or deafness, you can try a whistle to attract his or her attention and then use an exaggerated hand signal for the recall. Once your dog is looking at you, hold your arm out, palm down, at 90 degrees to your body and bring it down, keeping your arm straight, until your fingers point to your toes. This has worked very effectively with Max. (He looks, understands and then decides if he is going to come or not, but at least he knows what he should be doing! More often than not he does come back – especially if the arm signal is repeated while he is making up his

mind). Pictured is Lisa and Mark Mellor's Gracie (Catcombe Cut No Ice), of Goodgrace Retrievers, Essex, still looking good at age 11.

Weight - no matter how old your Goldie is, he still needs a waist! Maintaining a healthy weight with a balanced diet and regular, gentler exercise are two of the most important things you can do for your dog.

Environment - Make sure your dog has a nice soft place to rest his old bones, which may mean adding an extra blanket to his bed. This should be in a place that is not too hot or cold, as he may not be able to regulate his body temperature as well as when he was younger. He needs plenty of undisturbed sleep and should not be pestered and/or bullied by younger dogs, other animals or young children. If his eyesight is failing, move obstacles out of his way, reducing the chance of injuries.

Jumping on and off furniture or in or out of the car is high impact for his old joints and bones. He will need a helping hand on to and off the couch or your bed, if he's allowed up there, or even a little ramp to get in and out of the car. We bought a plastic ramp for Max as he has become hesitant to jump in or out of the car. However, this has proved to be a complete waste of money, as he doesn't like the feel of the non-slip surface on his paws and after the first couple of times, has steadfastly refused to set a paw on it!

Exercise - Take the lead from your dog, if he doesn't want to walk as far, then don't. But if your dog doesn't want to go out at all, you will have to coax him out. ALL old dogs need exercise, not only to keep their joints moving, but also to keep their heart, lungs and joints exercised and to help keep their minds engaged with different places, smells, etc. (Gracie is pictured below with her five-week-old granddaughter. Lisa says: "Gracie remains a very hands-on dog").

Consult a Professional - If your dog is showing any of these signs, get him checked out by a vet:

- ❧ Excessive increased urination or drinking - this can be a sign of something amiss, such as reduced liver or kidney function, Cushing's disease or diabetes

- ❧ Constipation or not urinating regularly could be a sign of something not functioning properly with the digestive system or organs

- ❧ Incontinence, which could be a sign of a mental or physical problem

- ❧ Cloudy eyes, which could be cataracts

- ❧ Decreased appetite – most Golden Retrievers love their food and loss of appetite is often a sign of an underlying problem

- Lumps or bumps on the body - which are most often benign, but can occasionally be malignant (cancerous)
- Excessive sleeping or a lack of interest in you and his/her surroundings
- Diarrhoea or vomiting
- A darkening and dryness of skin that never seems to get any better - this can be a sign of hypothyroidism
- Any other out-of-the-ordinary behaviour for your dog. A change in patterns or behaviour is often your dog's way of telling you that all is not well

The Last Lap

Huge advances in veterinary science have meant that there are countless procedures and medications that can prolong the life of your dog, and this is a good thing. But there comes a time when you do have to let go. If your dog is showing all the signs of ageing and has an ongoing medical condition from which he or she cannot recover, or is showing signs of pain, mental anxiety or distress and there is no hope of improvement, then the dreaded time has come to say goodbye. You owe it to him or her.

There is no point keeping an old dog alive if all he or she has to look forward to is pain and death. I'm even getting upset as I write this, as I think of parting from my 13-year-old in the not-too-distant future, as well as all the wonderful dogs we have had in the past. But we have their lives in our hands and we can give them the gift of passing away peacefully and humanely at the end when the time is right.

Losing our beloved companion, our best friend, a member of the family, is truly heart-breaking for most owners. But one of the things we realise at the back of our minds when we get that lively little puppy is the pain that comes with it; knowing that we will live longer than him or her and that we will probably have to make this most painful of decisions at some point.

It's the worst thing about being a dog owner.

If your Golden Retriever has had a long and happy life, then you could not have done any more. You were a great owner and your dog was lucky to have you.

Remember all the good times you had together. And try not to rush out and buy another dog; wait a while to grieve for your Golden Retriever. Assess your current life and lifestyle and, if your situation is right, only then consider getting another dog and all that that entails in terms of time, commitment and expense.

A Golden Retriever coming into a happy, stable household will get off to a much better start in life than a dog entering a home full of grief.

Whatever you decide to do, put the dog first.

Author's Notes:

The Golden Retriever is frequently referred to throughout this book by the popular terms 'Golden' or 'Goldie', and the masculine pronoun 'he' is often used to represent both male and female dogs.

The Complete Golden Retriever Handbook uses UK English, except where Americans have been quoted, when the original US English has been preserved.

Useful Contacts

Golden Retriever Club of America www.grca.org and advice on finding a breeder at: www.grca.org/find-a-golden/where-to-find-a-golden/grca-puppy-referral Rescue section: www.grca.org/find-a-golden/where-to-find-a-golden/rescue

American Kennel Club (AKC) http://www.akc.org/dog-breeds/golden-retriever Puppies via AKC marketplace: http://marketplace.akc.org/puppies/golden-retriever NOTE: Only Breeders of Merit have been vetted by the AKC Helps find lost or stolen dogs, register your dog's microchip www.akcreunite.org

Kennel Club (UK) www.thekennelclub.org.uk Kennel Club Assured Breeders: www.thekennelclub.org.uk/services/public/acbr/Default.aspx?breed=Retriever+(Golden) List of regional Golden Retriever Clubs and rescue organisations at: www.thekennelclub.org.uk/services/public/findaclub/breed/list.aspx?id=2047 Kennel Club Mate Select www.thekennelclub.org.uk/services/public/mateselect

The Golden Retriever Club (UK) https://thegoldenretrieverclub.co.uk Puppy advice: https://thegoldenretrieverclub.co.uk/puppies-page Rescue: https://thegoldenretrieverclub.co.uk/rescue-page Members' litters: https://thegoldenretrieverclub.co.uk/puppies-page/members-puppy-list

Champdogs (UK), puppies currently available– not all are KC members, not all of these breeders health test; check first: www.champdogs.co.uk/breeds/golden-retriever/puppies?start=all

Golden Retriever Breed Council www.goldenretrievers.co.uk/application/council/index.php

Association of Pet Dog Trainers USA www.apdt.com

Association of Pet Dog Trainers UK www.apdt.co.uk

Canadian Association of Professional Pet Dog Trainers www.cappdt.ca

Dog foods - useful information on grain-free and hypoallergenic www.dogfoodadvisor.com UK dog food advice www.allaboutdogfood.co.uk

There are also **internet forums** and **Facebook groups** that are a good source of information from other owners, including: http://www.goldenretrieverforum.com http://www.forum.breedia.com/dogs/golden-retriever www.facebook.com/officialgoldenretriever

....

List of Contributors

(Breeders listed alphabetically, by surname)

UK - all are Kennel Club Assured Breeders

Richard and Suzanne Clear, Arunsglory Golden Retrievers, West Sussex

Anna Cornelius-Jones, Mindieslodge Golden Retrievers, Dorset http://mindieslodge.simpl.com

George and Val Coxwell, Revaliac Golden Retrievers, Devon

Angie and Ray Gait, Sonodora Golden Retrievers, Hampshire www.sonodoragoldens.co.uk

Lesley Gunter and Geoff Brown, Moorvista, Derbyshire

Karen Ireland, Trikiti Golden Retrievers, Hampshire

Dee Johnson, Johnsongrace Golden Retrievers, North Cornwall www.johnsongrace.com

Nicholas Lock and Elaine Griffiths, Bonsaviour Retrievers, Shropshire bonsaviour.co.uk

Lisa and Mark Mellor, Goodgrace Golden Retrievers, Essex

Sue Page, Dormansue Golden Retrievers, Surrey

Karen Parsons, Arundel, West Sussex

Wendy Pickup, Blenstone Golden Retrievers, Flintshire www.blenstone.net

Julian Pottage, Yorkbeach Golden Retrievers, Mid Glamorgan, Wales www.yorkbeach.co.uk

Jan Schick, Mildenhall, Suffolk

Liz Spicer-Short, Priorschest Golden Retrievers, Dorset

Claire Underwood, of Bowcombe Golden Retrievers, Isle of Wight,

Jessica and Stephen Webb, HollyRoseFen Golden Retrievers, Lincolnshire www.webbspaws.co.uk

USA

Helen Dorrance, Ducat Goldens, Texas (AKC Breeder of Merit) www.ducatgoldens.com

Tim Hoke, Golden Meadows Retrievers, California (AKC Bred with H.E.A.R.T). www.GoldenMeadowsRetrievers.com

Karen Moore, Icewind Goldens, New Jersey www.icewindgoldens.com

Kelly Sisco and Jenica Belsha, Show Me Goldens, Missouri (AKC Bred with H.E.A.R.T). www.show-me-goldens.com

Other Contributor

Dr Sara Skiwski, The Western Dragon Integrated Veterinary Solutions, San Jose, California, USA www.thewesterndragon.com

Disclaimer

This book has been written to provide helpful information on Golden Retrievers. It is not meant to be used, nor should it be used, to diagnose or treat any medical condition. For diagnosis or treatment of any animal medical problem, consult a qualified veterinarian.

The author is not responsible for any specific health or allergy conditions that may require medical supervision and is not liable for any damages or negative consequences from any treatment, action, application or preparation, to any animal or to any person reading or following the information in this book.

The views expressed by contributors to this book are solely personal and do not necessarily represent those of the author. References are provided for informational purposes only and do not constitute endorsement of any websites or other sources.

Made in the USA
Las Vegas, NV
02 January 2021